# Honey Hunt

## 6 story and art by Miki Aihara

Honey Hunt 6

## CONTENTS

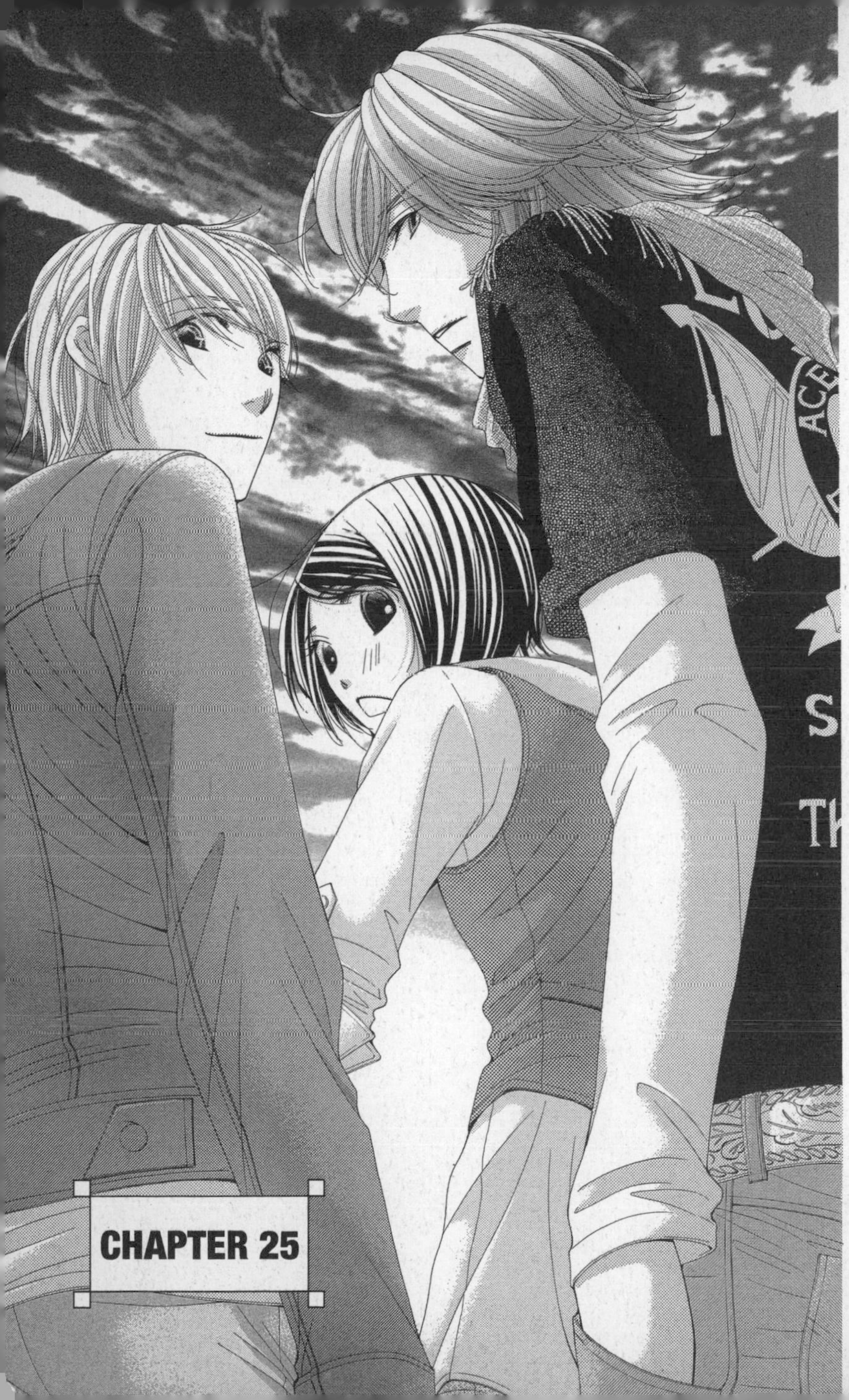
CHAPTER 25

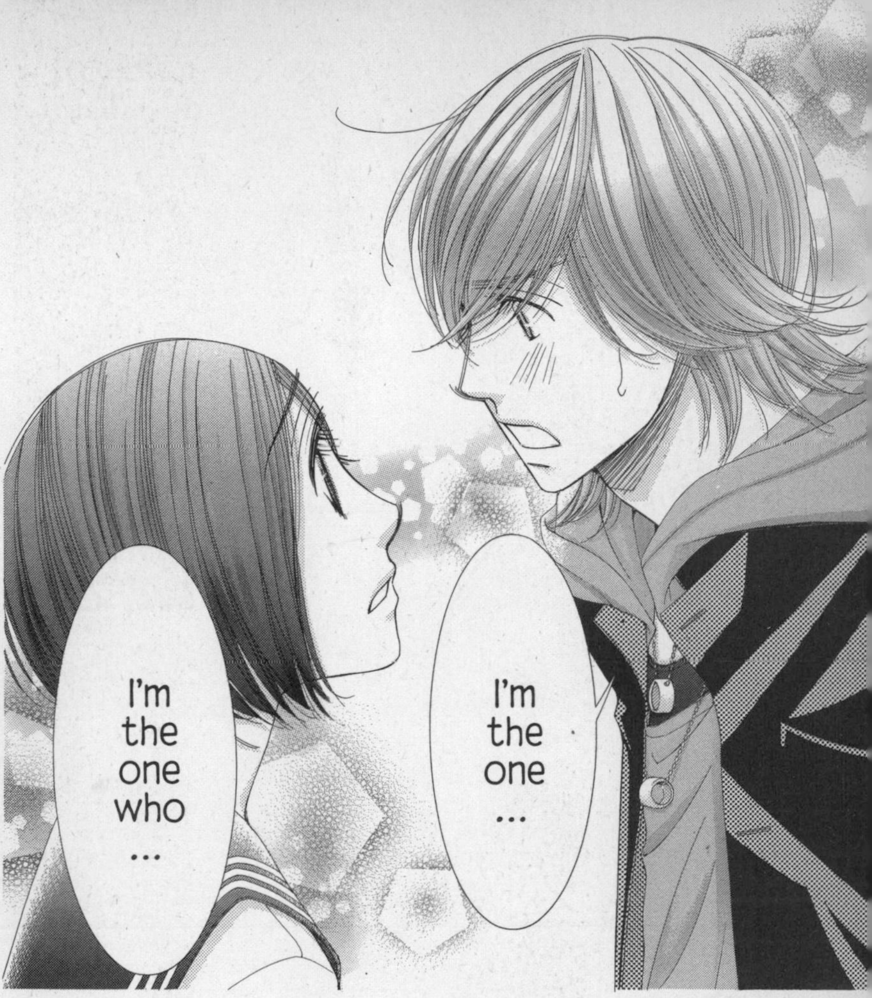
I'm the one ...
I'm the one who ...

Honey Hunt

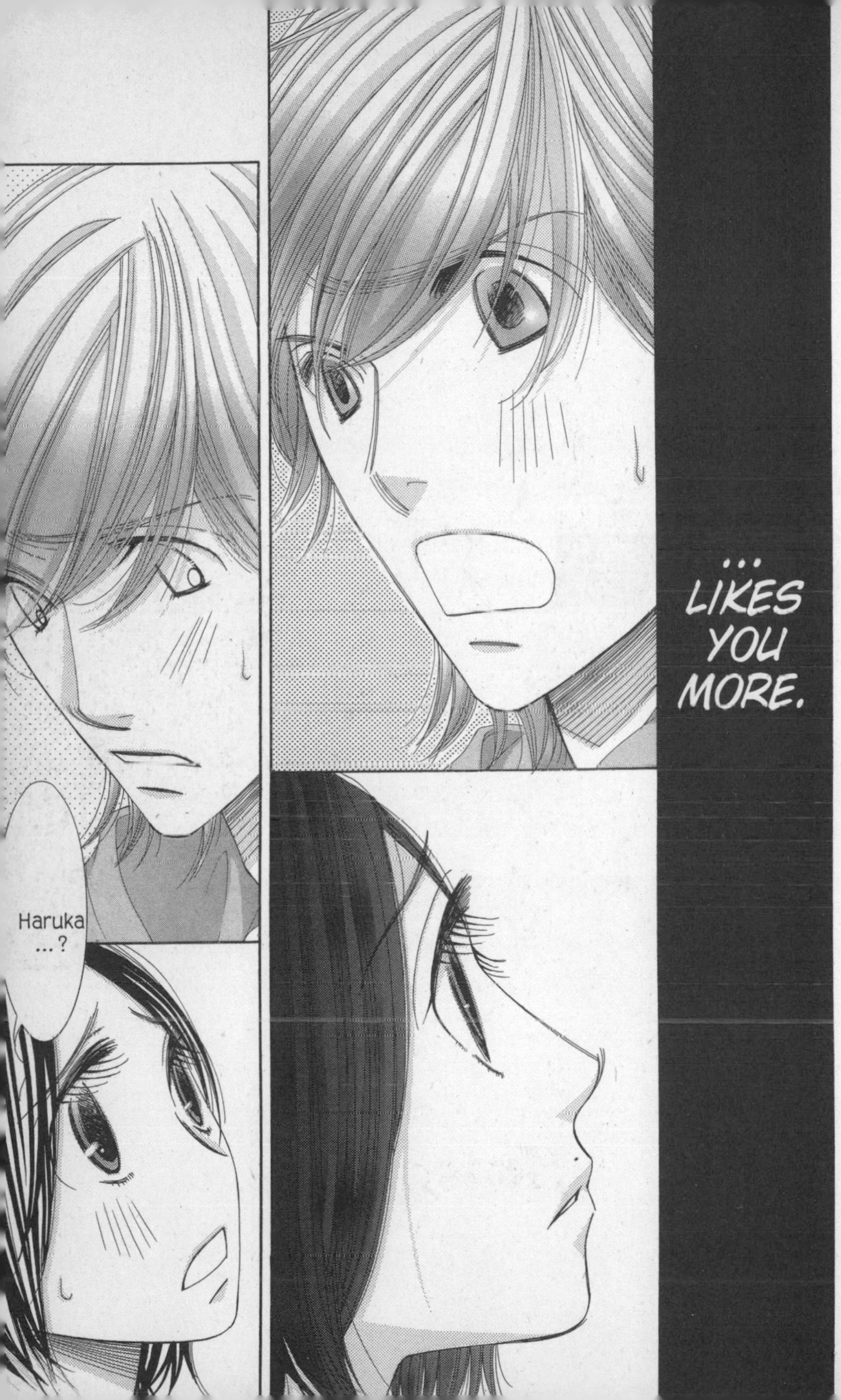
... LIKES YOU MORE.
Haruka ...?

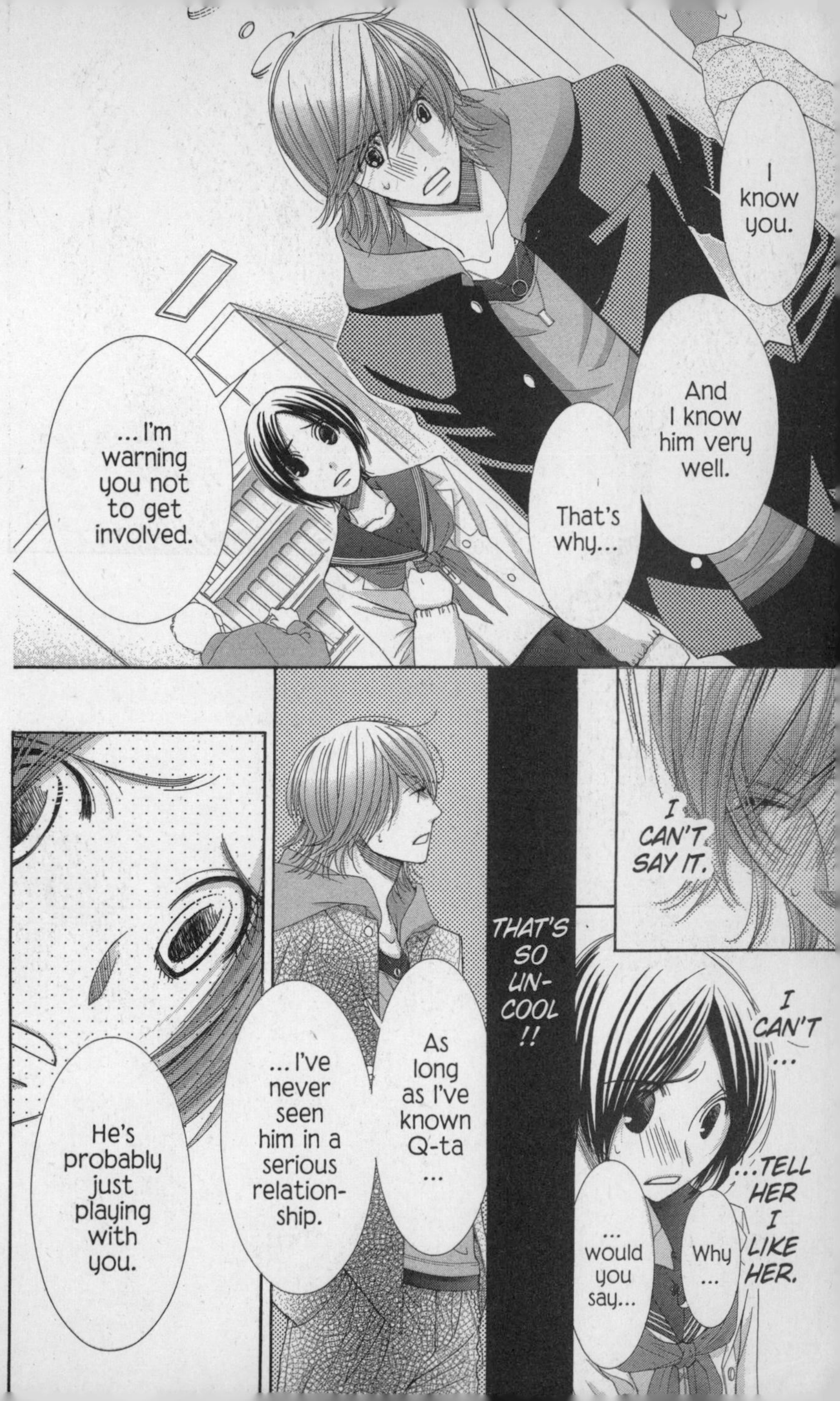
I know you.
And I know him very well.
That's why...
...I'm warning you not to get involved.
I CAN'T SAY IT.
I CAN'T...
...TELL HER I LIKE HER.
Why...
...would you say...
THAT'S SO UN-COOL!!
As long as I've known Q-ta...
...I've never seen him in a serious relationship.
He's probably just playing with you.

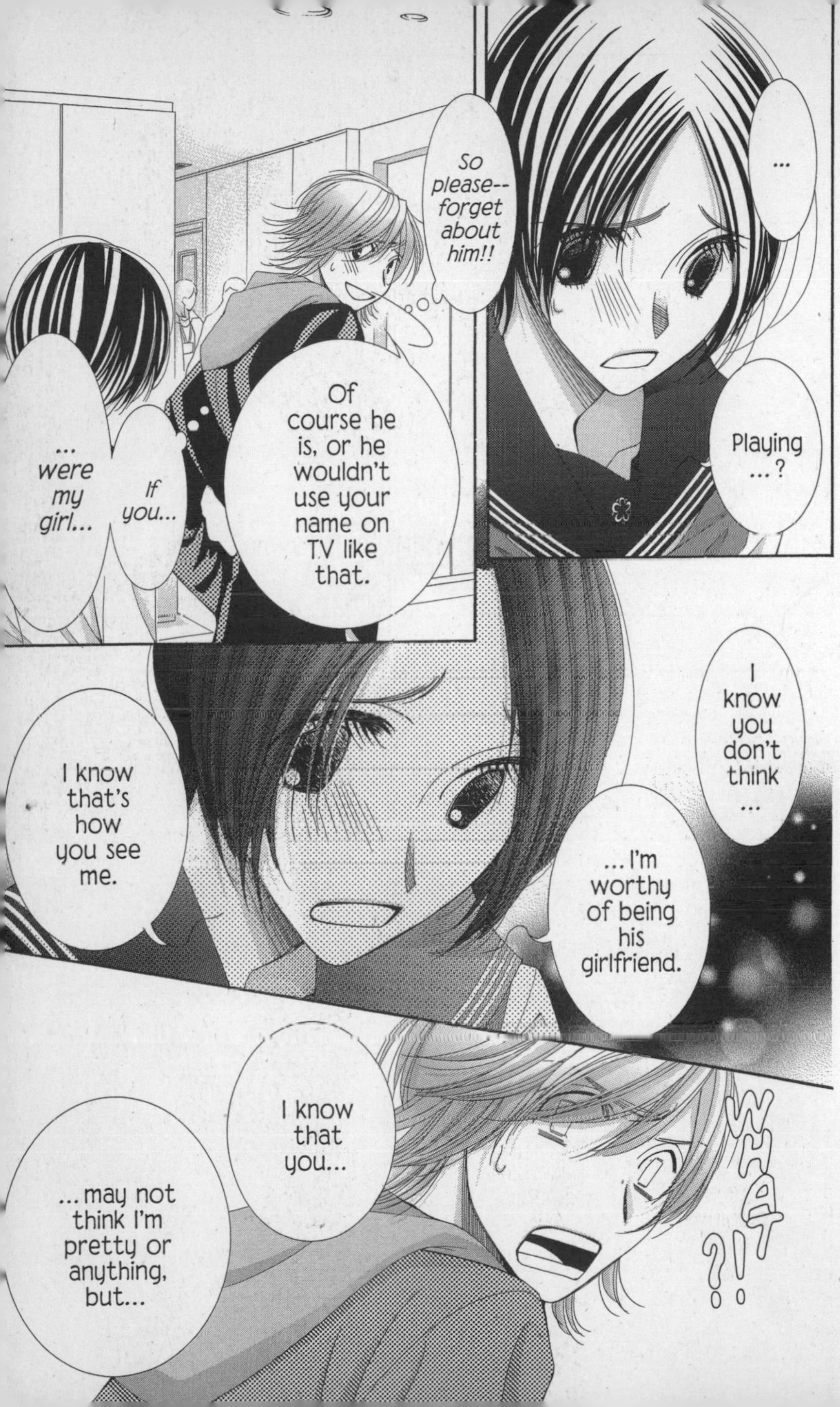
...
Playing ...?
So please-- forget about him!!
Of course he is, or he wouldn't use your name on T.V like that.
If you...
... were my girl...
I know you don't think ...
... I'm worthy of being his girlfriend.
I know that's how you see me.
WHAT ?!
I know that you...
... may not think I'm pretty or anything, but...

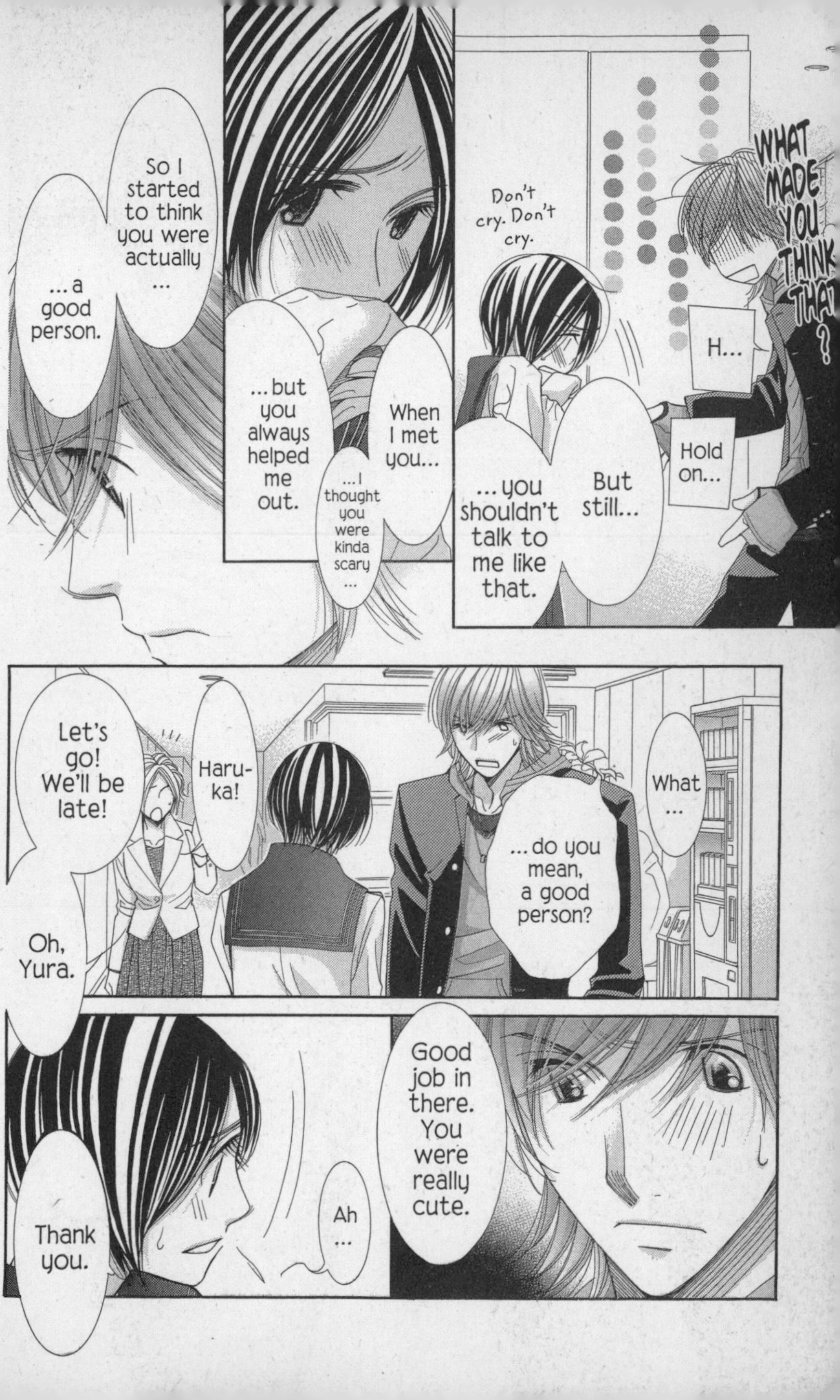
WHAT MADE YOU THINK THAT?
H...
Hold on...
Don't cry. Don't cry.
But still...
...you shouldn't talk to me like that.
When I met you...
...I thought you were kinda scary...
...but you always helped me out.
So I started to think you were actually...
...a good person.
What...
...do you mean, a good person?
Haruka!
Let's go! We'll be late!
Oh, Yura.
Good job in there. You were really cute.
Ah...
Thank you.

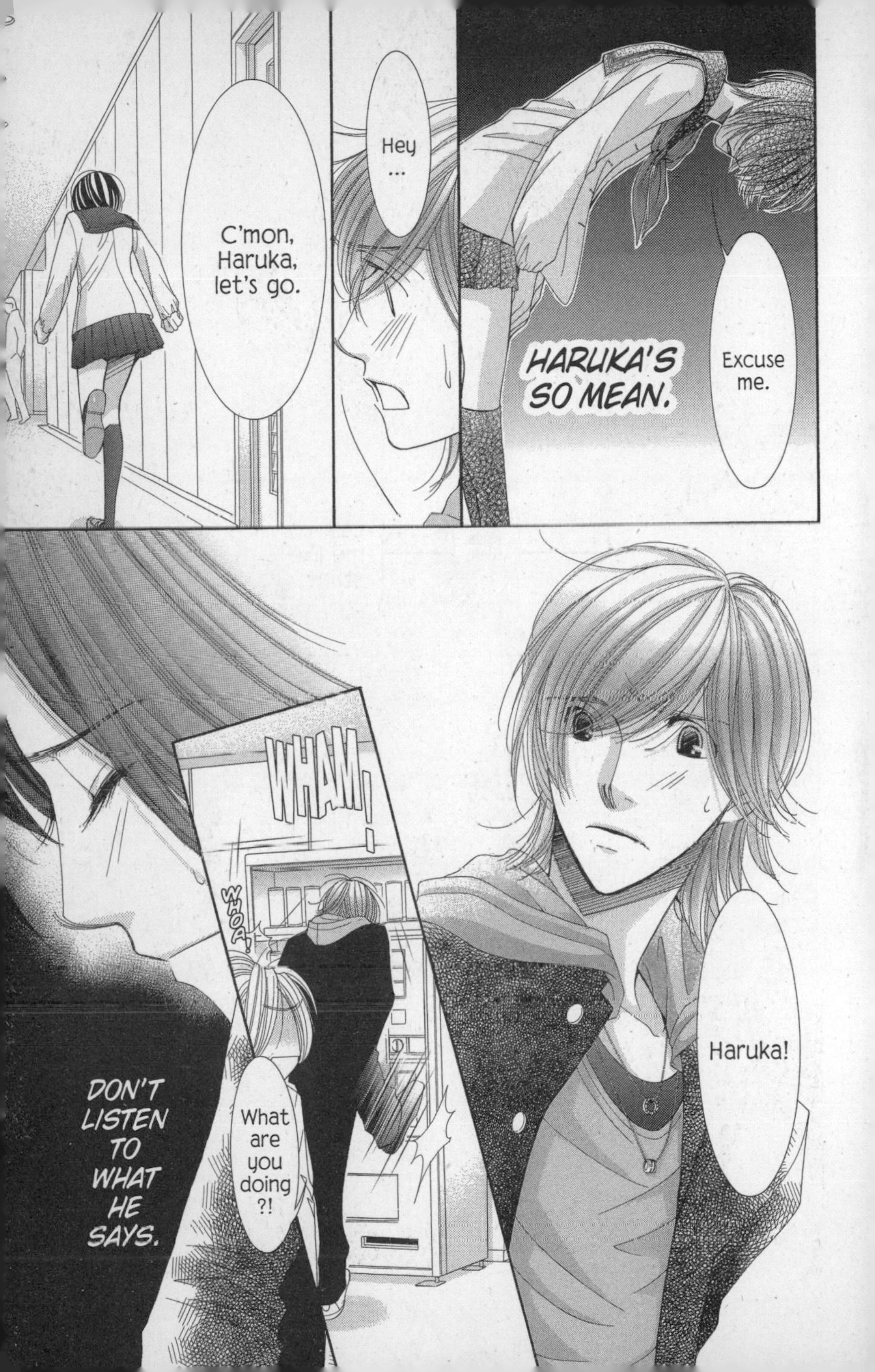
Excuse me.
HARUKA'S SO MEAN.
Hey ...
C'mon, Haruka, let's go.
Haruka!
WHAM!
WHOA!
What are you doing?!
DON'T LISTEN TO WHAT HE SAYS.

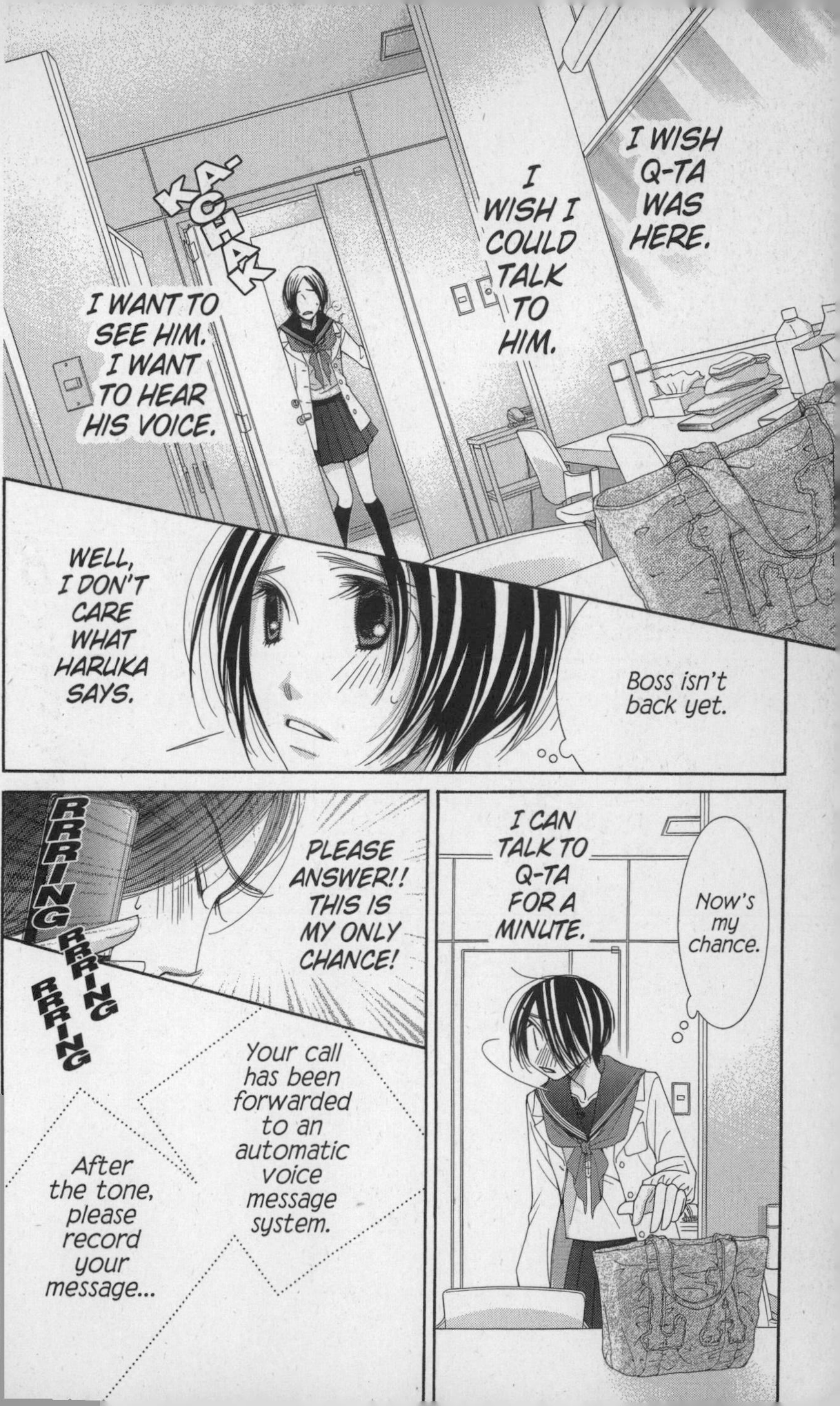
I WISH Q-TA WAS HERE.
I WISH I COULD TALK TO HIM.
KA-CHAK
I WANT TO SEE HIM. I WANT TO HEAR HIS VOICE.
Boss isn't back yet.
WELL, I DON'T CARE WHAT HARUKA SAYS.
Now's my chance.
I CAN TALK TO Q-TA FOR A MINUTE.
PLEASE ANSWER!! THIS IS MY ONLY CHANCE!
RRRING RRRING RRRING
Your call has been forwarded to an automatic voice message system.
After the tone, please record your message...

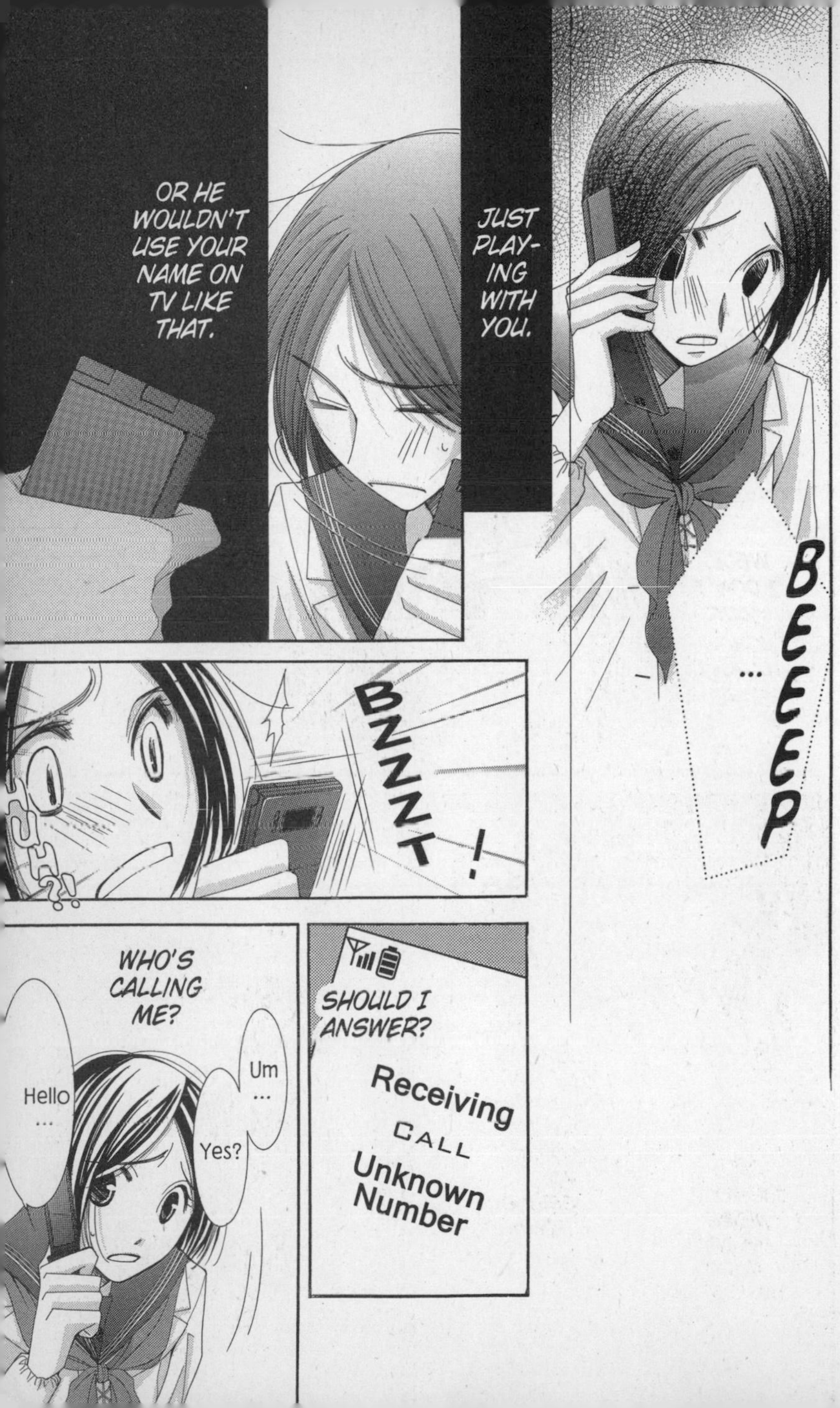

JUST PLAYING WITH YOU.
...
BEEEP
OR HE WOULDN'T USE YOUR NAME ON TV LIKE THAT.
BZZZT
!
SHOULD I ANSWER?
Receiving
CALL
Unknown Number
WHO'S CALLING ME?
Um ...
Yes?
Hello ...

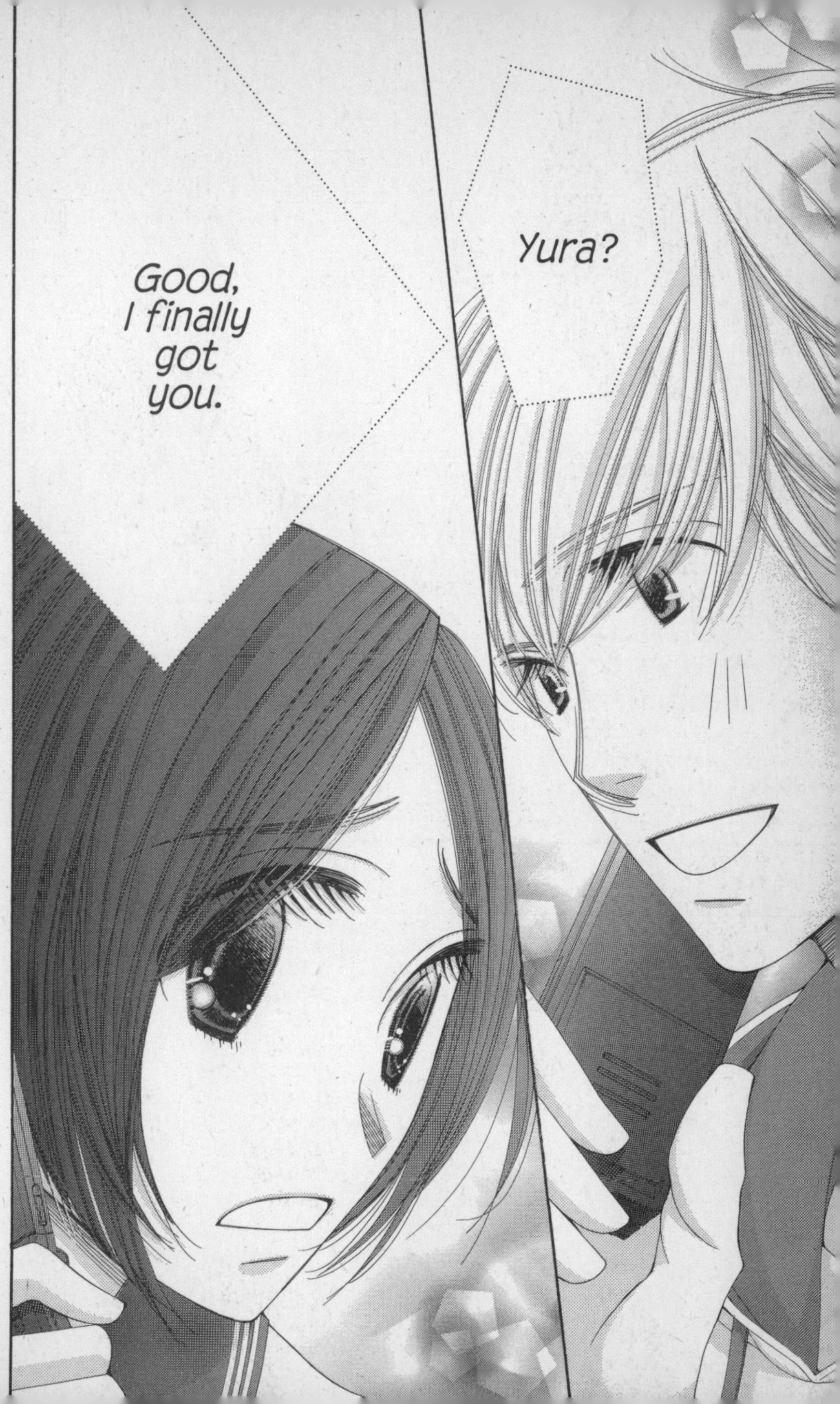
Yura?
Good, I finally got you.

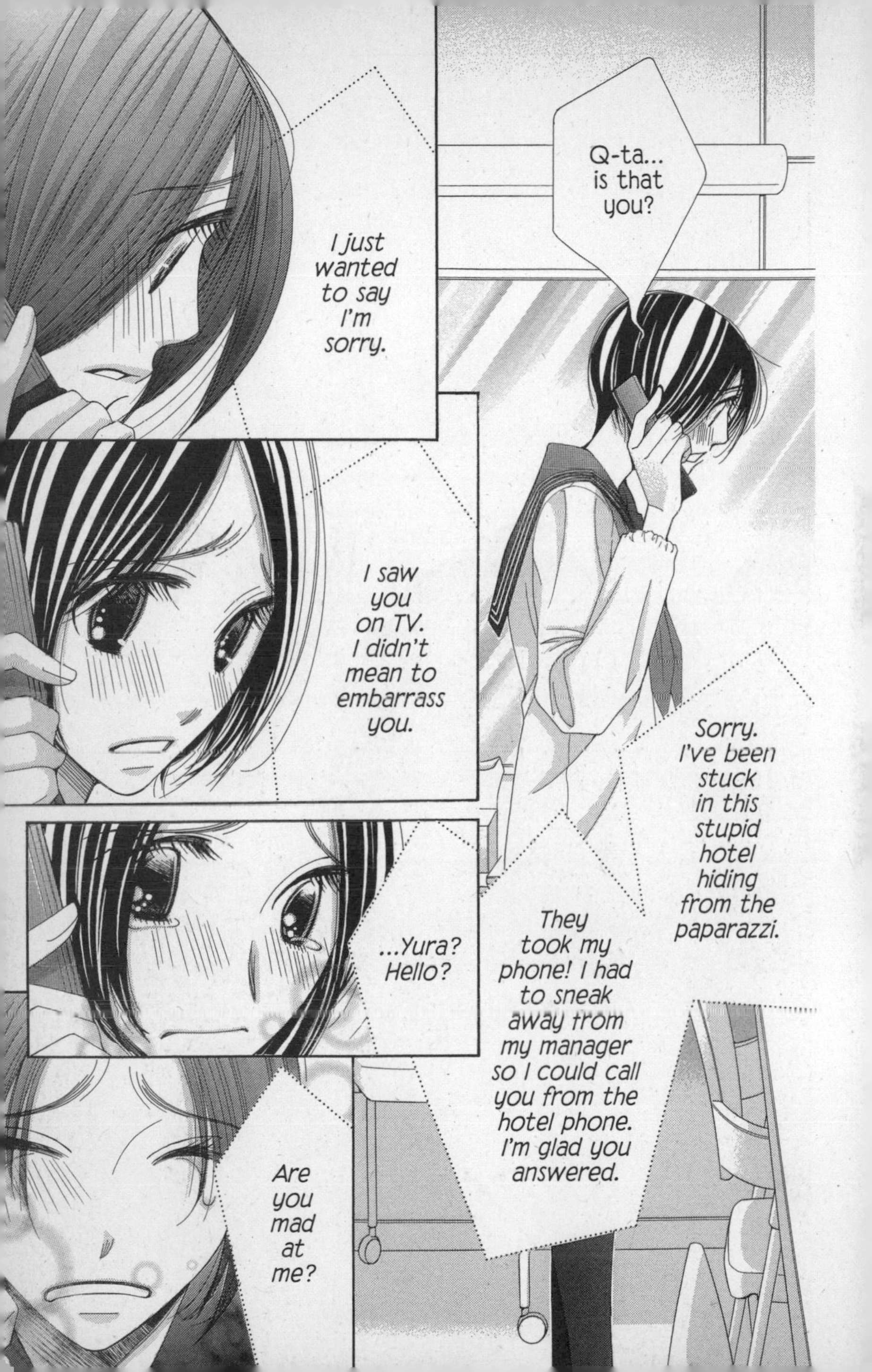
Q-ta... is that you?
I just wanted to say I'm sorry.
I saw you on TV. I didn't mean to embarrass you.
...Yura? Hello?
Sorry. I've been stuck in this stupid hotel hiding from the paparazzi.
They took my phone! I had to sneak away from my manager so I could call you from the hotel phone. I'm glad you answered.
Are you mad at me?

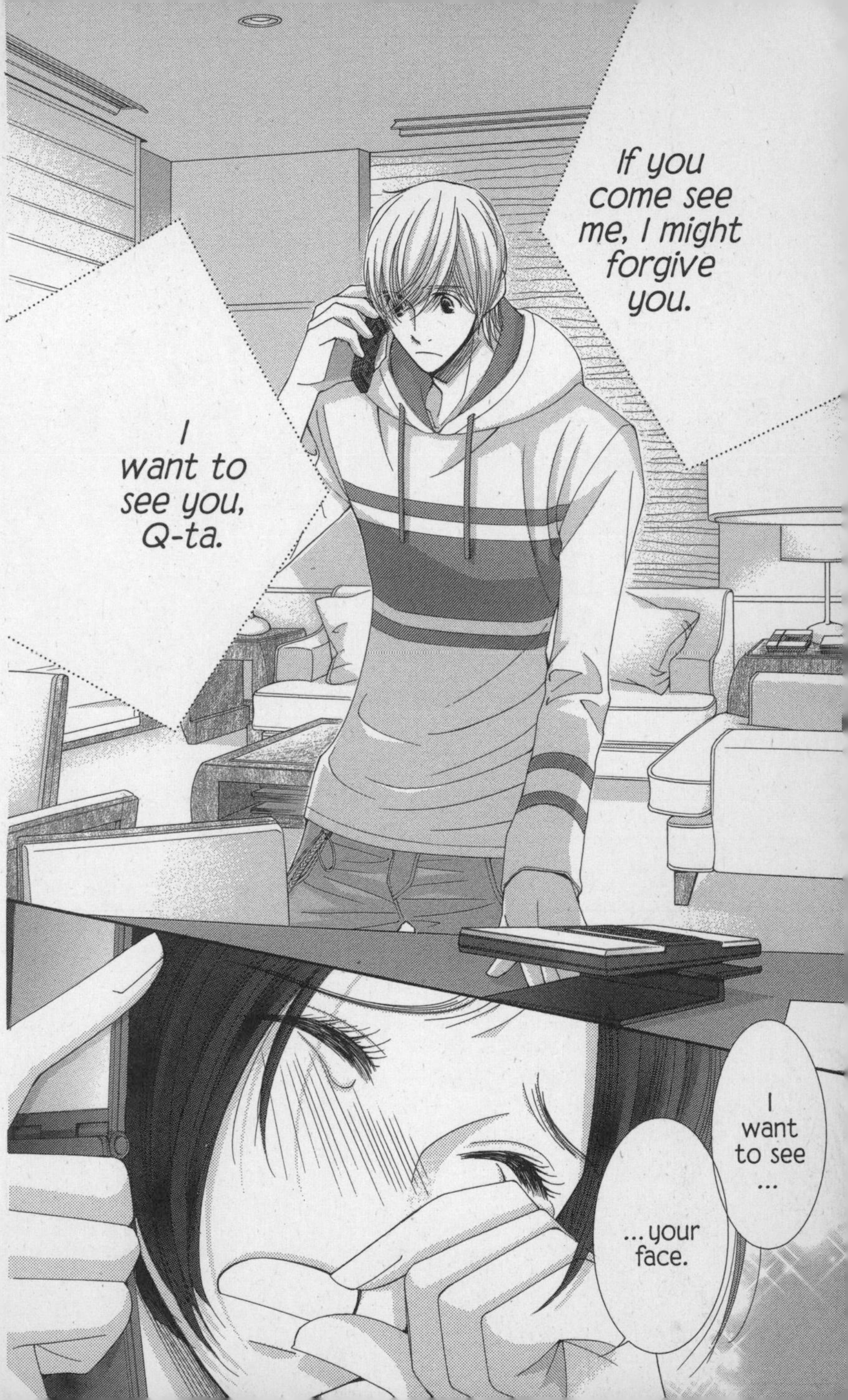
If you come see me, I might forgive you.
I want to see you, Q-ta.
I want to see ...
...your face.

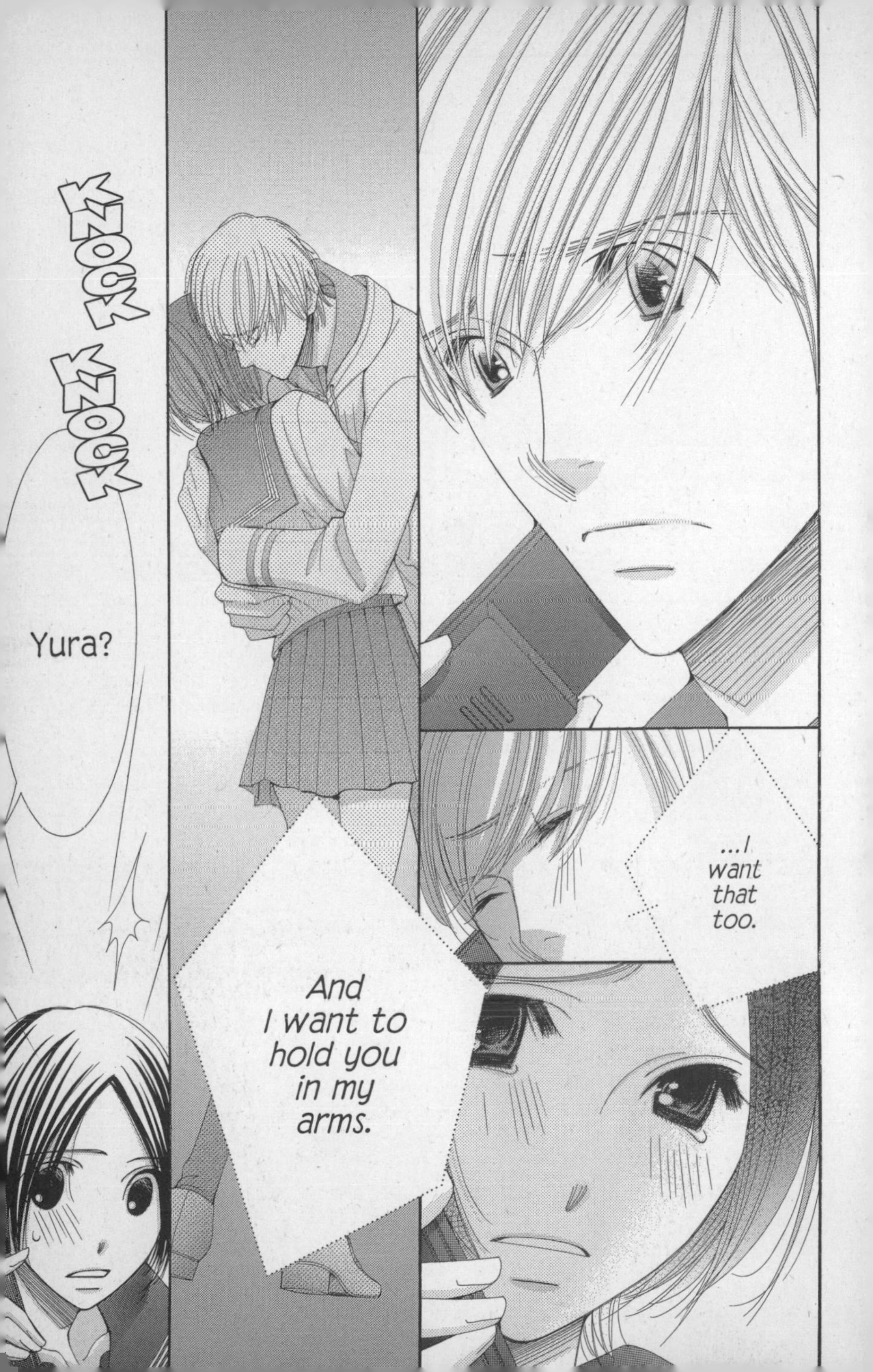
...I want that too.
And I want to hold you in my arms.
KNOCK KNOCK
Yura?

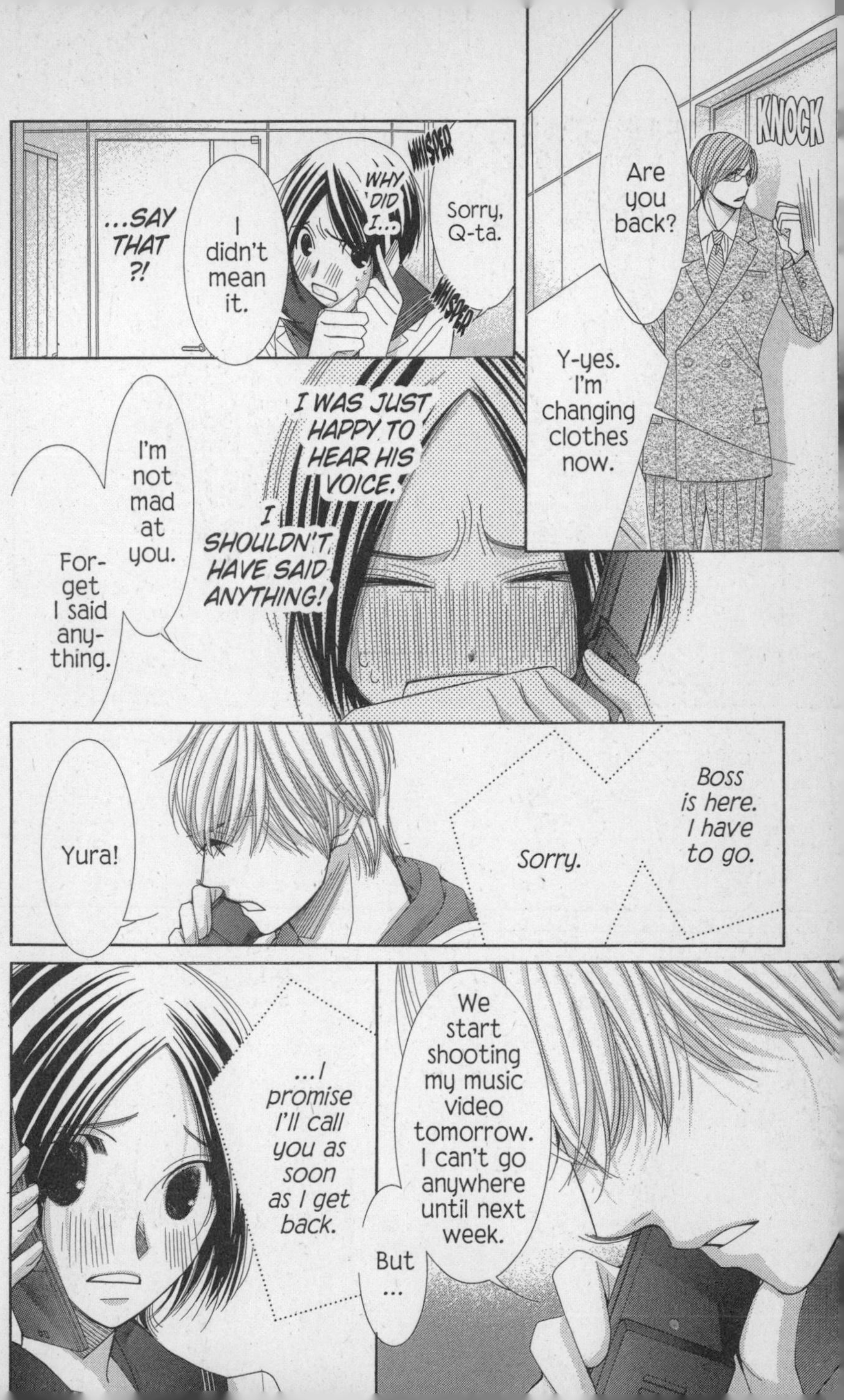
KNOCK
Are you back?
Y-yes. I'm changing clothes now.
Sorry, Q-ta.
WHISPER
WHY DID I...
I didn't mean it.
...SAY THAT?!
WHISPER
I WAS JUST HAPPY TO HEAR HIS VOICE.
I SHOULDN'T HAVE SAID ANYTHING!
I'm not mad at you.
For-get I said any-thing.
Boss is here. I have to go.
Sorry.
Yura!
We start shooting my music video tomorrow. I can't go anywhere until next week.
But ...
...I promise I'll call you as soon as I get back.

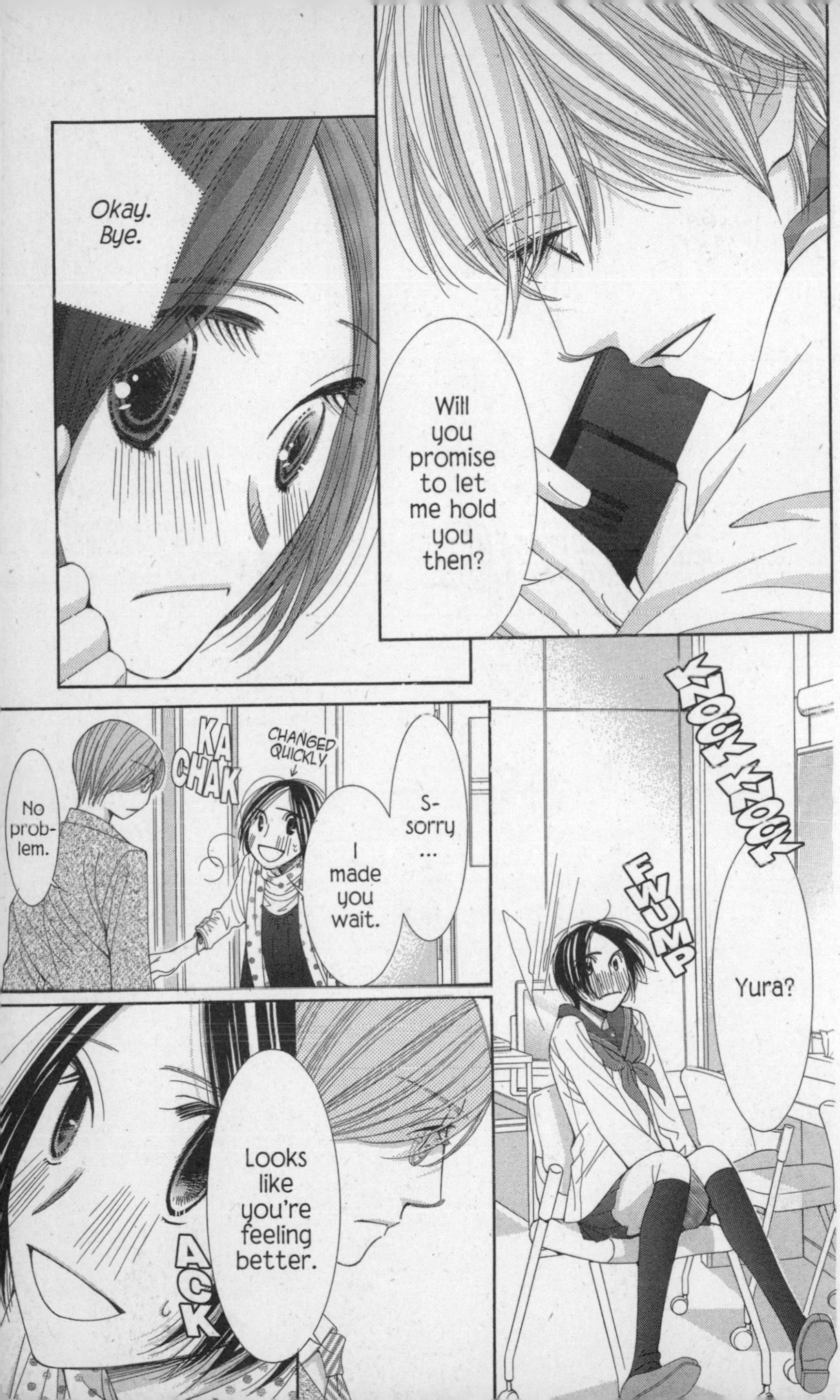
Will you promise to let me hold you then?
Okay. Bye.
KOOK KOOK
Yura?
FWUMP
KA CHAK
CHANGED QUICKLY
S-sorry...
I made you wait.
No prob-lem.
Looks like you're feeling better.
ACK

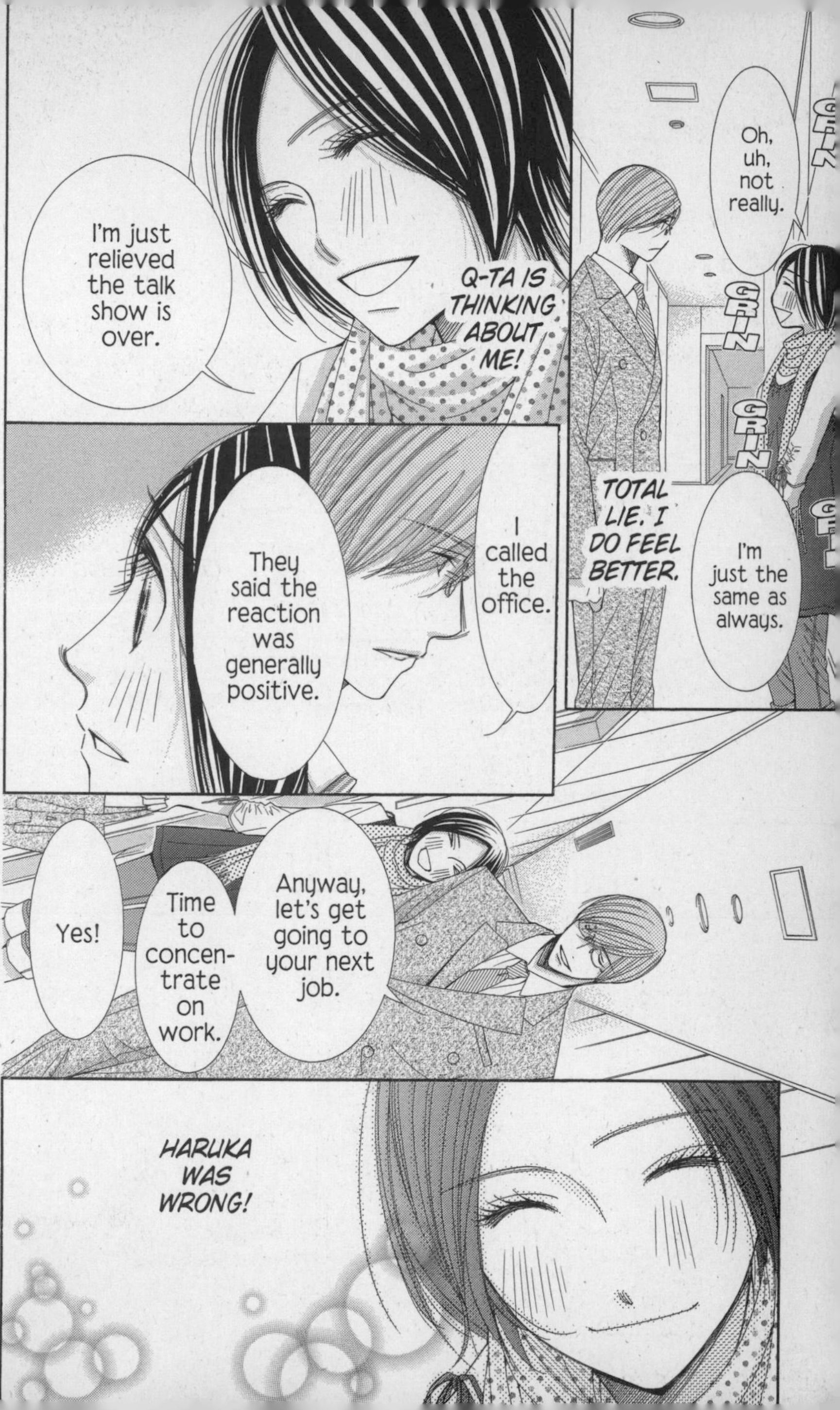
Oh, uh, not really.
GRIN
GRIN
TOTAL LIE. I DO FEEL BETTER.
I'm just the same as always.
Q-TA IS THINKING ABOUT ME!
I'm just relieved the talk show is over.
I called the office.
They said the reaction was generally positive.
Anyway, let's get going to your next job.
Time to concen-trate on work.
Yes!
HARUKA WAS WRONG!

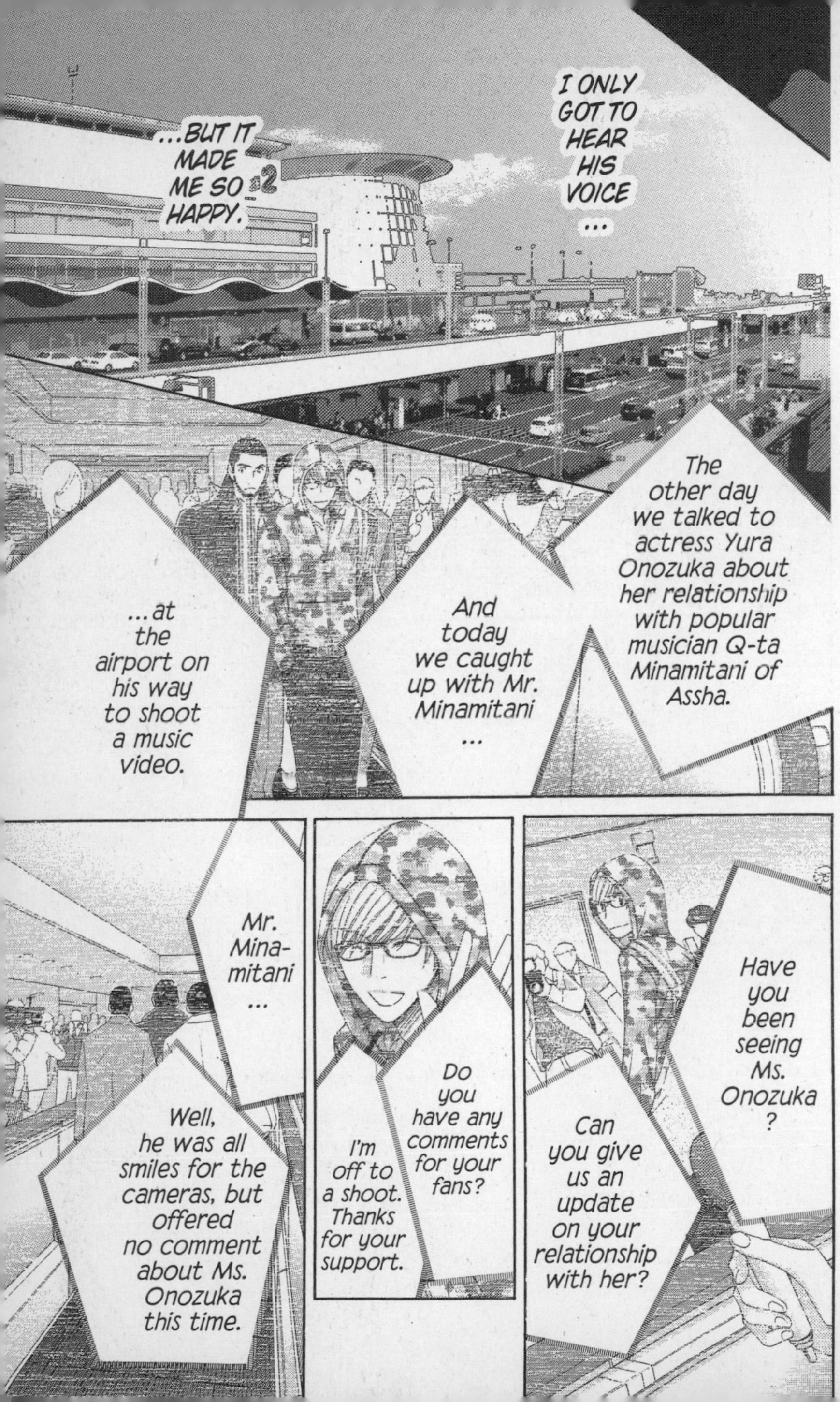
I ONLY GOT TO HEAR HIS VOICE...
...BUT IT MADE ME SO HAPPY.
The other day we talked to actress Yura Onozuka about her relationship with popular musician Q-ta Minamitani of Assha.
And today we caught up with Mr. Minamitani...
...at the airport on his way to shoot a music video.
Have you been seeing Ms. Onozuka?
Can you give us an update on your relationship with her?
Do you have any comments for your fans?
I'm off to a shoot. Thanks for your support.
Mr. Minamitani...
Well, he was all smiles for the cameras, but offered no comment about Ms. Onozuka this time.

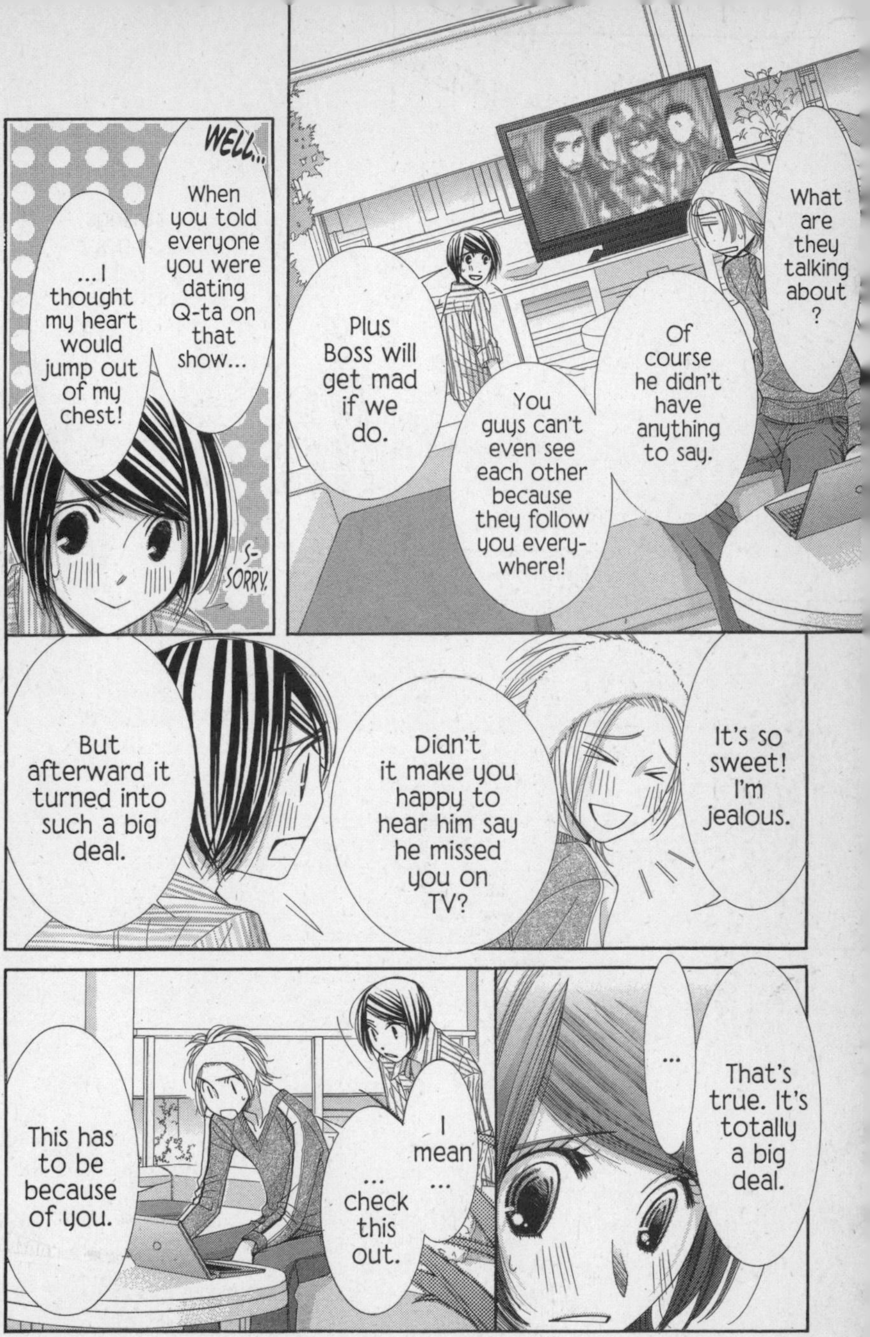
What are they talking about?
Of course he didn't have anything to say.
You guys can't even see each other because they follow you every-where!
Plus Boss will get mad if we do.
WELL...
When you told everyone you were dating Q-ta on that show...
...I thought my heart would jump out of my chest!
S-SORRY.
It's so sweet! I'm jealous.
Didn't it make you happy to hear him say he missed you on TV?
But afterward it turned into such a big deal.
...
That's true. It's totally a big deal.
I mean...
...check this out.
This has to be because of you.

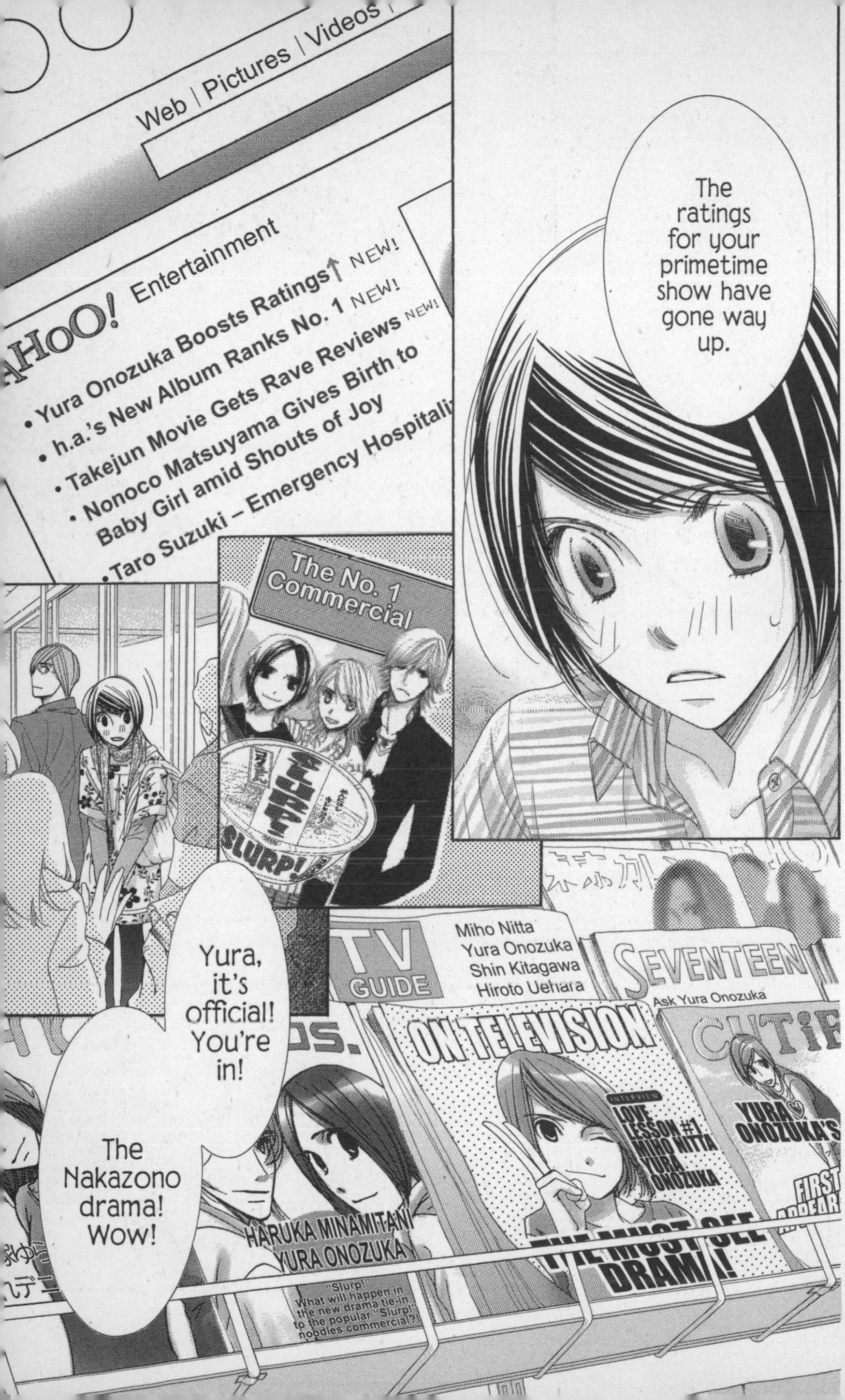
The ratings for your primetime show have gone way up.
Web | Pictures | Videos
AHoO! Entertainment
• Yura Onozuka Boosts Ratings↑ NEW!
• h.a.'s New Album Ranks No. 1 NEW!
• Takejun Movie Gets Rave Reviews NEW!
• Nonoco Matsuyama Gives Birth to Baby Girl amid Shouts of Joy
• Taro Suzuki – Emergency Hospitali
The No. 1 Commercial
SLURP!
Yura, it's official! You're in!
The Nakazono drama! Wow!
TV GUIDE
Miho Nitta
Yura Onozuka
Shin Kitagawa
Hiroto Uehara
SEVENTEEN
Ask Yura Onozuka
CUTiE
YURA ONOZUKA'S
FIRST APPEAR
ON TELEVISION
INTERVIEW
LOVE LESSON #1 MIHO NITTA YURA ONOZUKA
THE MUST SEE DRAMA!
HARUKA MINAMITANI YURA ONOZUKA
"Slurp!" What will happen in the new drama tie-in to the popular "Slurp!" noodles commercial?

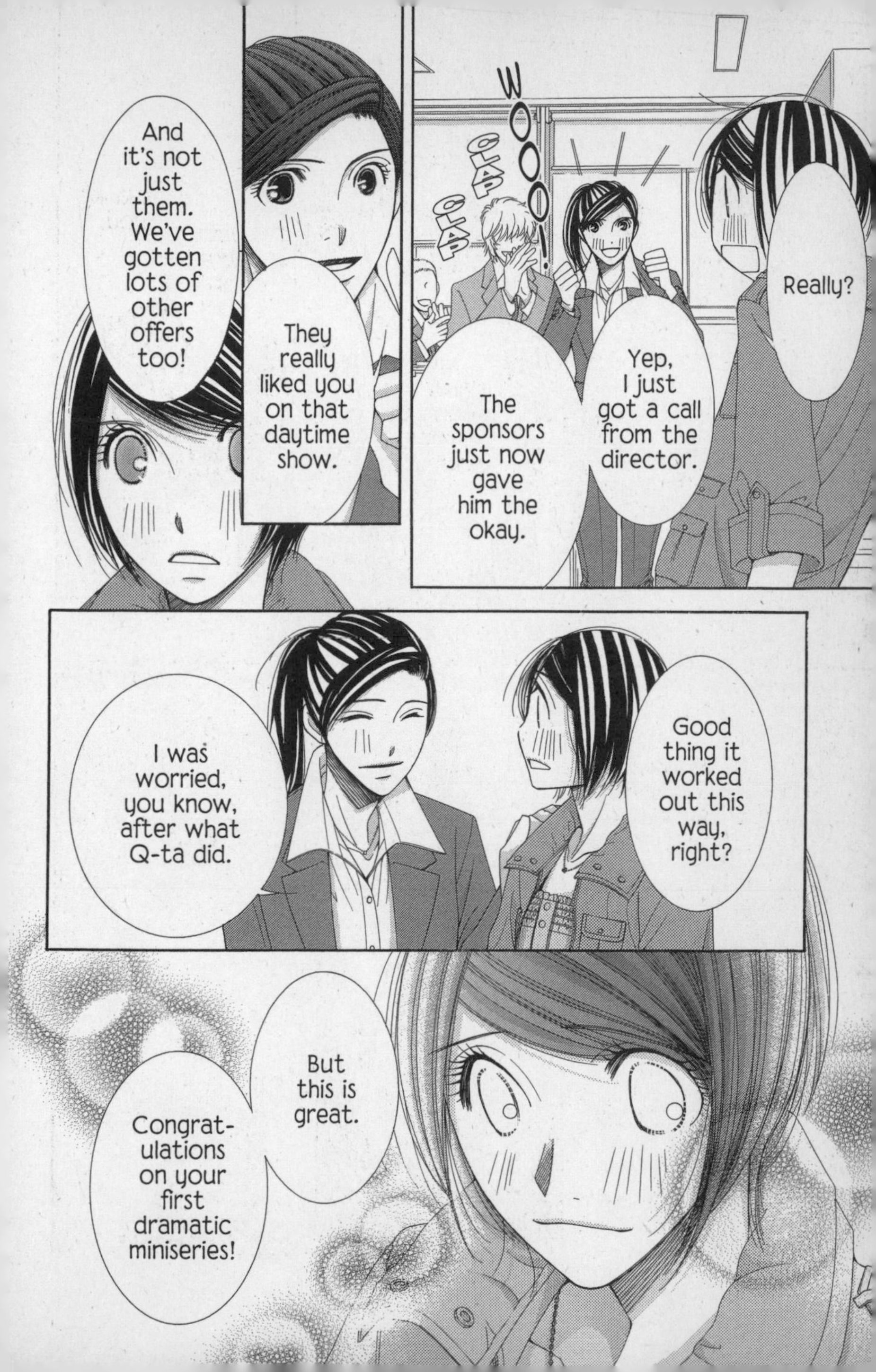
Really?
WOOO!
CLAP CLAP
Yep, I just got a call from the director.
The sponsors just now gave him the okay.
They really liked you on that daytime show.
And it's not just them. We've gotten lots of other offers too!
Good thing it worked out this way, right?
I was worried, you know, after what Q-ta did.
But this is great.
Congrat-ulations on your first dramatic miniseries!

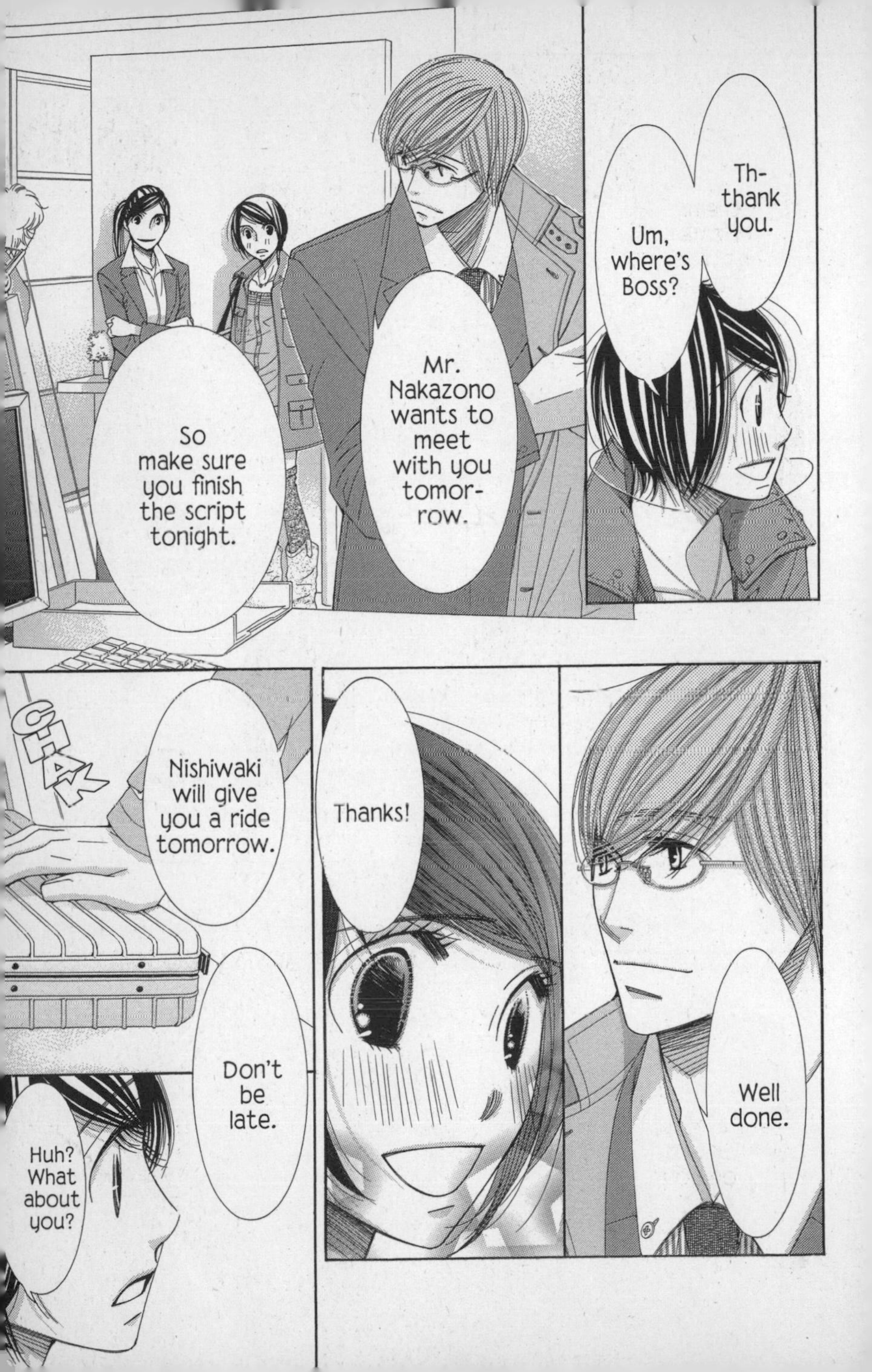
Th-thank you.
Um, where's Boss?
Mr. Nakazono wants to meet with you tomorrow.
So make sure you finish the script tonight.
Well done.
Thanks!
Nishiwaki will give you a ride tomorrow.
CHAK
Don't be late.
Huh? What about you?

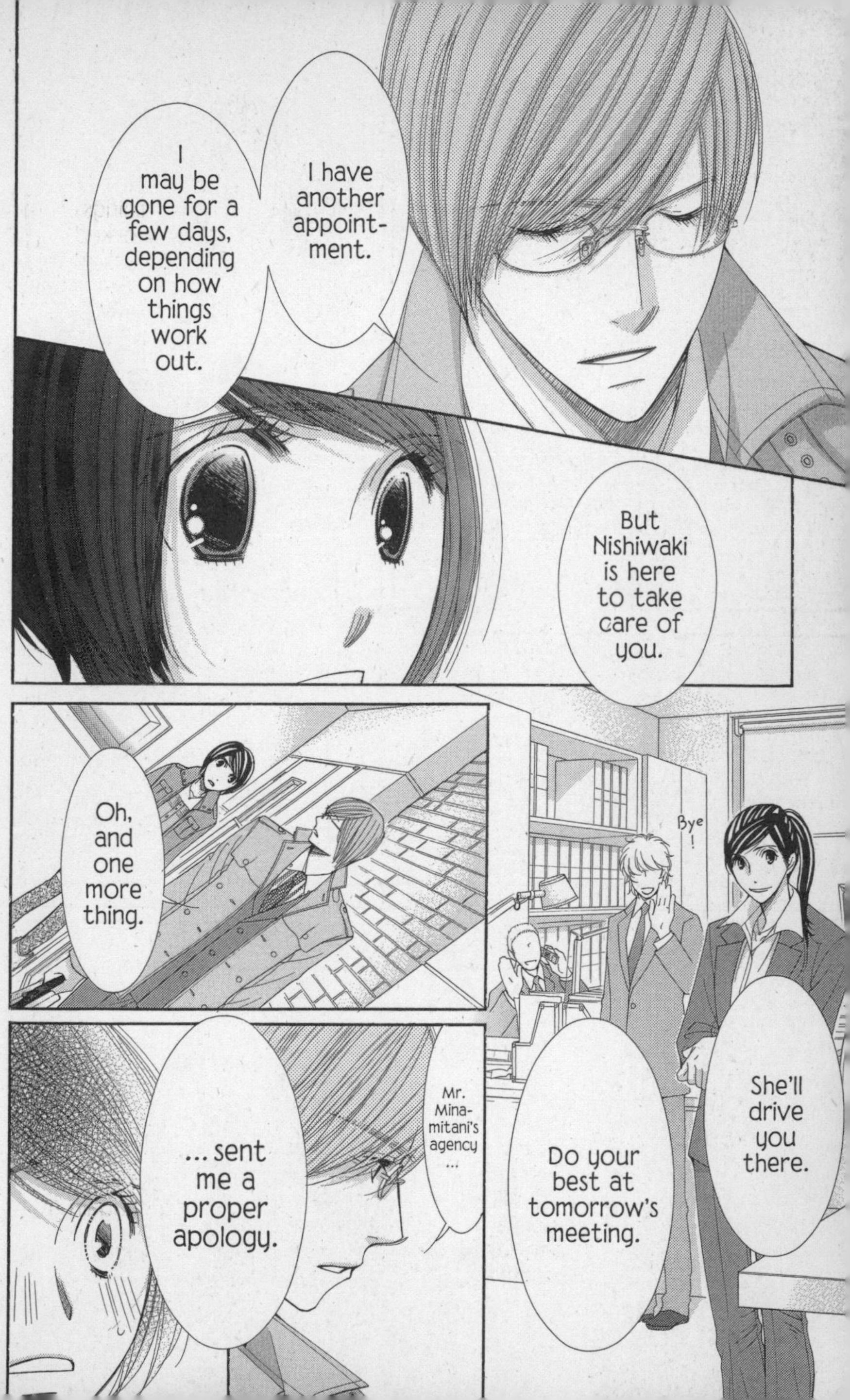
I have another appointment.
I may be gone for a few days, depending on how things work out.
But Nishiwaki is here to take care of you.
Bye!
She'll drive you there.
Do your best at tomorrow's meeting.
Oh, and one more thing.
Mr. Minamitani's agency...
...sent me a proper apology.

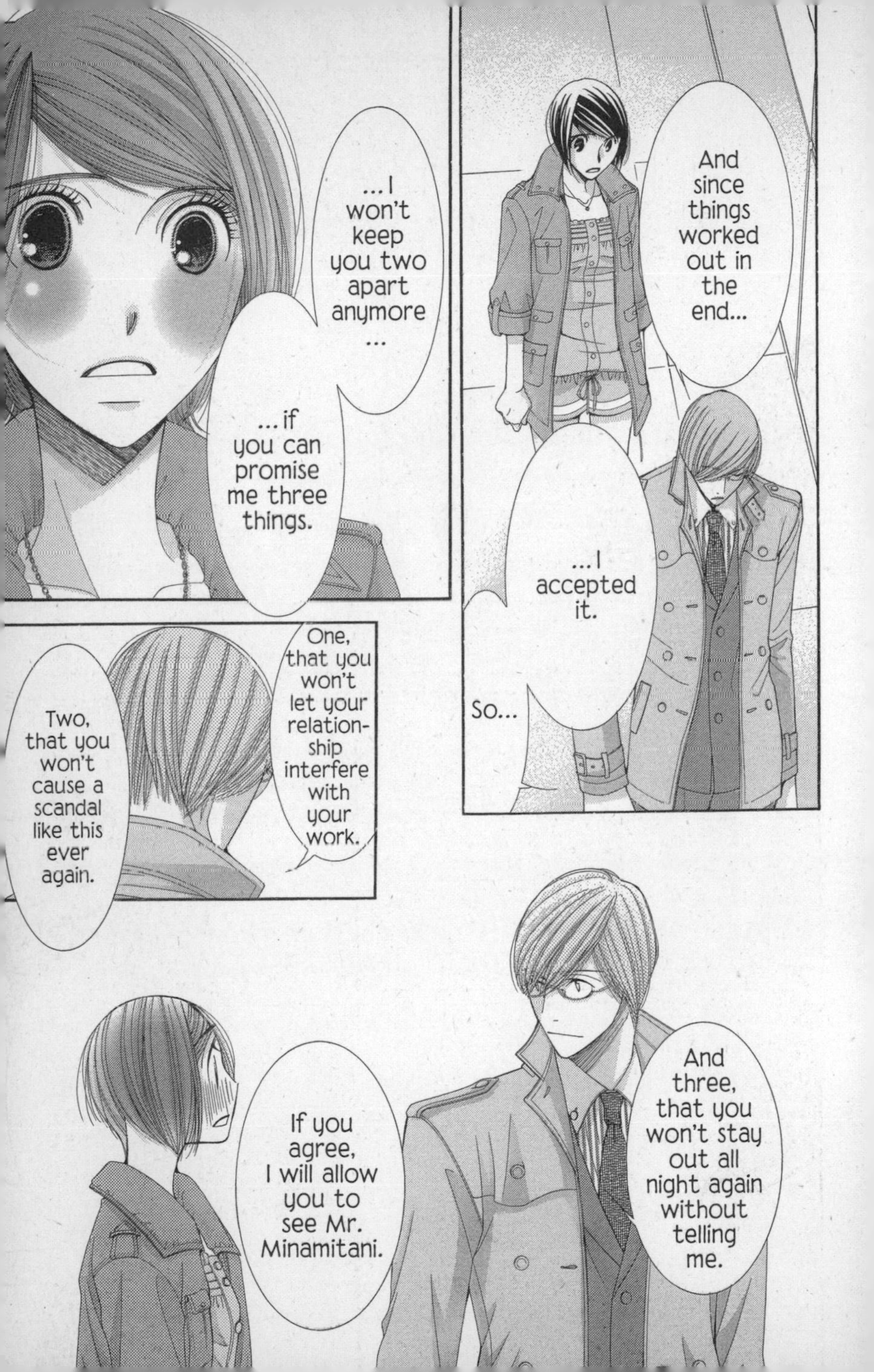
And since things worked out in the end...
...I accepted it.
So...
...I won't keep you two apart anymore...
...if you can promise me three things.
One, that you won't let your relationship interfere with your work.
Two, that you won't cause a scandal like this ever again.
And three, that you won't stay out all night again without telling me.
If you agree, I will allow you to see Mr. Minamitani.

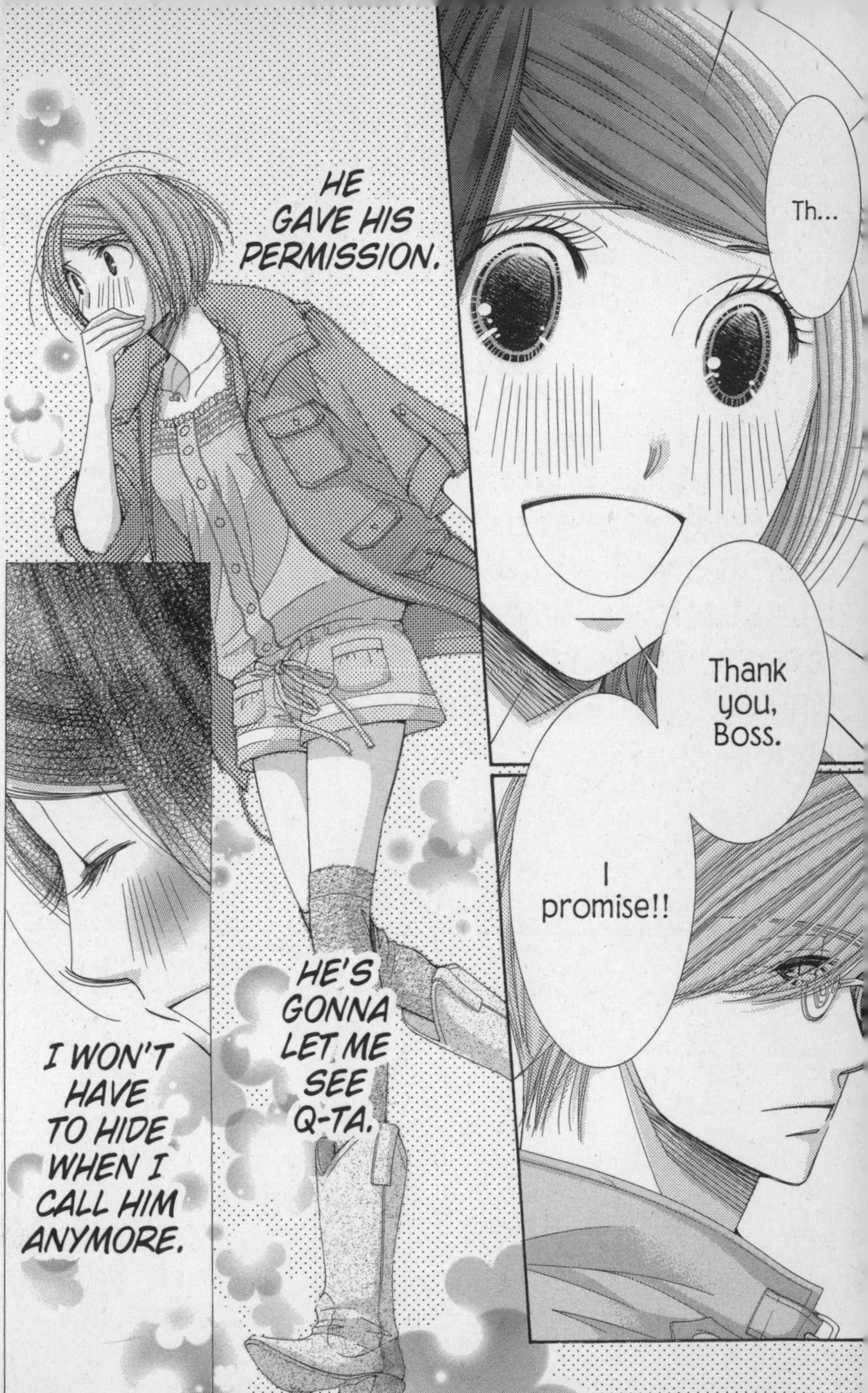
Th...
Thank you, Boss.
I promise!!
HE GAVE HIS PERMISSION.
HE'S GONNA LET ME SEE Q-TA.
I WON'T HAVE TO HIDE WHEN I CALL HIM ANYMORE.

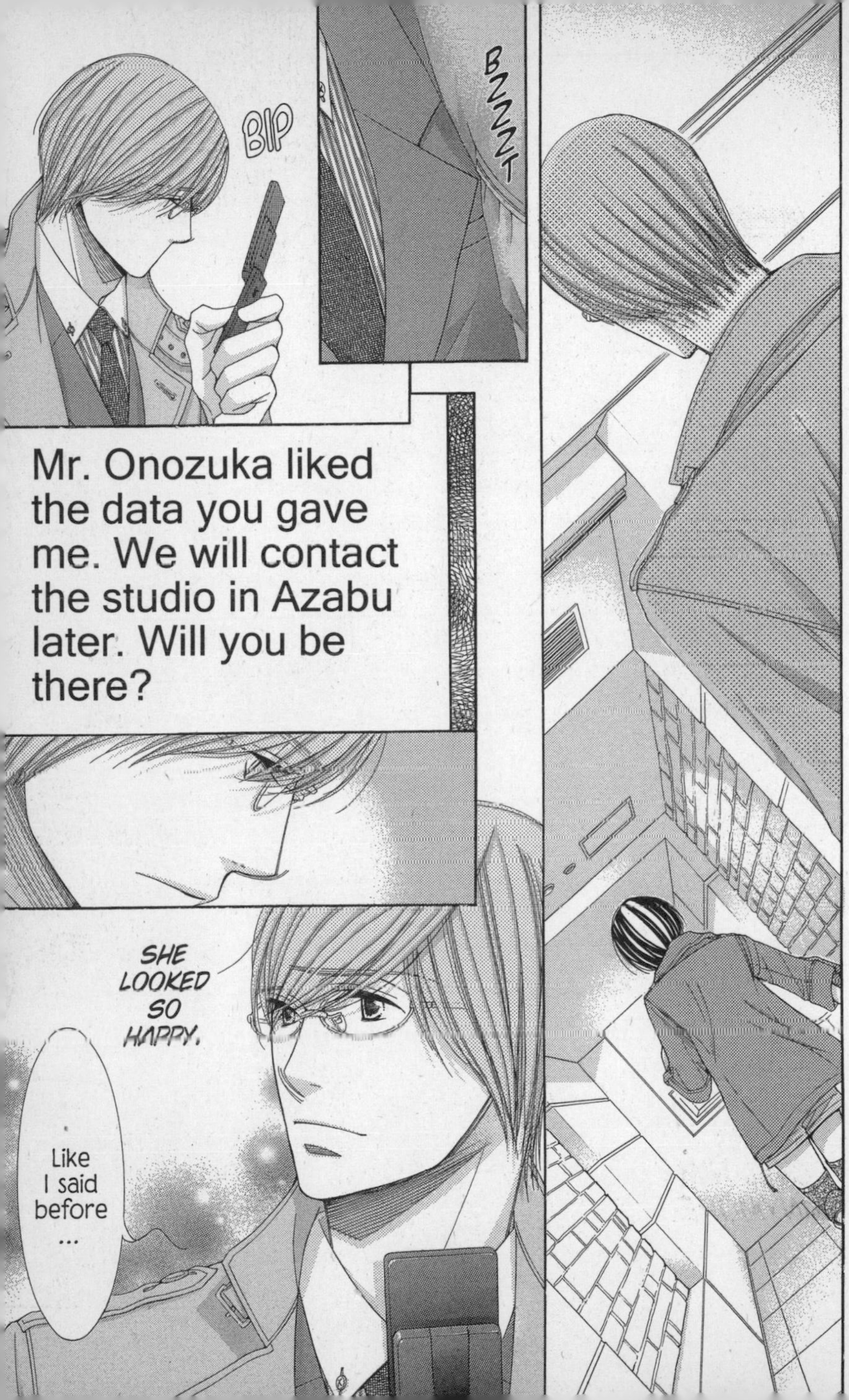
BZZZT
BIP
Mr. Onozuka liked the data you gave me. We will contact the studio in Azabu later. Will you be there?
SHE LOOKED SO HAPPY.
Like I said before ...

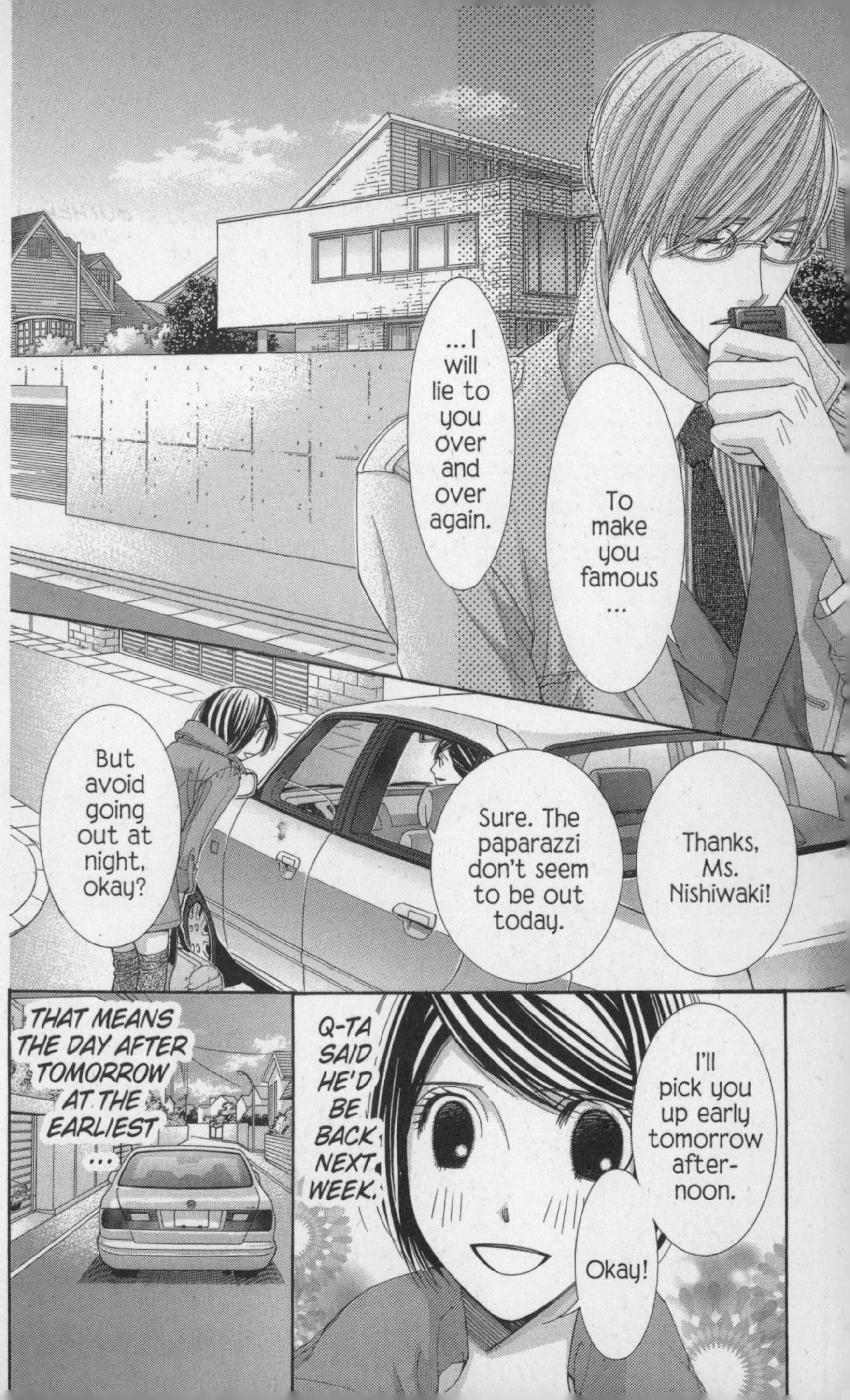
To make you famous...
...I will lie to you over and over again.
Thanks, Ms. Nishiwaki!
Sure. The paparazzi don't seem to be out today.
But avoid going out at night, okay?
I'll pick you up early tomorrow after-noon.
Okay!
Q-TA SAID HE'D BE BACK NEXT WEEK.
THAT MEANS THE DAY AFTER TOMORROW AT THE EARLIEST...

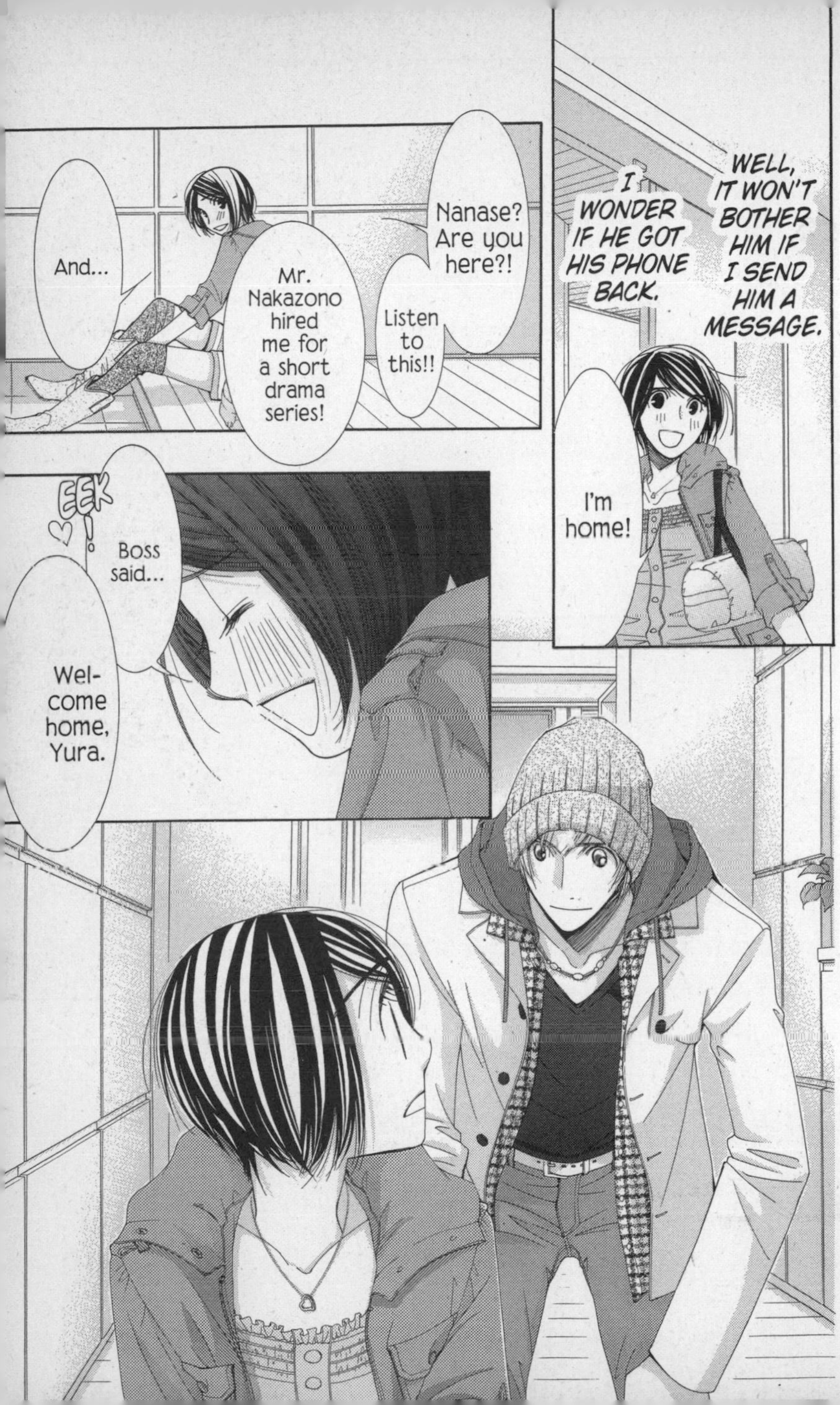
WELL, IT WON'T BOTHER HIM IF I SEND HIM A MESSAGE.
I WONDER IF HE GOT HIS PHONE BACK.
I'm home!
Nanase? Are you here?!
Listen to this!!
Mr. Nakazono hired me for a short drama series!
And...
Boss said...
EEK!
Wel-come home, Yura.

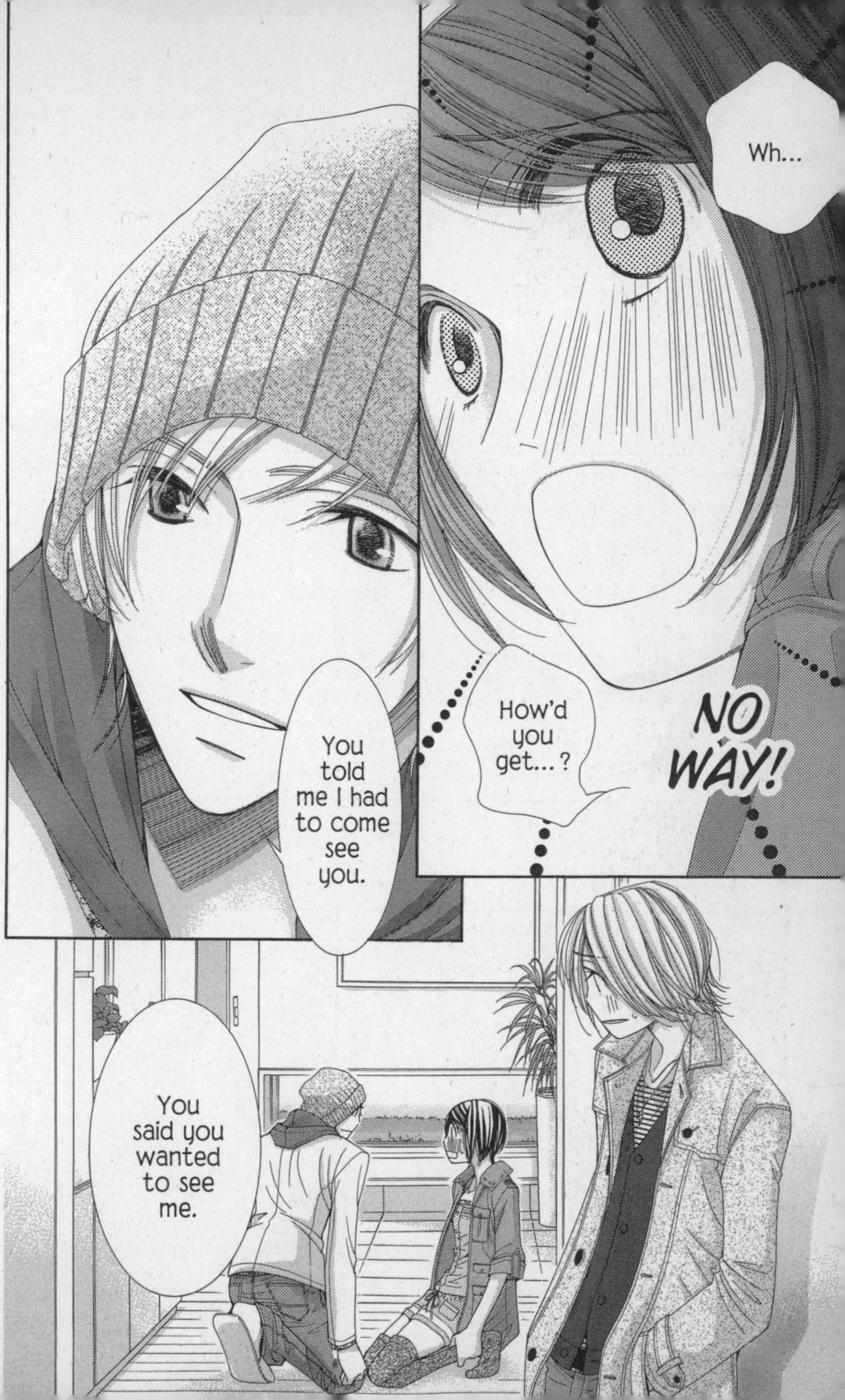
Wh...
NO WAY!
How'd you get...?
You told me I had to come see you.
You said you wanted to see me.

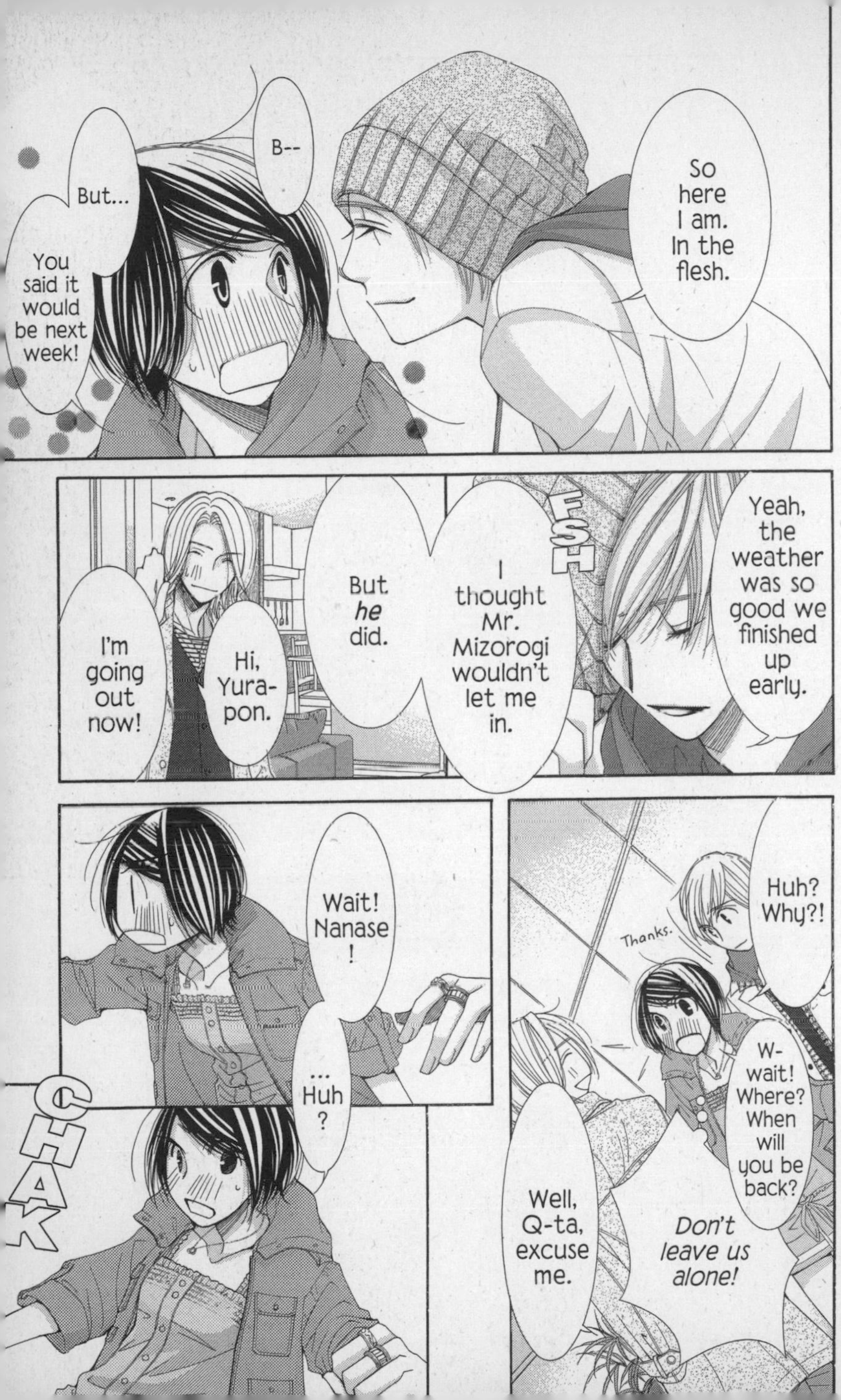
So here I am. In the flesh.
B--
But...
You said it would be next week!
Yeah, the weather was so good we finished up early.
FSH
I thought Mr. Mizorogi wouldn't let me in.
But *he* did.
Hi, Yura-pon.
I'm going out now!
Huh? Why?!
Thanks.
W-wait! Where? When will you be back?
*Don't leave us alone!*
Well, Q-ta, excuse me.
Wait! Nanase!
...Huh?
CHAK

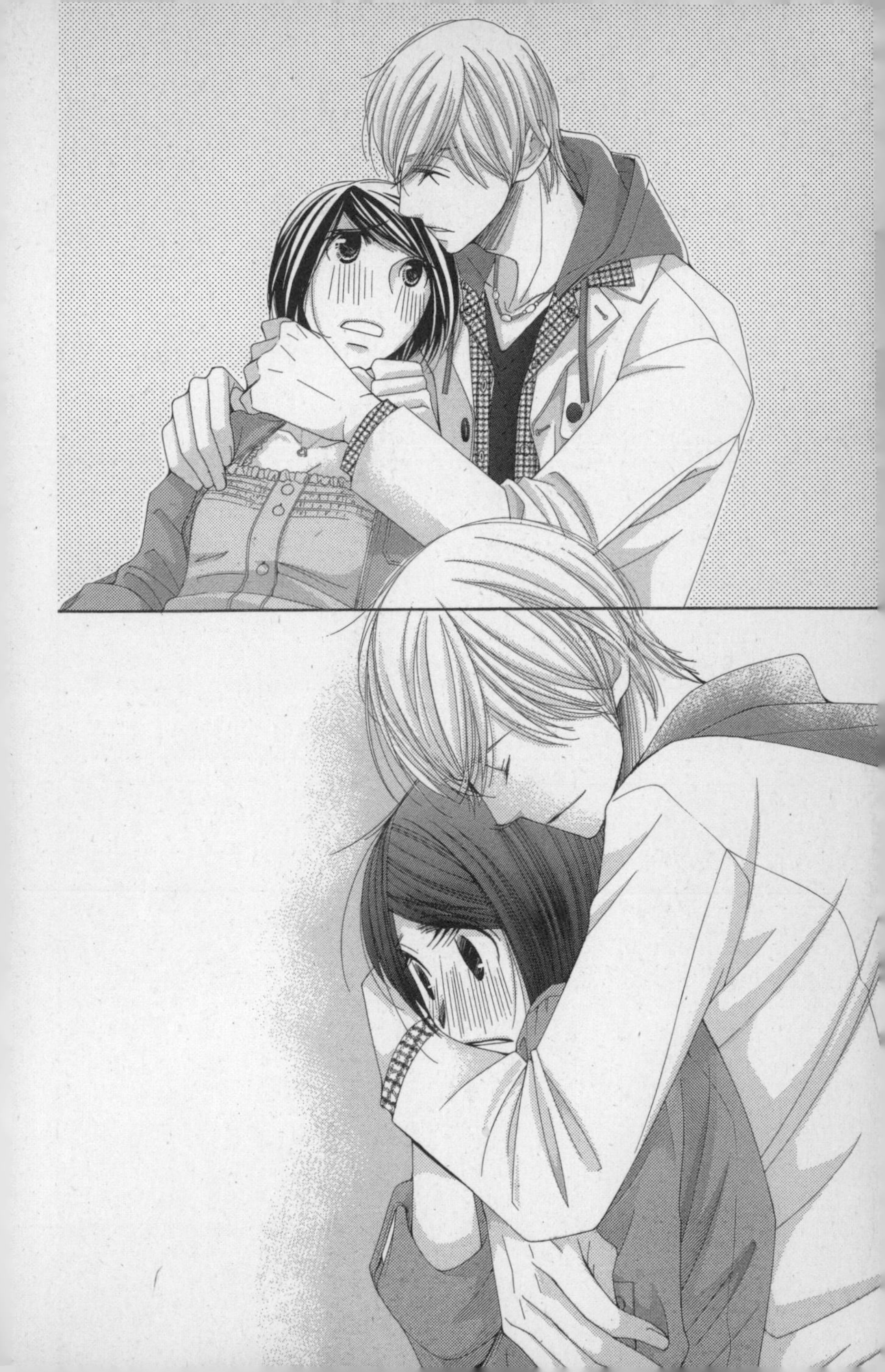

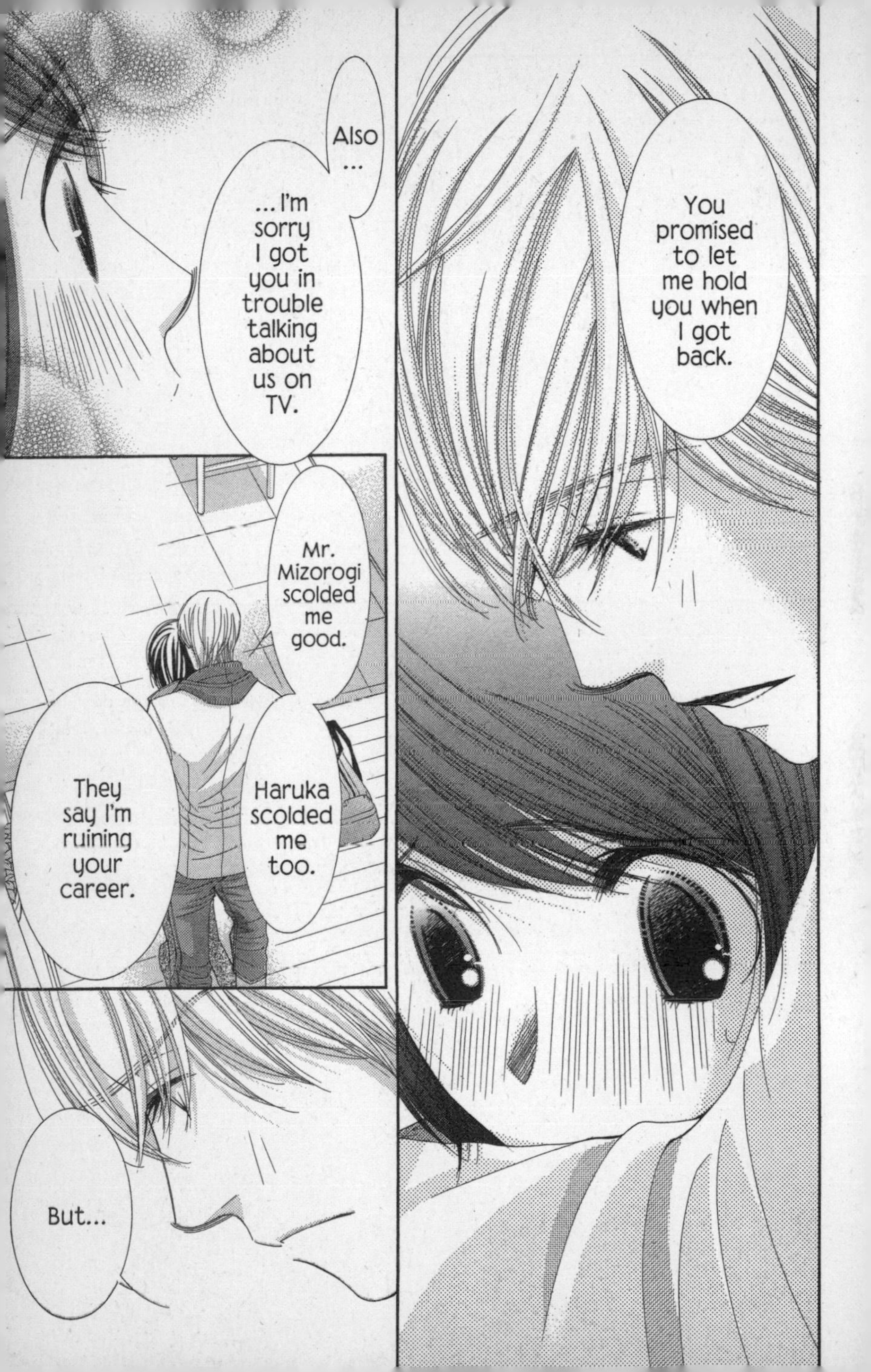
You promised to let me hold you when I got back.
Also...
...I'm sorry I got you in trouble talking about us on TV.
Mr. Mizorogi scolded me good.
Haruka scolded me too.
They say I'm ruining your career.
But...

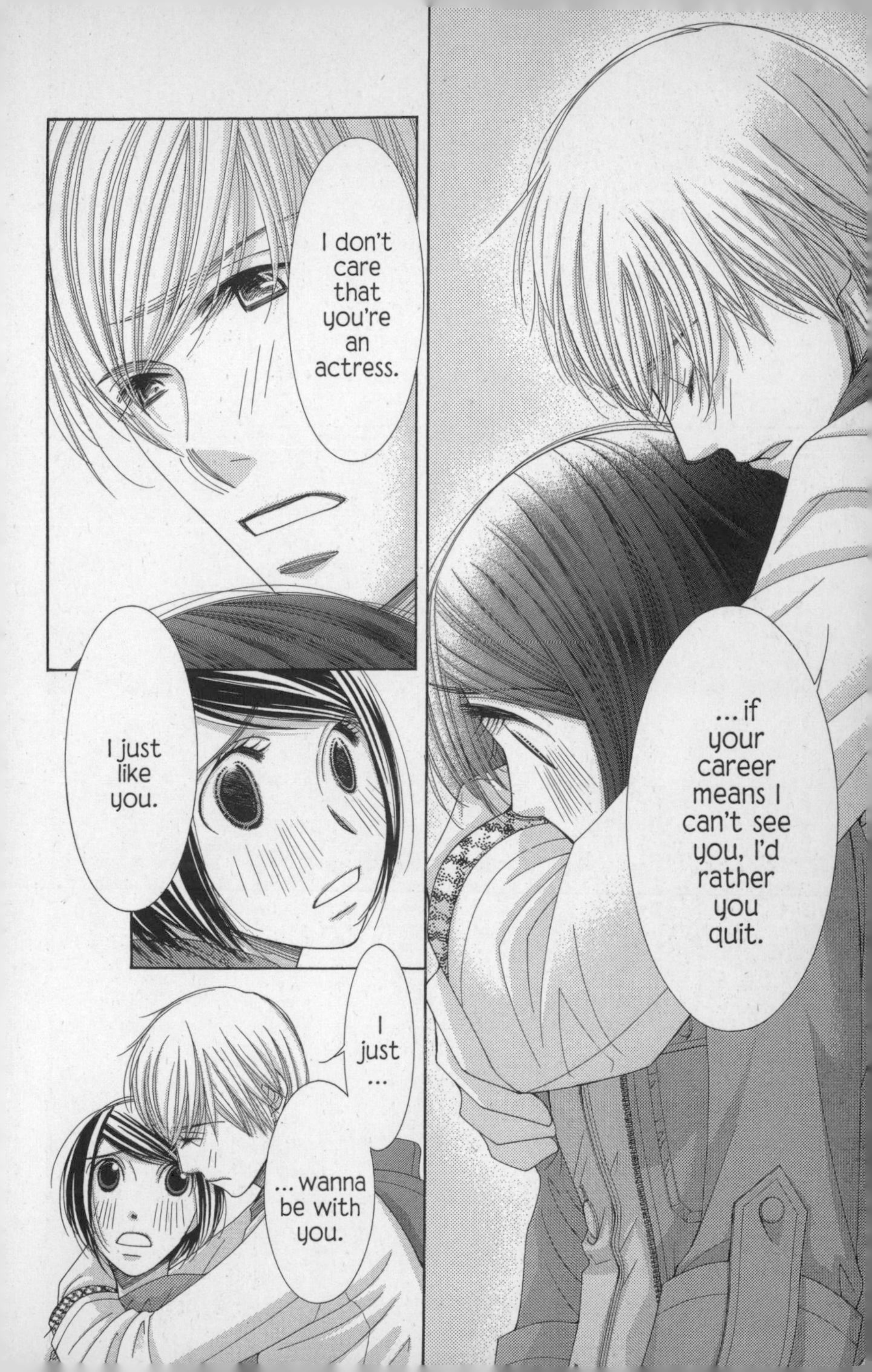
I don't care that you're an actress.
I just like you.
I just ...
...wanna be with you.
...if your career means I can't see you, I'd rather you quit.

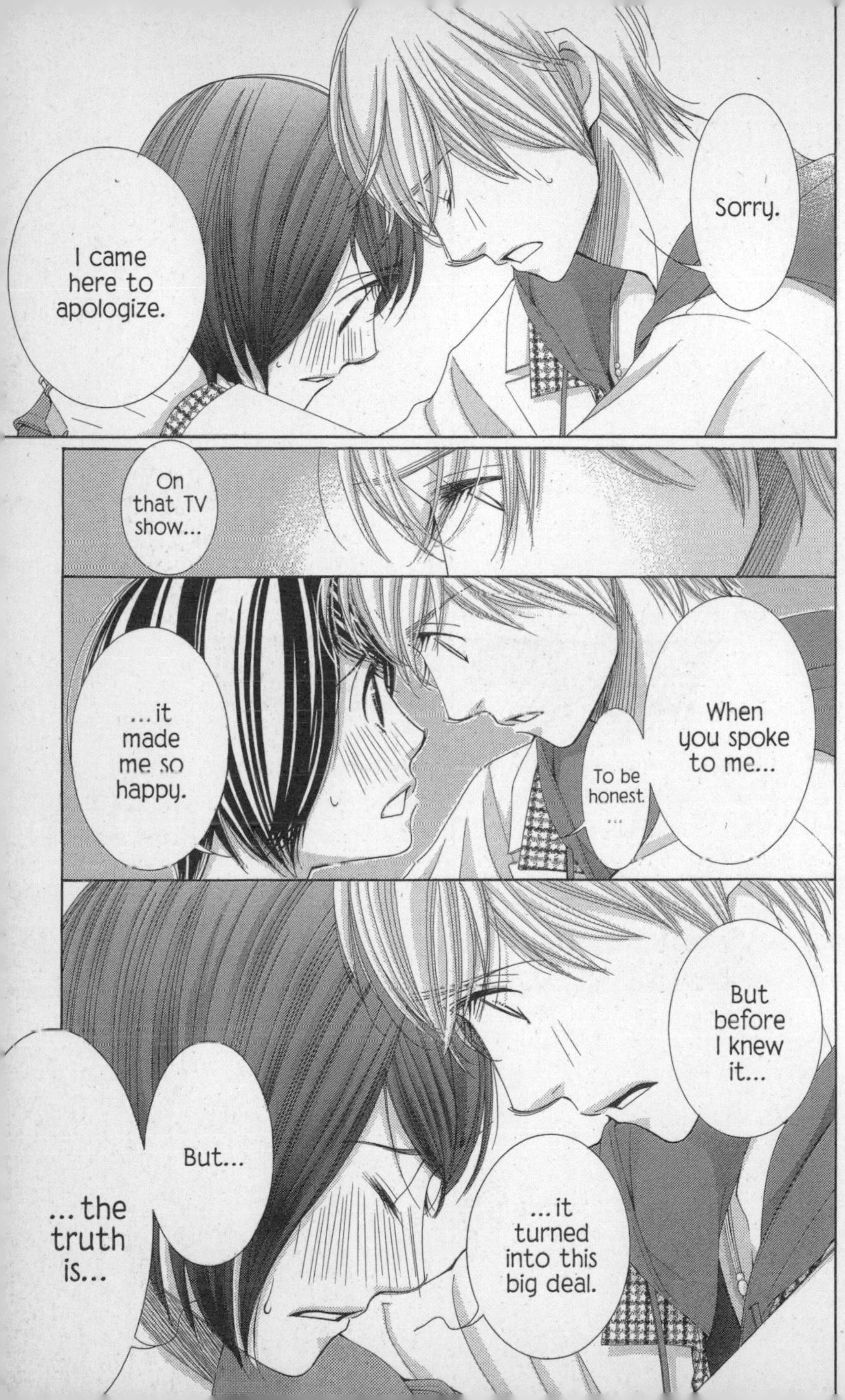
Sorry.
I came here to apologize.
On that TV show...
When you spoke to me...
To be honest...
...it made me so happy.
But before I knew it...
...it turned into this big deal.
But...
...the truth is...

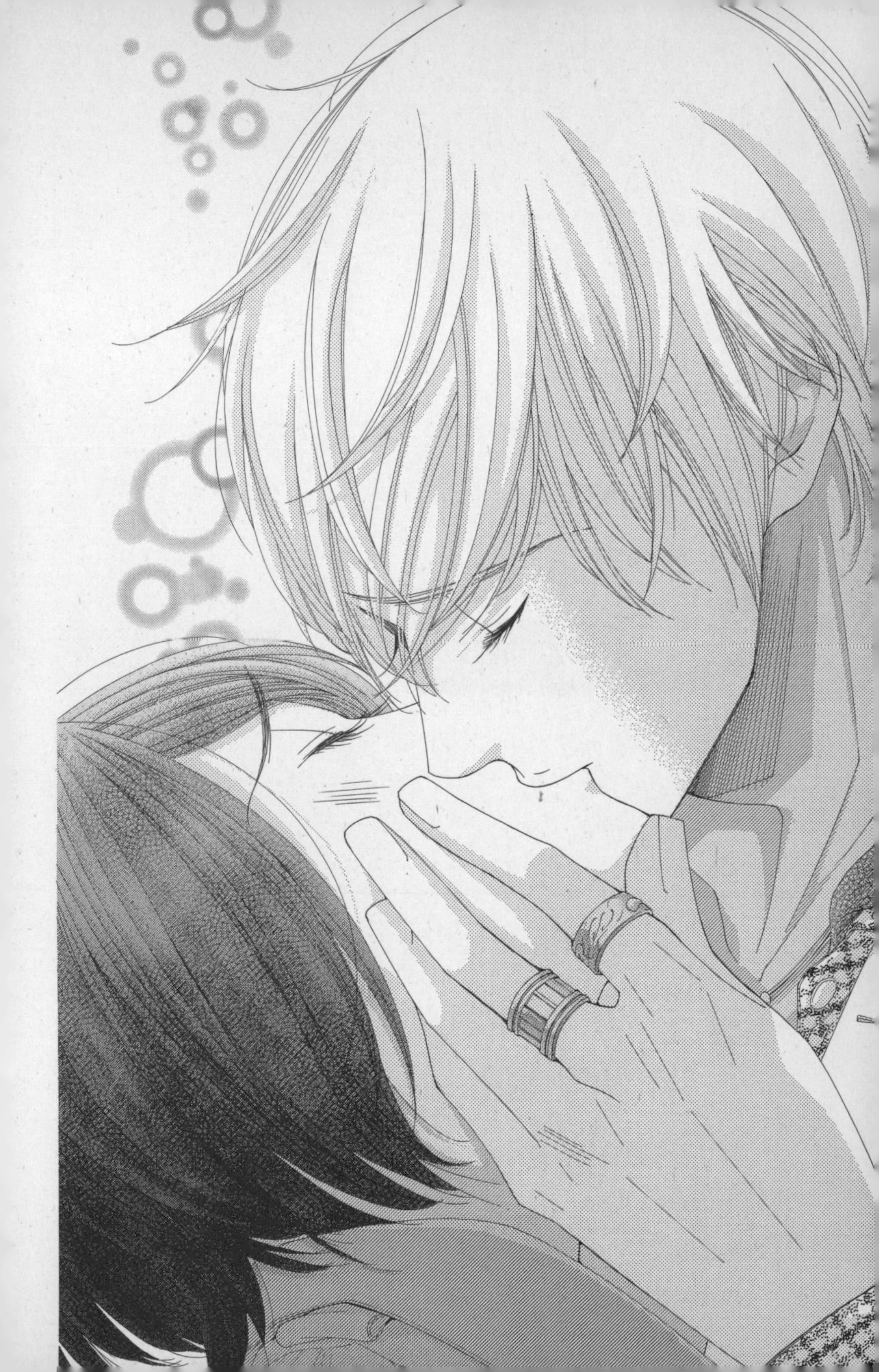

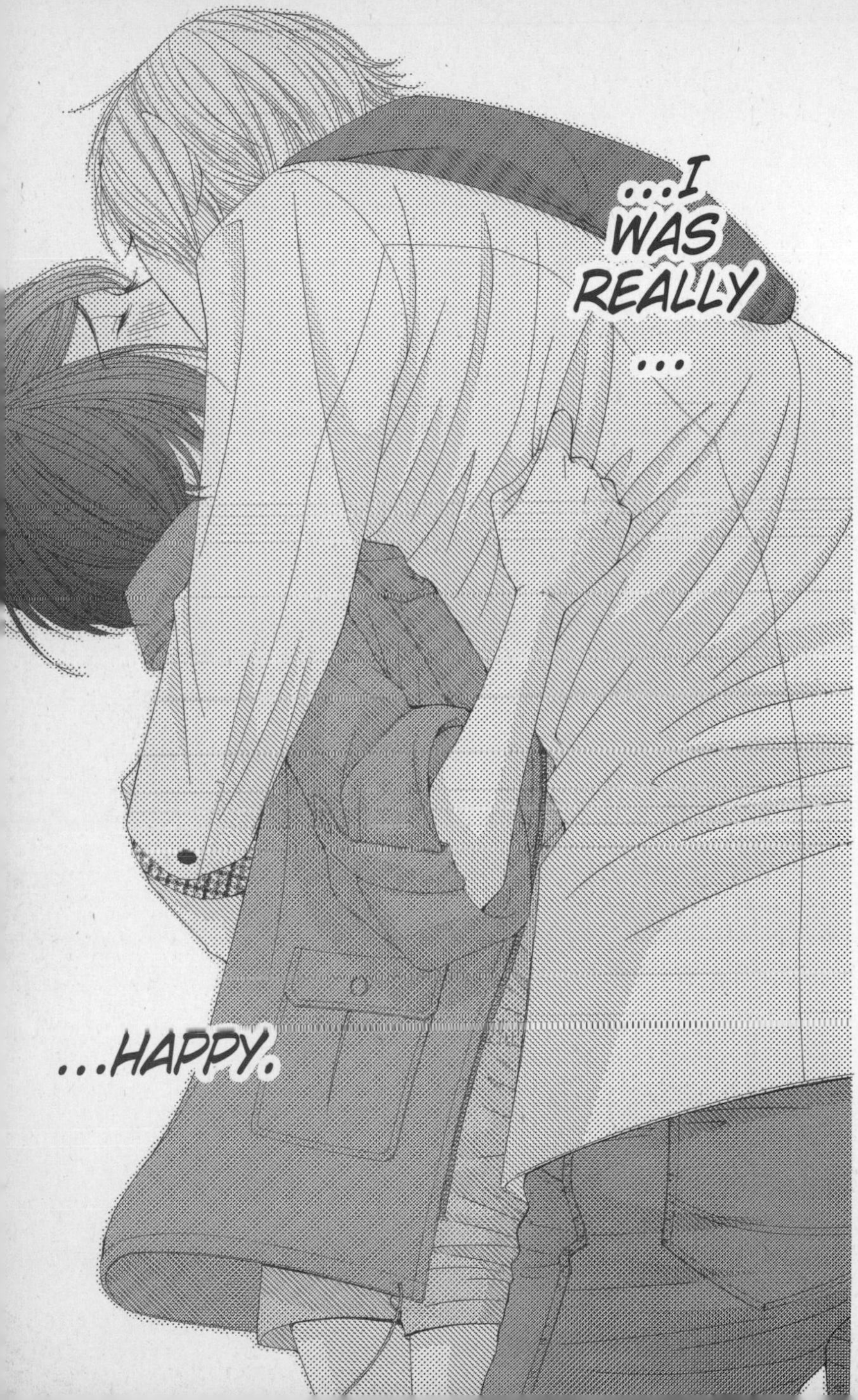
...I WAS REALLY ...
...HAPPY.

Honey Hunt 06

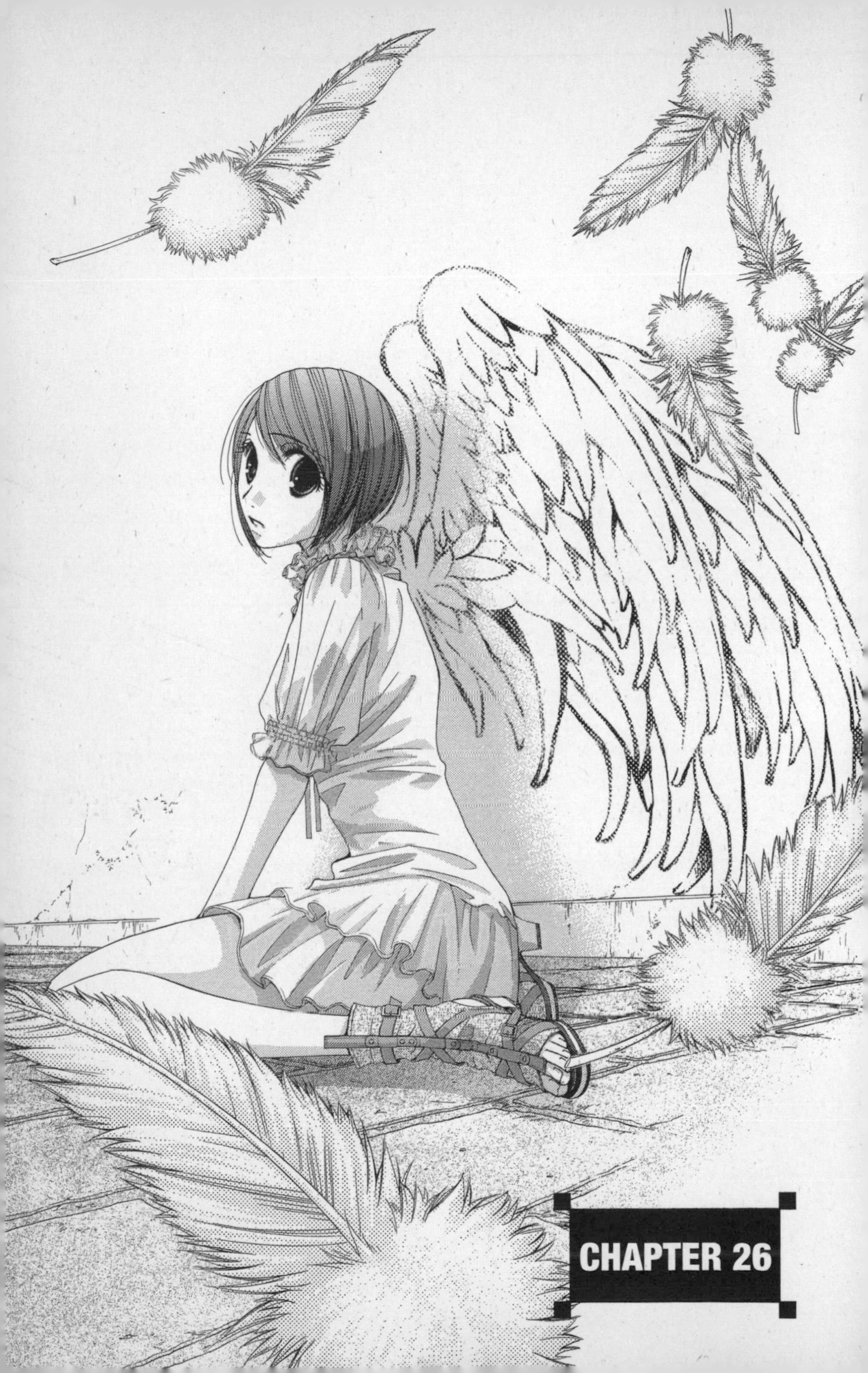
CHAPTER 26

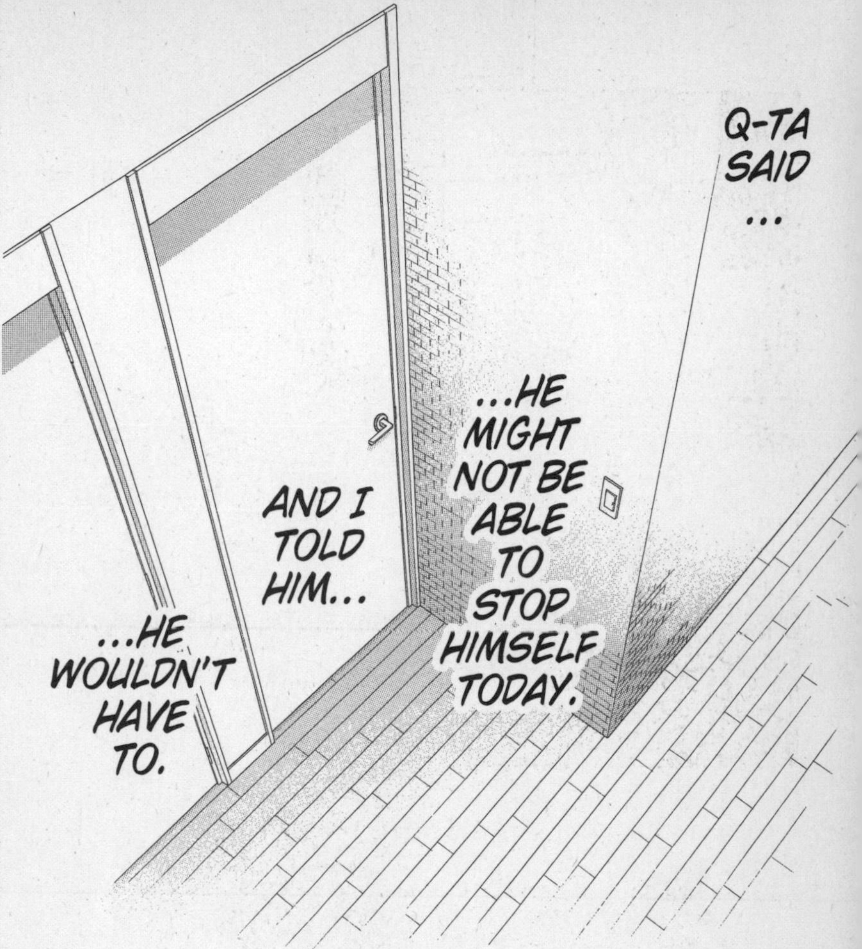
Q-TA SAID ...
...HE MIGHT NOT BE ABLE TO STOP HIMSELF TODAY.
AND I TOLD HIM...
...HE WOULDN'T HAVE TO.

Honey Hunt

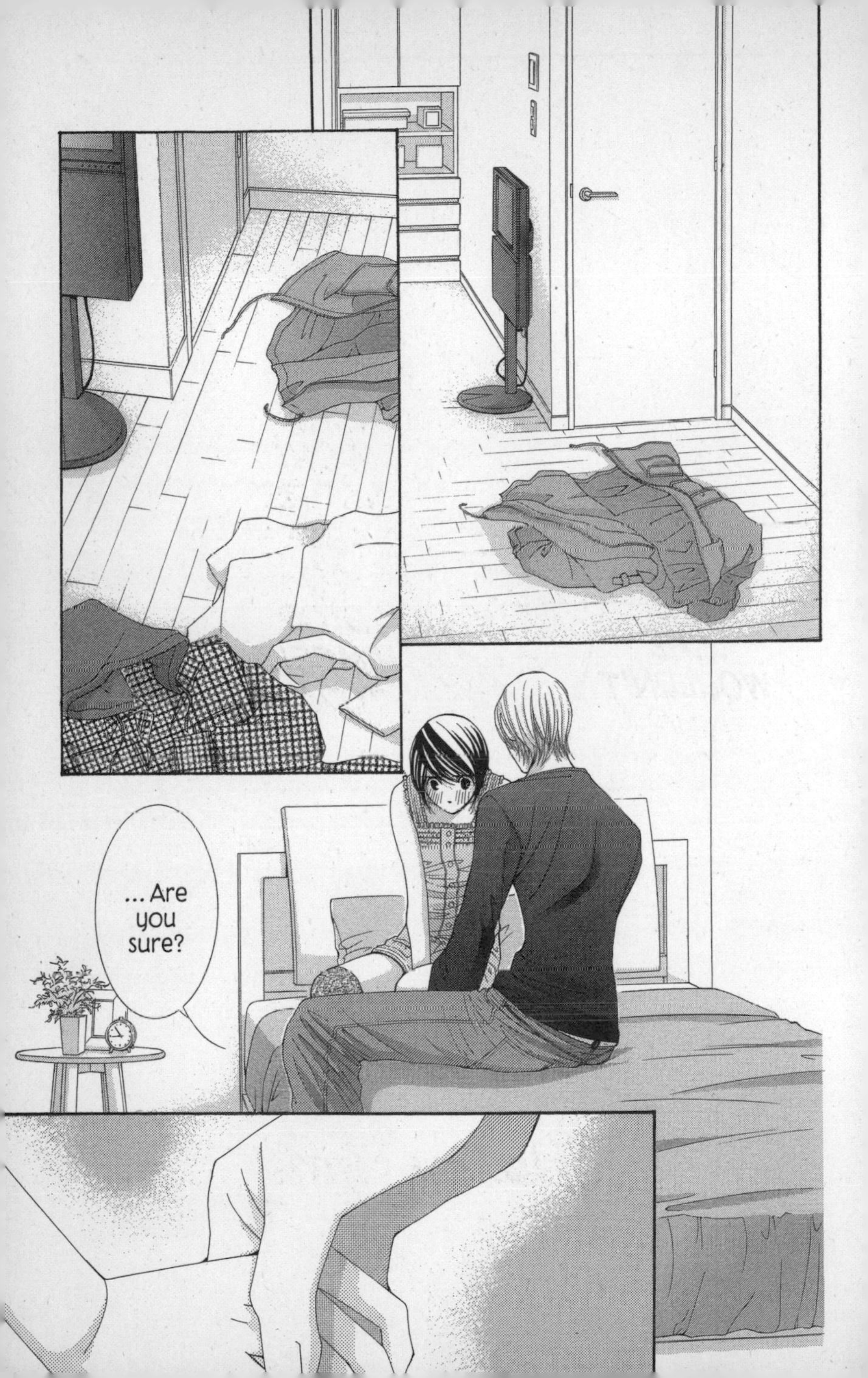
... Are you sure?

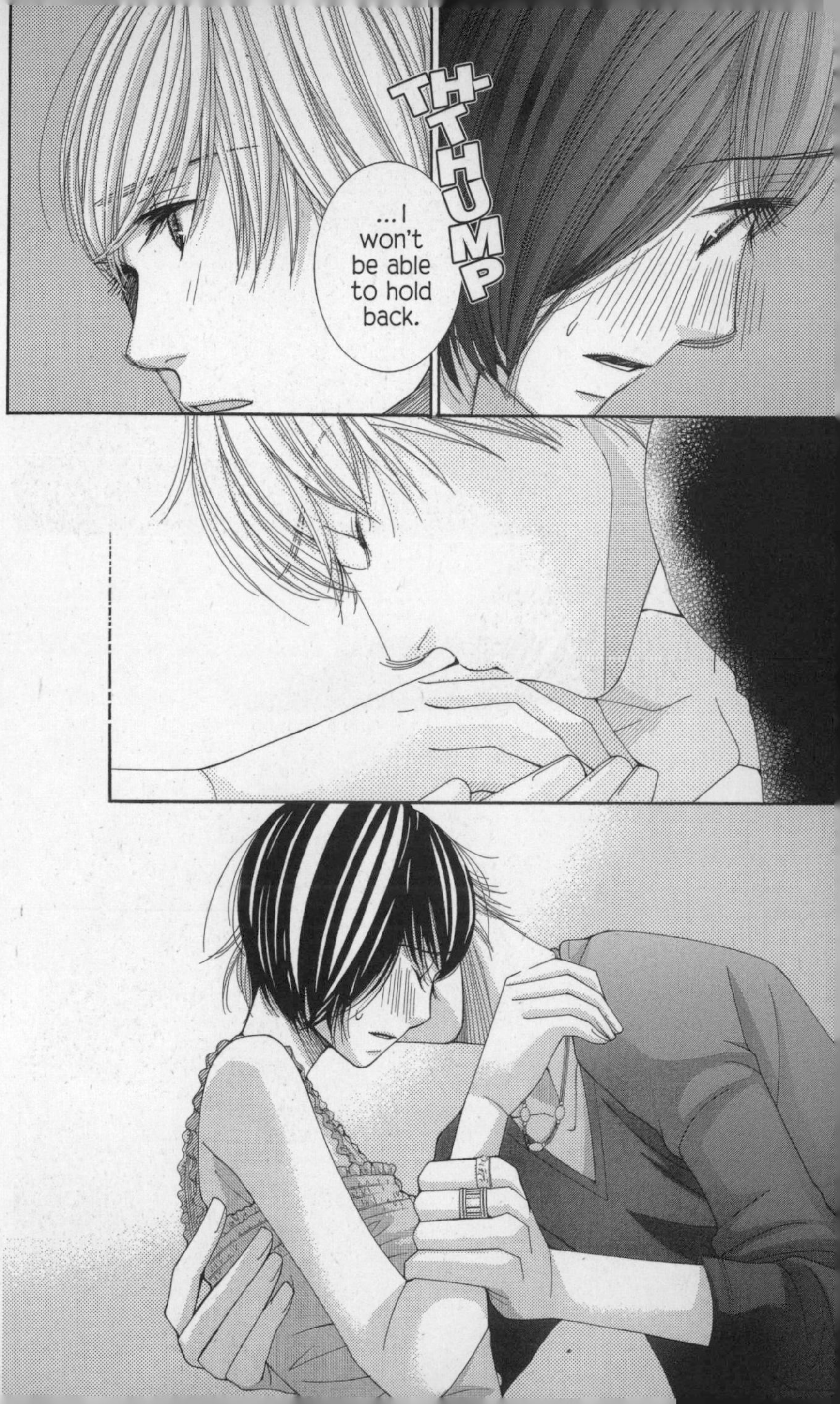
TH-THUMP
...I won't be able to hold back.

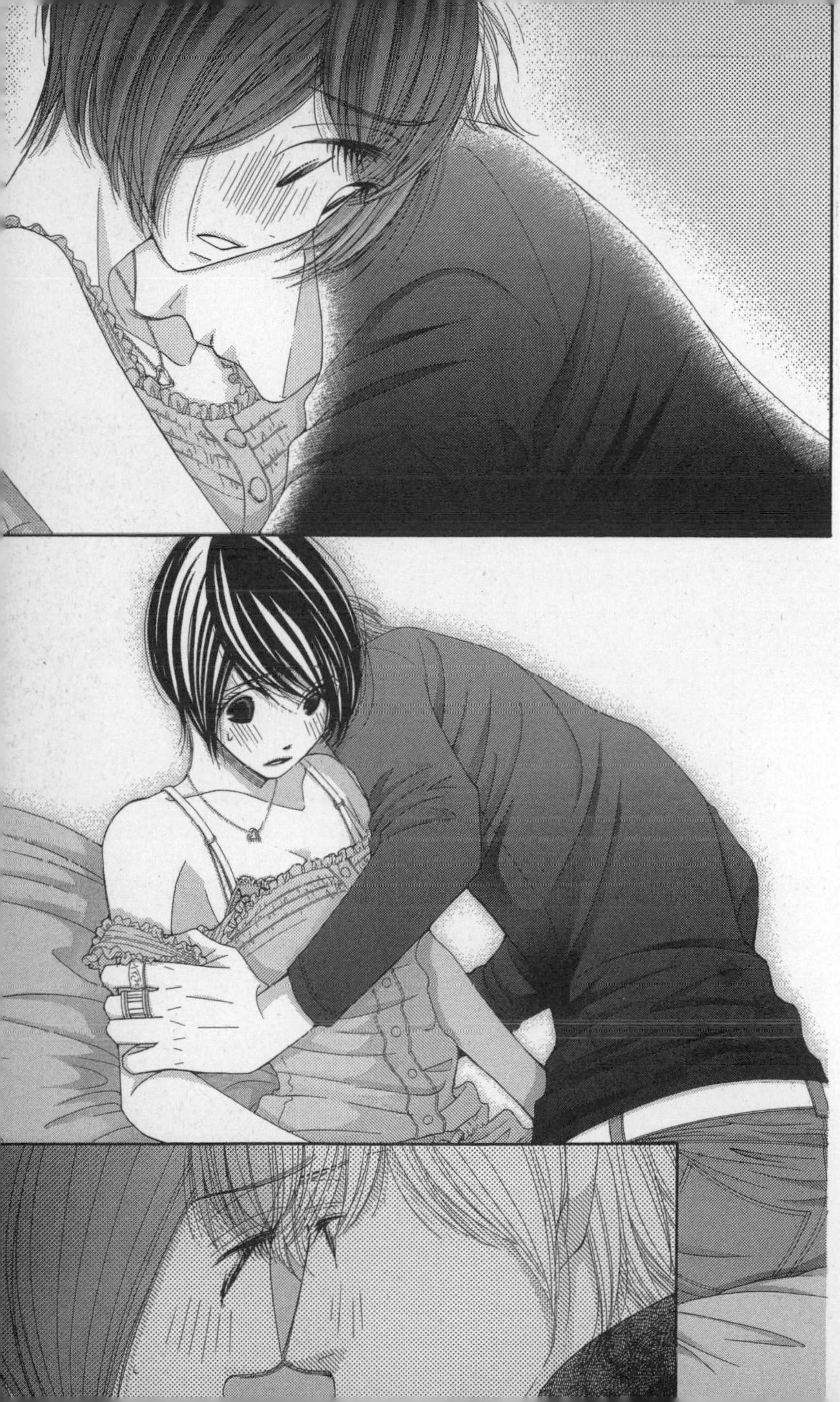

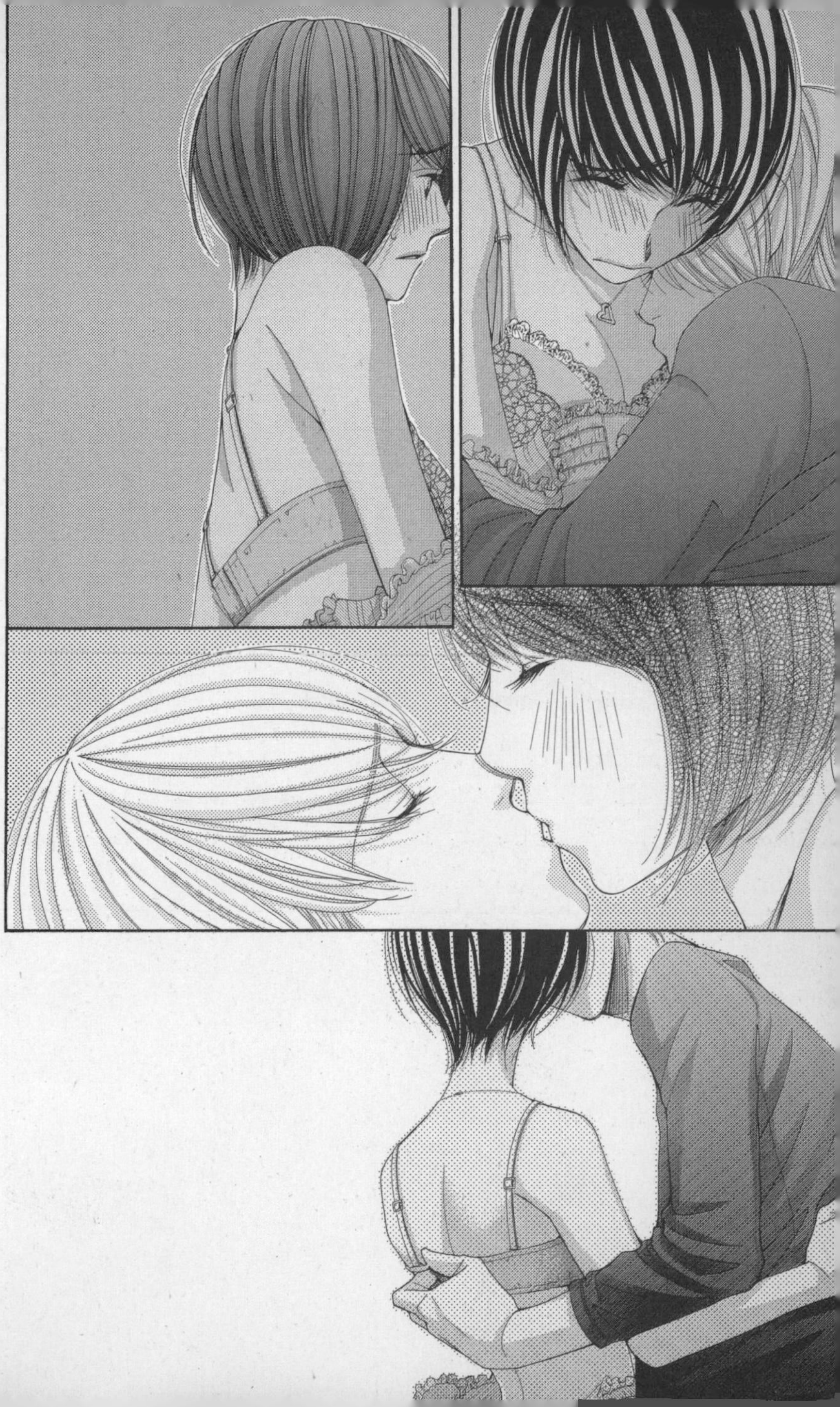

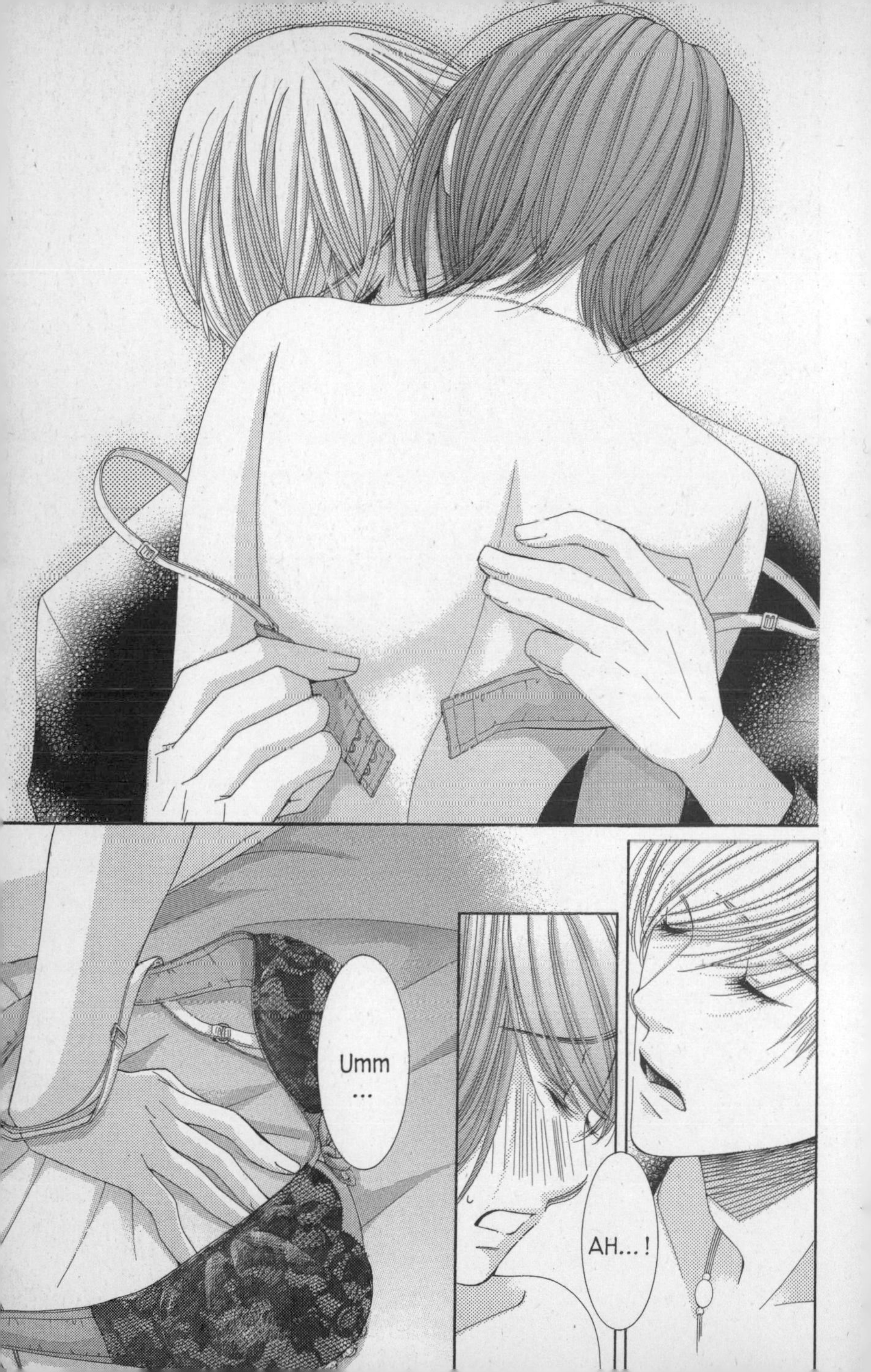
AH... !
Umm ...

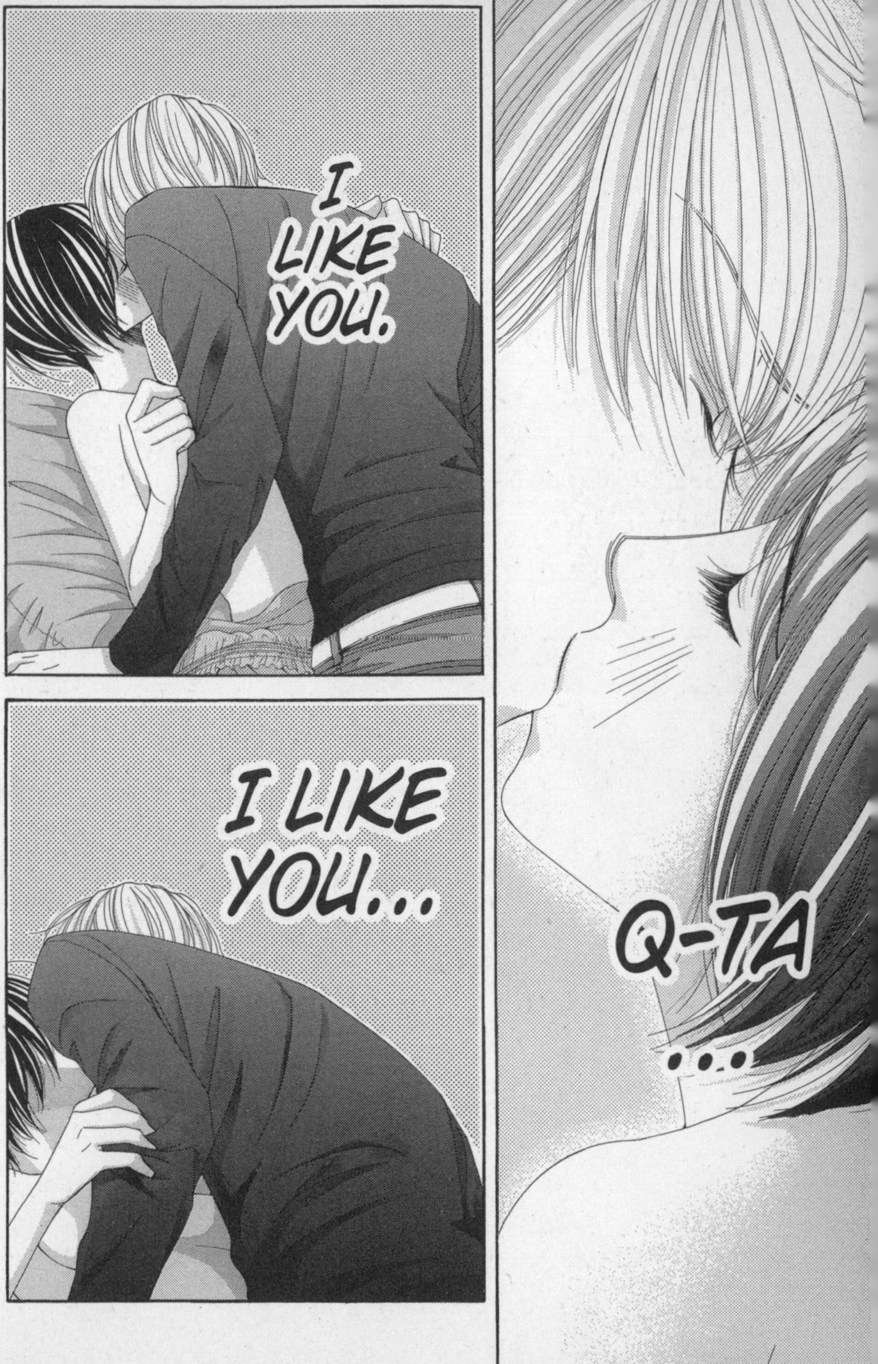
Q-TA
...
I LIKE YOU.
I LIKE YOU...

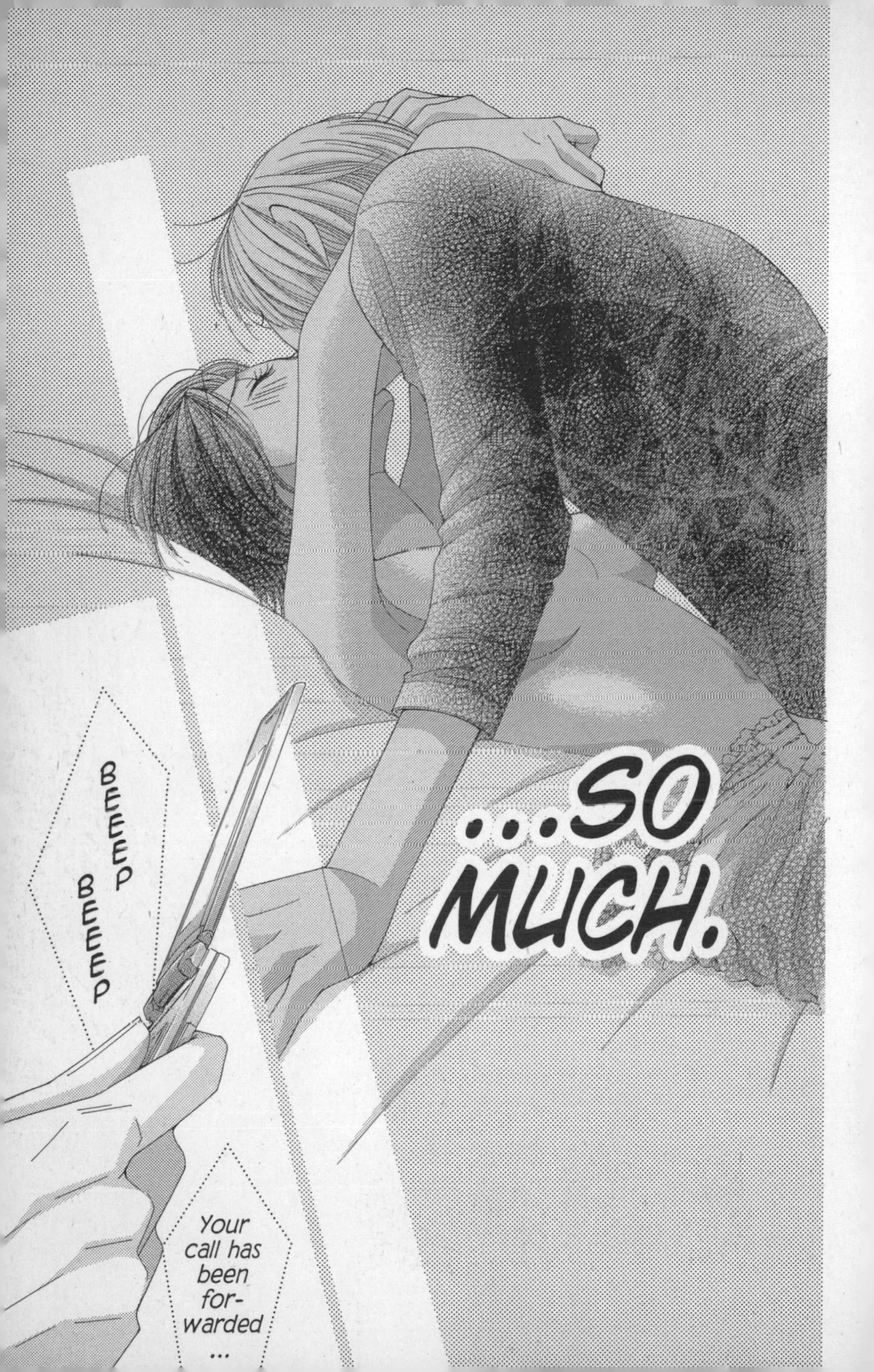
...SO MUCH.
BEEEP BEEEP
Your call has been for-warded ...

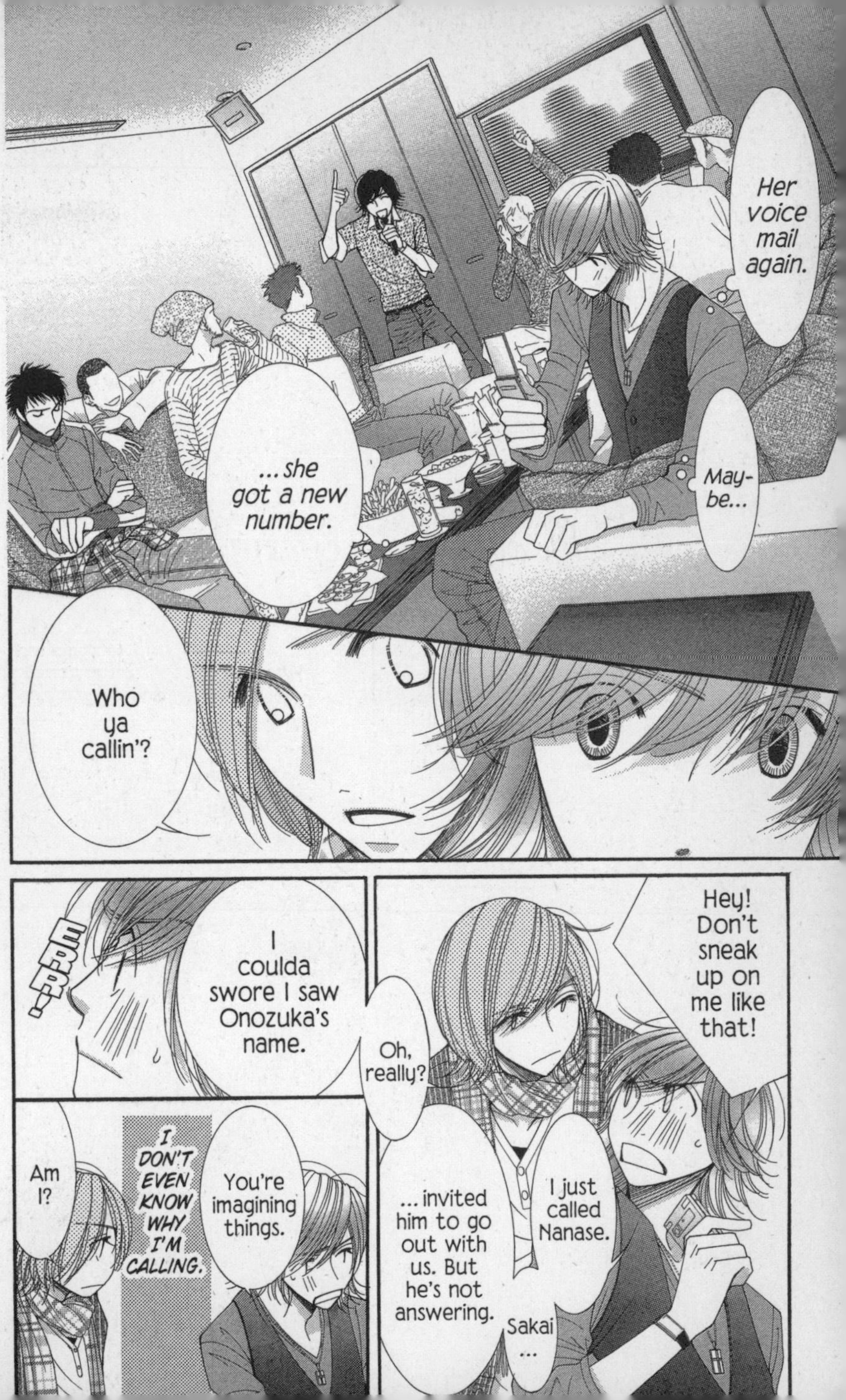
Her voice mail again.
May-be...
...she got a new number.
Who ya callin'?
Hey! Don't sneak up on me like that!
I coulda swore I saw Onozuka's name.
Oh, really?
Sakai ...
I just called Nanase.
...invited him to go out with us. But he's not answering.
You're imagining things.
I DON'T EVEN KNOW WHY I'M CALLING.
Am I?

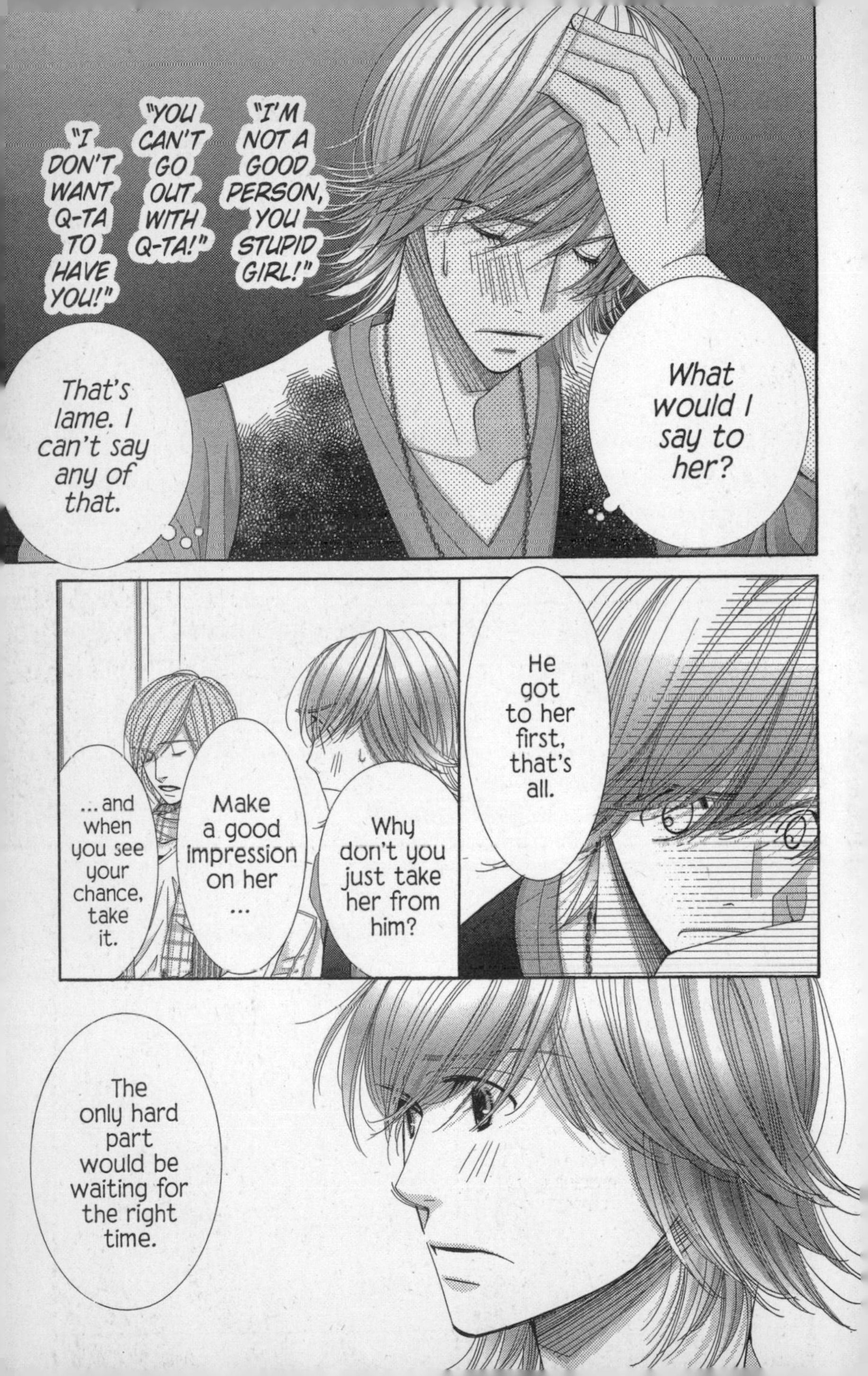
What would I say to her?
"I'M NOT A GOOD PERSON, YOU STUPID GIRL!"
"YOU CAN'T GO OUT WITH Q-TA!"
"I DON'T WANT Q-TA TO HAVE YOU!"
That's lame. I can't say any of that.
He got to her first, that's all.
Why don't you just take her from him?
Make a good impression on her ...
...and when you see your chance, take it.
The only hard part would be waiting for the right time.

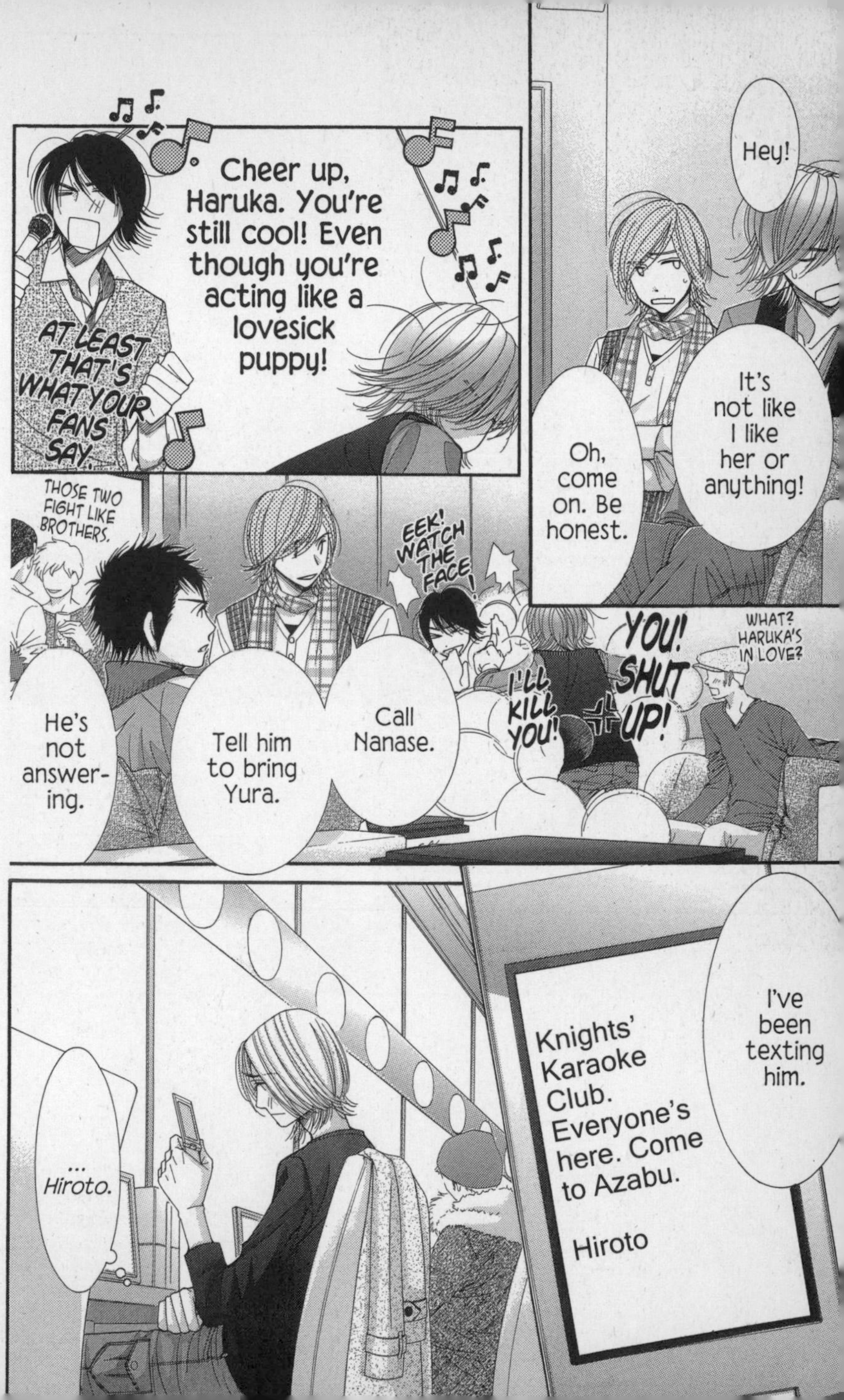
Hey!
It's not like I like her or anything!
Oh, come on. Be honest.
Cheer up, Haruka. You're still cool! Even though you're acting like a lovesick puppy!
AT LEAST THAT'S WHAT YOUR FANS SAY.
WHAT? HARUKA'S IN LOVE?
YOU! SHUT UP!
I'LL KILL YOU!
EEK! WATCH THE FACE!
Call Nanase.
Tell him to bring Yura.
He's not answering.
THOSE TWO FIGHT LIKE BROTHERS.
I've been texting him.
Knights' Karaoke Club. Everyone's here. Come to Azabu.
Hiroto
... Hiroto.

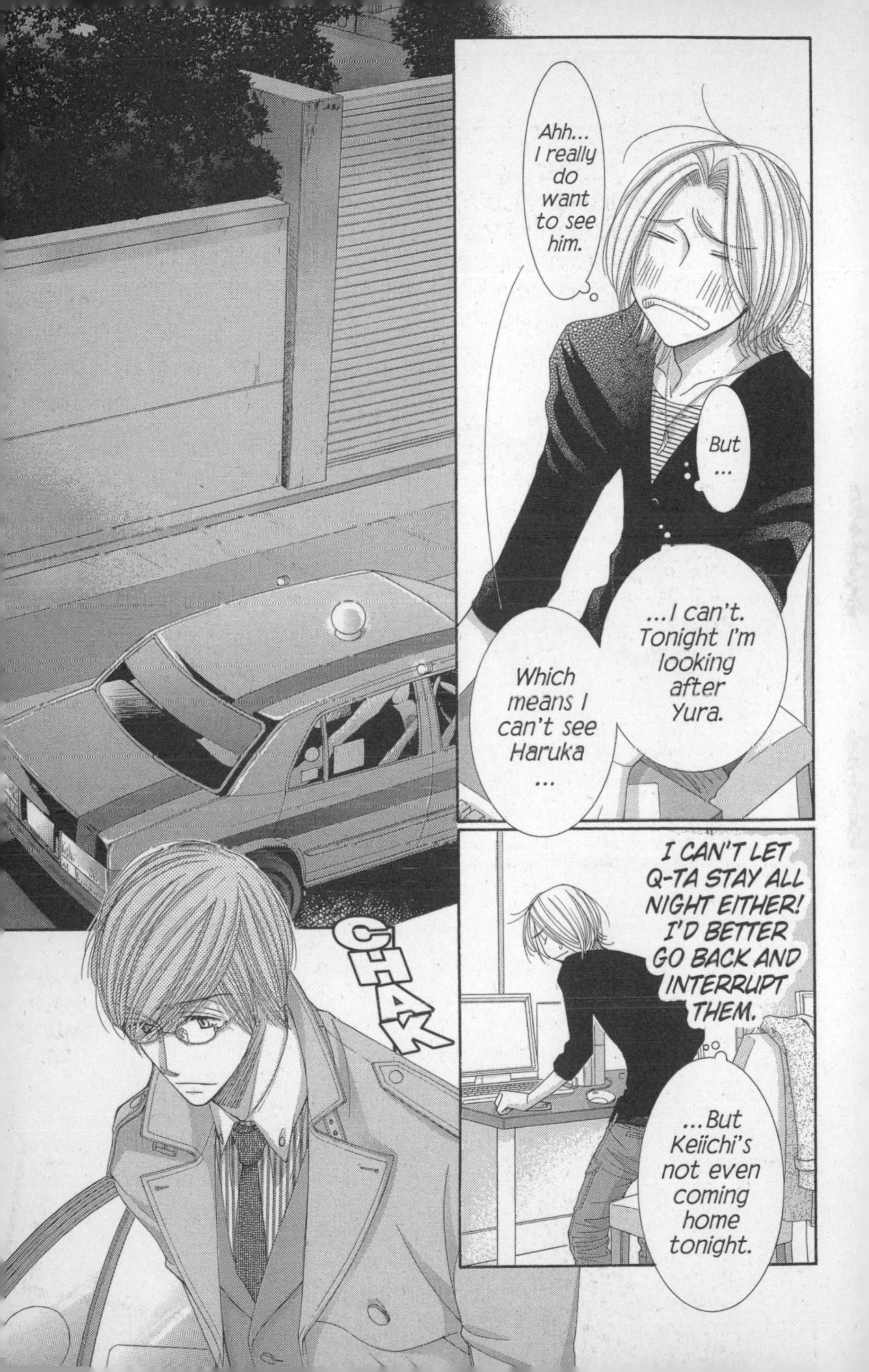

Ahh... I really do want to see him.
But ...
...I can't. Tonight I'm looking after Yura.
Which means I can't see Haruka ...
I CAN'T LET Q-TA STAY ALL NIGHT EITHER! I'D BETTER GO BACK AND INTERRUPT THEM.
...But Keiichi's not even coming home tonight.
CHAK

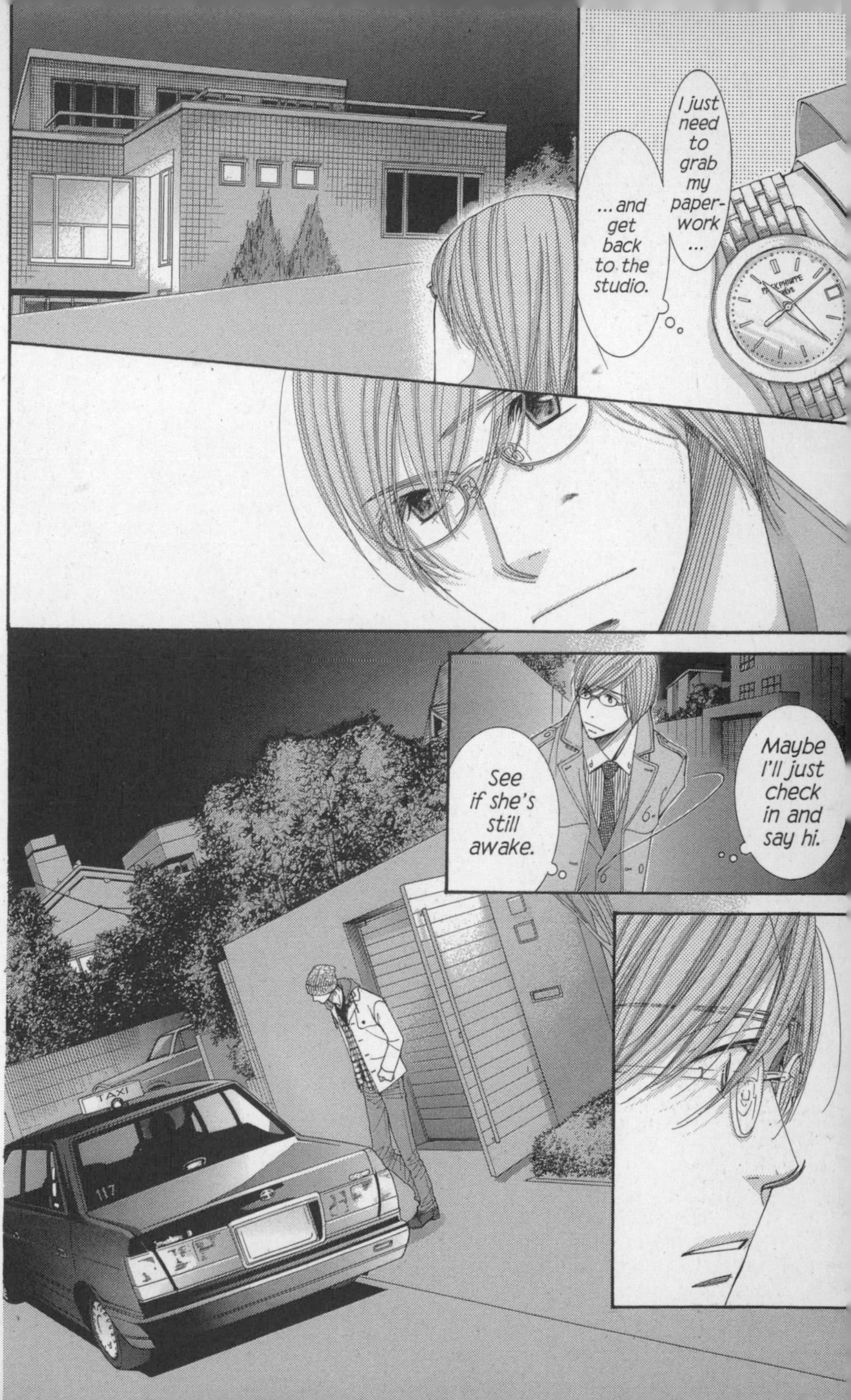
I just need to grab my paper-work ...
... and get back to the studio.
Maybe I'll just check in and say hi.
See if she's still awake.

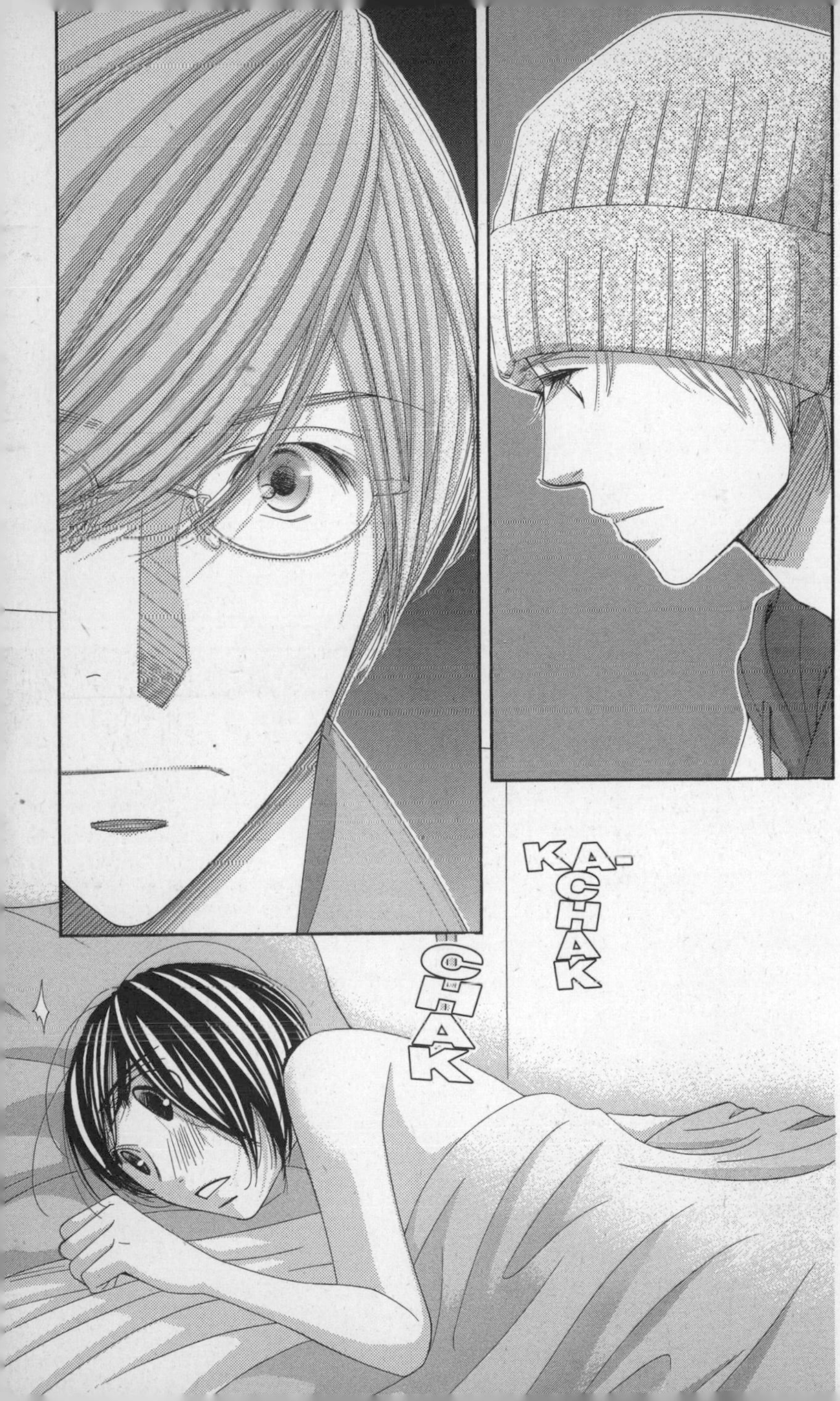
KA-CHAK
CHAK

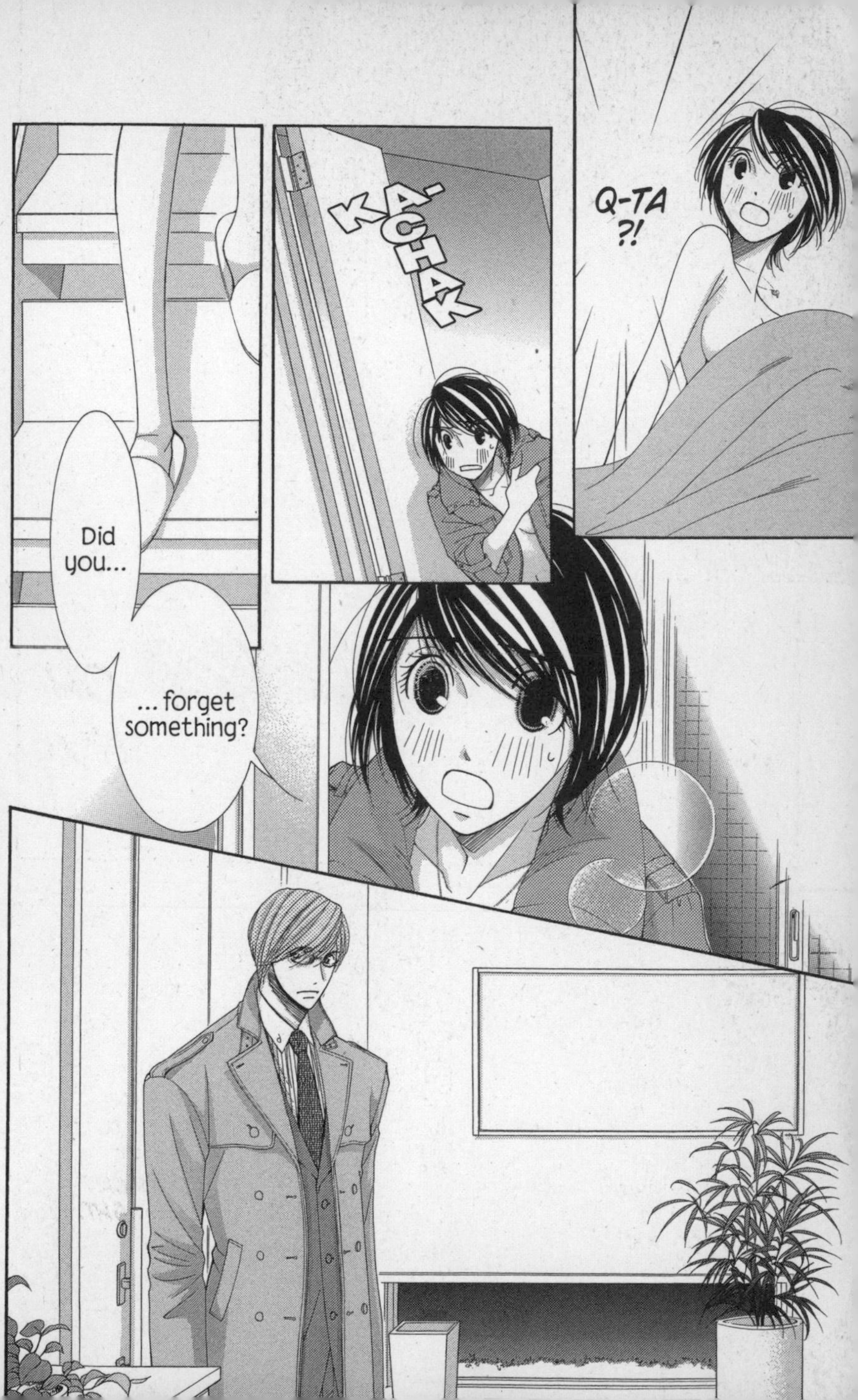
Q-TA ?!
KA'CHAK
Did you...
... forget something?

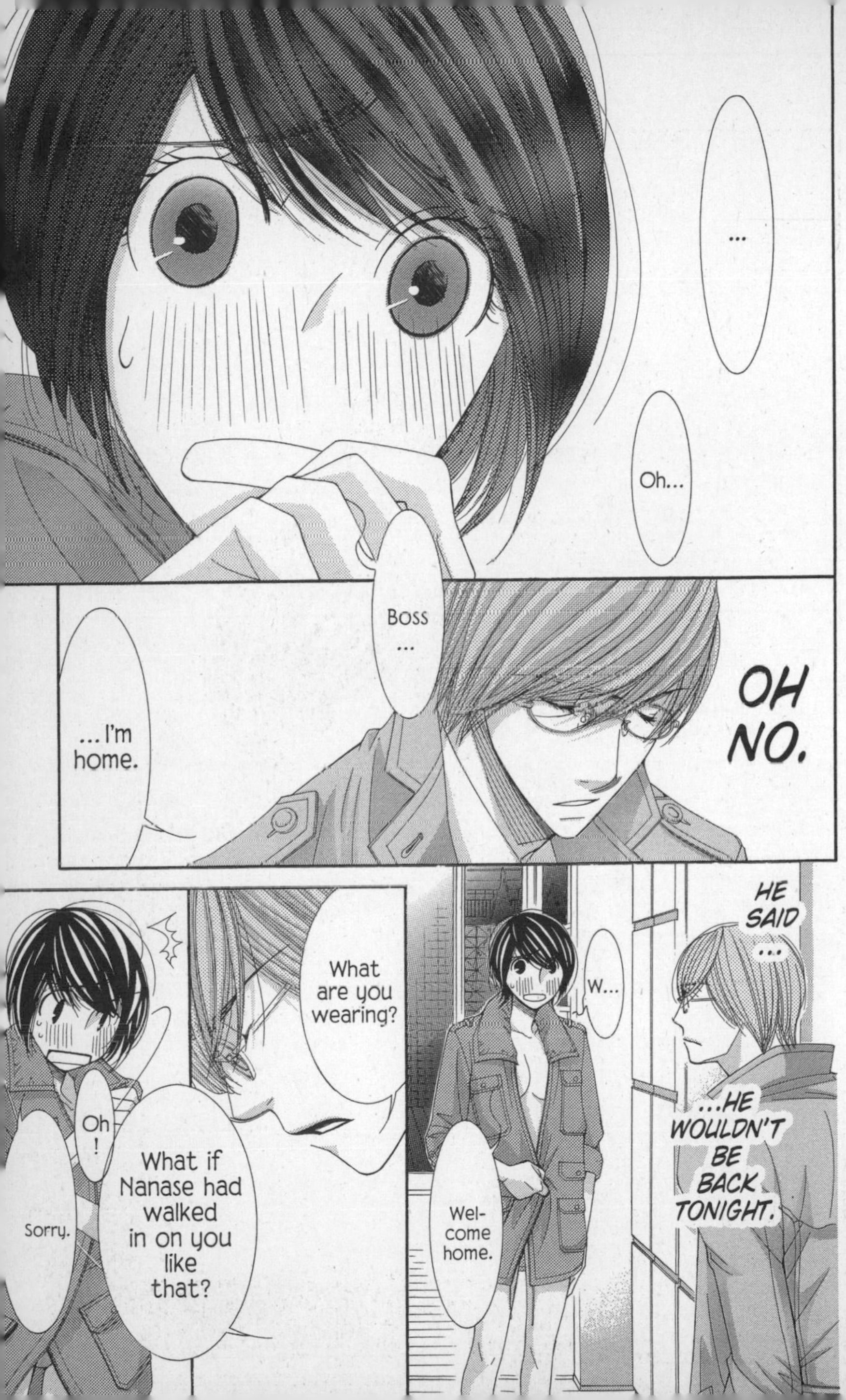
...
Oh...
Boss ...
OH NO.
...I'm home.
HE SAID ...
...HE WOULDN'T BE BACK TONIGHT.
W...
Wel- come home.
What are you wearing?
What if Nanase had walked in on you like that?
Oh!
Sorry.

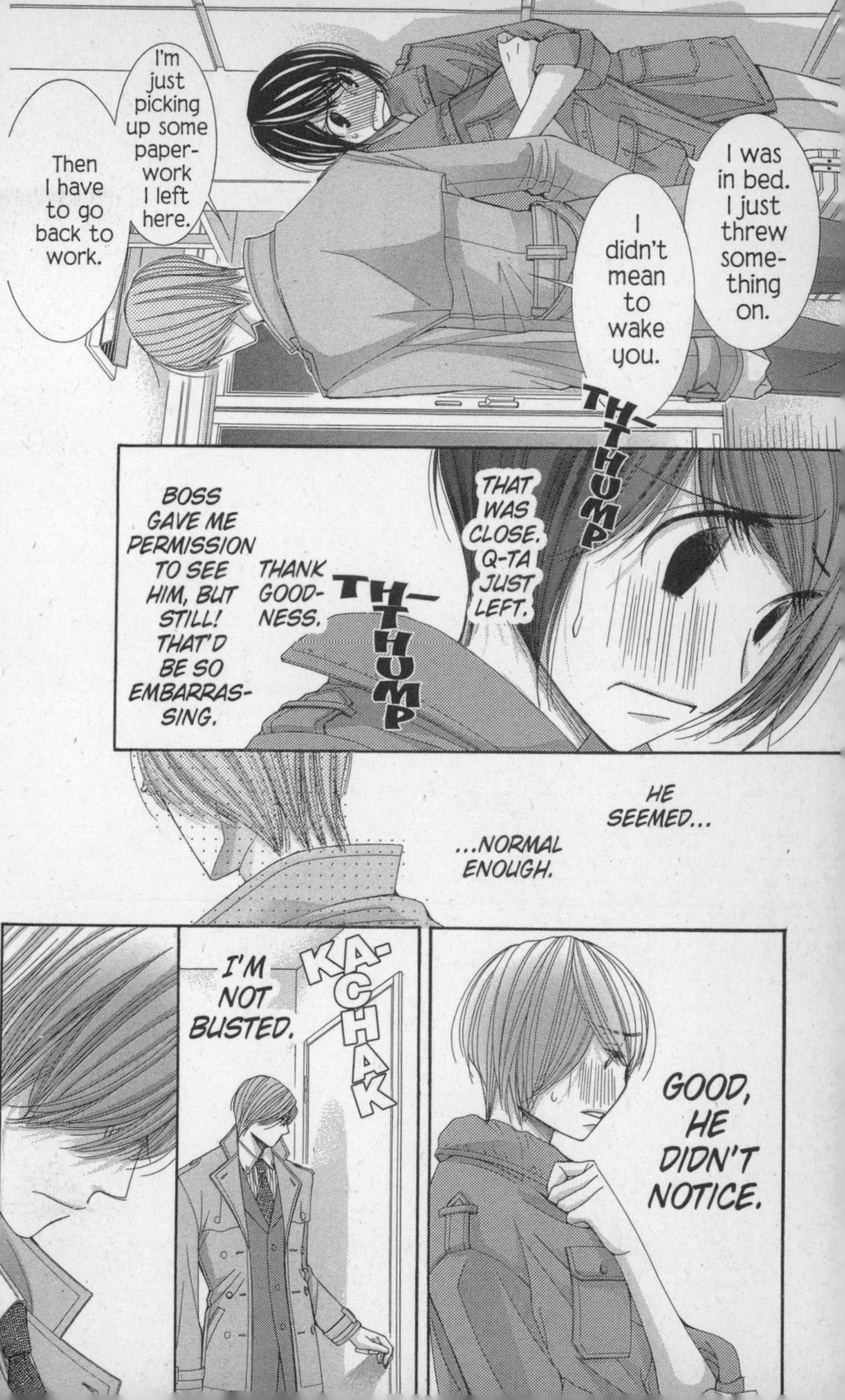
I was in bed. I just threw something on.
I didn't mean to wake you.
TH-THUMP
I'm just picking up some paperwork I left here.
Then I have to go back to work.
THAT WAS CLOSE. Q-TA JUST LEFT.
TH-THUMP
THANK GOODNESS.
BOSS GAVE ME PERMISSION TO SEE HIM, BUT STILL! THAT'D BE SO EMBARRASSING.
HE SEEMED...
...NORMAL ENOUGH.
GOOD, HE DIDN'T NOTICE.
KA-CHAK
I'M NOT BUSTED.

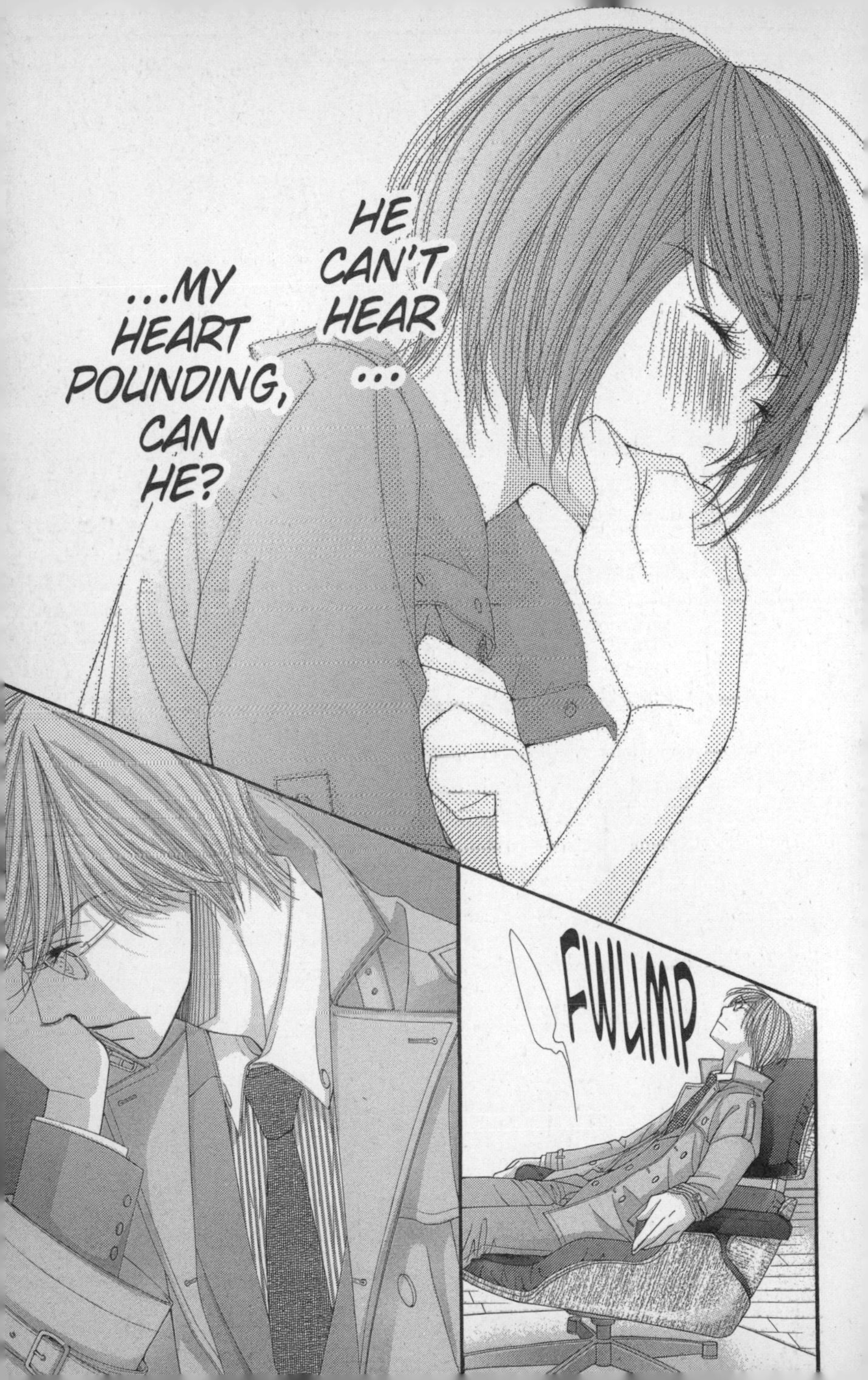
HE CAN'T HEAR...
...MY HEART POUNDING, CAN HE?
FWUMP

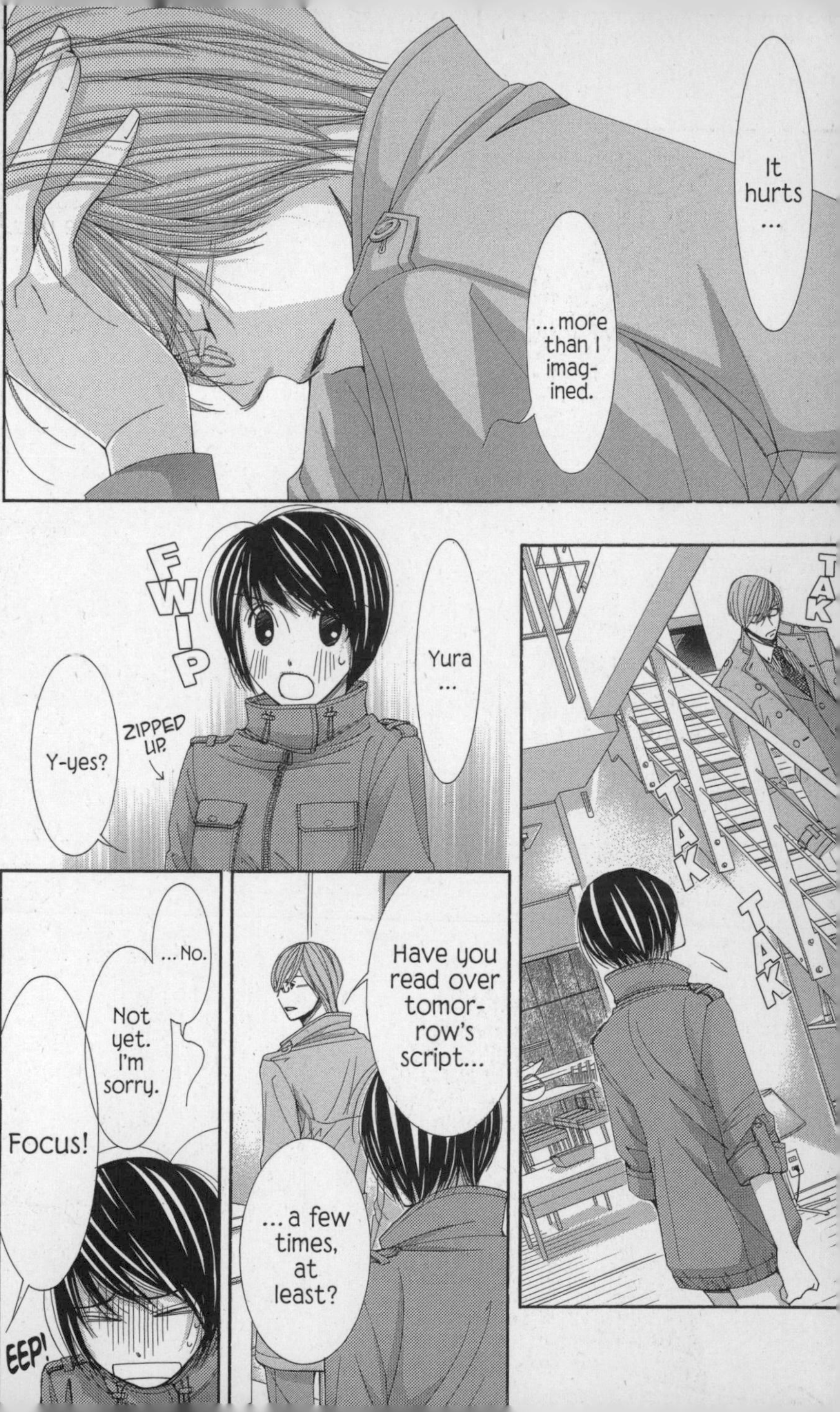
It hurts...
...more than I imagined.
TAK
TAK
TAK
TAK
Yura...
FWIP
Y-yes?
ZIPPED UP.
Have you read over tomorrow's script...
...a few times, at least?
...No.
Not yet. I'm sorry.
Focus!
EEP!

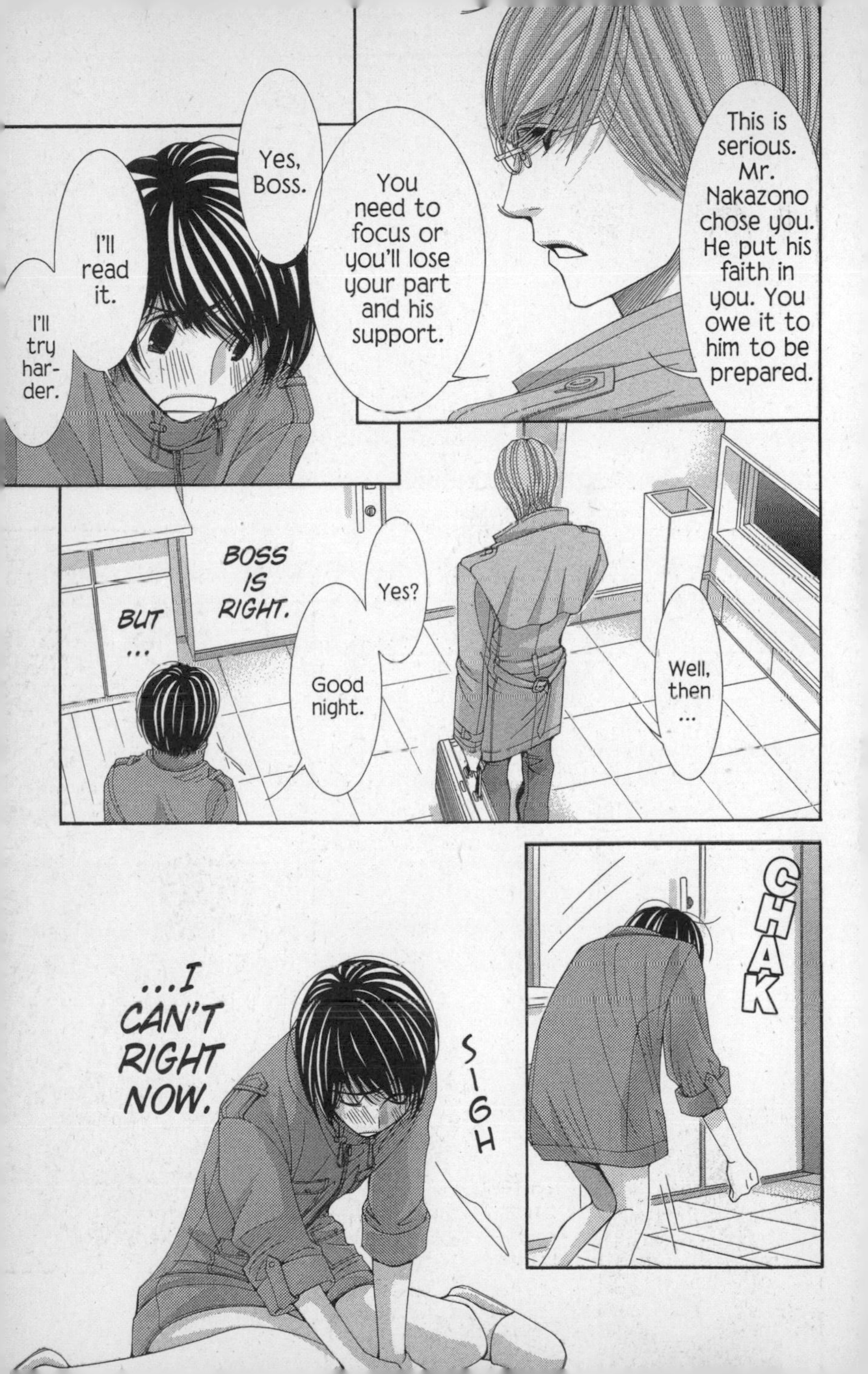
This is serious. Mr. Nakazono chose you. He put his faith in you. You owe it to him to be prepared.
You need to focus or you'll lose your part and his support.
Yes, Boss.
I'll read it.
I'll try harder.
Well, then ...
Yes?
Good night.
BOSS IS RIGHT.
BUT ...
CHAK
SIGH
...I CAN'T RIGHT NOW.

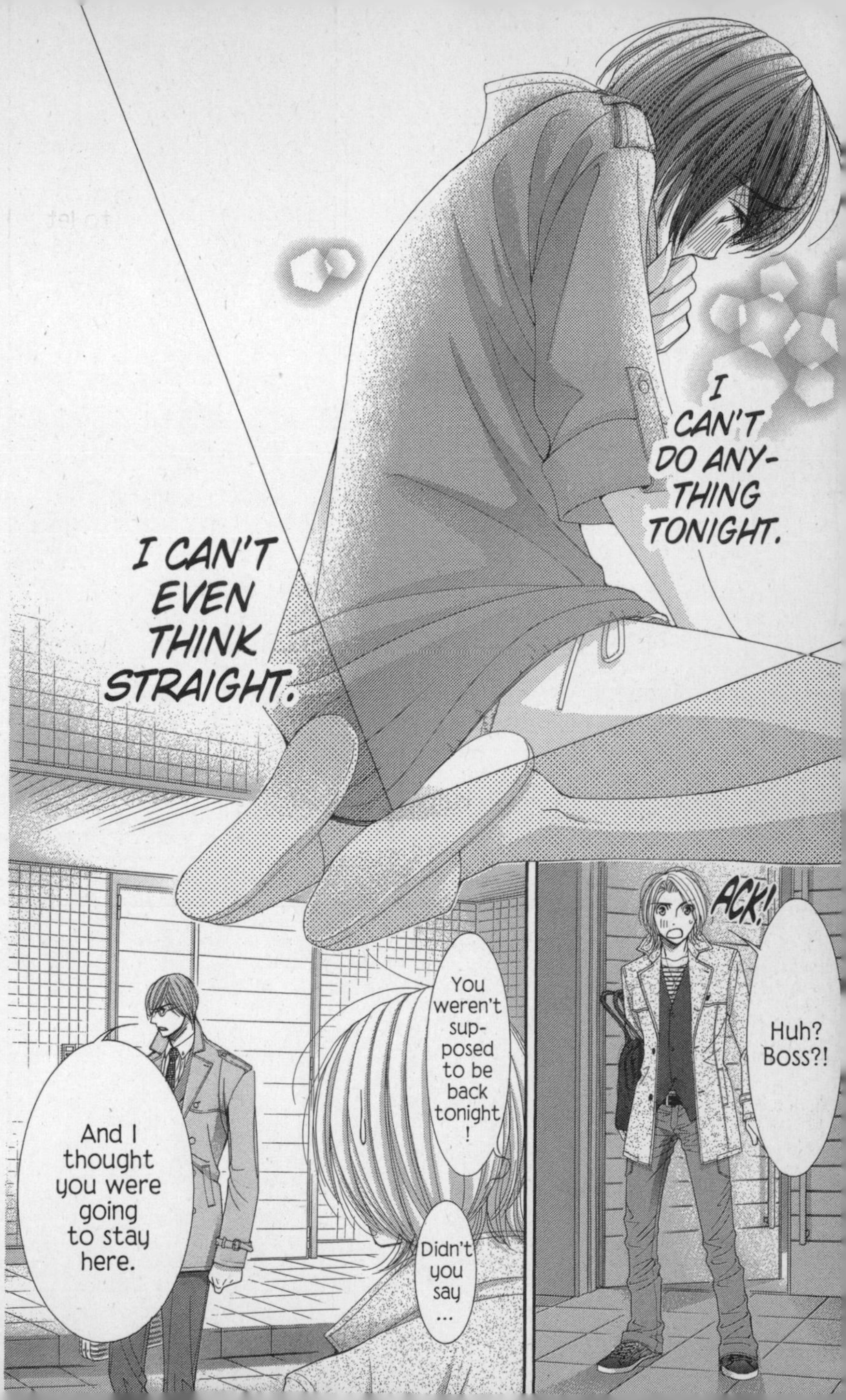

I CAN'T DO ANY-THING TONIGHT.
I CAN'T EVEN THINK STRAIGHT.
ACK!
Huh? Boss?!
You weren't sup-posed to be back tonight!
Didn't you say...
And I thought you were going to stay here.

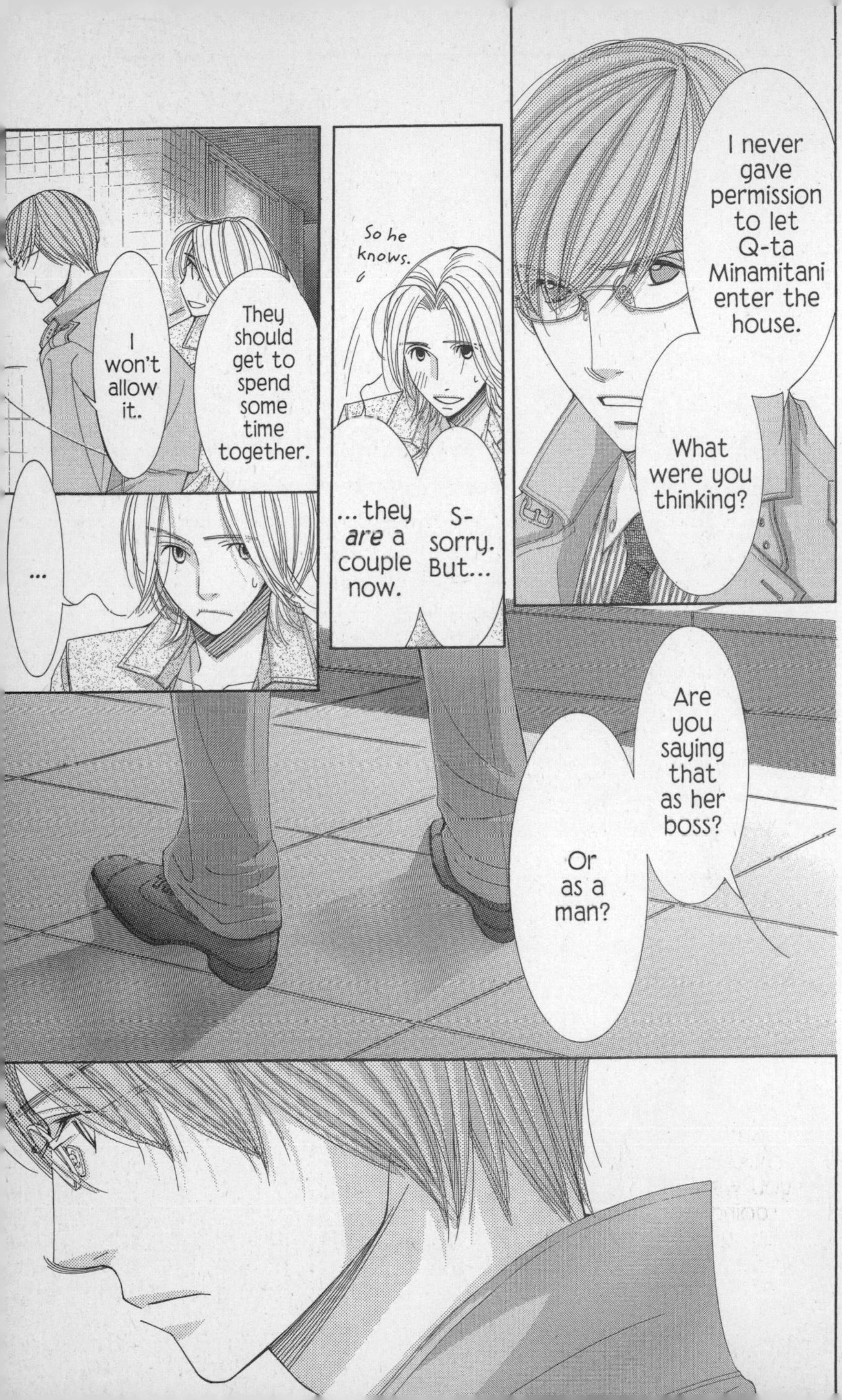
I never gave permission to let Q-ta Minamitani enter the house.
What were you thinking?
So he knows.
S-sorry. But...
...they *are* a couple now.
They should get to spend some time together.
I won't allow it.
...
Are you saying that as her boss?
Or as a man?

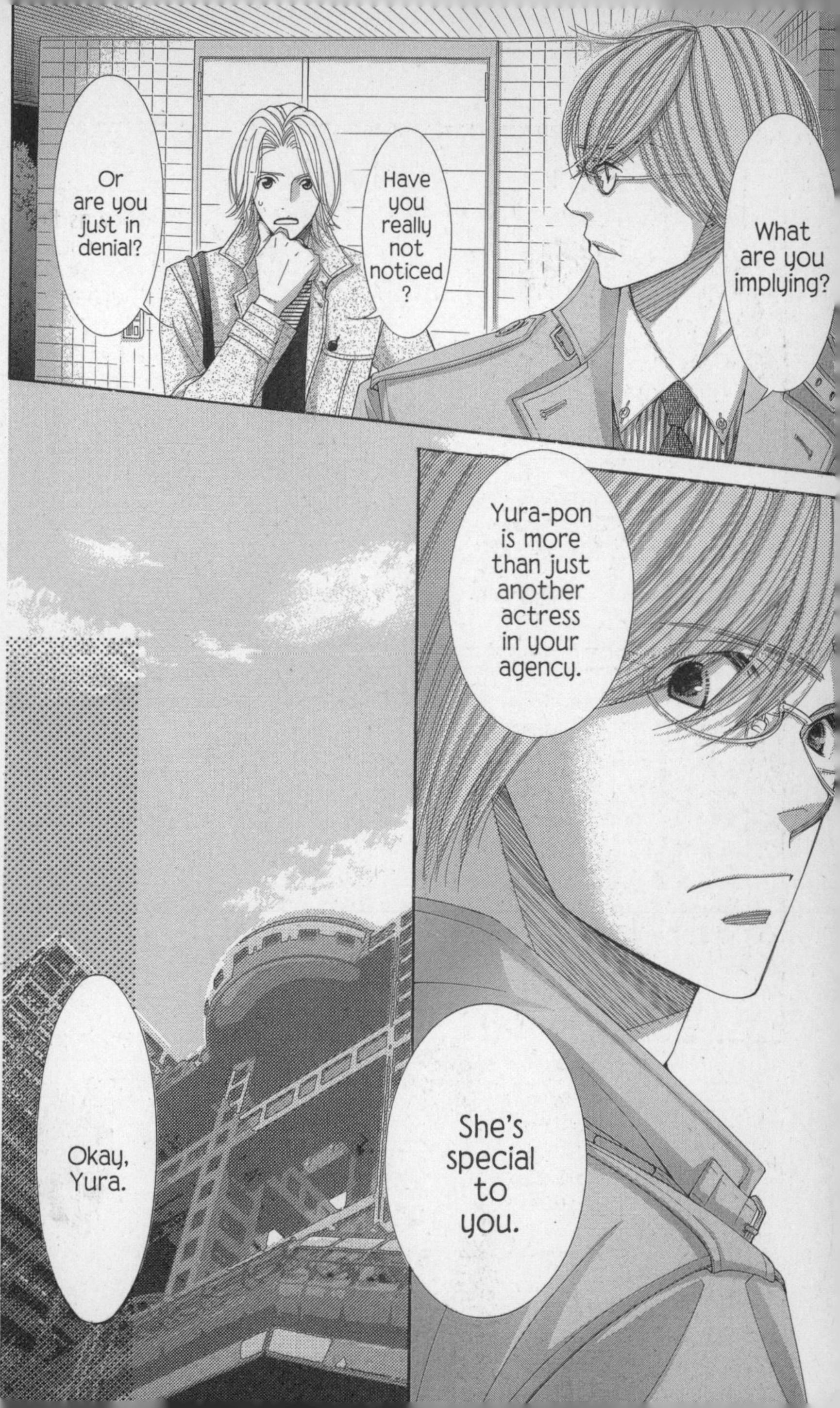
What are you implying?
Have you really not noticed?
Or are you just in denial?
Yura-pon is more than just another actress in your agency.
She's special to you.
Okay, Yura.

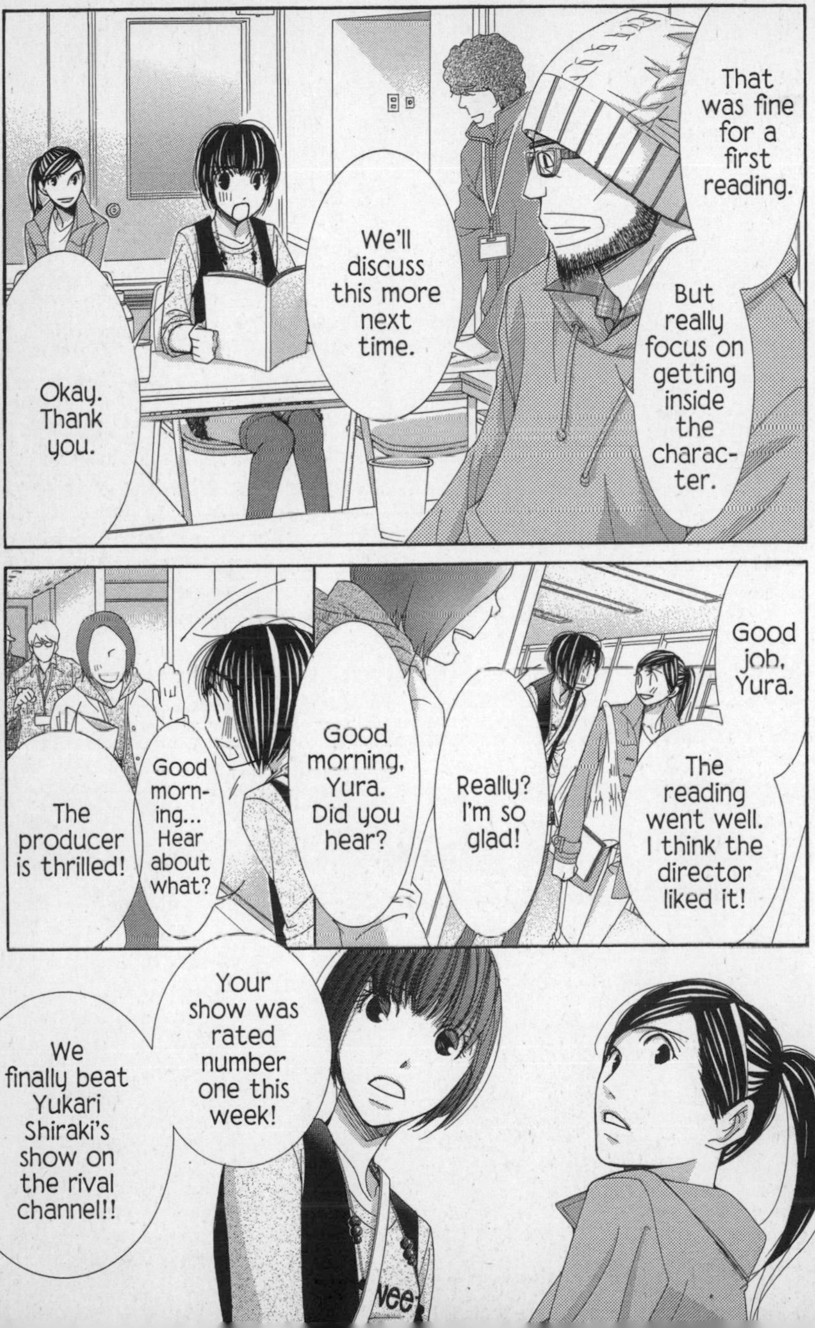
That was fine for a first reading.
But really focus on getting inside the charac-ter.
We'll discuss this more next time.
Okay. Thank you.
Good job, Yura.
The reading went well. I think the director liked it!
Really? I'm so glad!
Good morning, Yura. Did you hear?
Good morn-ing... Hear about what?
The producer is thrilled!
Your show was rated number one this week!
We finally beat Yukari Shiraki's show on the rival channel!!

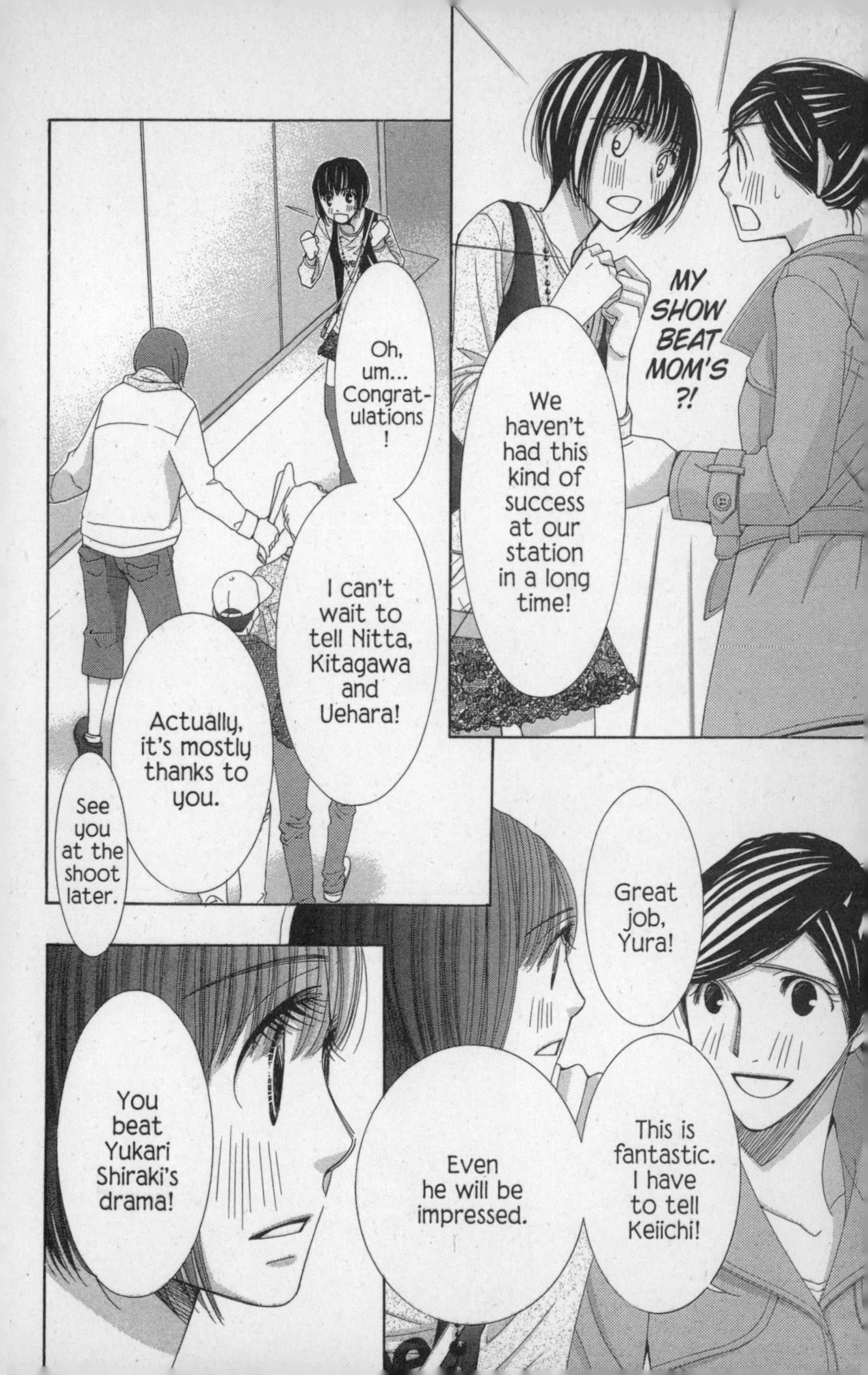
MY SHOW BEAT MOM'S ?!
We haven't had this kind of success at our station in a long time!
Oh, um... Congratulations!
I can't wait to tell Nitta, Kitagawa and Uehara!
Actually, it's mostly thanks to you.
See you at the shoot later.
Great job, Yura!
This is fantastic. I have to tell Keiichi!
Even he will be impressed.
You beat Yukari Shiraki's drama!

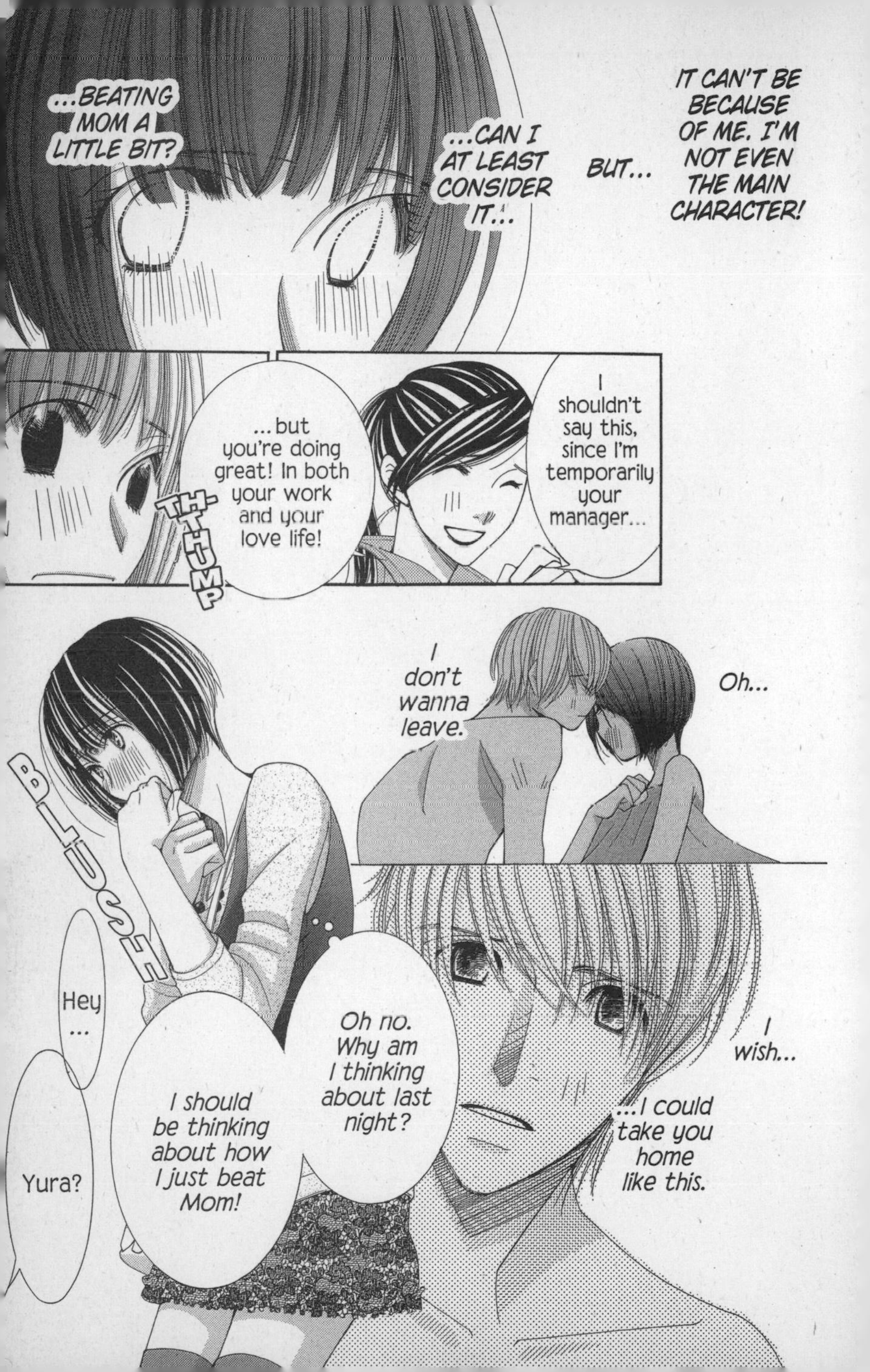
IT CAN'T BE BECAUSE OF ME. I'M NOT EVEN THE MAIN CHARACTER!
BUT...
...CAN I AT LEAST CONSIDER IT...
...BEATING MOM A LITTLE BIT?
I shouldn't say this, since I'm temporarily your manager...
...but you're doing great! In both your work and your love life!
TH-THUMP
Oh...
I don't wanna leave.
I wish...
...I could take you home like this.
BLUSH
Oh no. Why am I thinking about last night?
I should be thinking about how I just beat Mom!
Hey...
Yura?

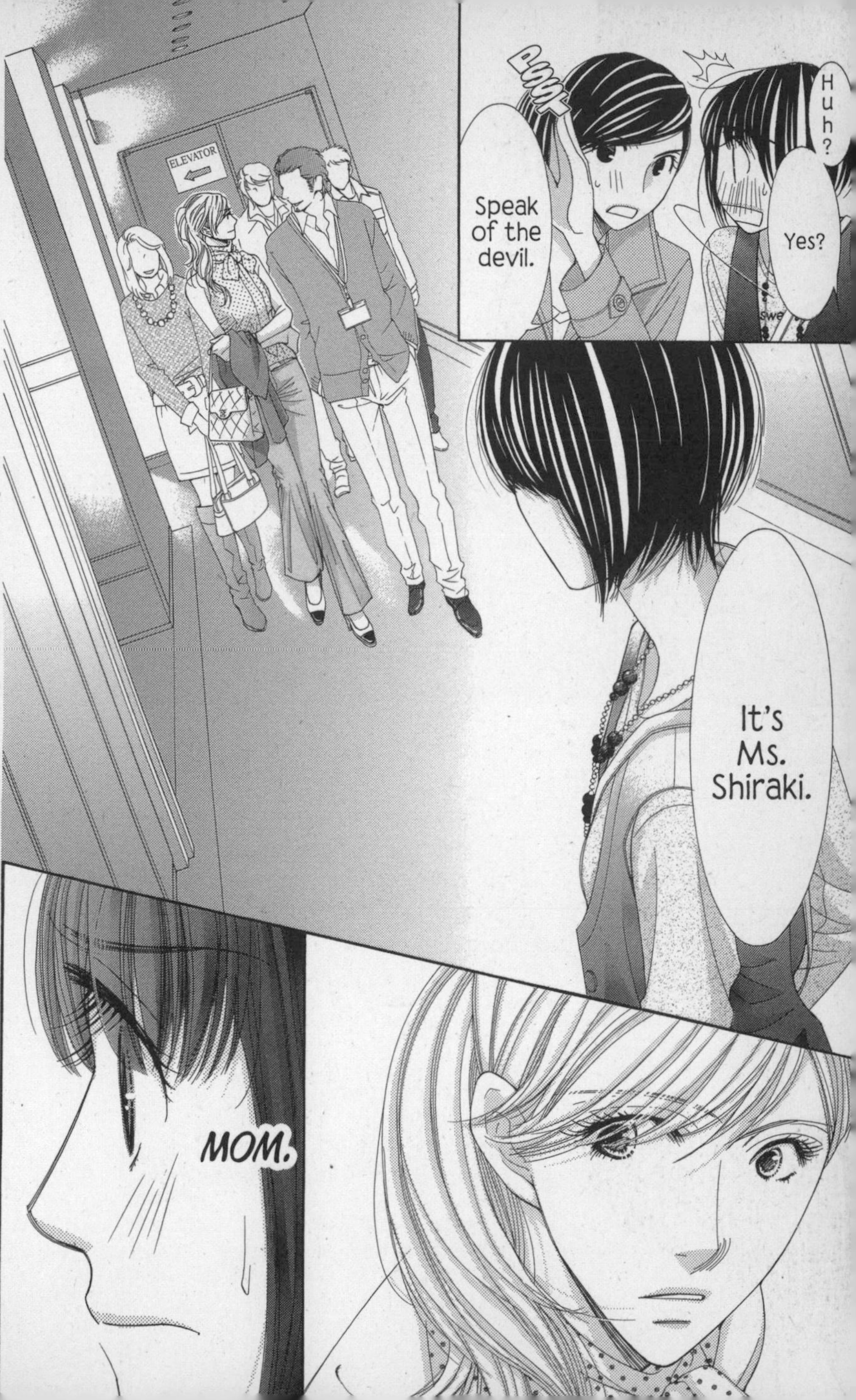
Huh?
Yes?
Speak of the devil.
ELEVATOR
It's Ms. Shiraki.
MOM.

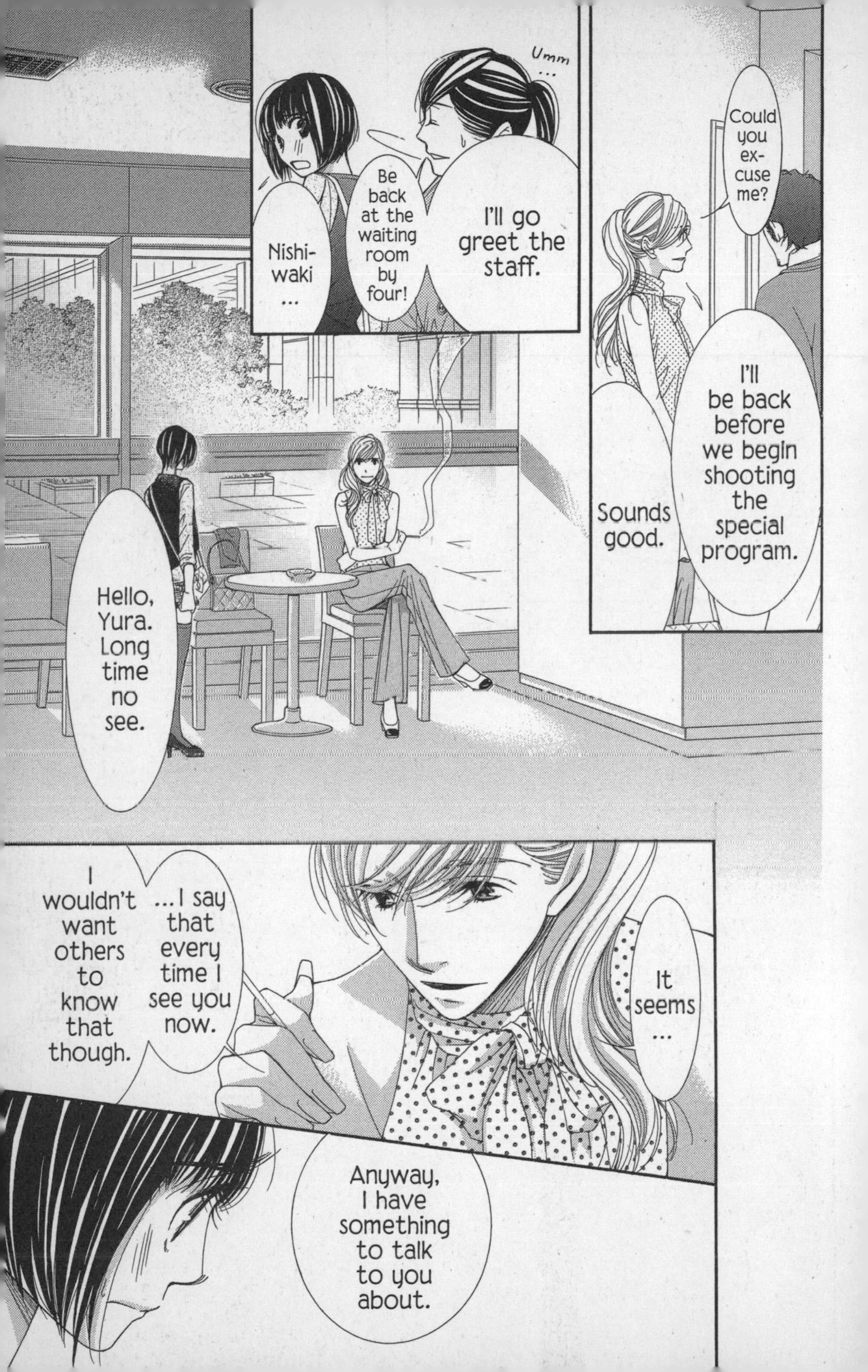
Could you ex-cuse me?
I'll be back before we begin shooting the special program.
Sounds good.
Umm...
I'll go greet the staff.
Be back at the waiting room by four!
Nishi-waki...
Hello, Yura. Long time no see.
It seems...
...I say that every time I see you now.
I wouldn't want others to know that though.
Anyway, I have something to talk to you about.

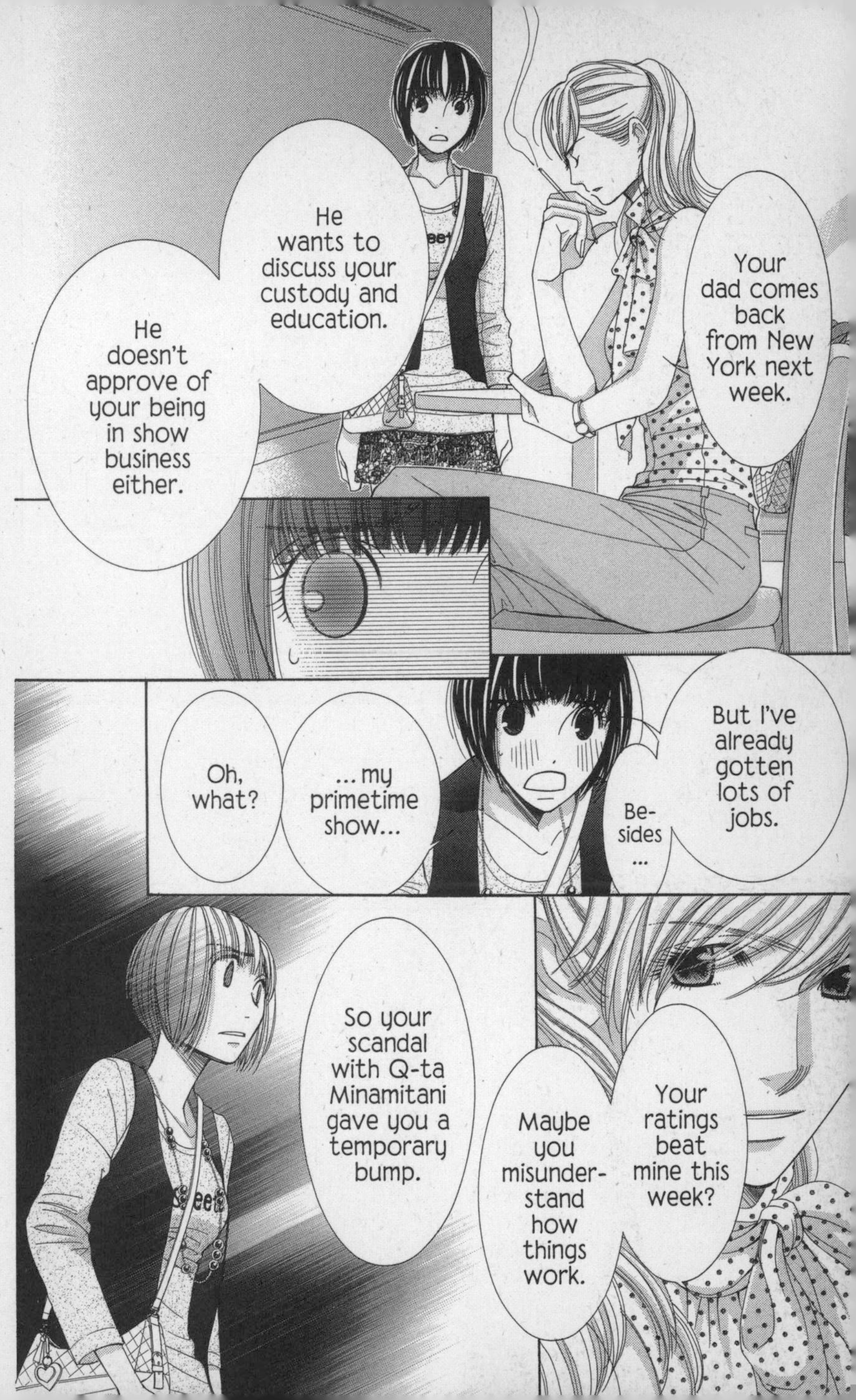
Your dad comes back from New York next week.
He wants to discuss your custody and education.
He doesn't approve of your being in show business either.
But I've already gotten lots of jobs.
Be-sides ...
... my primetime show...
Oh, what?
Your ratings beat mine this week?
Maybe you misunder-stand how things work.
So your scandal with Q-ta Minamitani gave you a temporary bump.

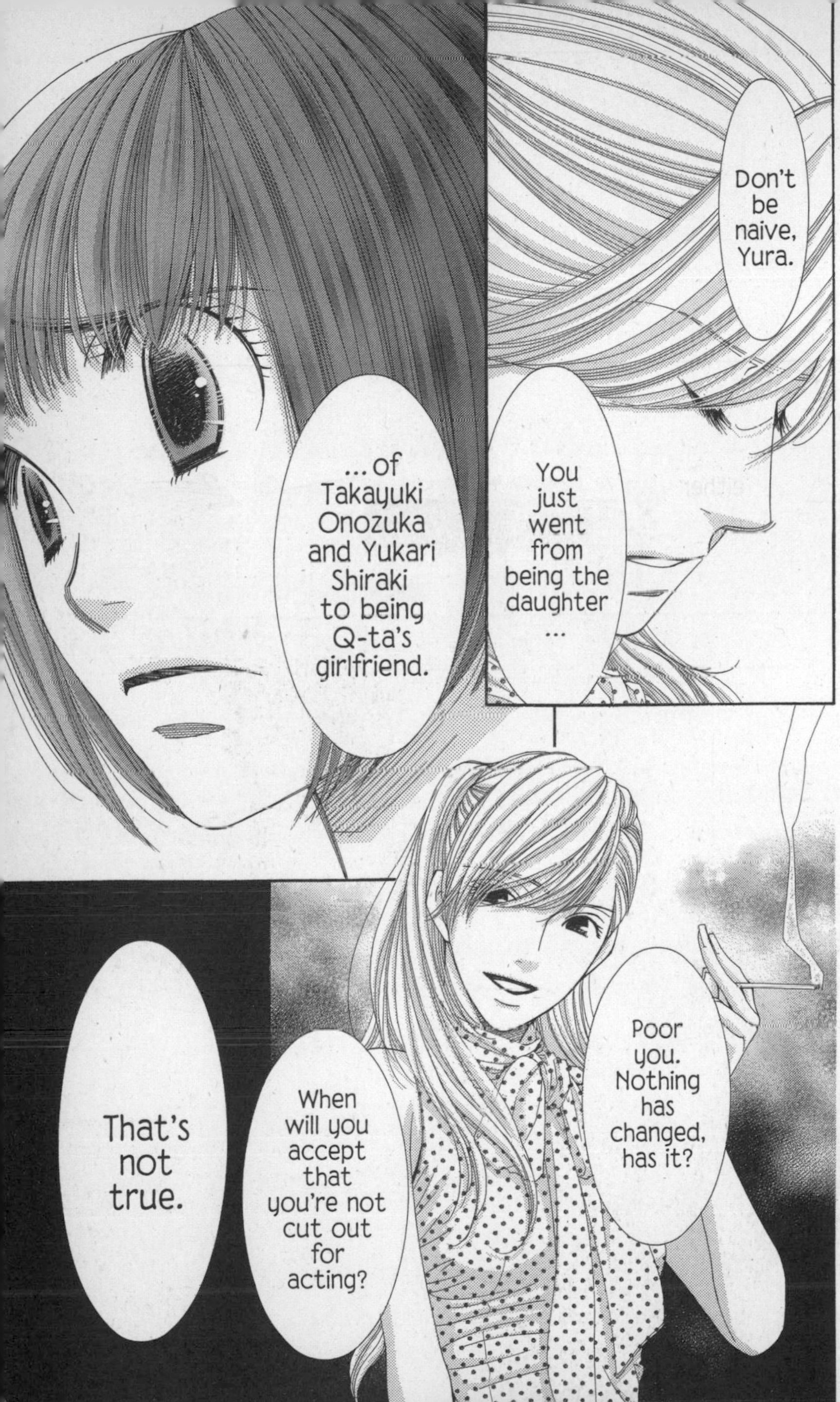
Don't be naive, Yura.
You just went from being the daughter ...
...of Takayuki Onozuka and Yukari Shiraki to being Q-ta's girlfriend.
Poor you. Nothing has changed, has it?
When will you accept that you're not cut out for acting?
That's not true.

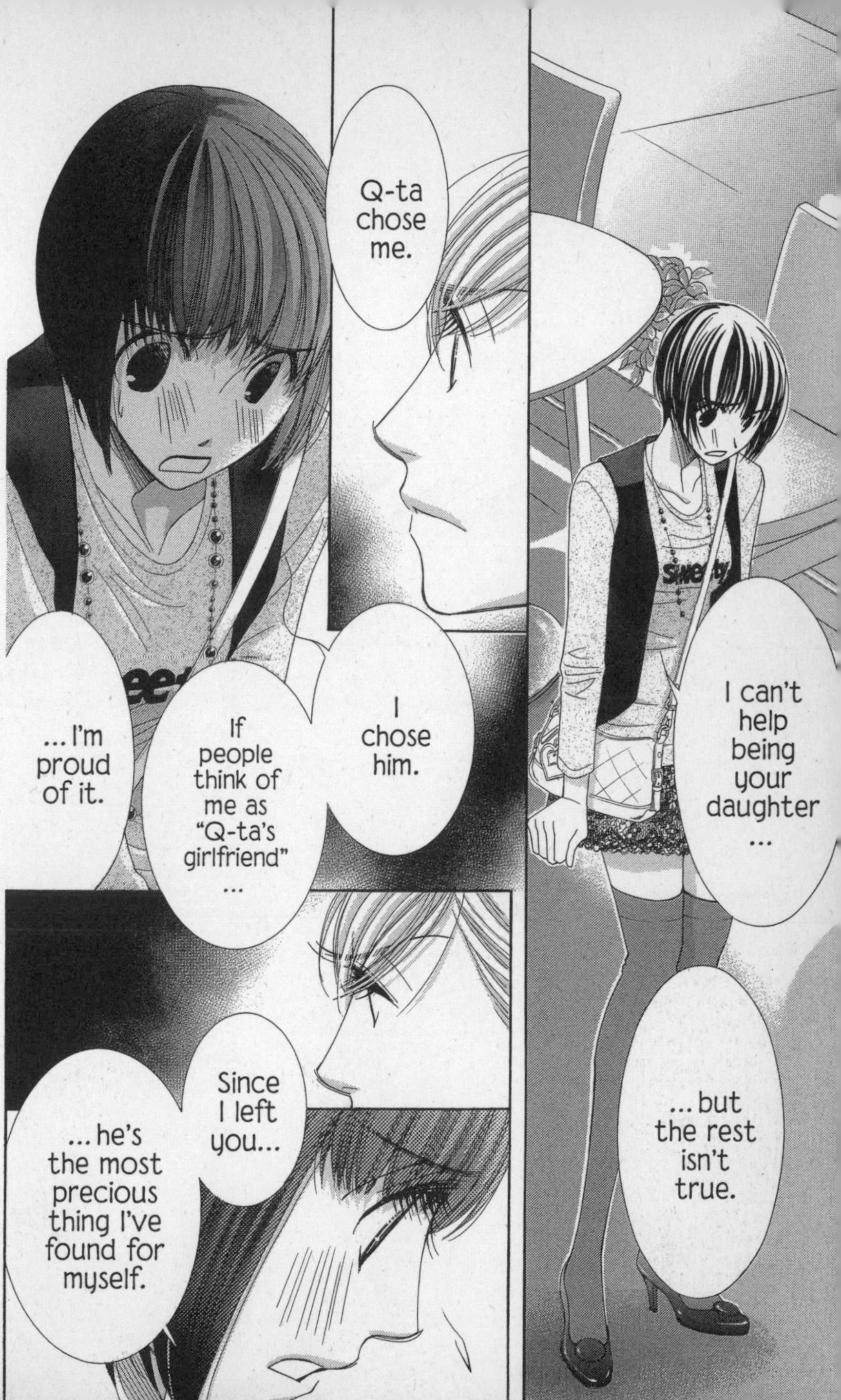
I can't help being your daughter...
...but the rest isn't true.
Q-ta chose me.
I chose him.
If people think of me as "Q-ta's girlfriend"...
...I'm proud of it.
Since I left you...
...he's the most precious thing I've found for myself.

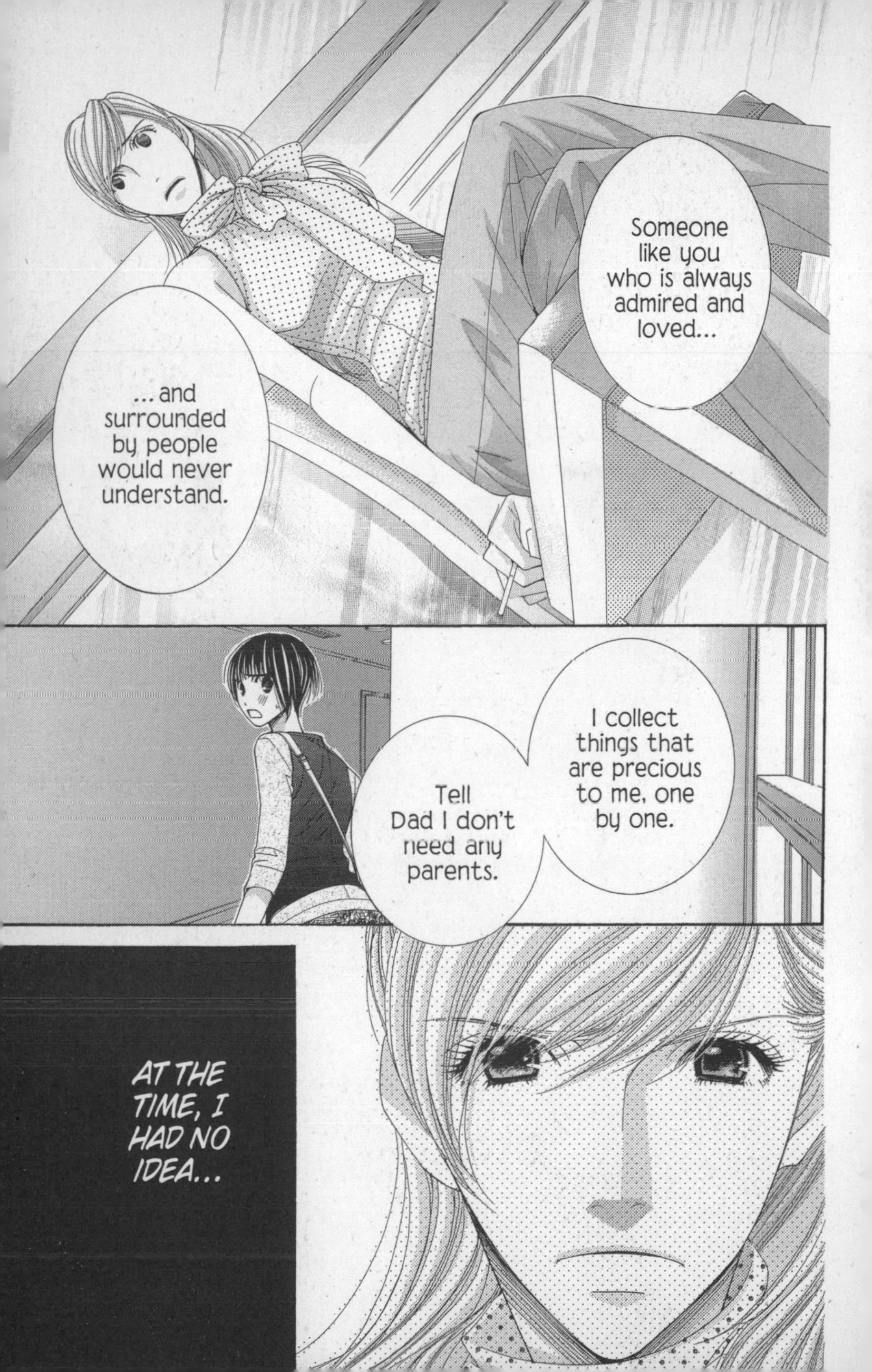
Someone like you who is always admired and loved...
...and surrounded by people would never understand.
I collect things that are precious to me, one by one.
Tell Dad I don't need any parents.
AT THE TIME, I HAD NO IDEA...

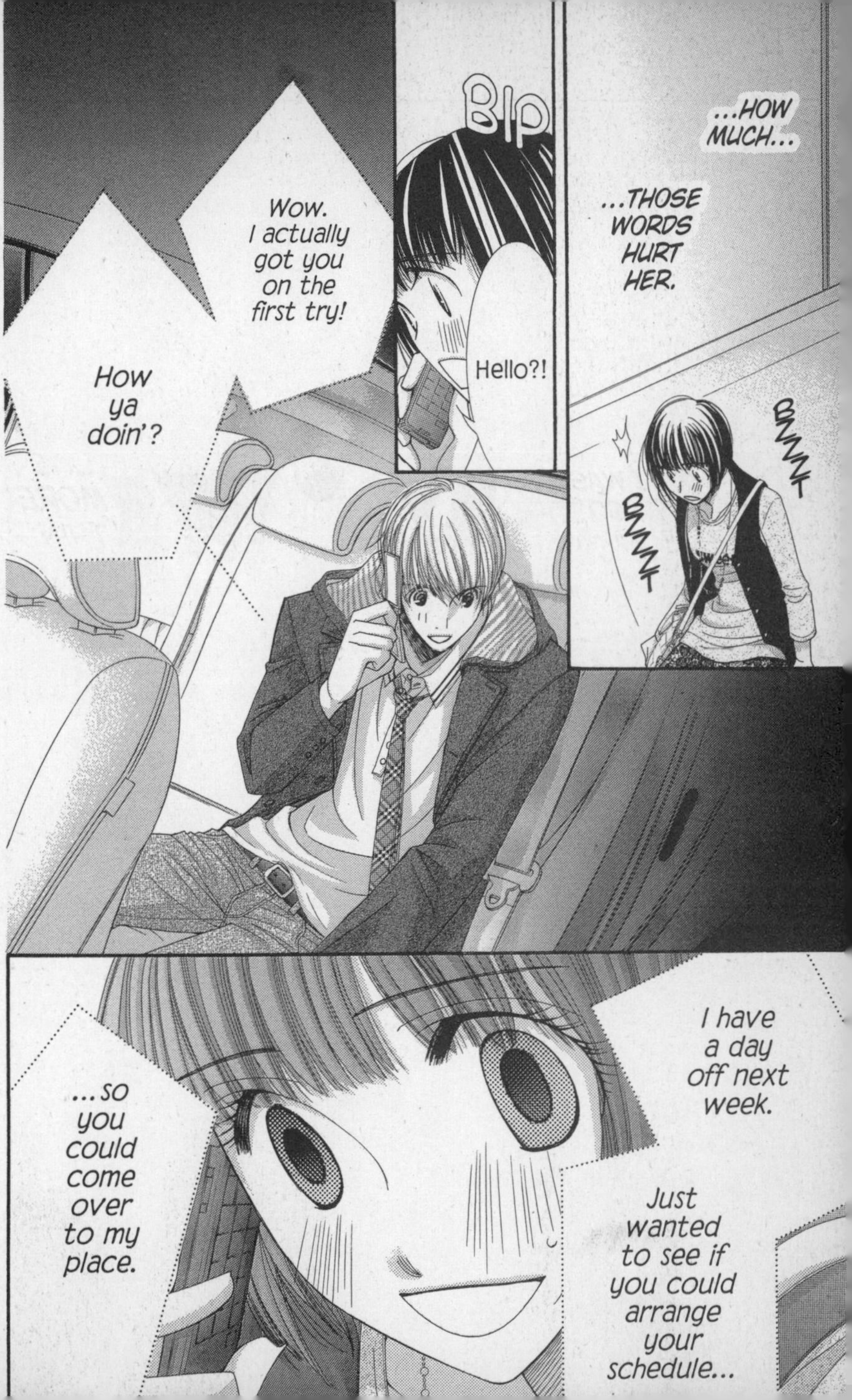
...HOW MUCH...
...THOSE WORDS HURT HER.
BZZZK
BZZZK
BIP
Hello?!
Wow. I actually got you on the first try!
How ya doin'?
I have a day off next week.
Just wanted to see if you could arrange your schedule...
...so you could come over to my place.

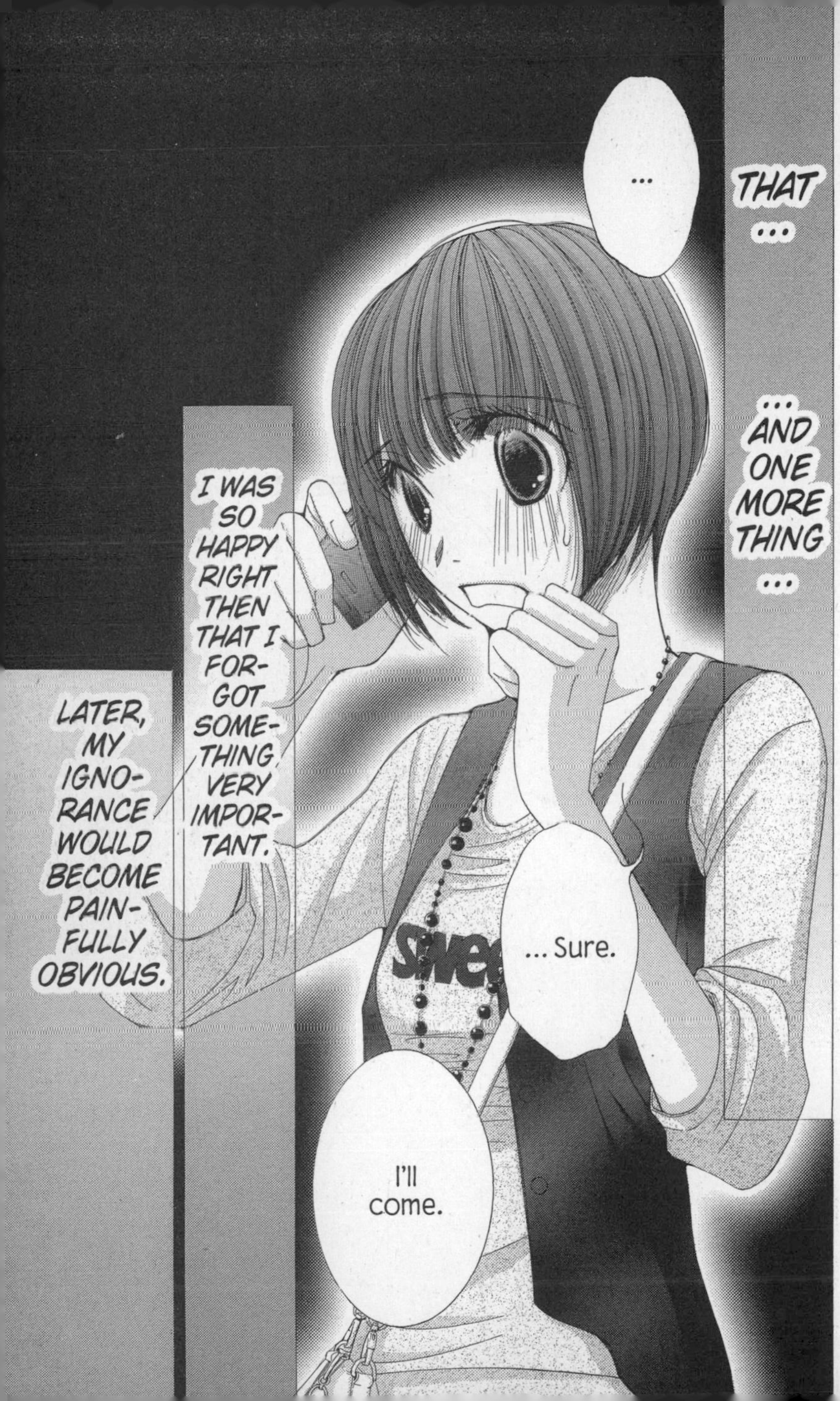
THAT...
...
...AND ONE MORE THING...
I WAS SO HAPPY RIGHT THEN THAT I FORGOT SOMETHING VERY IMPORTANT.
LATER, MY IGNORANCE WOULD BECOME PAINFULLY OBVIOUS.
...Sure.
I'll come.

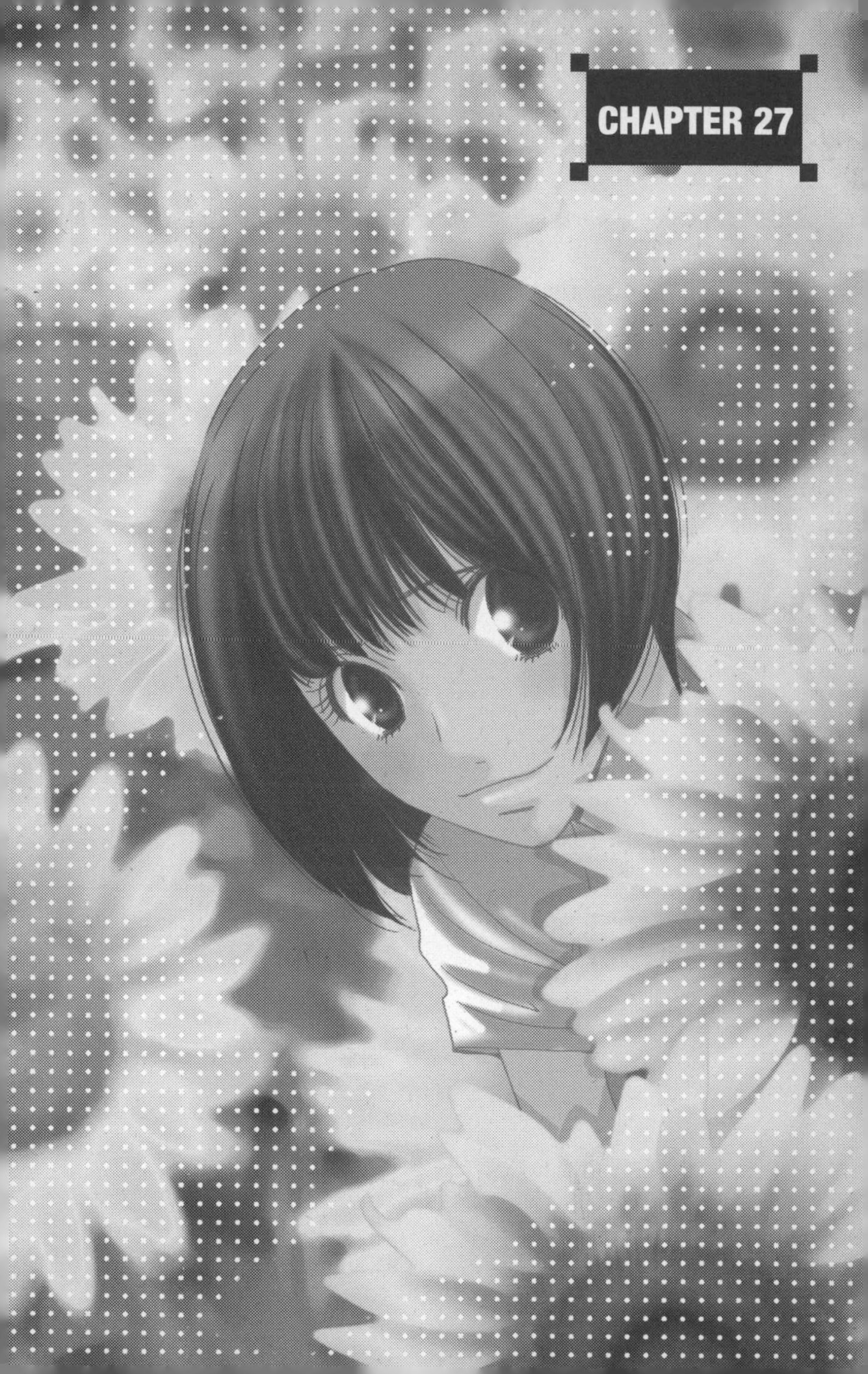
CHAPTER 27

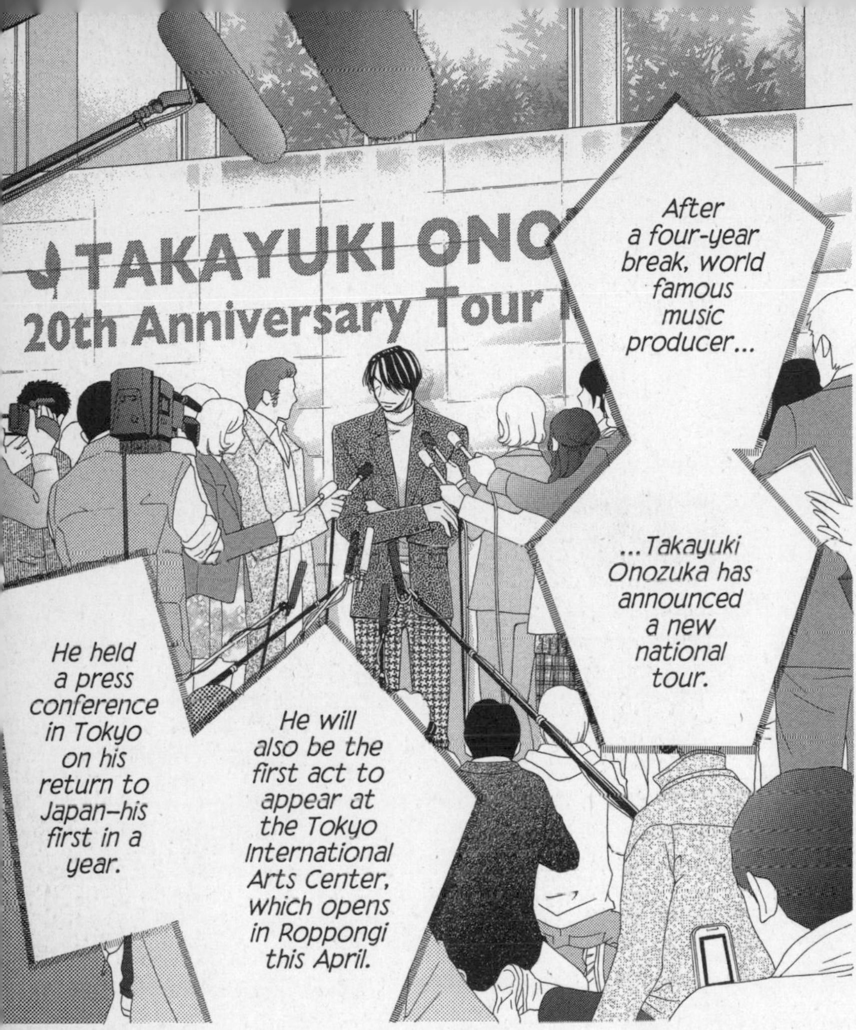
After a four-year break, world famous music producer...
...Takayuki Onozuka has announced a new national tour.
TAKAYUKI ONO
20th Anniversary Tour
He will also be the first act to appear at the Tokyo International Arts Center, which opens in Roppongi this April.
He held a press conference in Tokyo on his return to Japan—his first in a year.

Honey Hunt

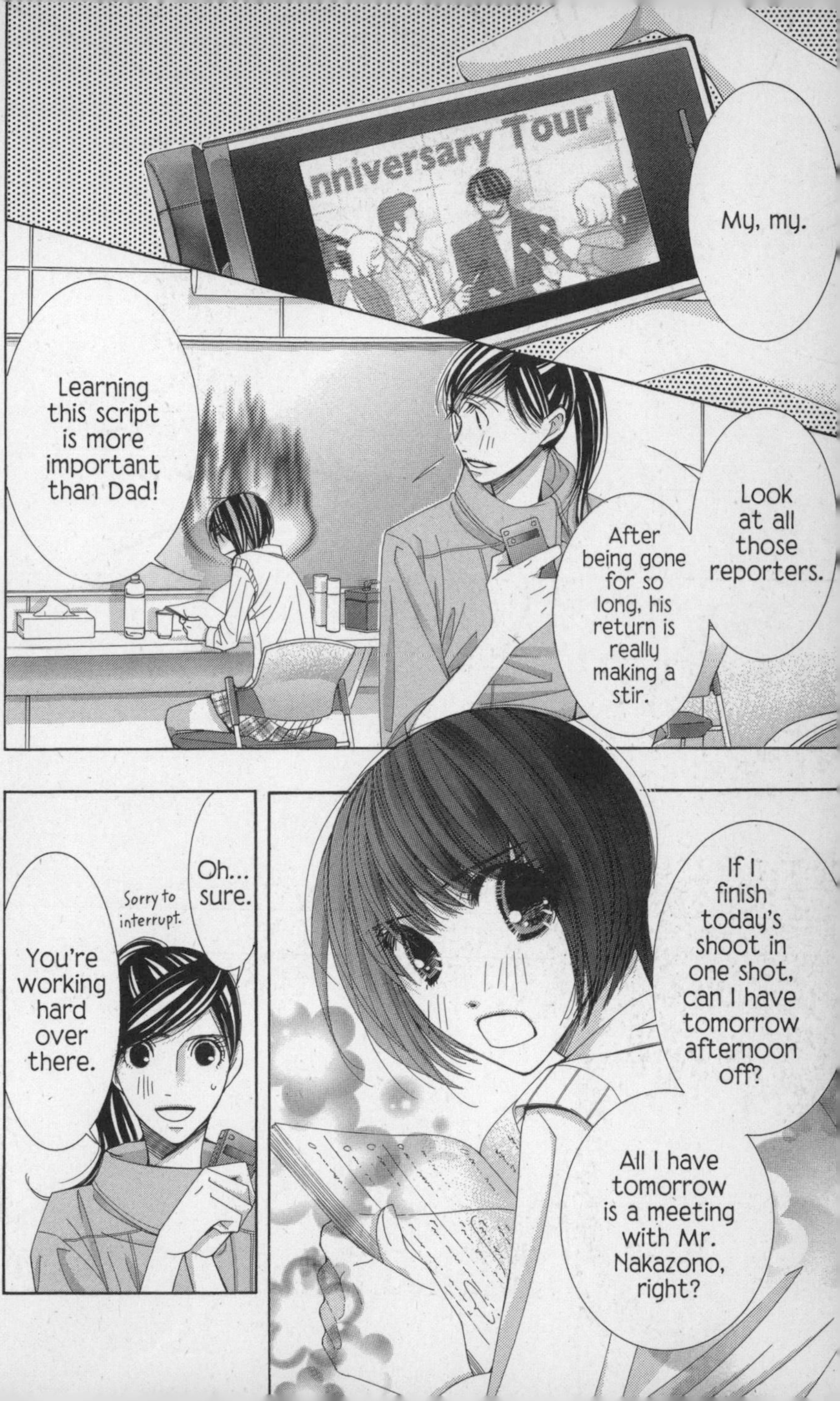
nniversary Tour
My, my.
Look at all those reporters.
After being gone for so long, his return is really making a stir.
Learning this script is more important than Dad!
If I finish today's shoot in one shot, can I have tomorrow afternoon off?
All I have tomorrow is a meeting with Mr. Nakazono, right?
Oh... sure.
Sorry to interrupt.
You're working hard over there.

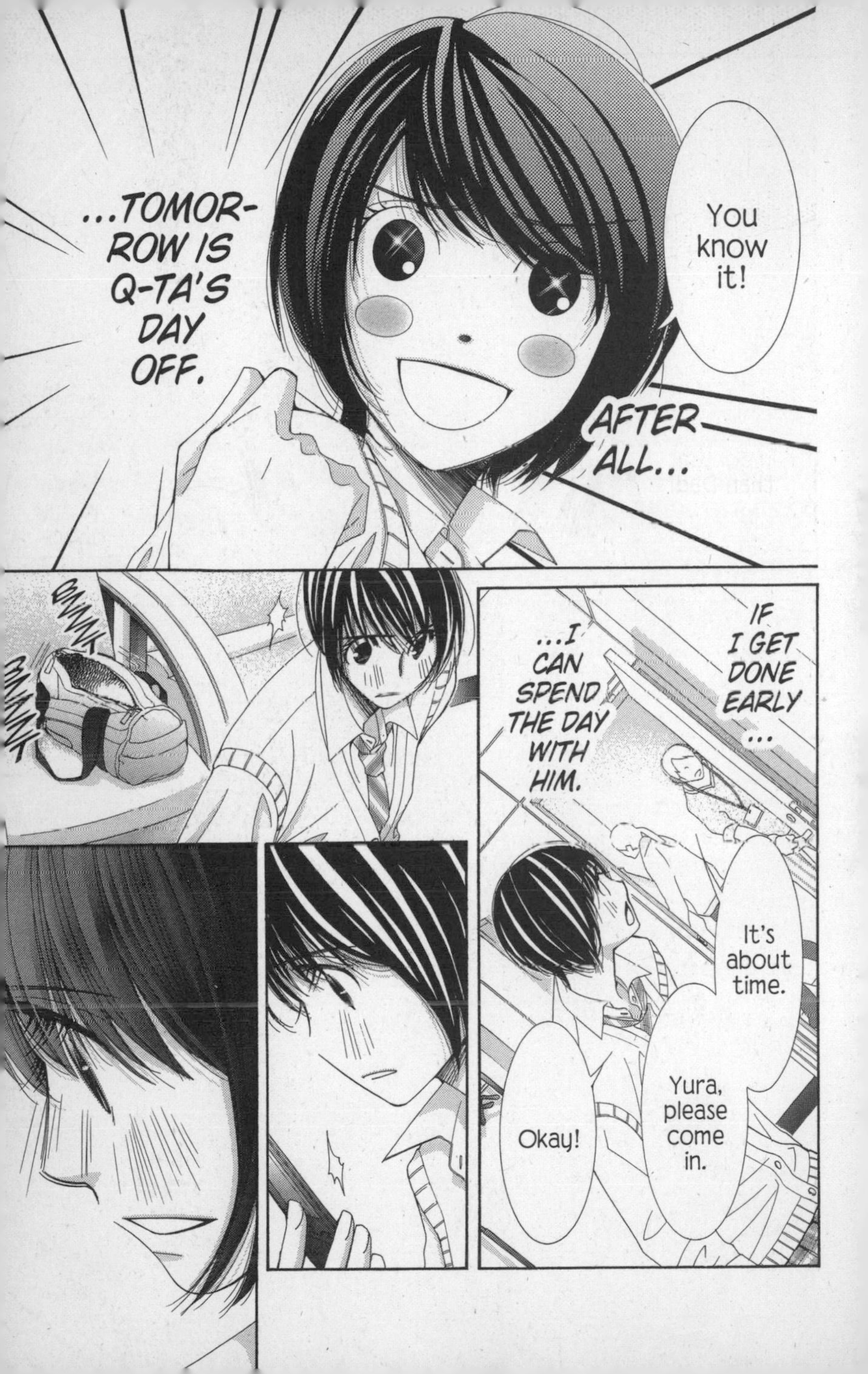
You know it!
AFTER ALL...
...TOMORROW IS Q-TA'S DAY OFF.
IF I GET DONE EARLY...
...I CAN SPEND THE DAY WITH HIM.
It's about time.
Yura, please come in.
Okay!

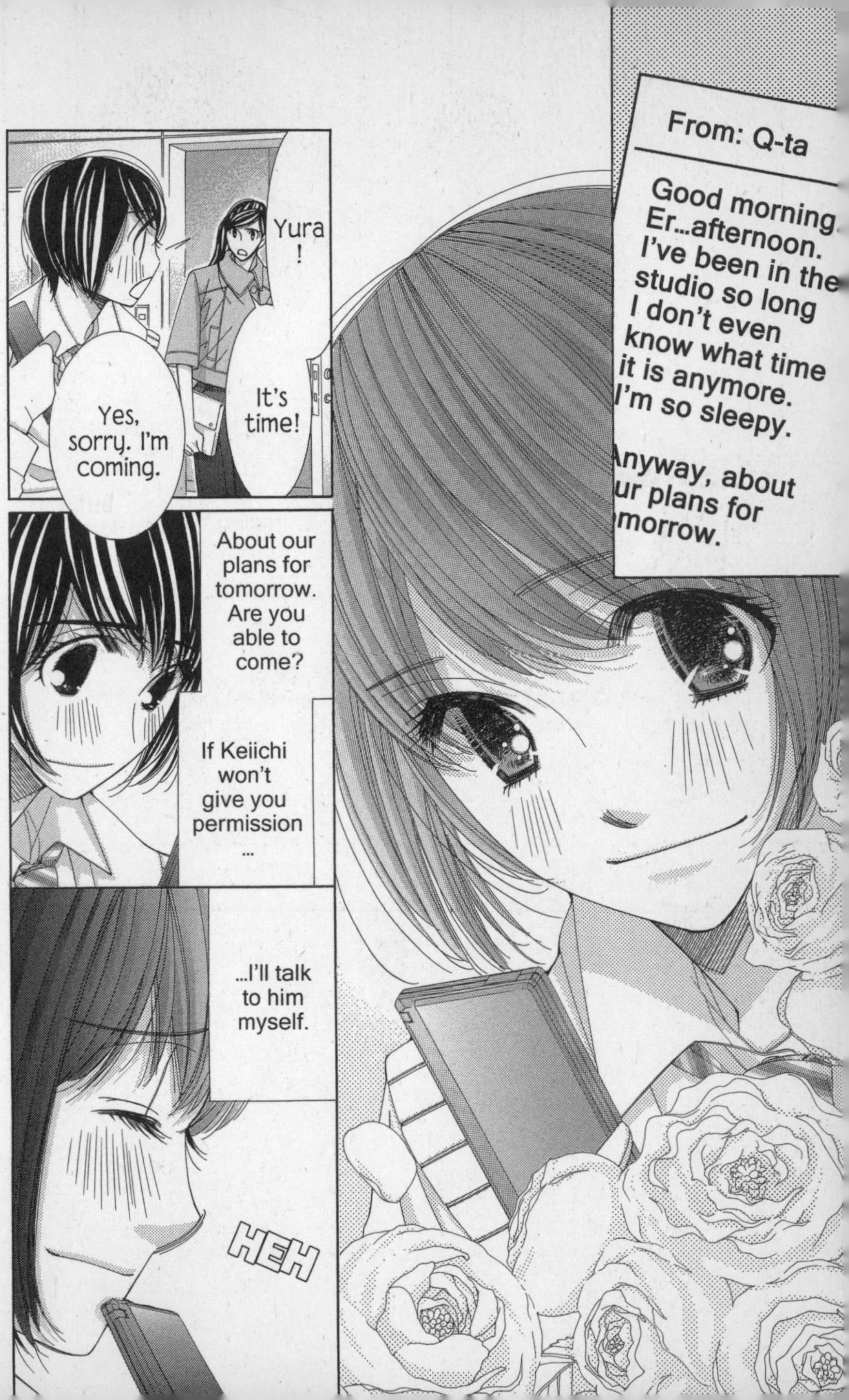
From: Q-ta
Good morning. Er...afternoon. I've been in the studio so long I don't even know what time it is anymore. I'm so sleepy.
Anyway, about ur plans for morrow.
Yura!
It's time!
Yes, sorry. I'm coming.
About our plans for tomorrow. Are you able to come?
If Keiichi won't give you permission...
...I'll talk to him myself.
HEH

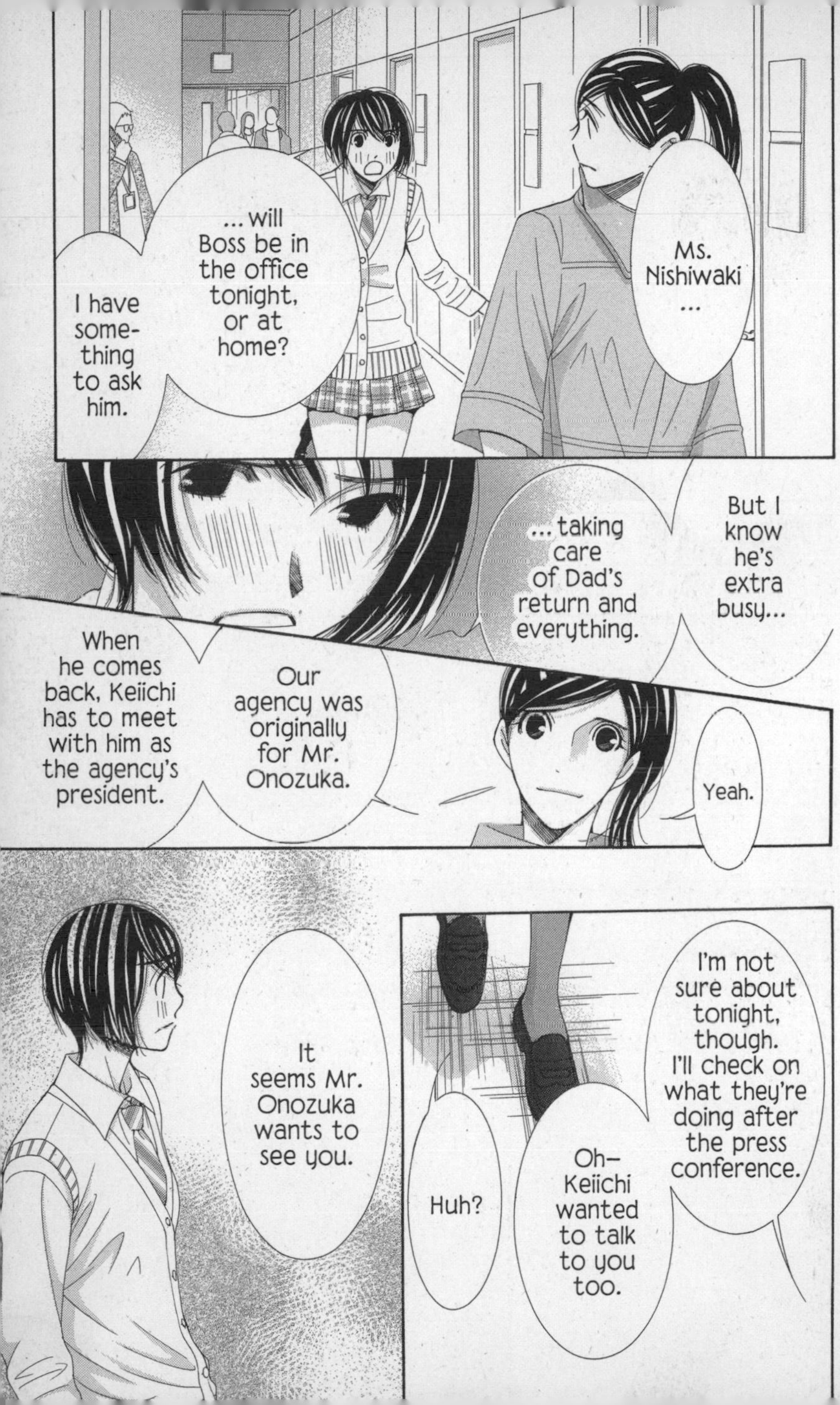
Ms. Nishiwaki ...
... will Boss be in the office tonight, or at home?
I have some-thing to ask him.
But I know he's extra busy...
... taking care of Dad's return and everything.
Yeah.
Our agency was originally for Mr. Onozuka.
When he comes back, Keiichi has to meet with him as the agency's president.
I'm not sure about tonight, though. I'll check on what they're doing after the press conference.
Oh– Keiichi wanted to talk to you too.
Huh?
It seems Mr. Onozuka wants to see you.

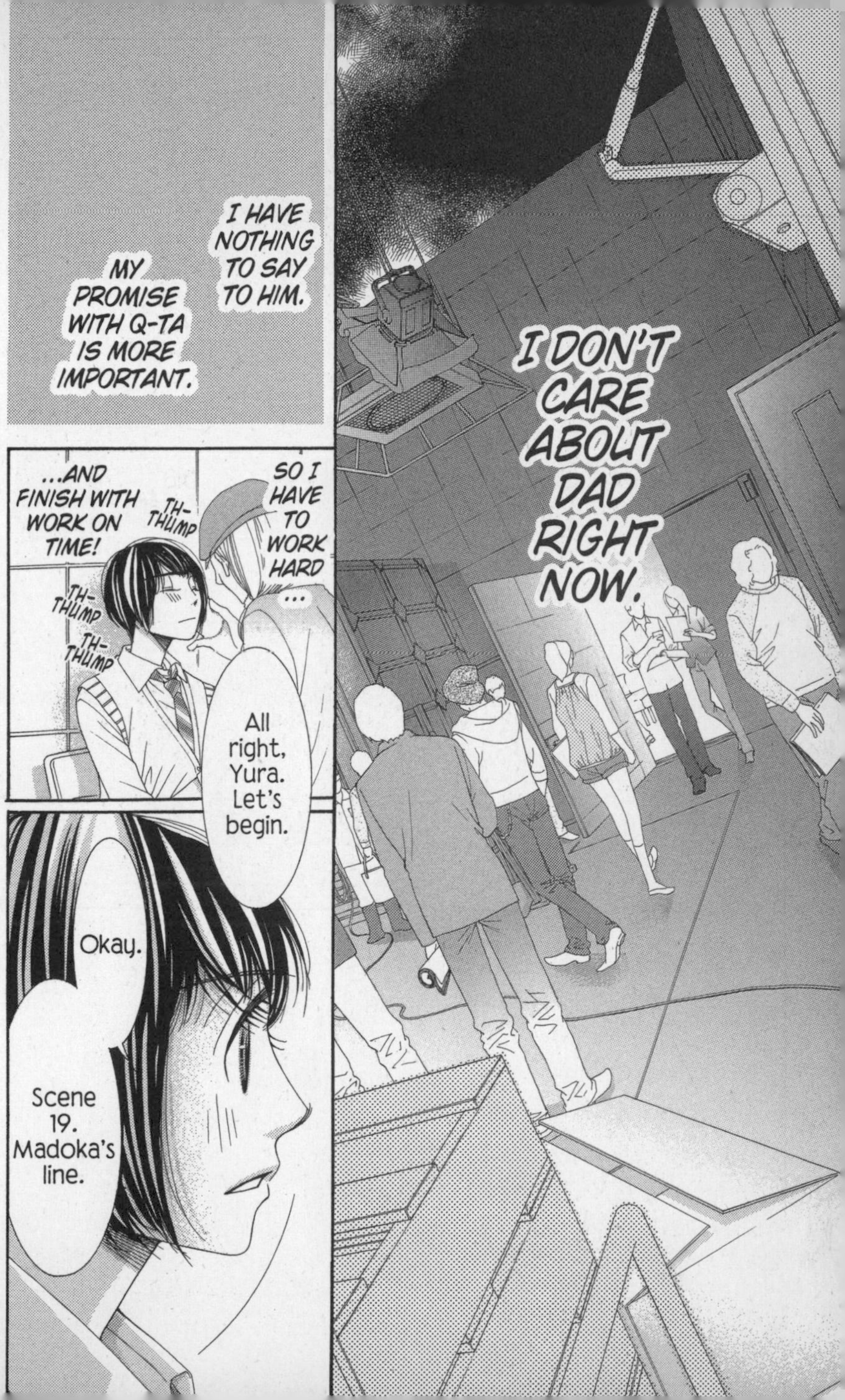
I DON'T CARE ABOUT DAD RIGHT NOW.
I HAVE NOTHING TO SAY TO HIM.
MY PROMISE WITH Q-TA IS MORE IMPORTANT.
SO I HAVE TO WORK HARD...
TH-THUMP
...AND FINISH WITH WORK ON TIME!
TH-THUMP
TH-THUMP
All right, Yura. Let's begin.
Okay.
Scene 19. Madoka's line.

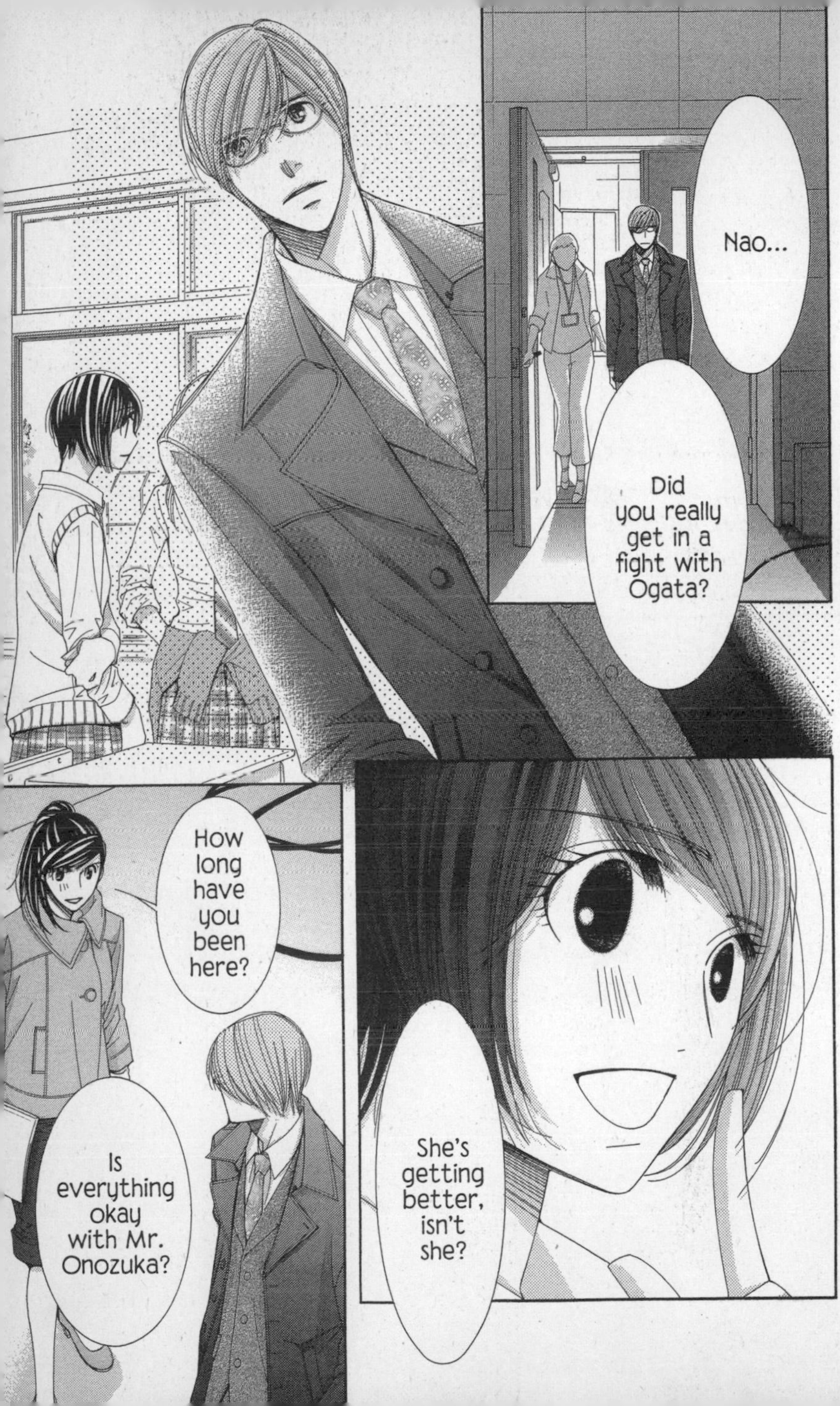
Nao...
Did you really get in a fight with Ogata?
She's getting better, isn't she?
How long have you been here?
Is everything okay with Mr. Onozuka?

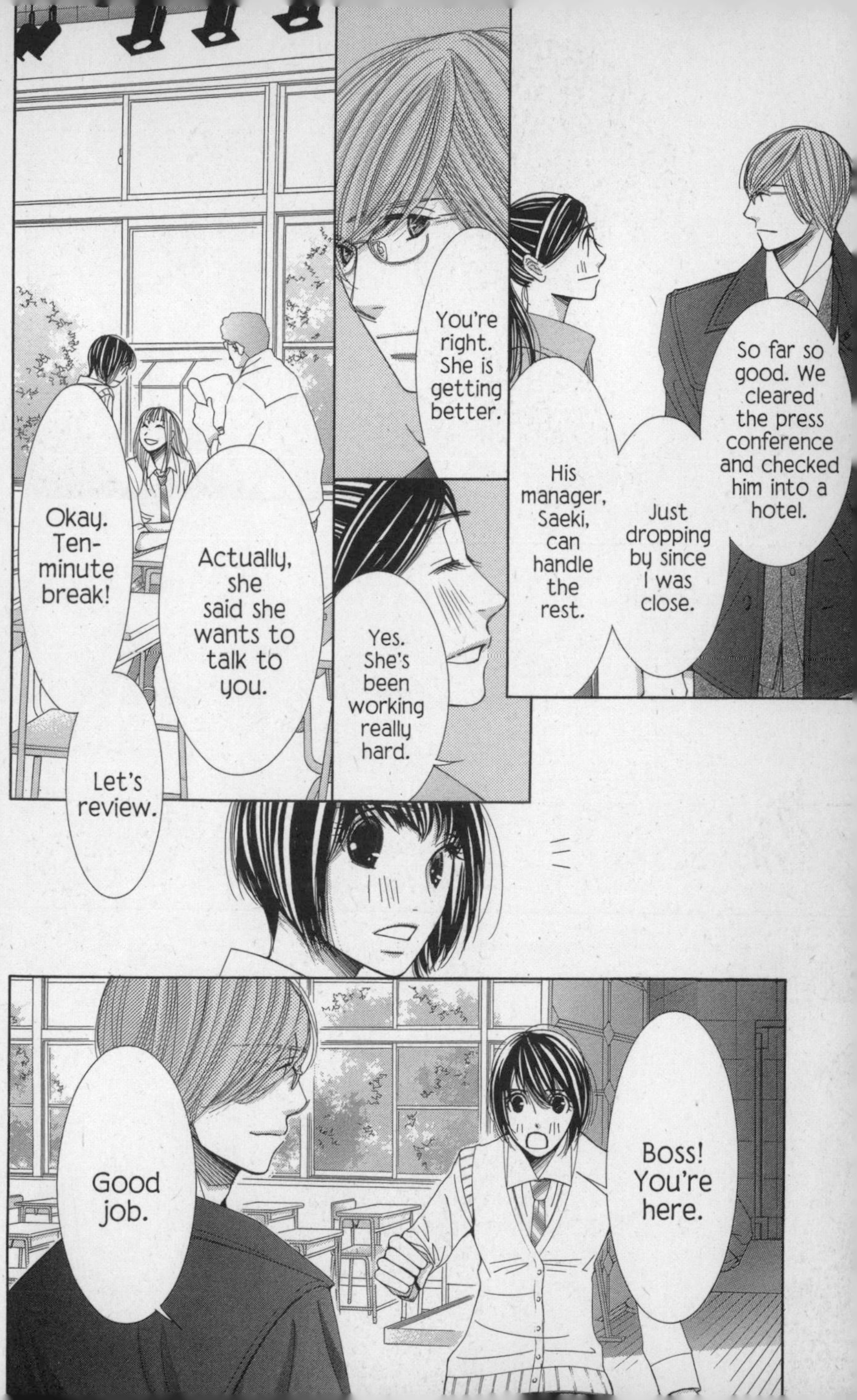
So far so good. We cleared the press conference and checked him into a hotel.
Just dropping by since I was close.
His manager, Saeki, can handle the rest.
You're right. She is getting better.
Yes. She's been working really hard.
Actually, she said she wants to talk to you.
Okay. Ten-minute break!
Let's review.
Boss! You're here.
Good job.

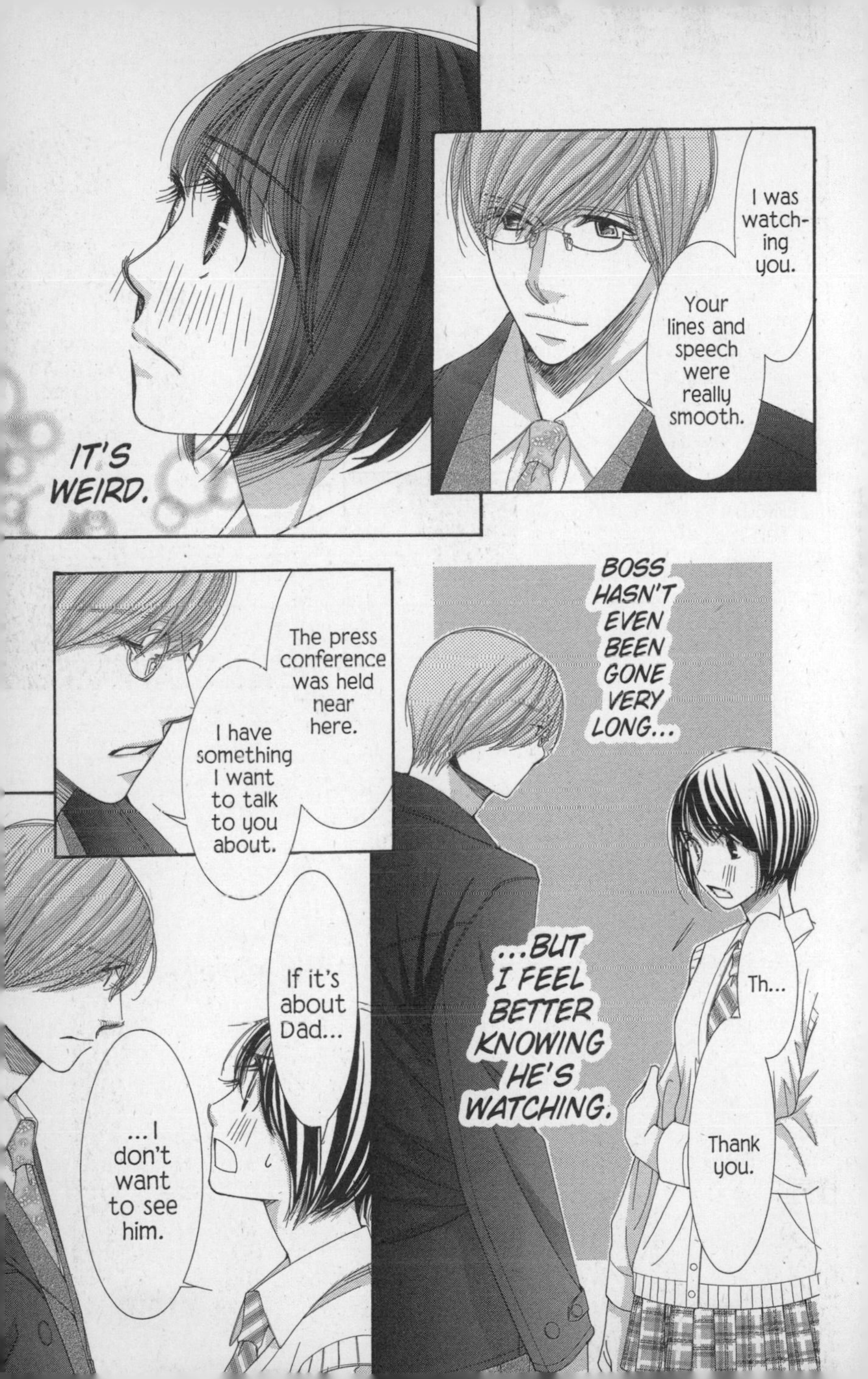
I was watching you.
Your lines and speech were really smooth.
IT'S WEIRD.
BOSS HASN'T EVEN BEEN GONE VERY LONG...
...BUT I FEEL BETTER KNOWING HE'S WATCHING.
Th...
Thank you.
The press conference was held near here.
I have something I want to talk to you about.
If it's about Dad...
...I don't want to see him.

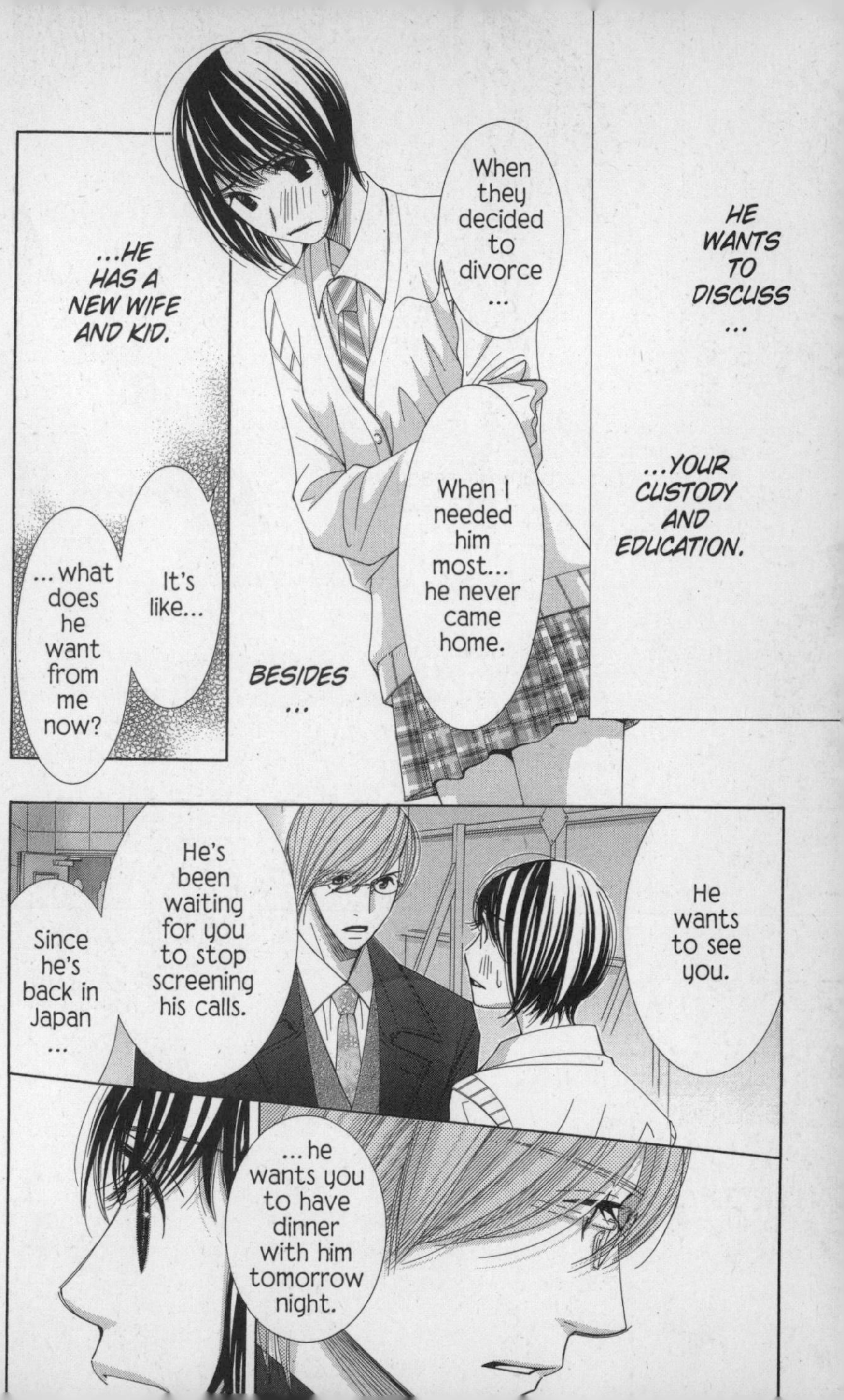
HE WANTS TO DISCUSS...
...YOUR CUSTODY AND EDUCATION.
When they decided to divorce...
When I needed him most... he never came home.
BESIDES...
...HE HAS A NEW WIFE AND KID.
It's like...
...what does he want from me now?
He wants to see you.
He's been waiting for you to stop screening his calls.
Since he's back in Japan...
...he wants you to have dinner with him tomorrow night.

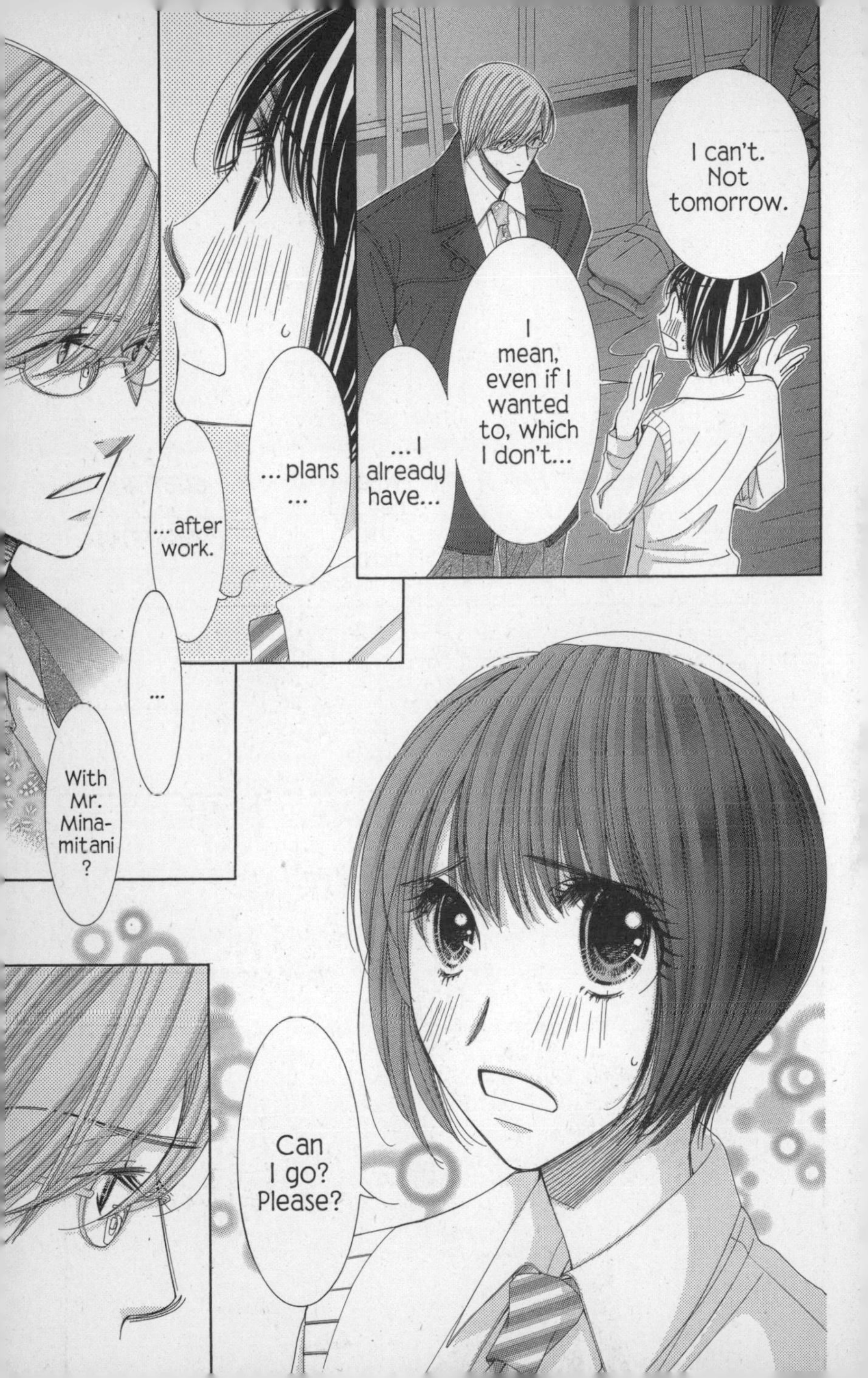
I can't. Not tomorrow.
I mean, even if I wanted to, which I don't...
...I already have...
...plans...
...after work.
...
With Mr. Minamitani?
Can I go? Please?

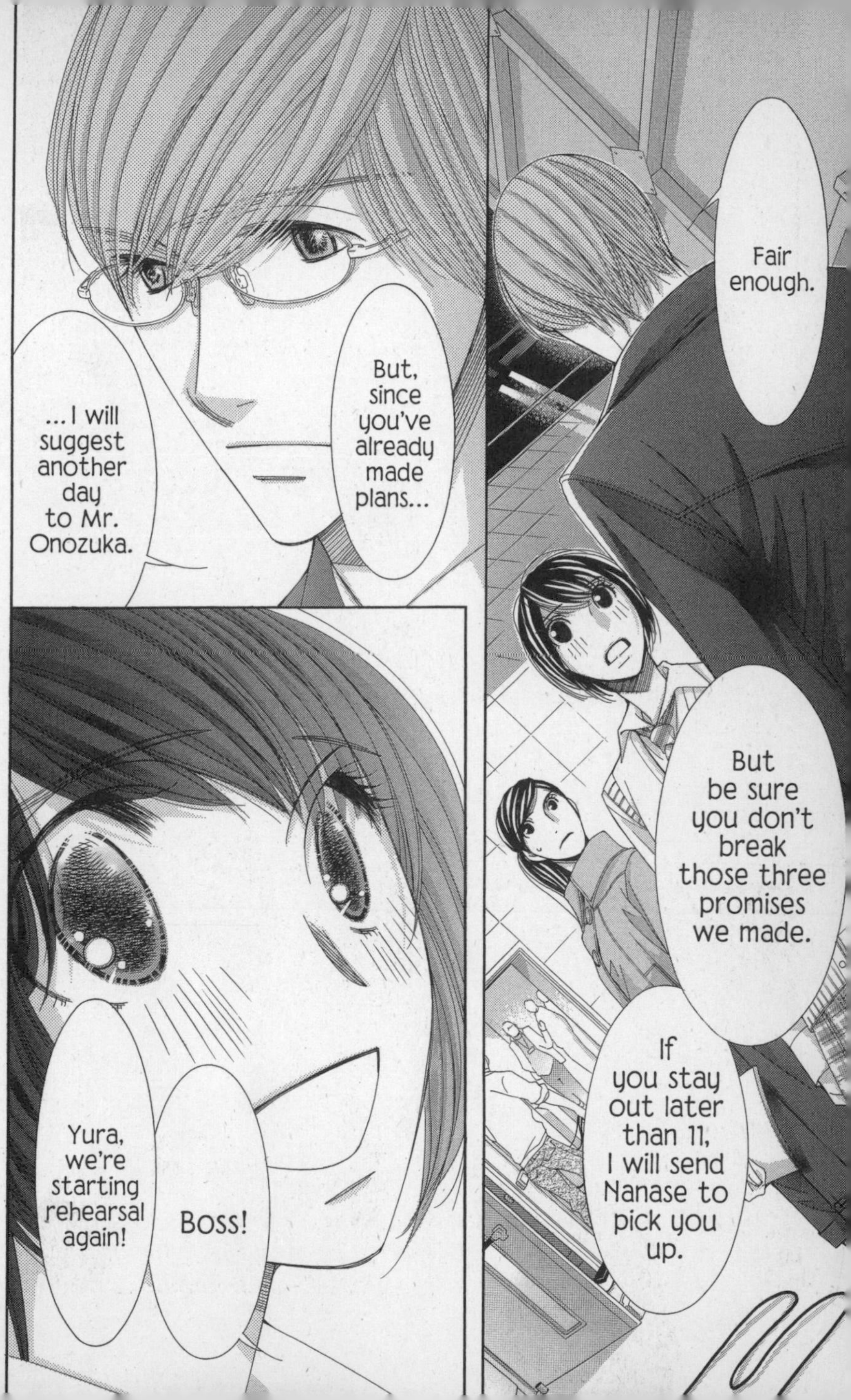
Fair enough.
But be sure you don't break those three promises we made.
If you stay out later than 11, I will send Nanase to pick you up.
But, since you've already made plans...
...I will suggest another day to Mr. Onozuka.
Boss!
Yura, we're starting rehearsal again!

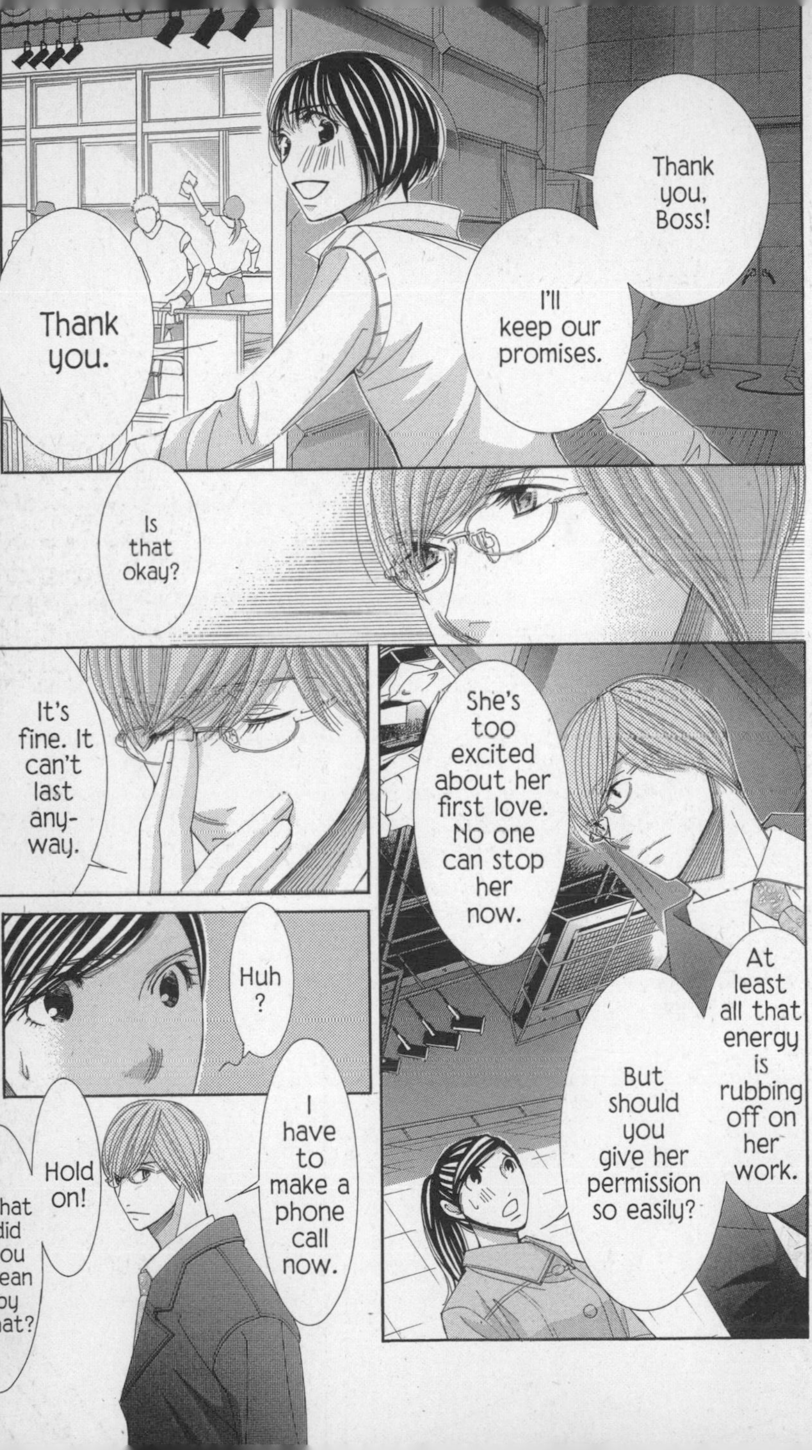
Thank you, Boss!
I'll keep our promises.
Thank you.
Is that okay?
She's too excited about her first love. No one can stop her now.
At least all that energy is rubbing off on her work.
But should you give her permission so easily?
It's fine. It can't last any-way.
Huh?
I have to make a phone call now.
Hold on!
What did you mean by that?

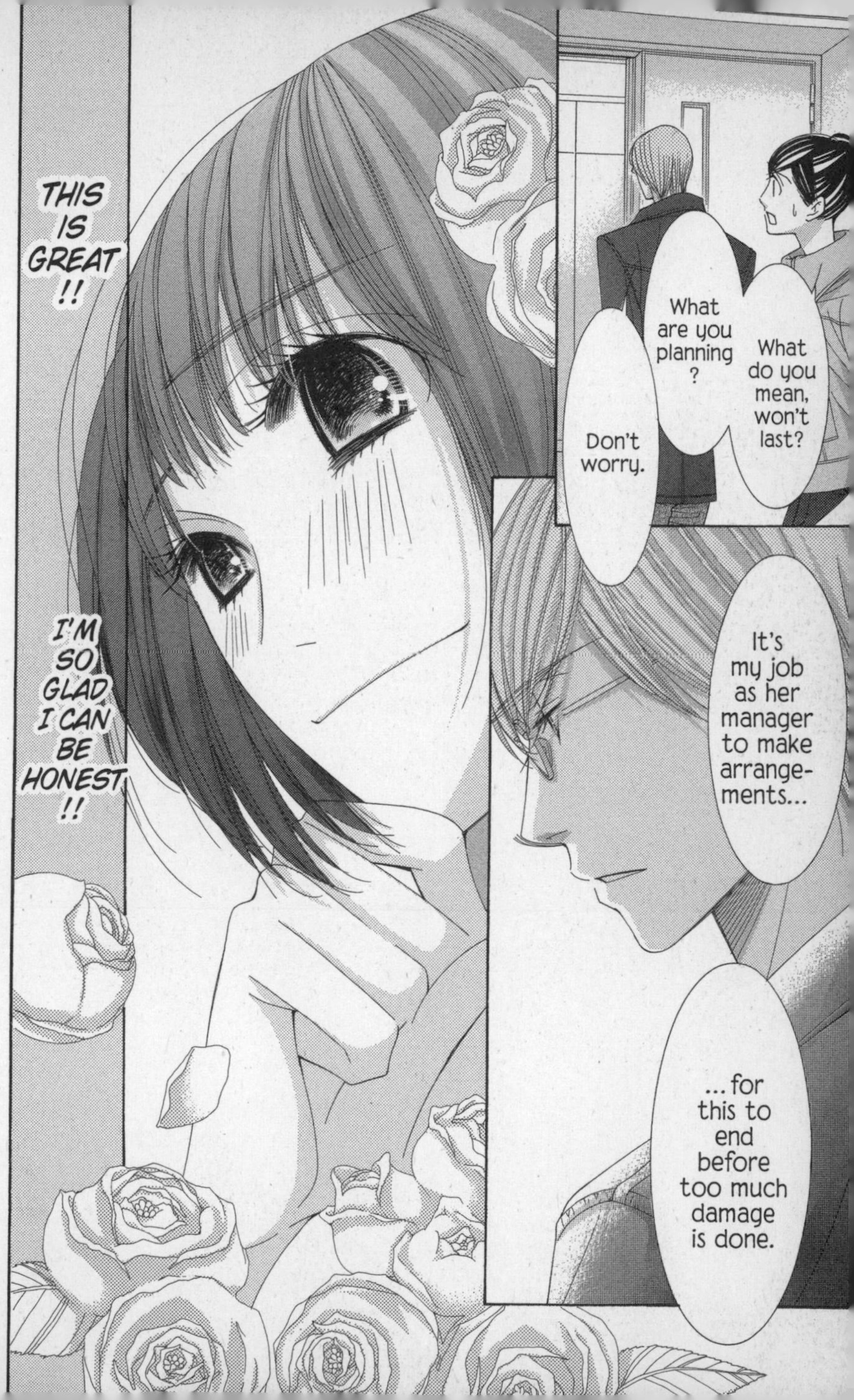
What do you mean, won't last?
What are you planning?
Don't worry.
It's my job as her manager to make arrangements...
...for this to end before too much damage is done.
THIS IS GREAT!!
I'M SO GLAD I CAN BE HONEST!!

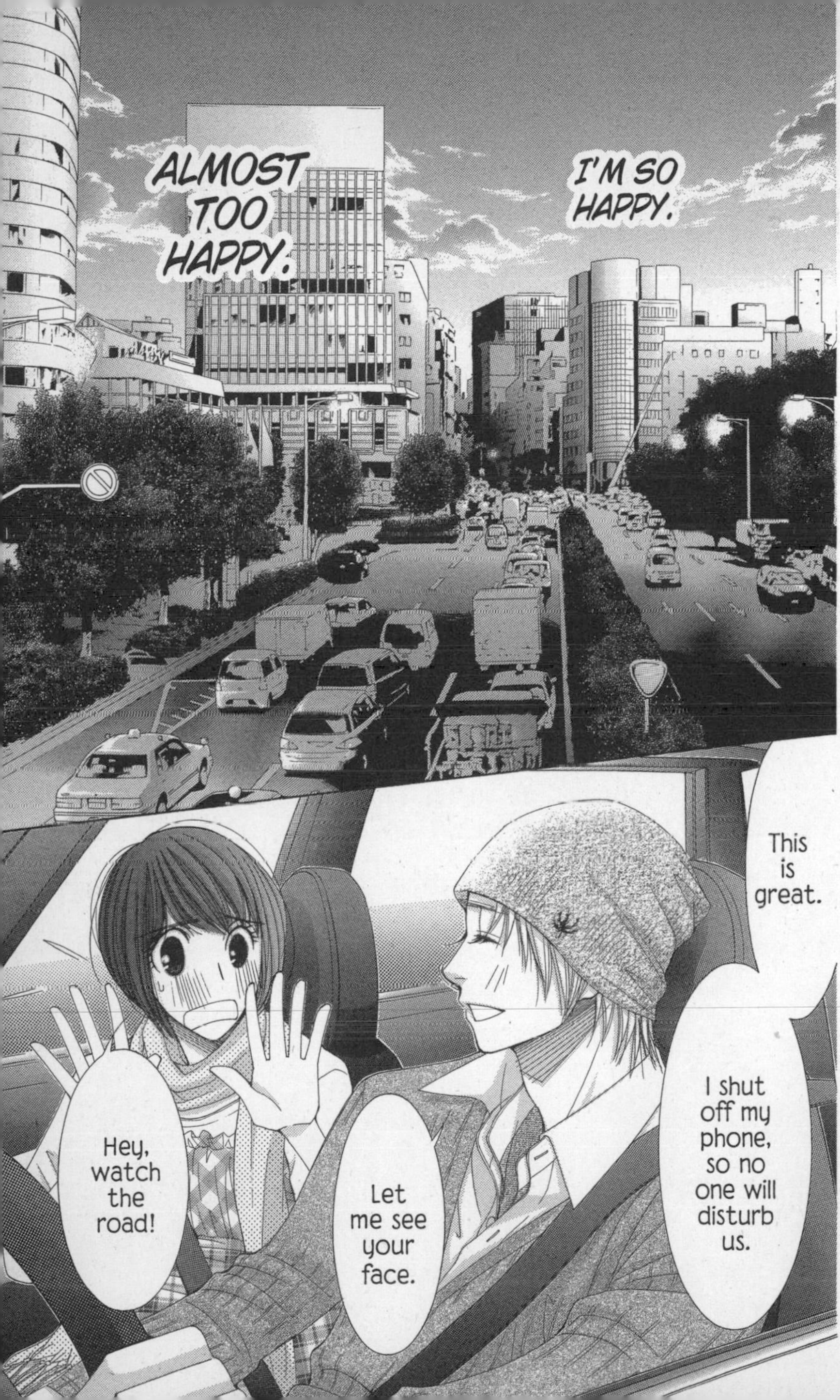
I'M SO HAPPY.
ALMOST TOO HAPPY.
This is great.
I shut off my phone, so no one will disturb us.
Let me see your face.
Hey, watch the road!

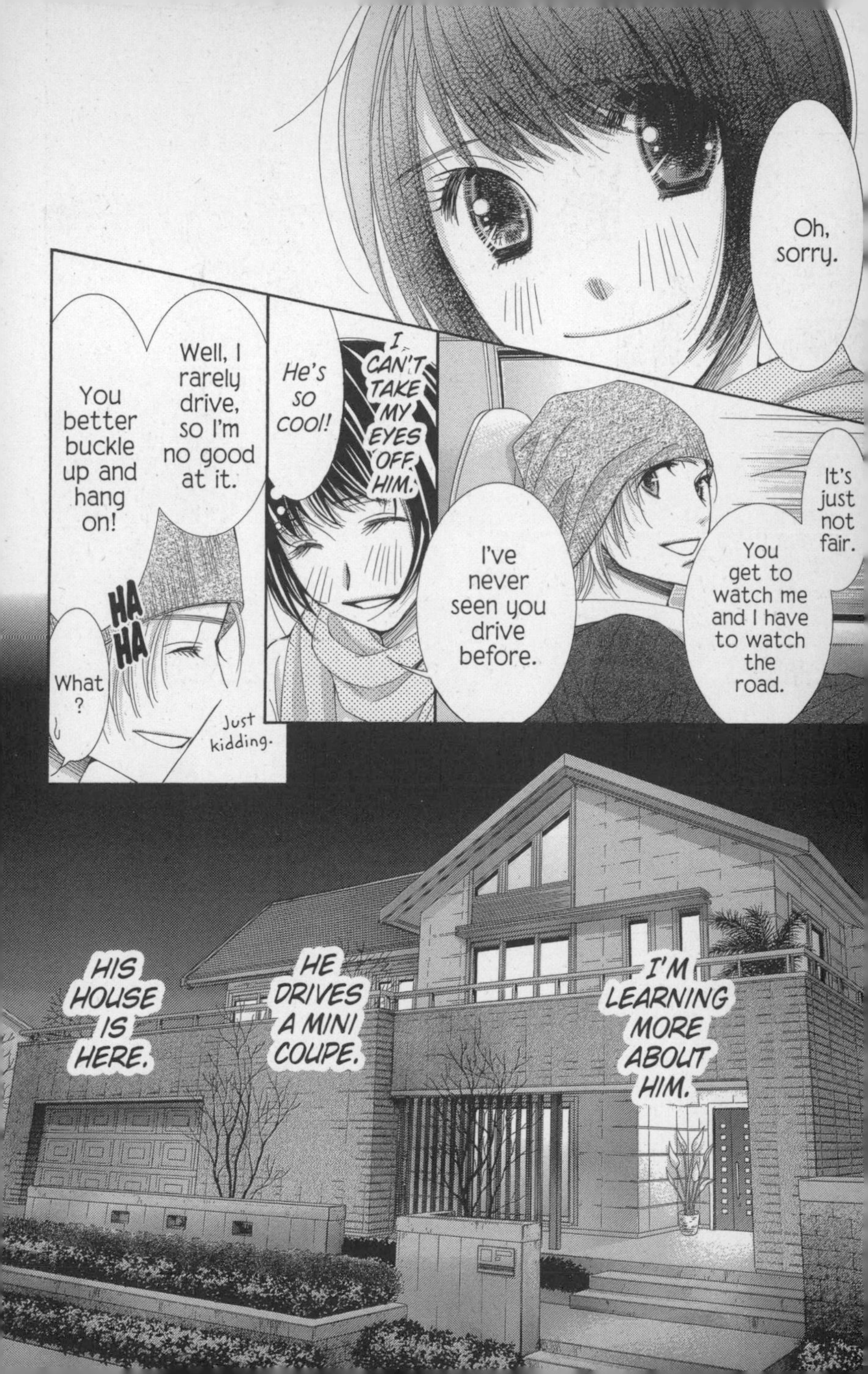
Oh, sorry.
It's just not fair.
You get to watch me and I have to watch the road.
I've never seen you drive before.
I CAN'T TAKE MY EYES OFF HIM.
He's so cool!
Well, I rarely drive, so I'm no good at it.
You better buckle up and hang on!
HA HA
What?
Just kidding.
I'M LEARNING MORE ABOUT HIM.
HE DRIVES A MINI COUPE.
HIS HOUSE IS HERE.

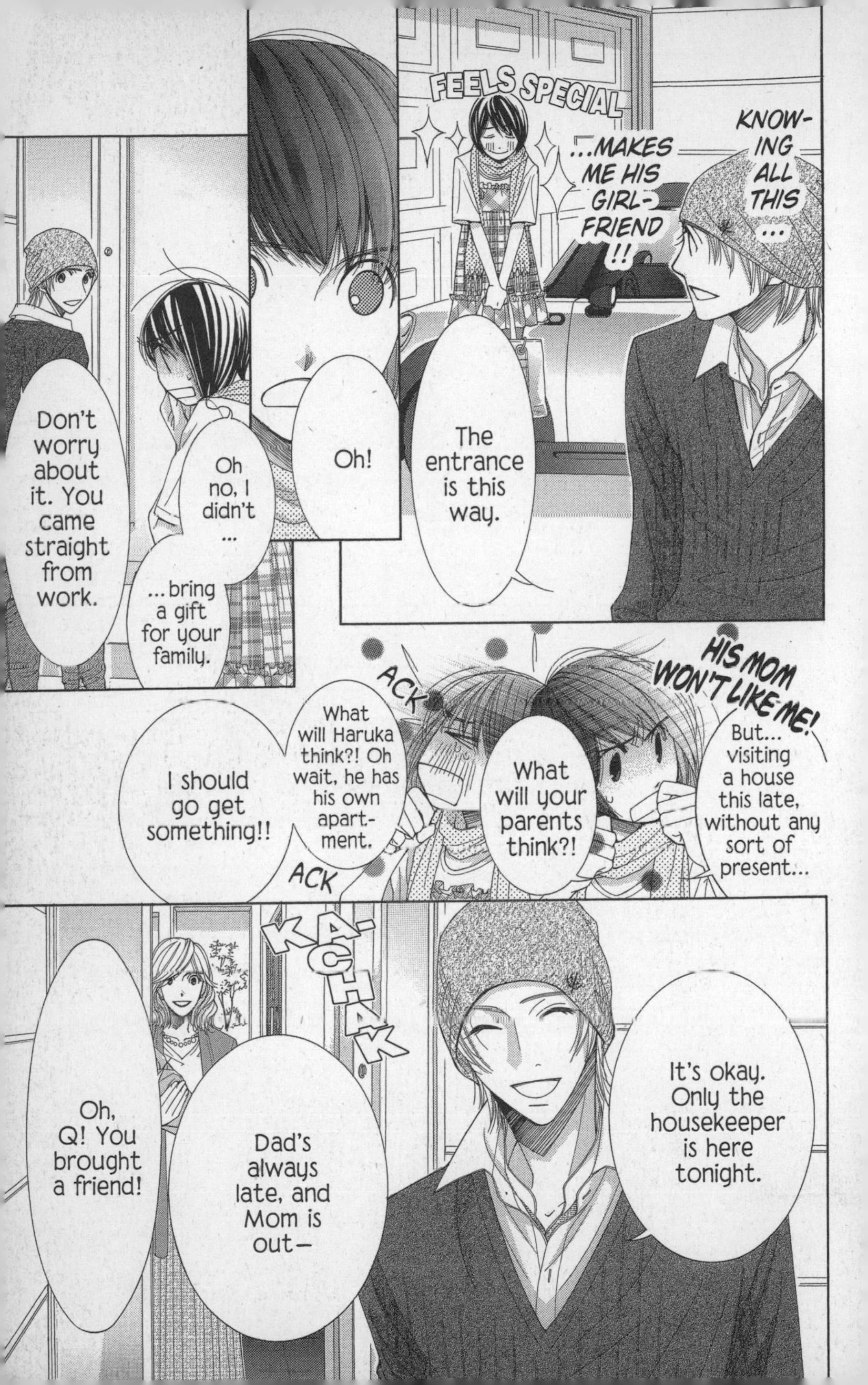
KNOWING ALL THIS...
...MAKES ME HIS GIRLFRIEND!!
FEELS SPECIAL
The entrance is this way.
Oh!
Oh no, I didn't...
...bring a gift for your family.
Don't worry about it. You came straight from work.
HIS MOM WON'T LIKE ME!
But... visiting a house this late, without any sort of present...
What will your parents think?!
ACK
What will Haruka think?! Oh wait, he has his own apartment.
I should go get something!!
ACK
It's okay. Only the housekeeper is here tonight.
KA-CHAK
Dad's always late, and Mom is out—
Oh, Q! You brought a friend!

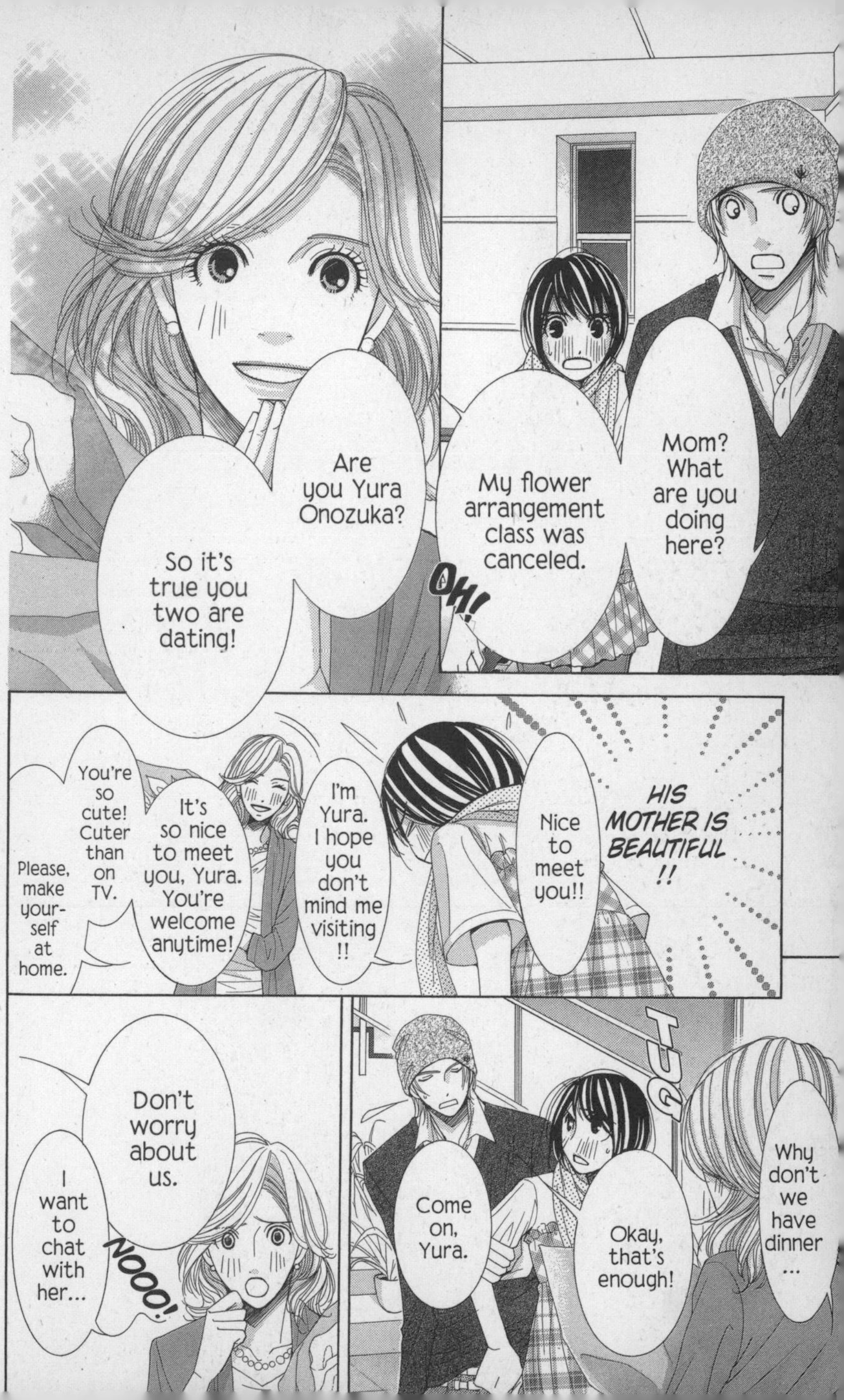
Mom? What are you doing here?
My flower arrangement class was canceled.
OH!
Are you Yura Onozuka?
So it's true you two are dating!
HIS MOTHER IS BEAUTIFUL!!
Nice to meet you!!
I'm Yura. I hope you don't mind me visiting!!
It's so nice to meet you, Yura. You're welcome anytime!
You're so cute! Cuter than on TV.
Please, make your-self at home.
Why don't we have dinner...
Okay, that's enough!
TUG
Come on, Yura.
Don't worry about us.
I want to chat with her...
NOOO!

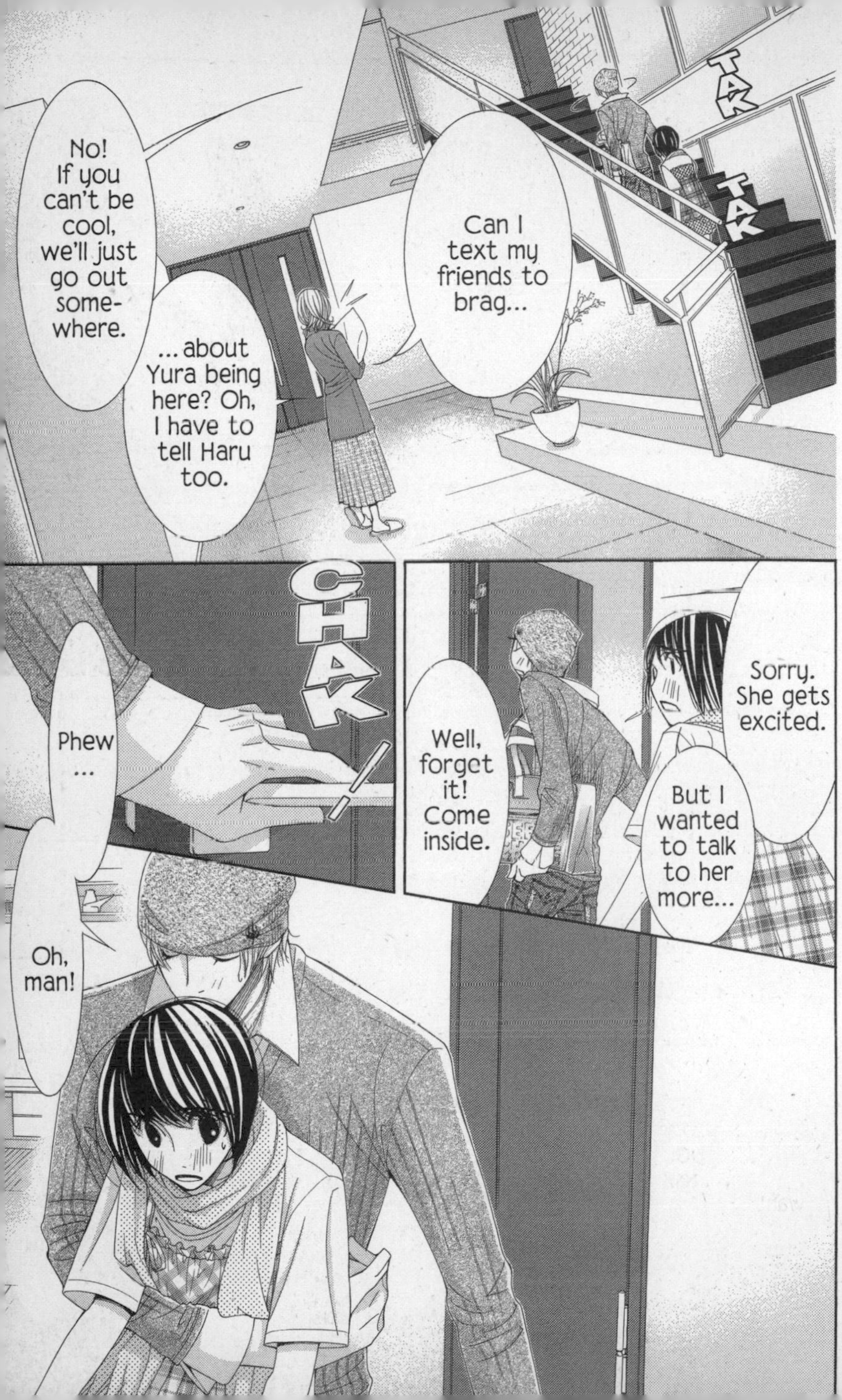
TAK
TAK
Can I text my friends to brag...
...about Yura being here? Oh, I have to tell Haru too.
No! If you can't be cool, we'll just go out some-where.
Sorry. She gets excited.
But I wanted to talk to her more...
Well, forget it! Come inside.
CHAK
Phew...
Oh, man!

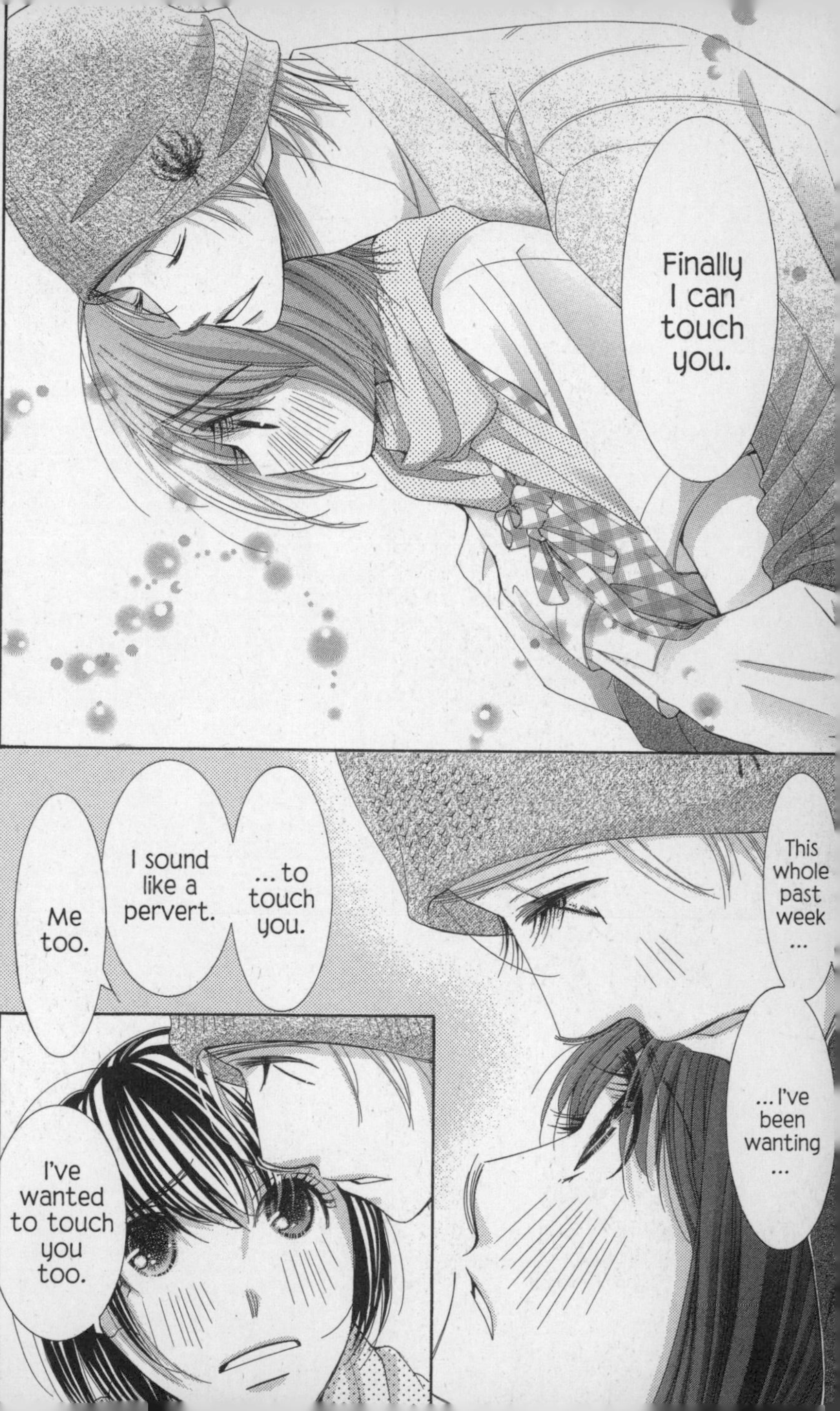
Finally I can touch you.
This whole past week ...
... I've been wanting ...
... to touch you.
I sound like a pervert.
Me too.
I've wanted to touch you too.

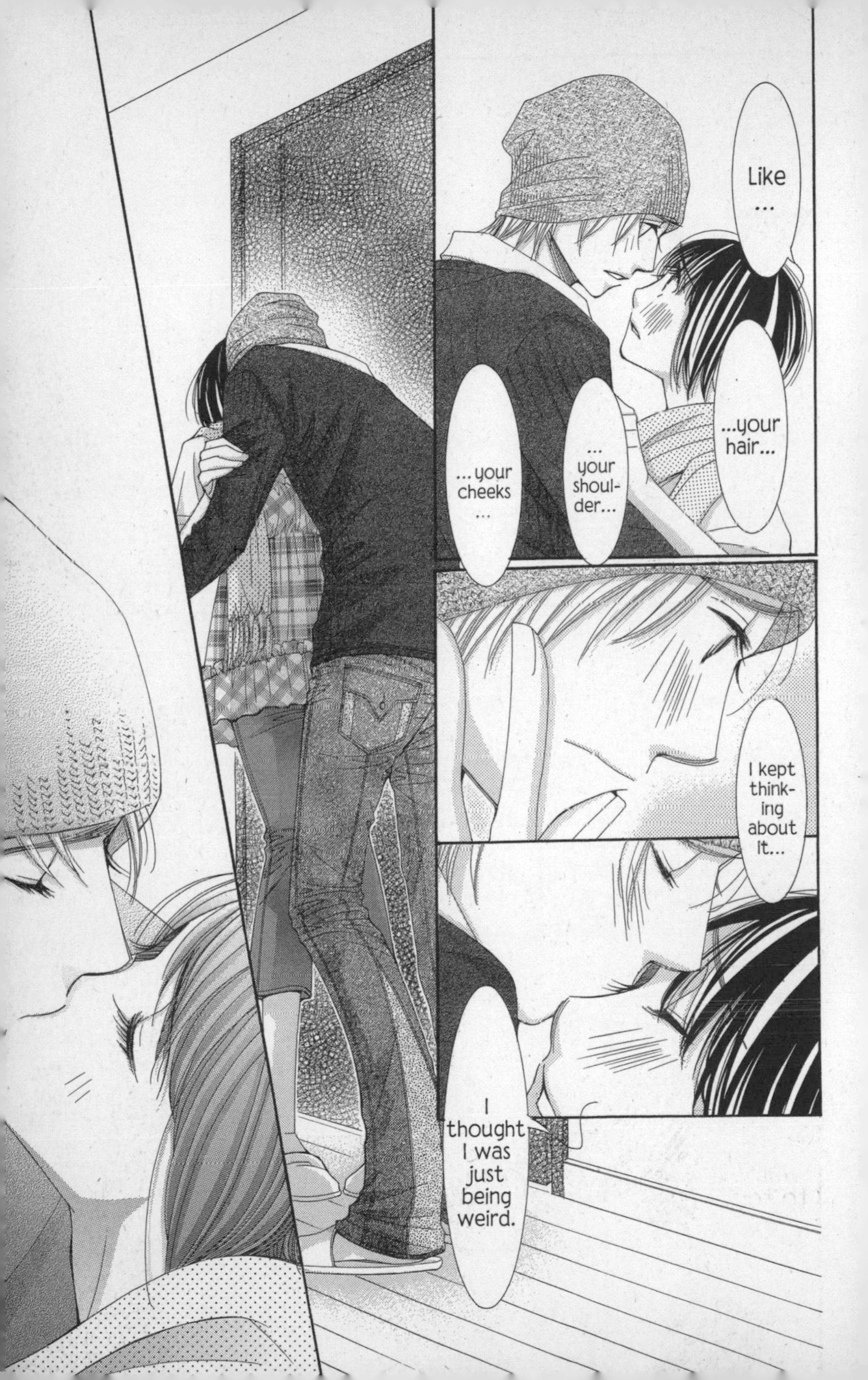
Like...
...your hair...
...your shoulder...
...your cheeks...
I kept thinking about it...
I thought I was just being weird.

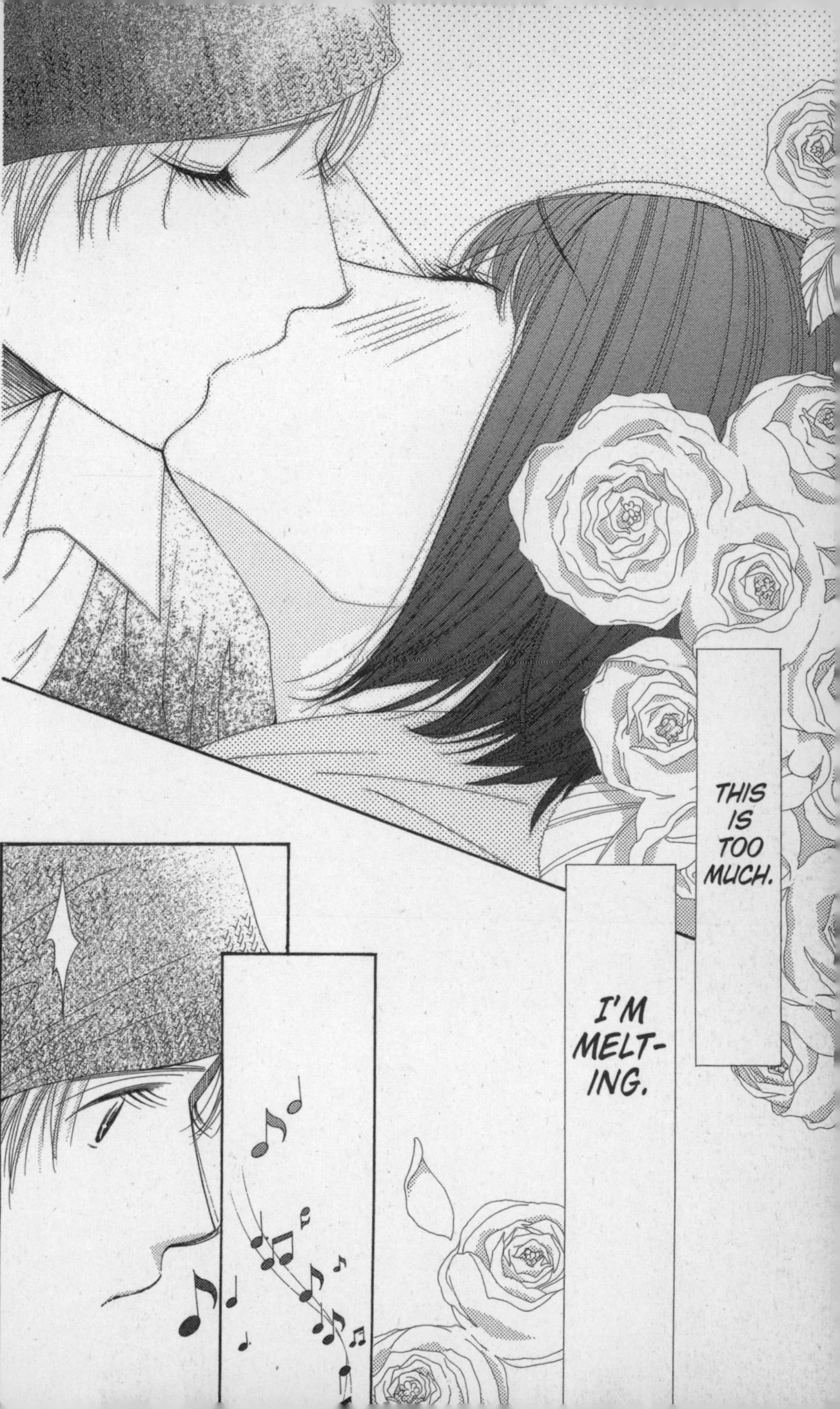
THIS IS TOO MUCH.
I'M MELTING.

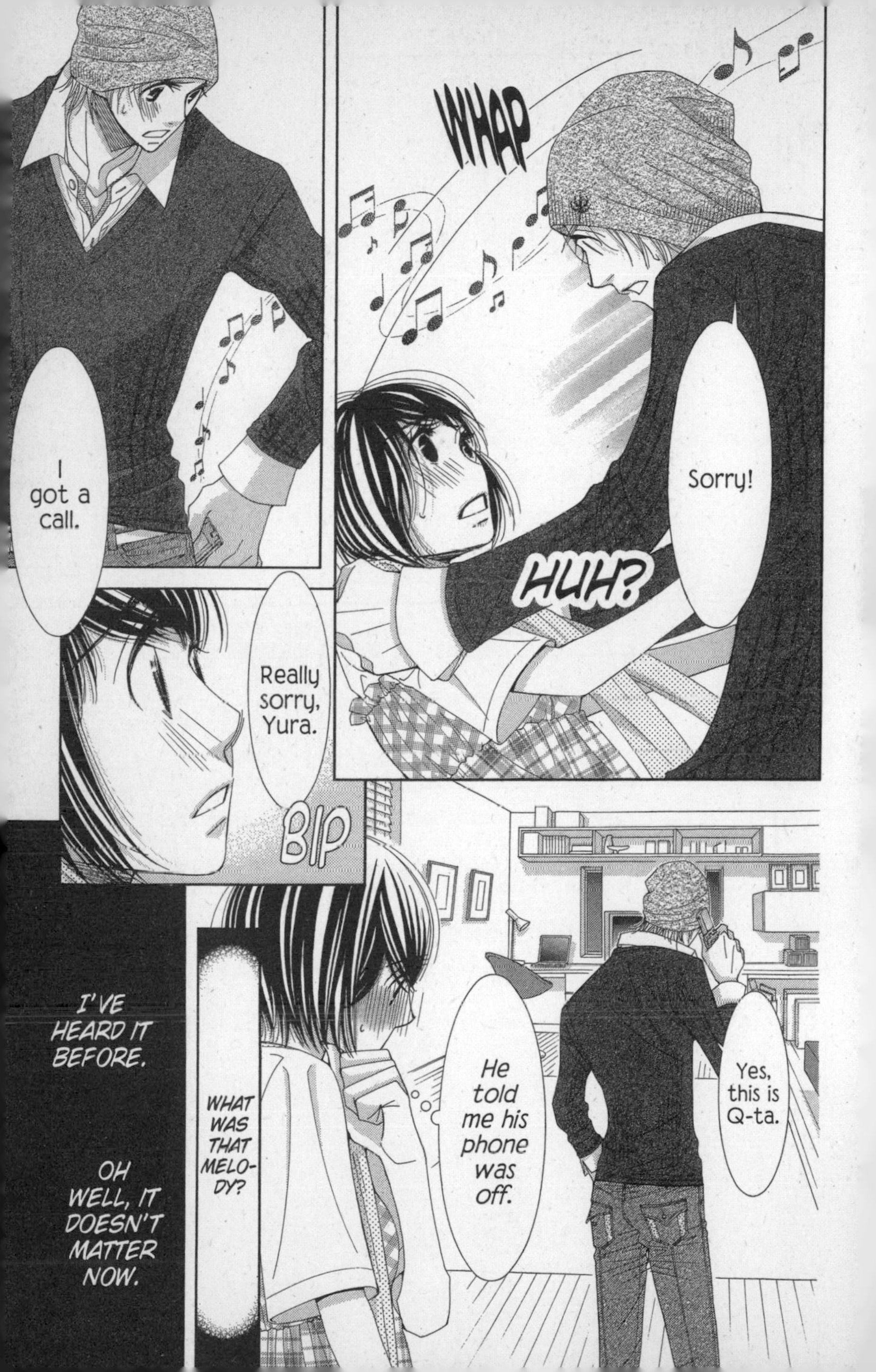
WHAP
Sorry!
HUH?
I got a call.
Really sorry, Yura.
BIP
Yes, this is Q-ta.
He told me his phone was off.
WHAT WAS THAT MELODY?
I'VE HEARD IT BEFORE.
OH WELL, IT DOESN'T MATTER NOW.

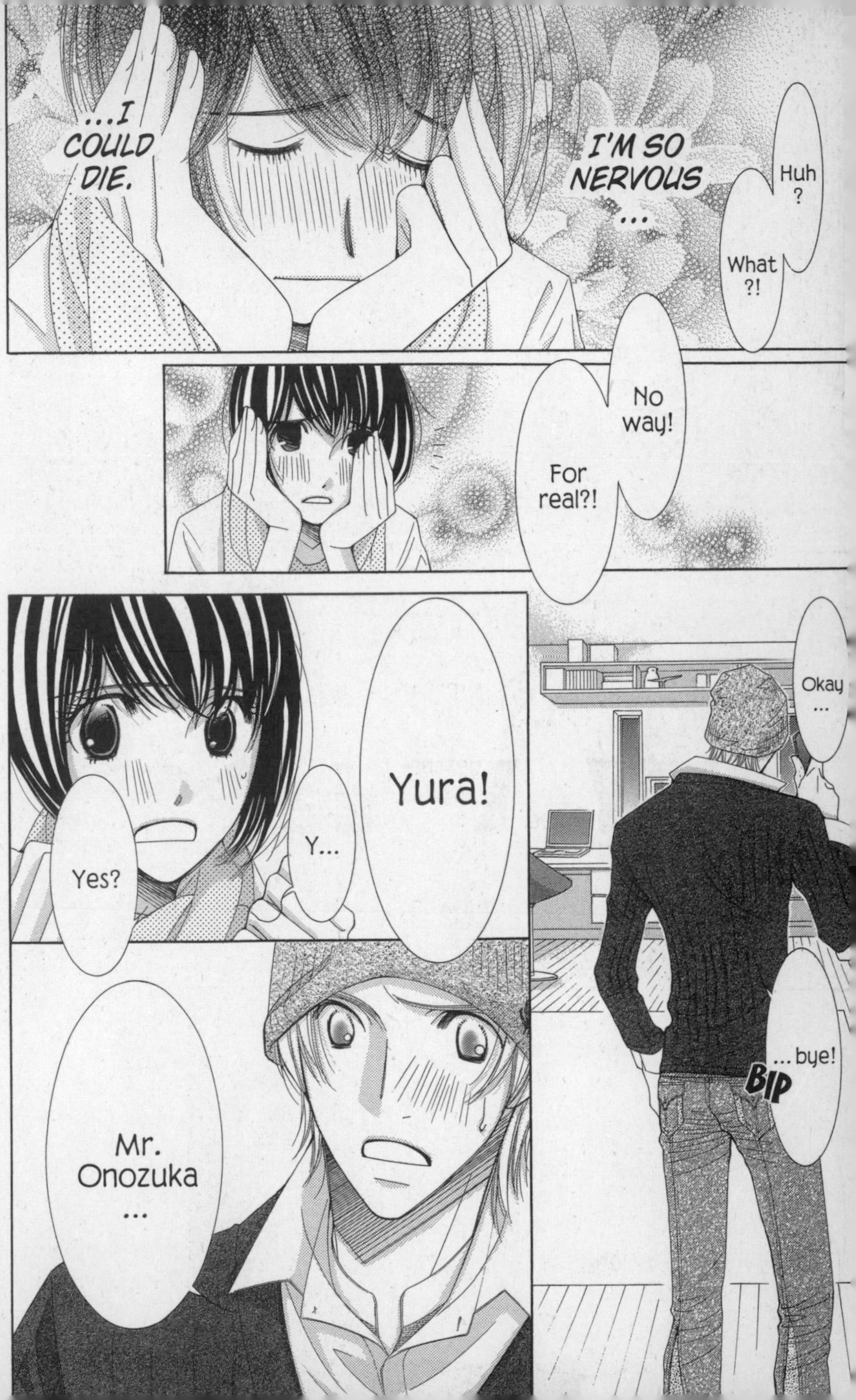
Huh?
What?!
I'M SO NERVOUS...
...I COULD DIE.
No way!
For real?!
Okay...
BIP
...bye!
Yura!
Y...
Yes?
Mr. Onozuka...

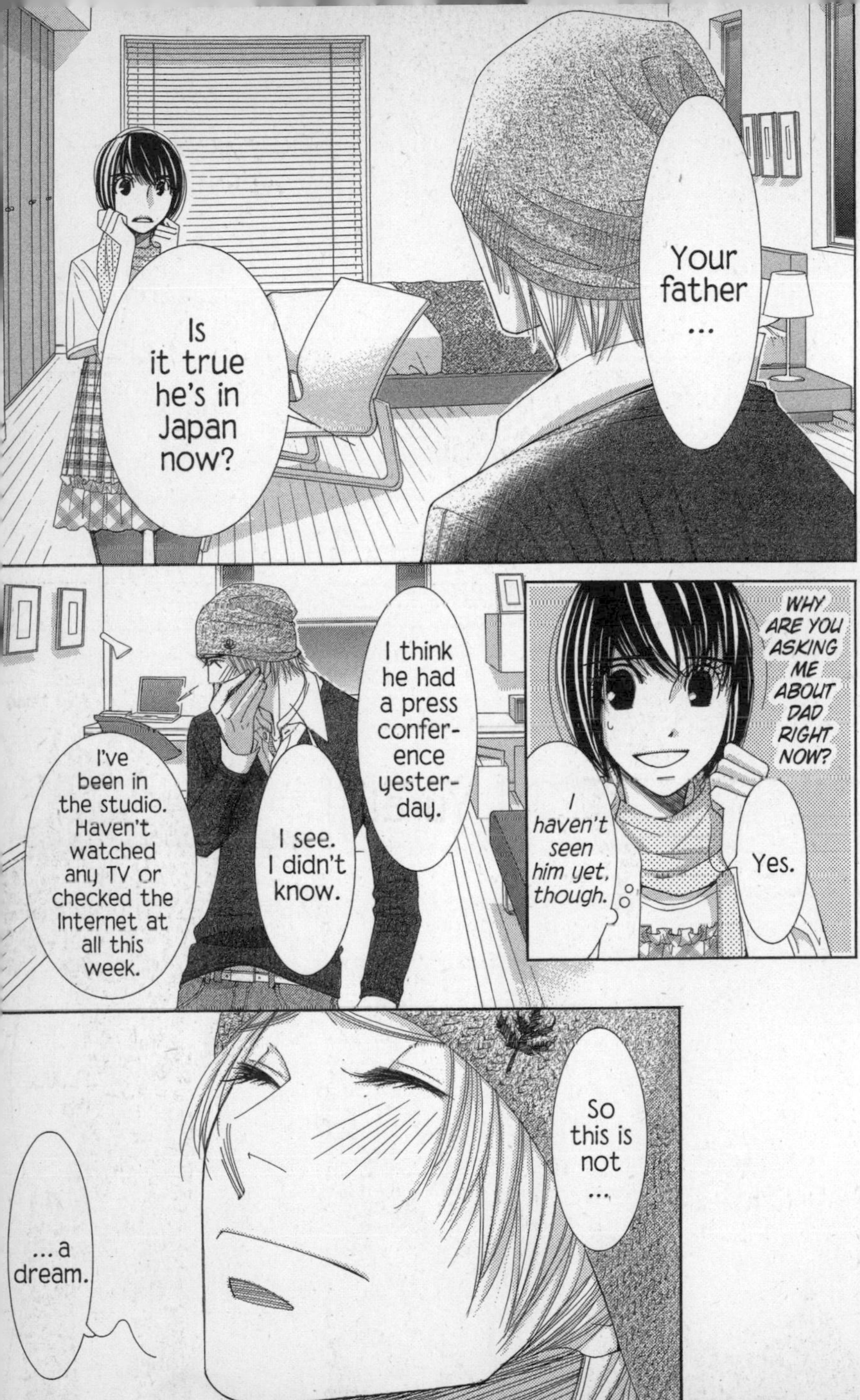
Your father ...
Is it true he's in Japan now?
WHY ARE YOU ASKING ME ABOUT DAD RIGHT NOW?
Yes.
I haven't seen him yet, though.
I think he had a press conference yesterday.
I see. I didn't know.
I've been in the studio. Haven't watched any TV or checked the Internet at all this week.
So this is not ...
... a dream.

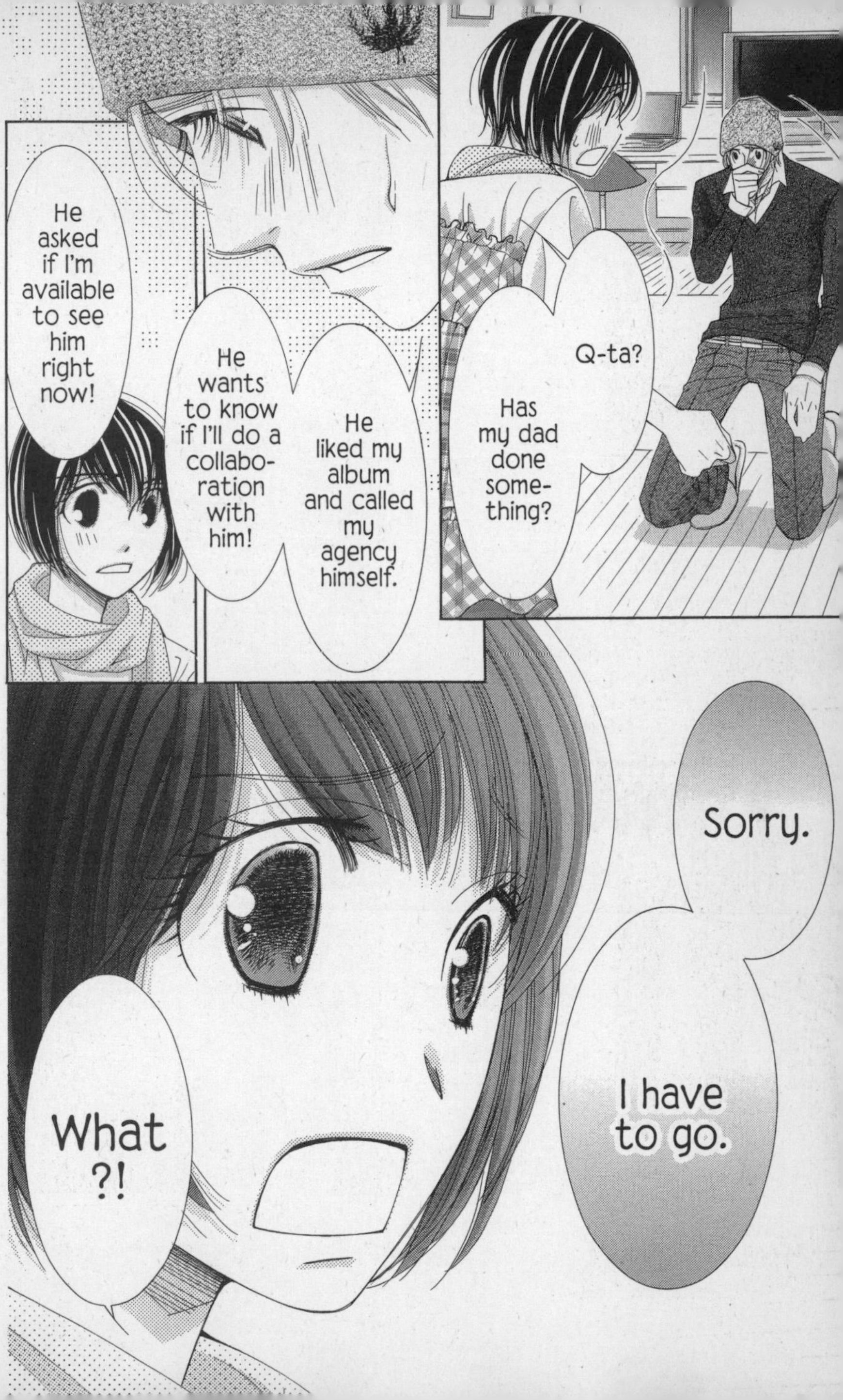
Q-ta?
Has my dad done some-thing?
He liked my album and called my agency himself.
He wants to know if I'll do a collabo-ration with him!
He asked if I'm available to see him right now!
Sorry.
I have to go.
What?!

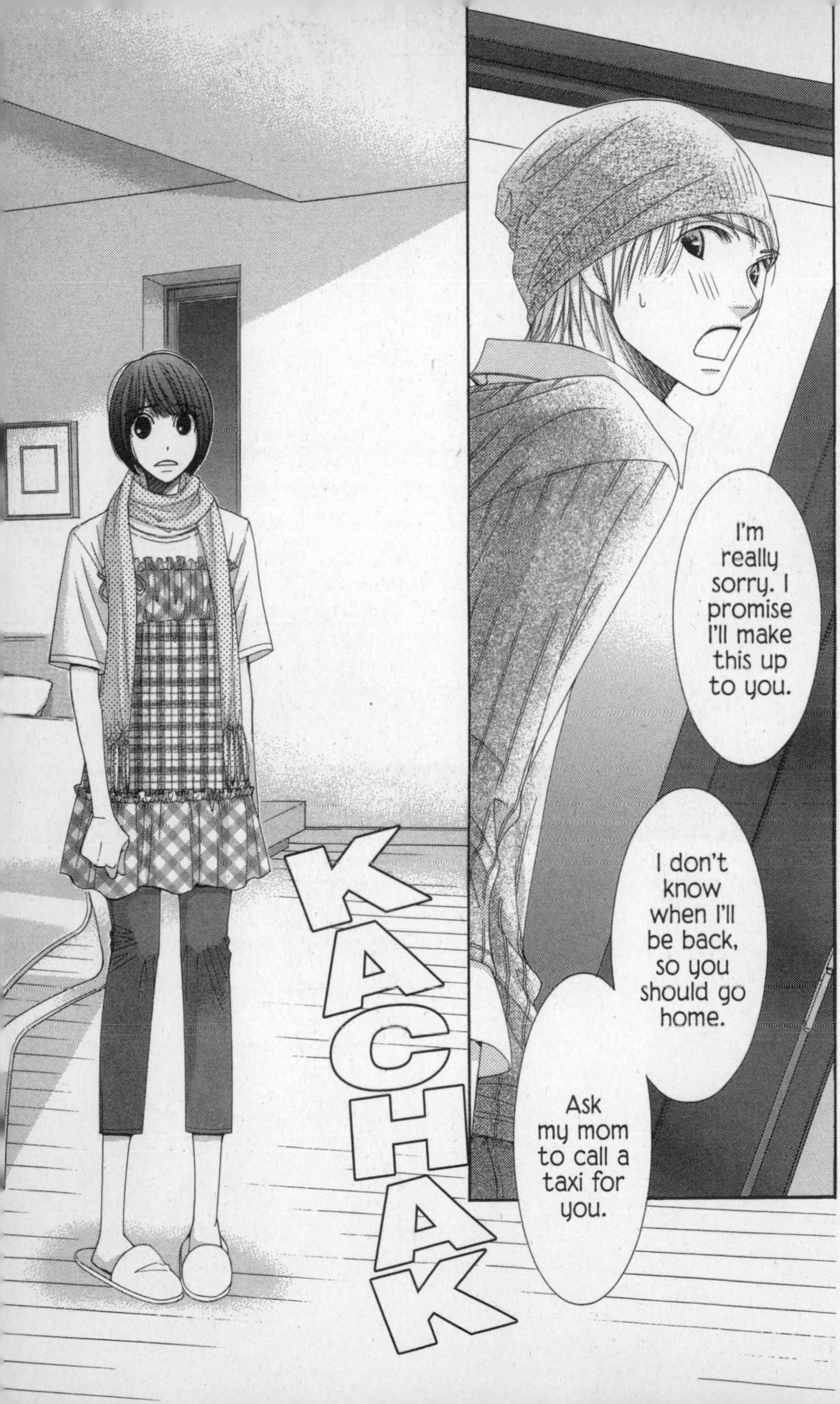
I'm really sorry. I promise I'll make this up to you.
I don't know when I'll be back, so you should go home.
Ask my mom to call a taxi for you.
KACHAK

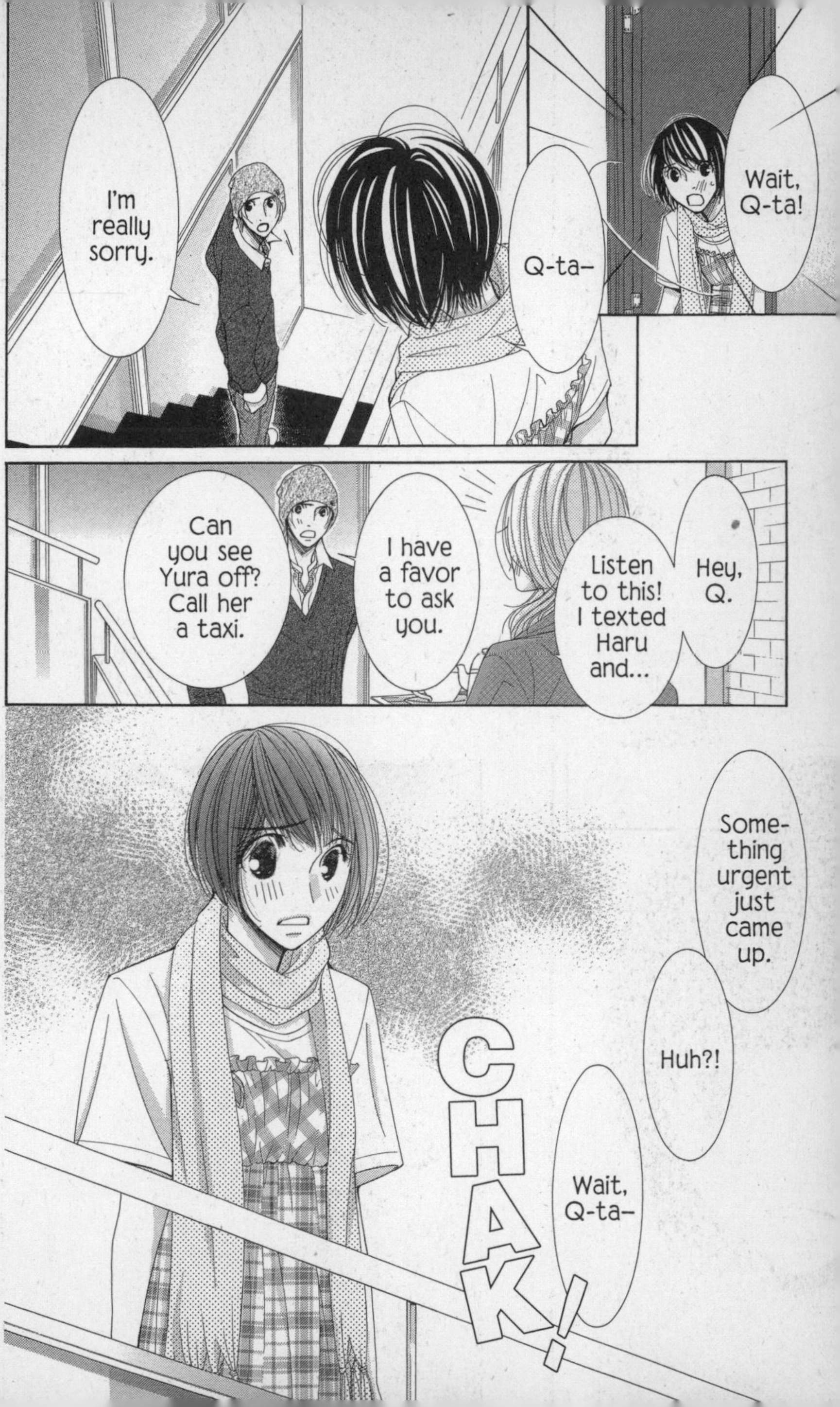
Wait, Q-ta!
Q-ta–
I'm really sorry.
Hey, Q.
Listen to this! I texted Haru and...
I have a favor to ask you.
Can you see Yura off? Call her a taxi.
Some-thing urgent just came up.
Huh?!
Wait, Q-ta–
CHAK!

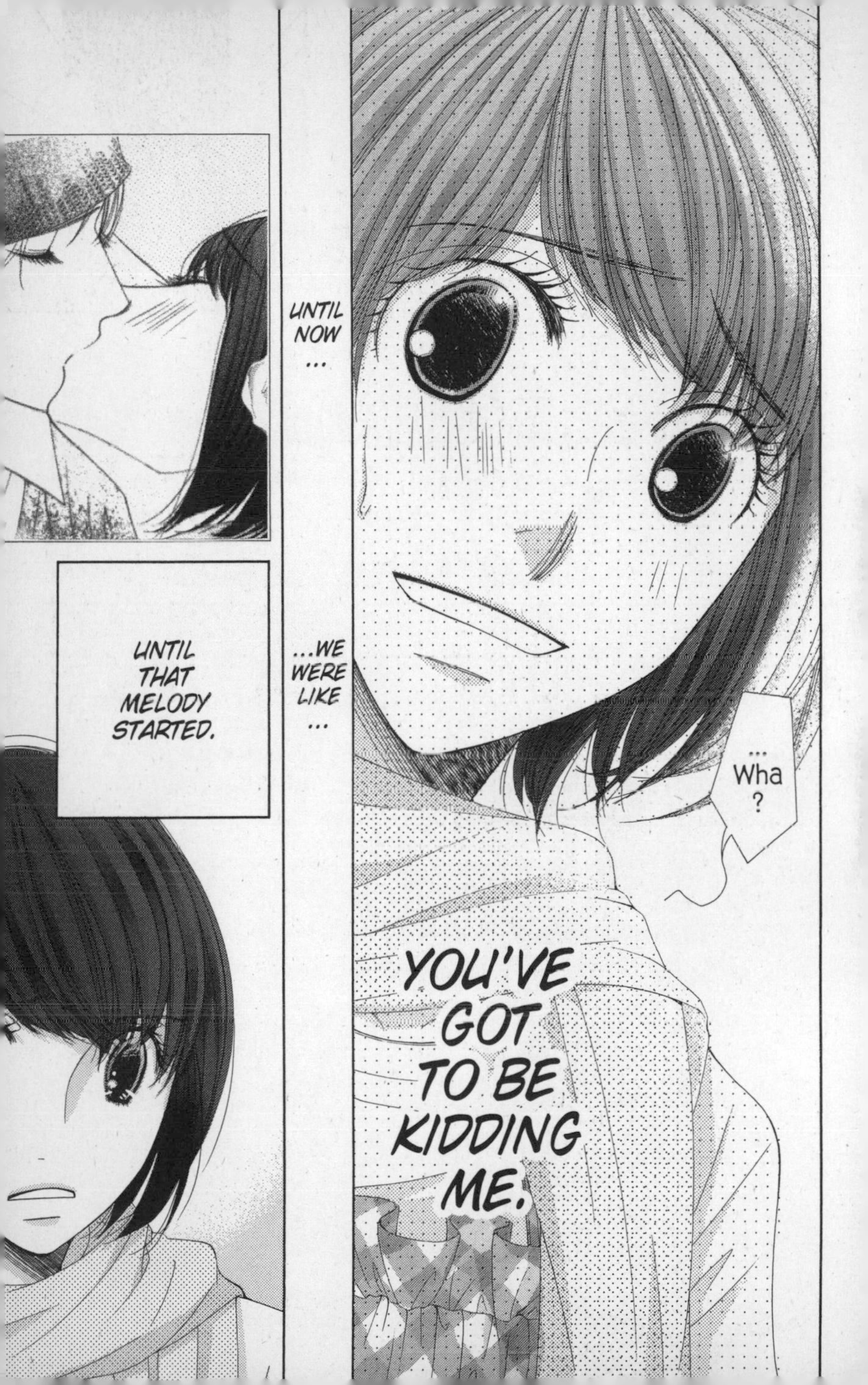
UNTIL NOW ...
...WE WERE LIKE ...
... Wha ?
YOU'VE GOT TO BE KIDDING ME.
UNTIL THAT MELODY STARTED.

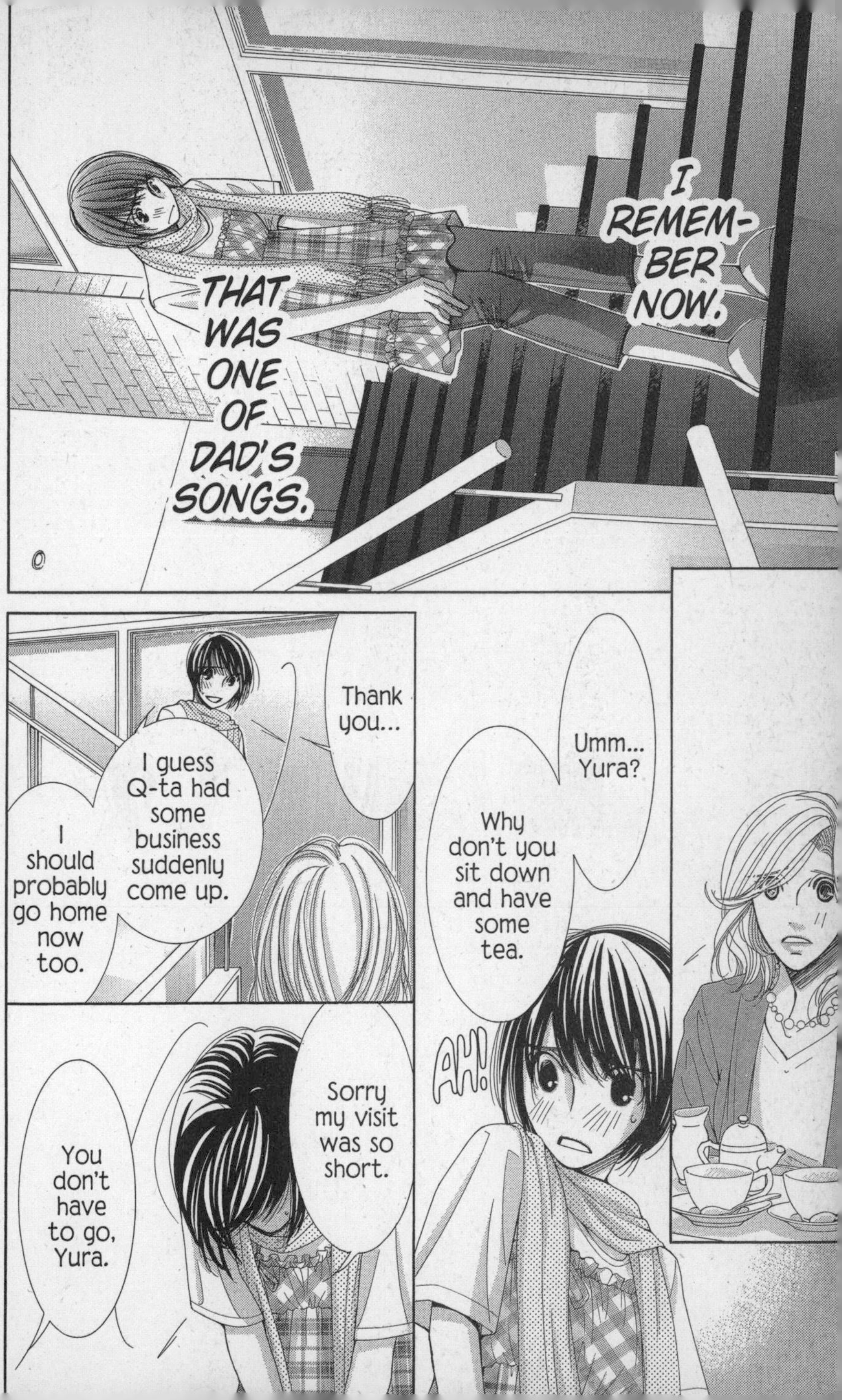

I REMEMBER NOW.
THAT WAS ONE OF DAD'S SONGS.
Umm... Yura?
Why don't you sit down and have some tea.
AH!
Thank you...
I guess Q-ta had some business suddenly come up.
I should probably go home now too.
Sorry my visit was so short.
You don't have to go, Yura.

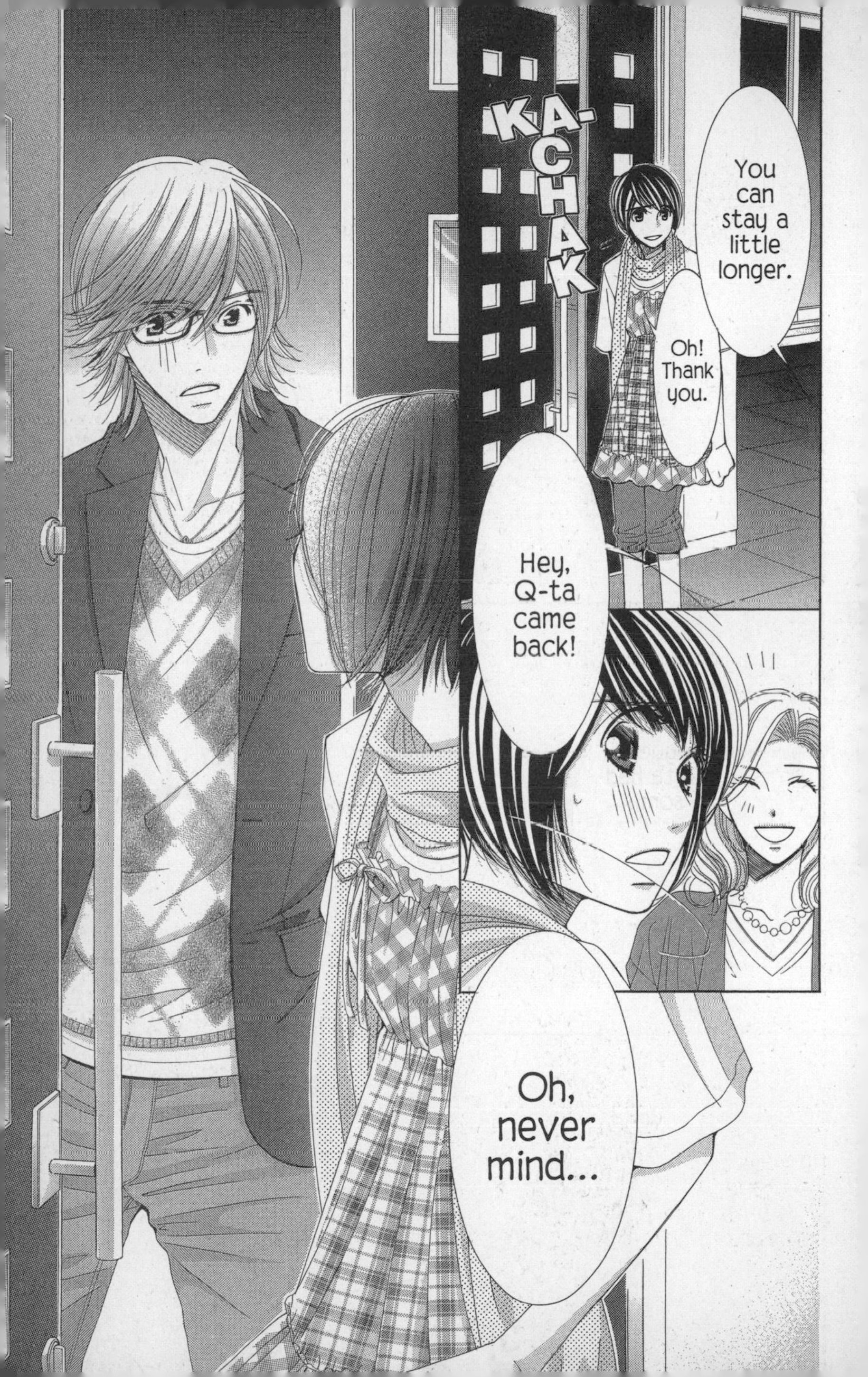
You can stay a little longer.
Oh! Thank you.
KA-CHAK
Hey, Q-ta came back!
Oh, never mind...

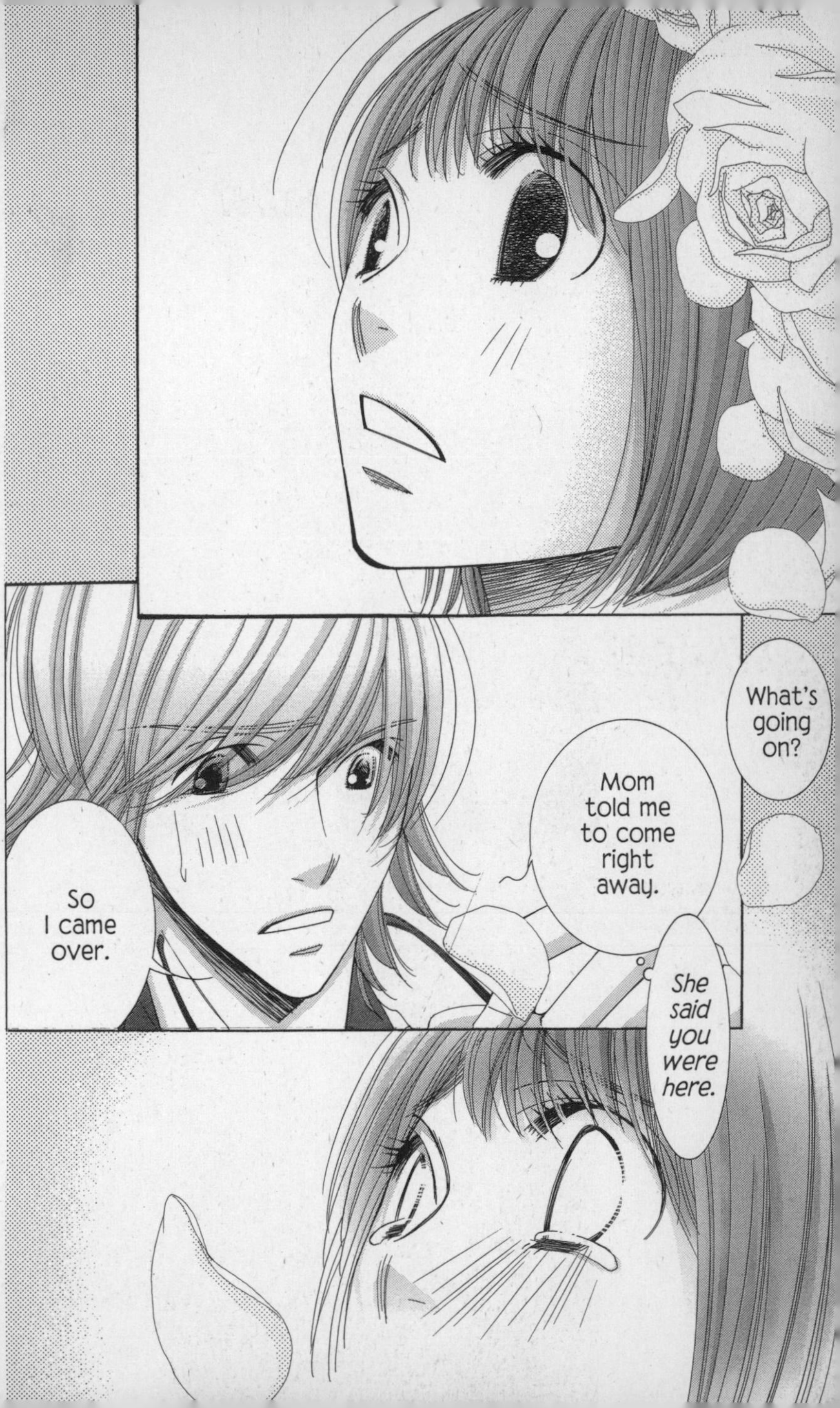
What's going on?
Mom told me to come right away.
So I came over.
She said you were here.

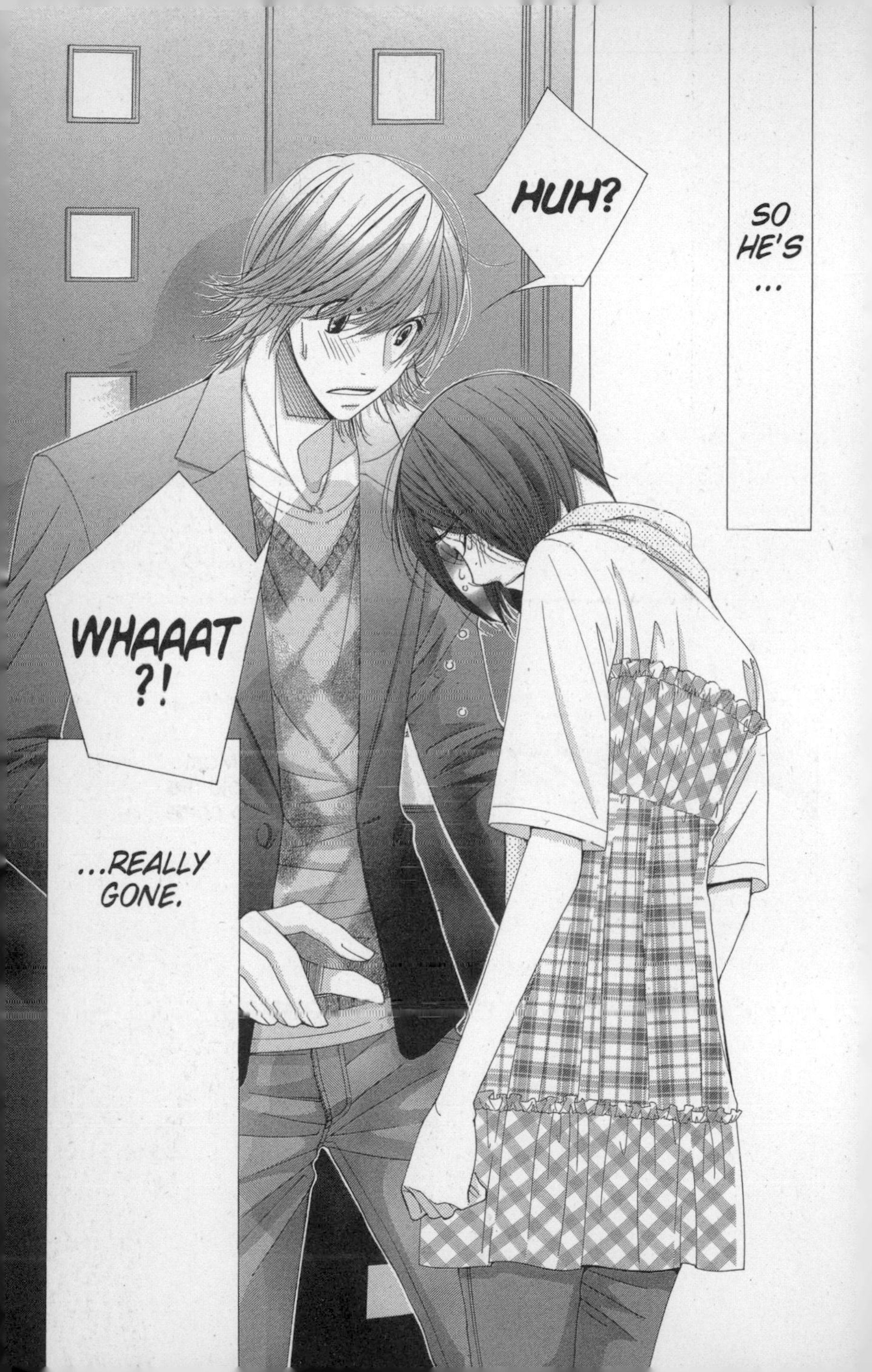
SO HE'S ...
HUH?
WHAAAT ?!
...REALLY GONE.

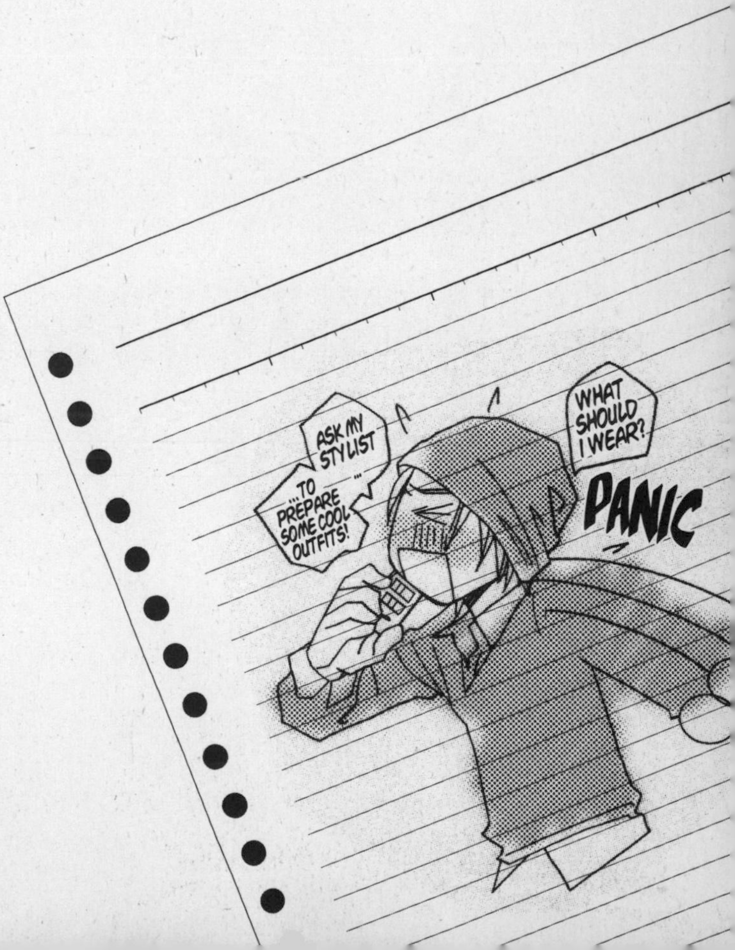
WHAT SHOULD I WEAR?
PANIC
ASK MY STYLIST ...
...TO PREPARE SOME COOL OUTFITS!

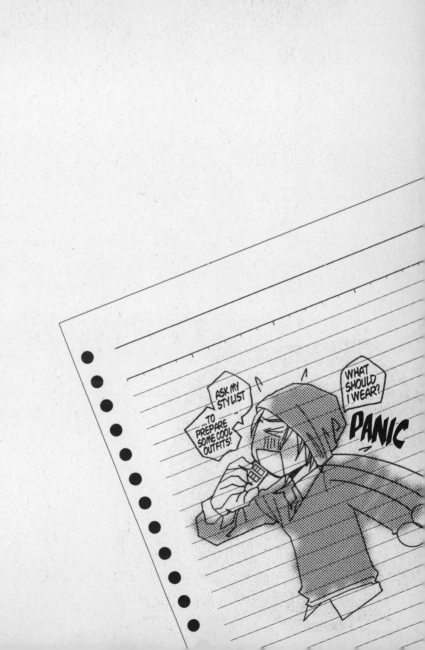

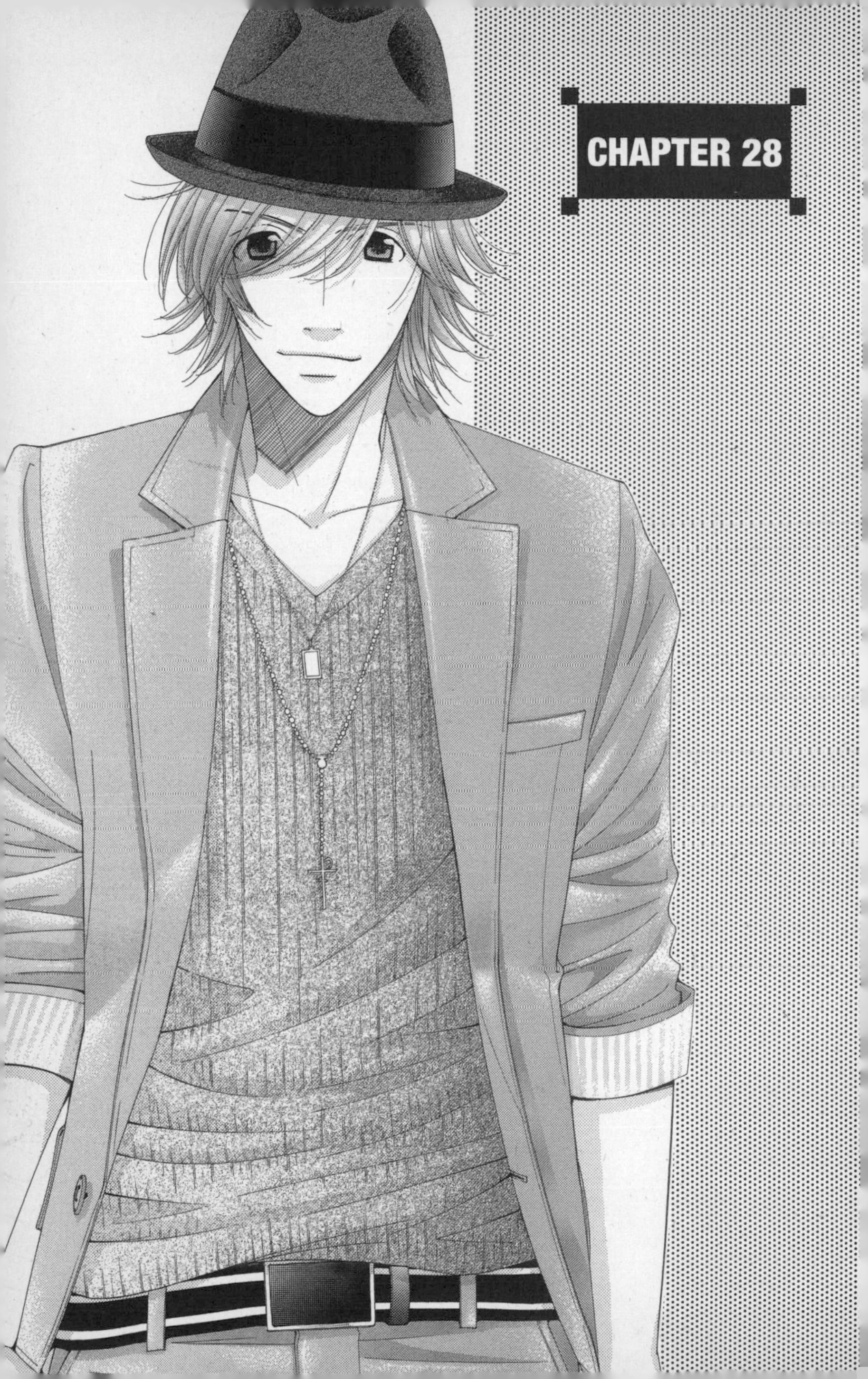
CHAPTER 28

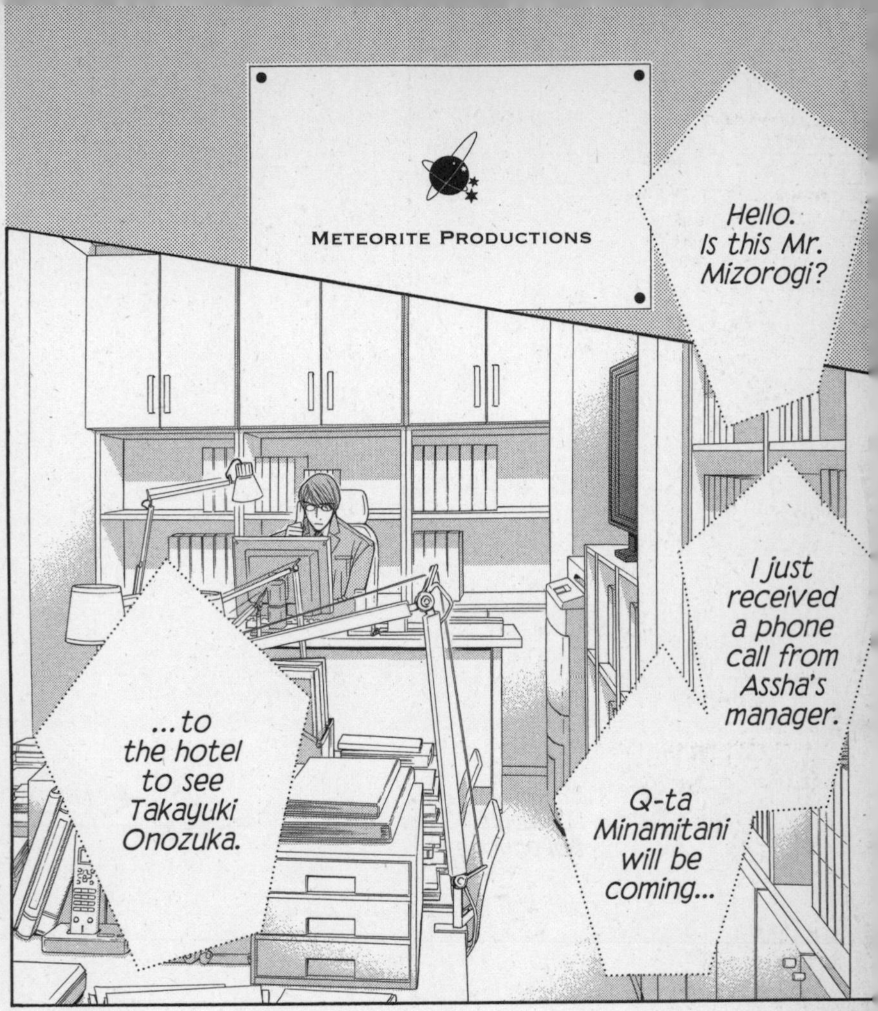
METEORITE PRODUCTIONS
Hello. Is this Mr. Mizorogi?
I just received a phone call from Assha's manager.
Q-ta Minamitani will be coming...
...to the hotel to see Takayuki Onozuka.

Honey Hunt

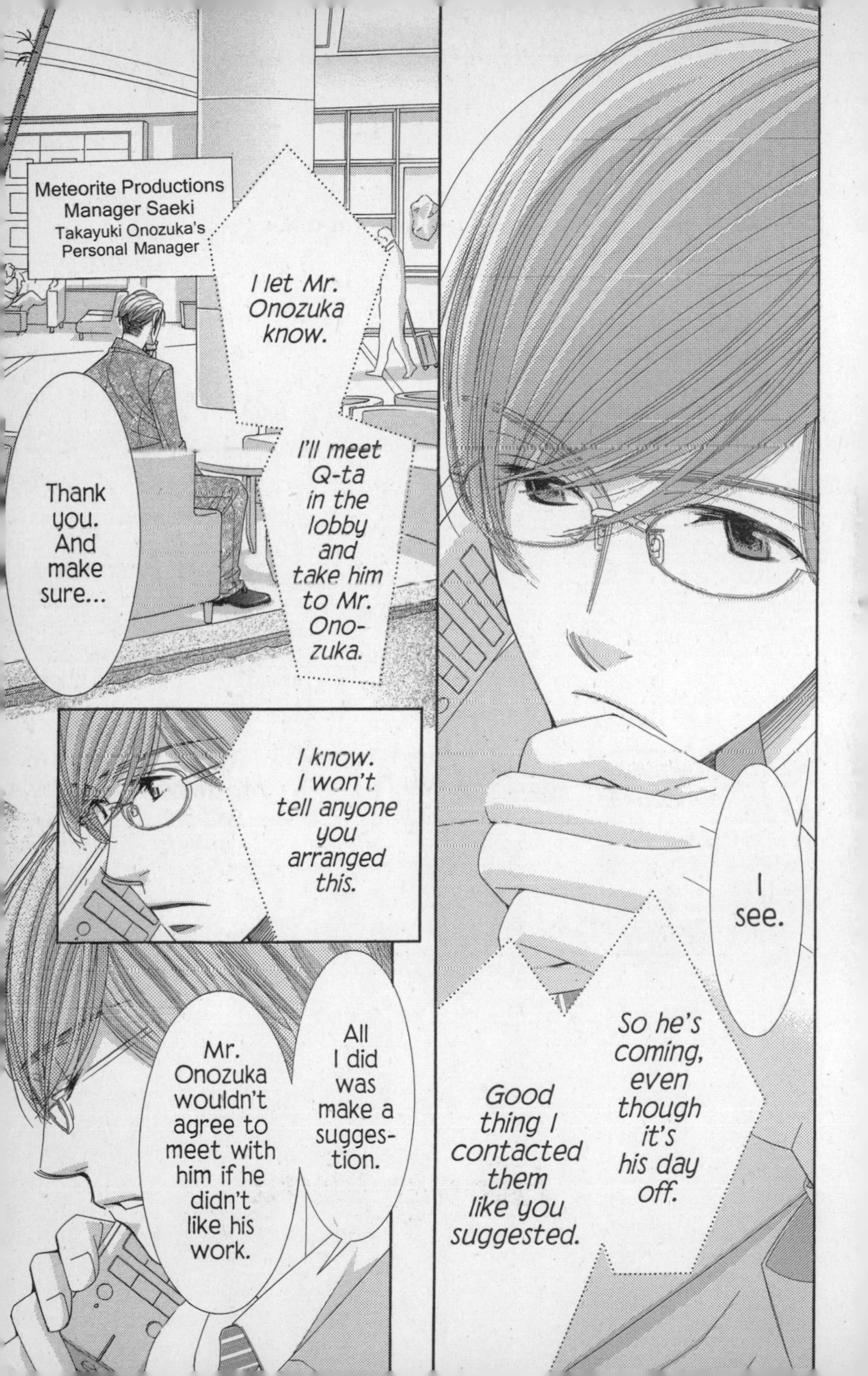
I see.
So he's coming, even though it's his day off.
Good thing I contacted them like you suggested.
Meteorite Productions Manager Saeki Takayuki Onozuka's Personal Manager
I let Mr. Onozuka know.
I'll meet Q-ta in the lobby and take him to Mr. Onozuka.
Thank you. And make sure...
I know. I won't tell anyone you arranged this.
All I did was make a suggestion.
Mr. Onozuka wouldn't agree to meet with him if he didn't like his work.

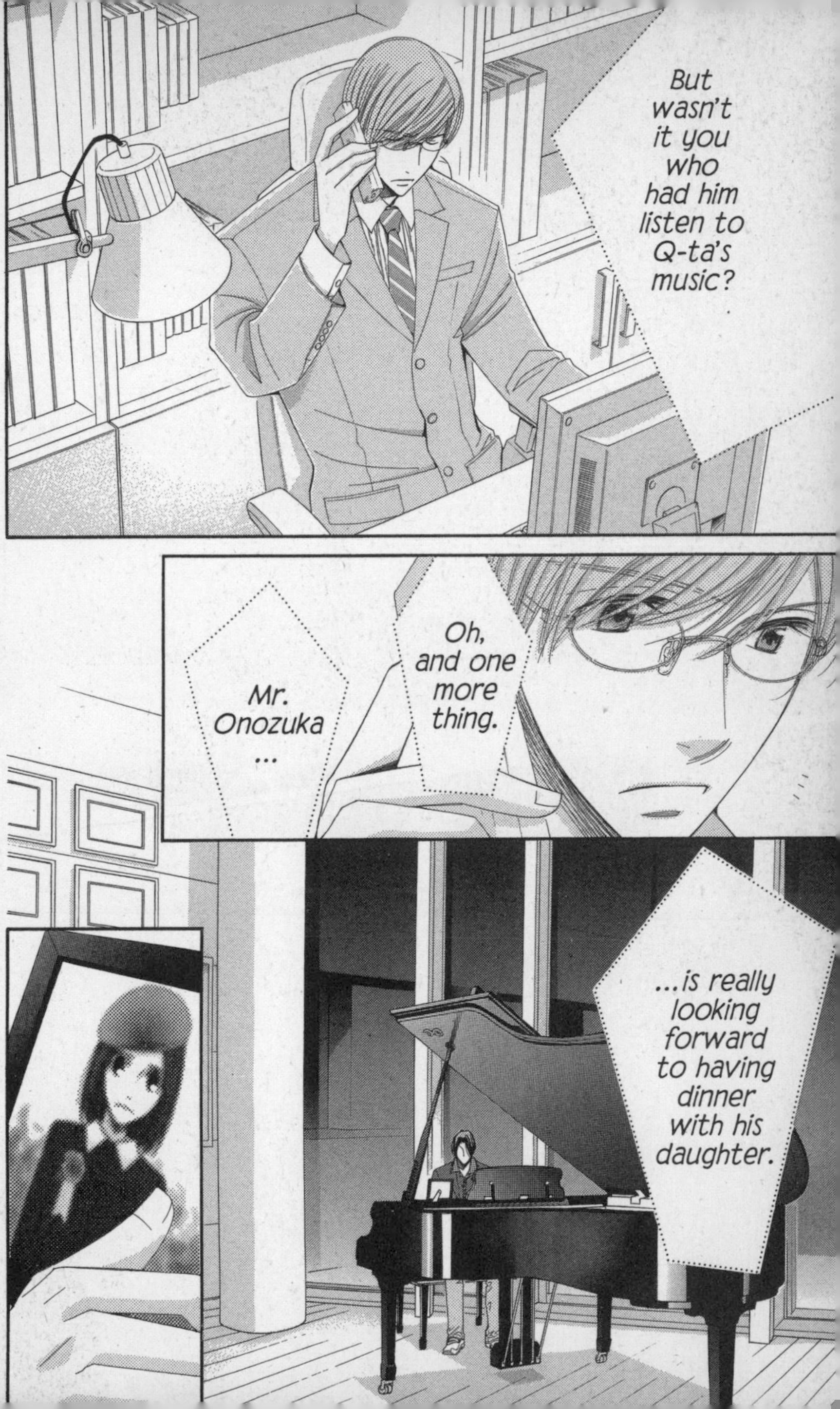
But wasn't it you who had him listen to Q-ta's music?
Oh, and one more thing.
Mr. Onozuka ...
...is really looking forward to having dinner with his daughter.

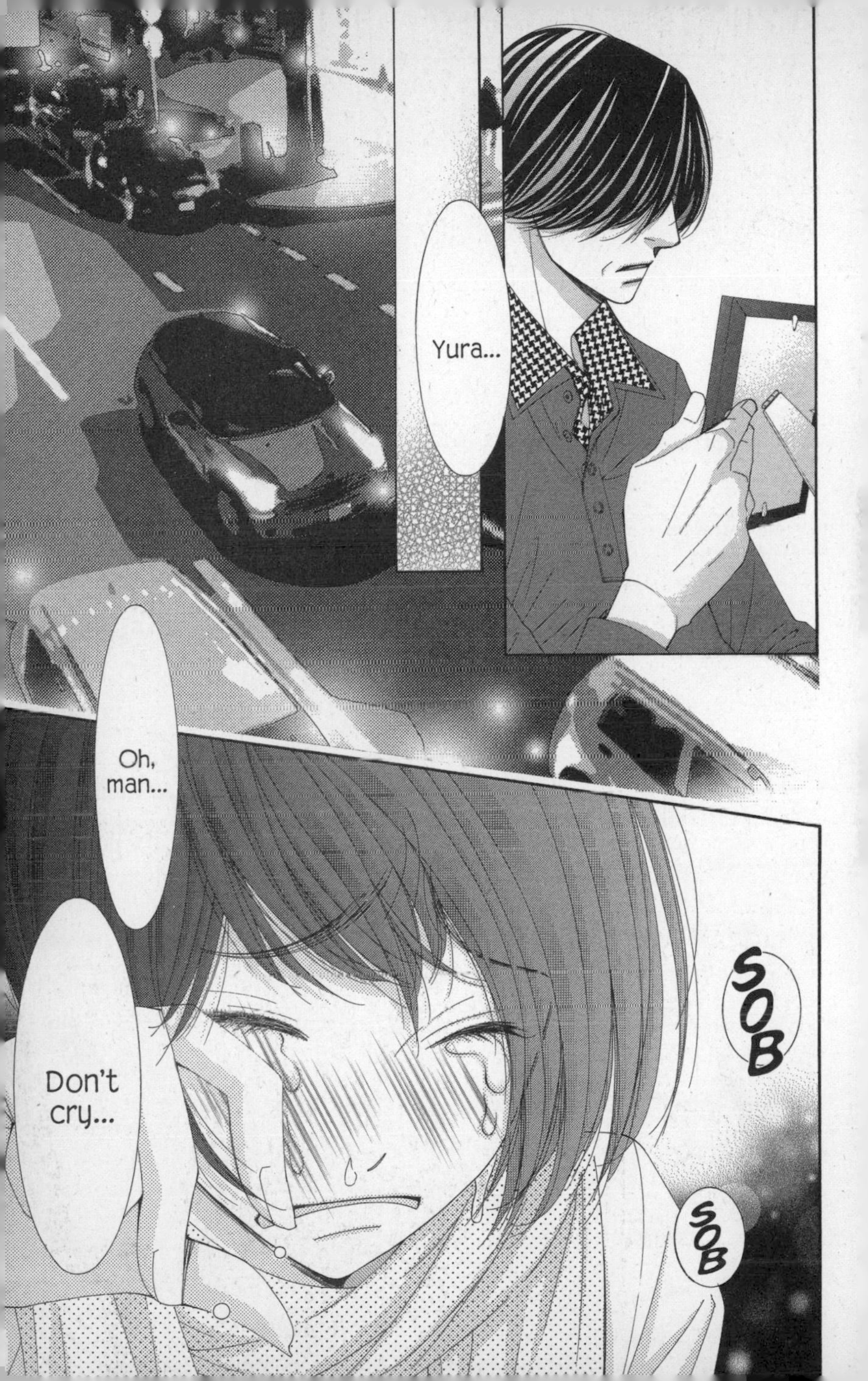
Yura...
Oh, man...
SOB
SOB
Don't cry...

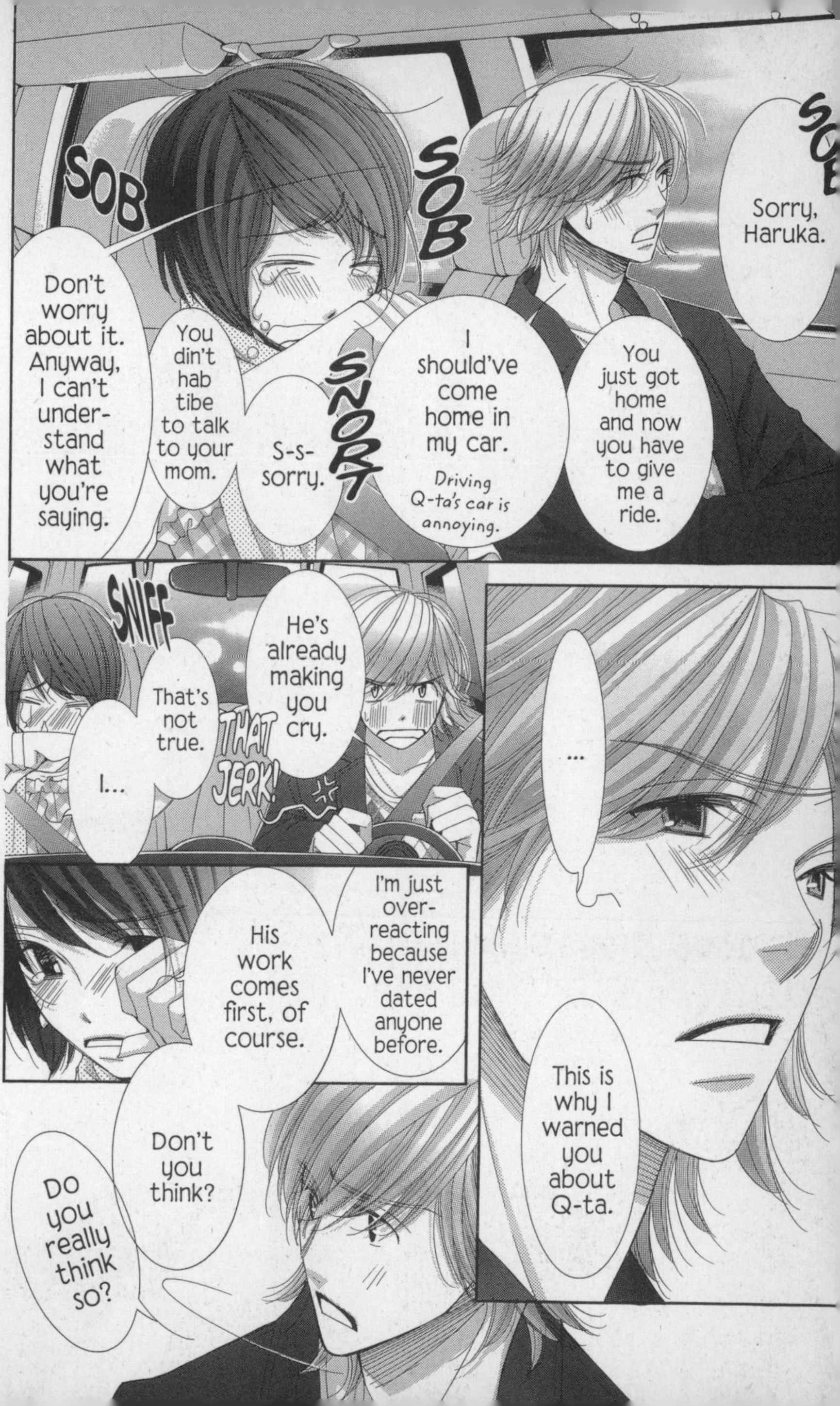
SOB
Sorry, Haruka.
You just got home and now you have to give me a ride.
I should've come home in my car.
Driving Q-ta's car is annoying.
SNORT
SOB
S-s-sorry.
You din't hab tibe to talk to your mom.
SOB
Don't worry about it. Anyway, I can't under-stand what you're saying.
...
This is why I warned you about Q-ta.
He's already making you cry.
THAT JERK!
SNIFF
That's not true.
I...
I'm just over-reacting because I've never dated anyone before.
His work comes first, of course.
Don't you think?
Do you really think so?

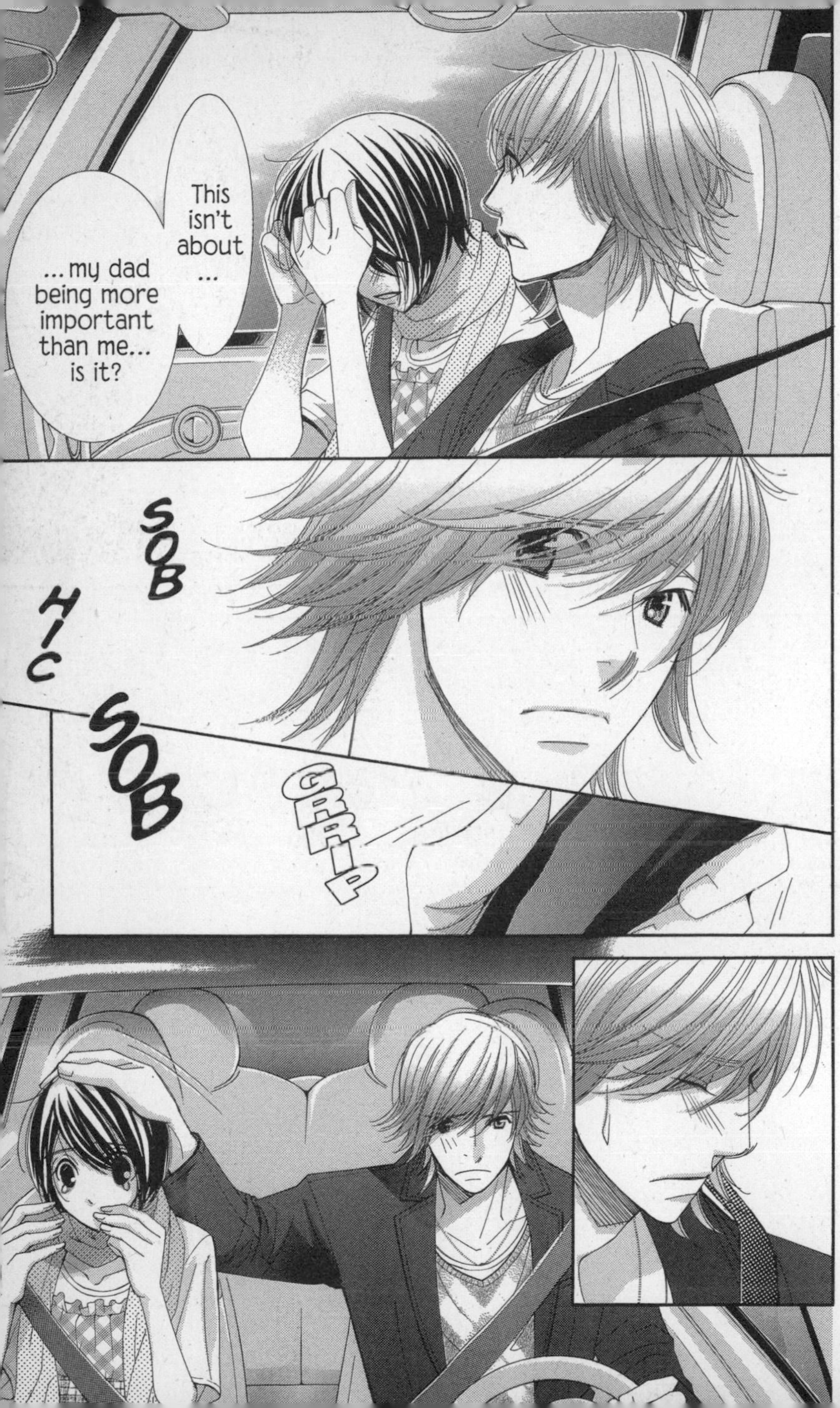
This isn't about ...
... my dad being more important than me... is it?
SOB
HIC
SOB
GRRIP

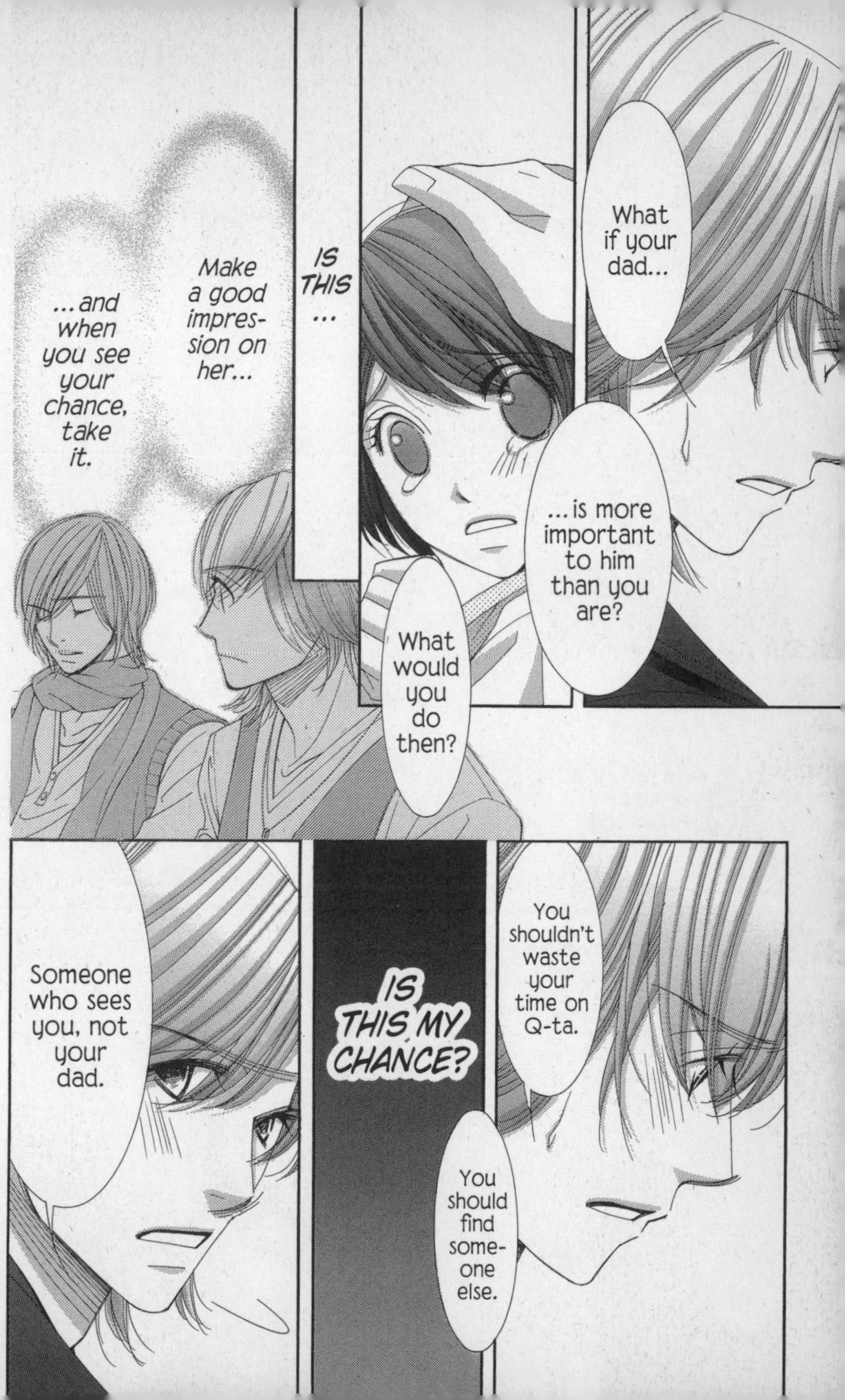
What if your dad...
...is more important to him than you are?
What would you do then?
IS THIS ...
Make a good impression on her...
...and when you see your chance, take it.
You shouldn't waste your time on Q-ta.
You should find someone else.
IS THIS MY CHANCE?
Someone who sees you, not your dad.

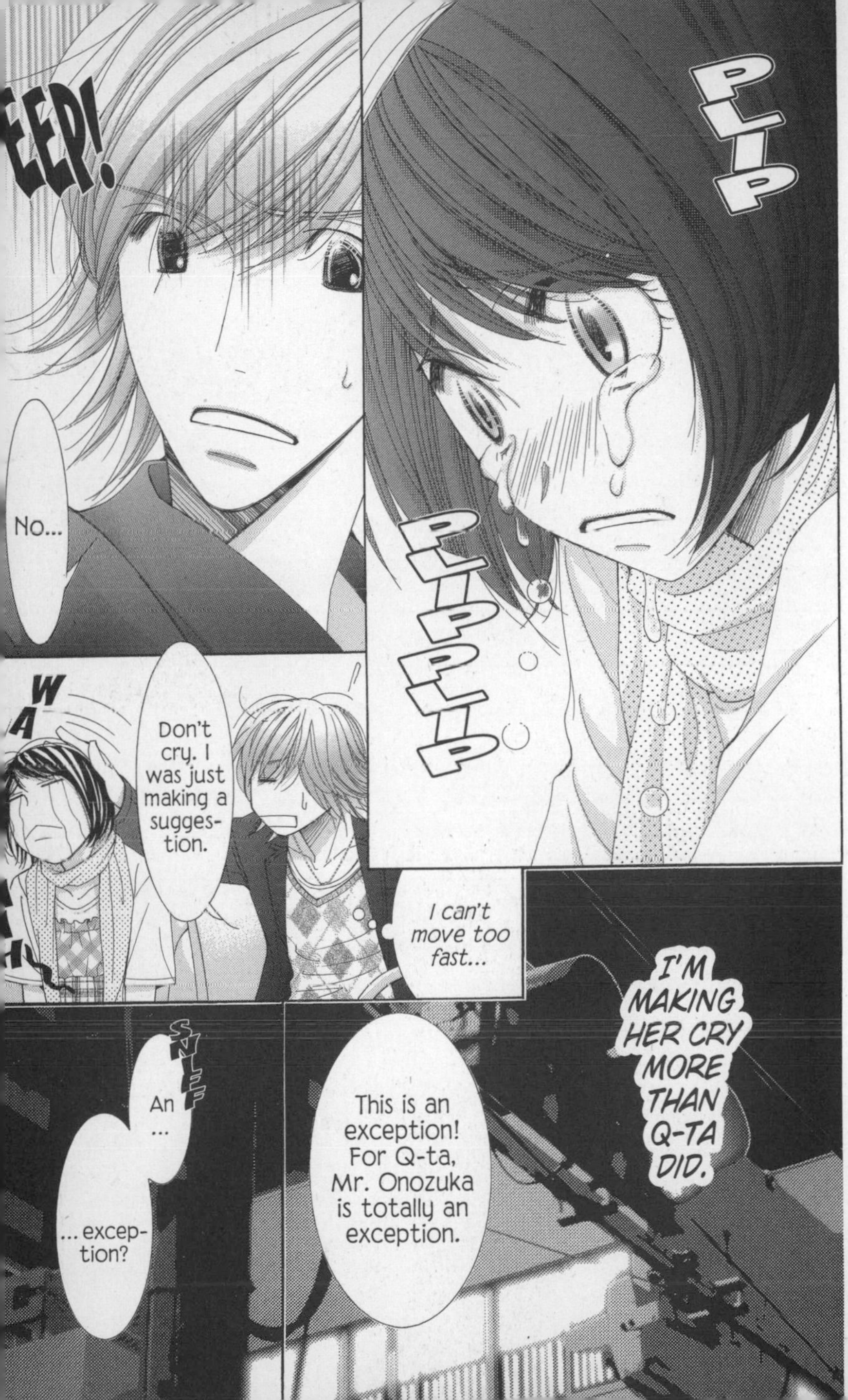
PLIP
EEP!
No...
PLIP
PLIP
PLIP
WAA
Don't cry. I was just making a sugges-tion.
I can't move too fast...
I'M MAKING HER CRY MORE THAN Q-TA DID.
This is an exception! For Q-ta, Mr. Onozuka is totally an exception.
SNIFF
An ...
... excep-tion?

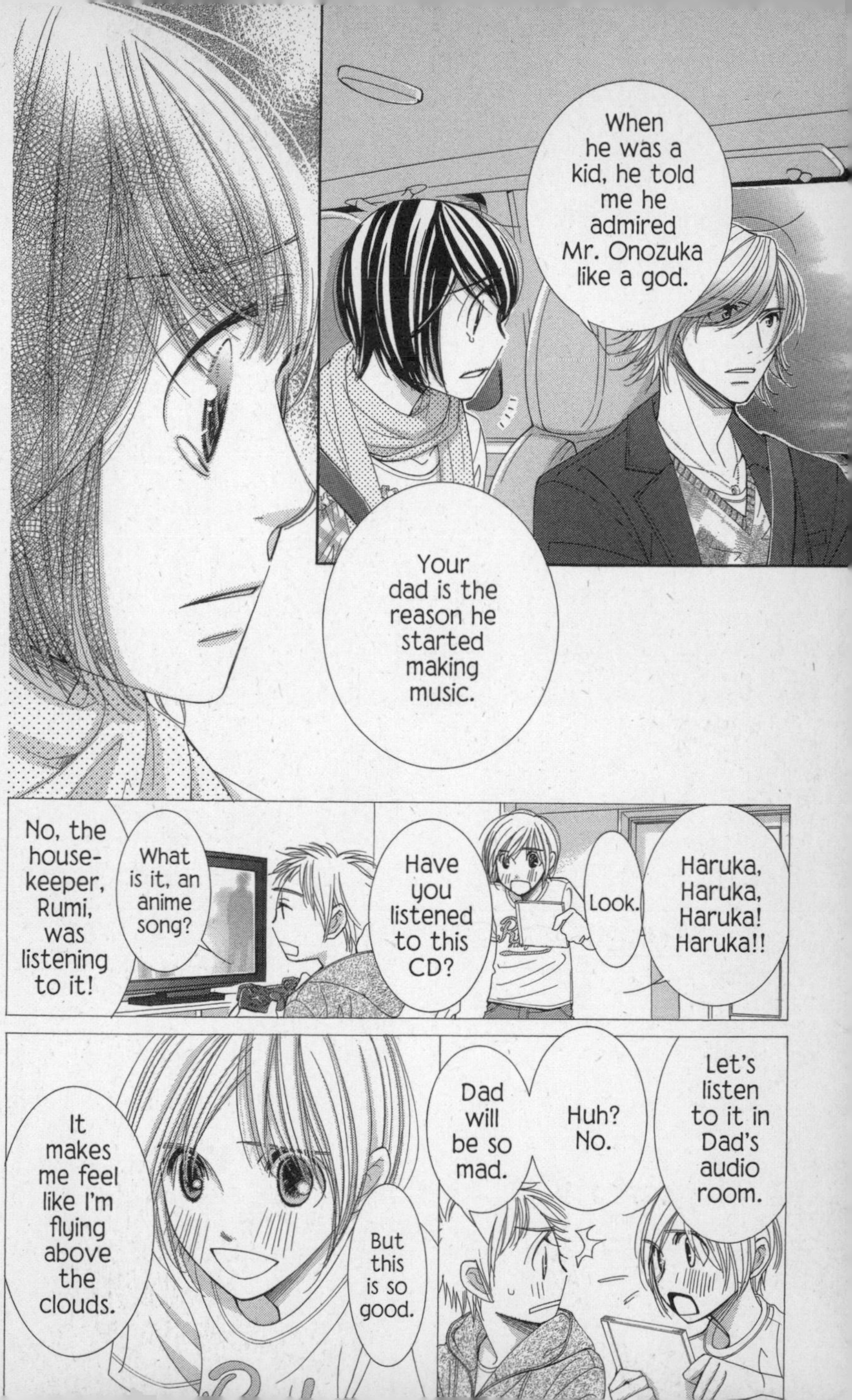
When he was a kid, he told me he admired Mr. Onozuka like a god.
Your dad is the reason he started making music.
Haruka, Haruka, Haruka! Haruka!!
Look.
Have you listened to this CD?
What is it, an anime song?
No, the housekeeper, Rumi, was listening to it!
Let's listen to it in Dad's audio room.
Huh? No.
Dad will be so mad.
But this is so good.
It makes me feel like I'm flying above the clouds.

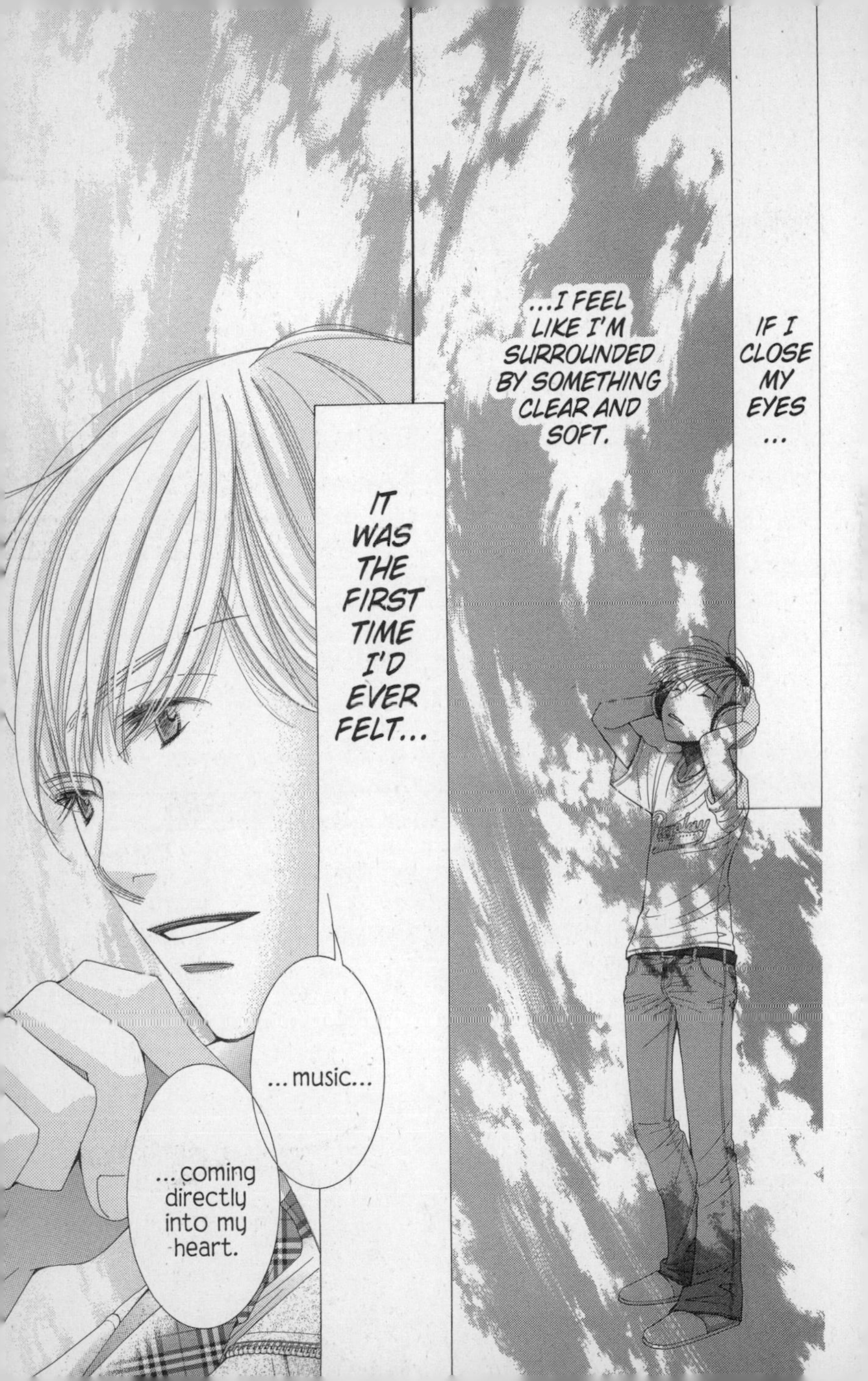
IF I CLOSE MY EYES...
...I FEEL LIKE I'M SURROUNDED BY SOMETHING CLEAR AND SOFT.
IT WAS THE FIRST TIME I'D EVER FELT...
...music...
...coming directly into my heart.

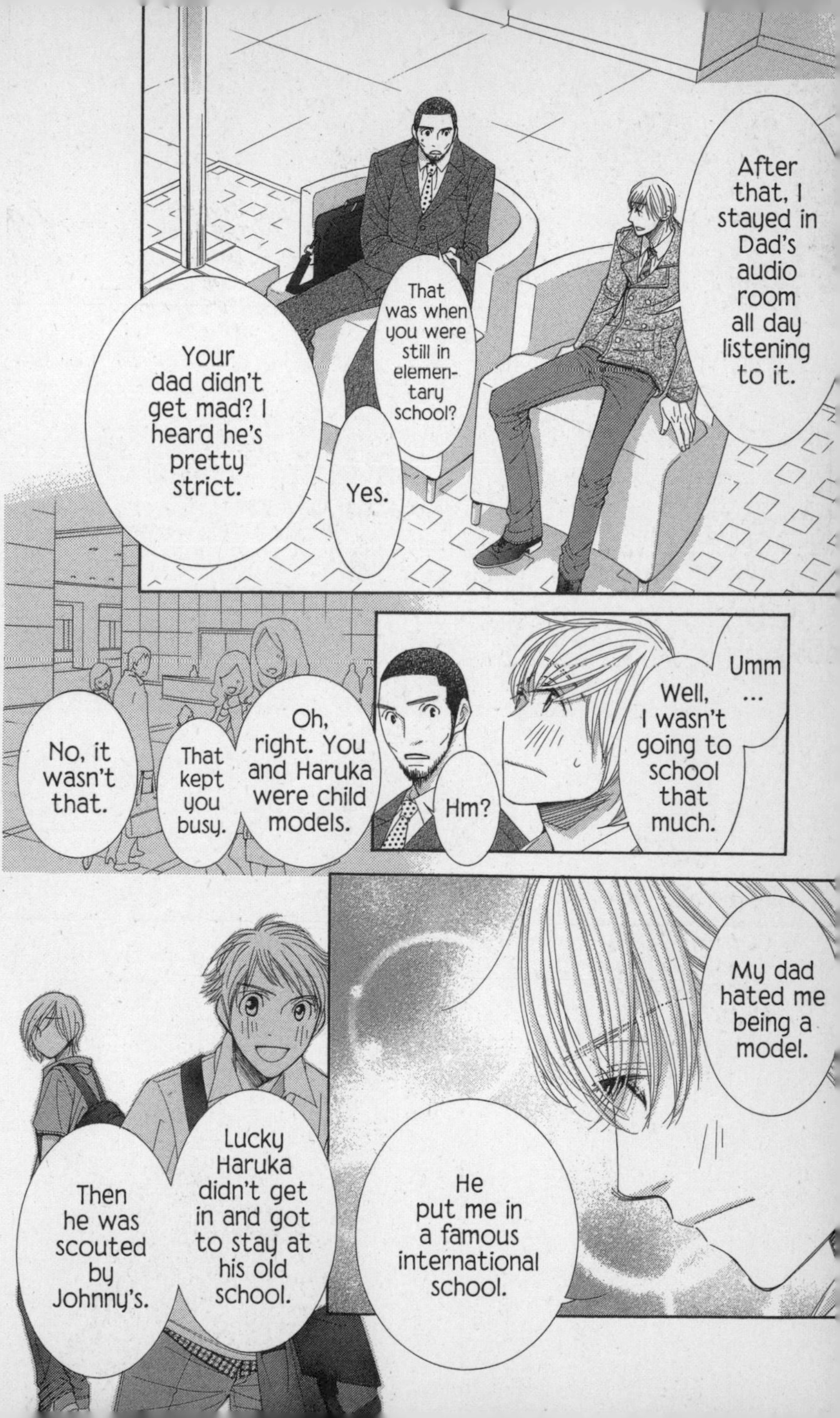
After that, I stayed in Dad's audio room all day listening to it.
That was when you were still in elementary school?
Yes.
Your dad didn't get mad? I heard he's pretty strict.
Umm ...
Well, I wasn't going to school that much.
Hm?
Oh, right. You and Haruka were child models.
That kept you busy.
No, it wasn't that.
My dad hated me being a model.
He put me in a famous international school.
Lucky Haruka didn't get in and got to stay at his old school.
Then he was scouted by Johnny's.

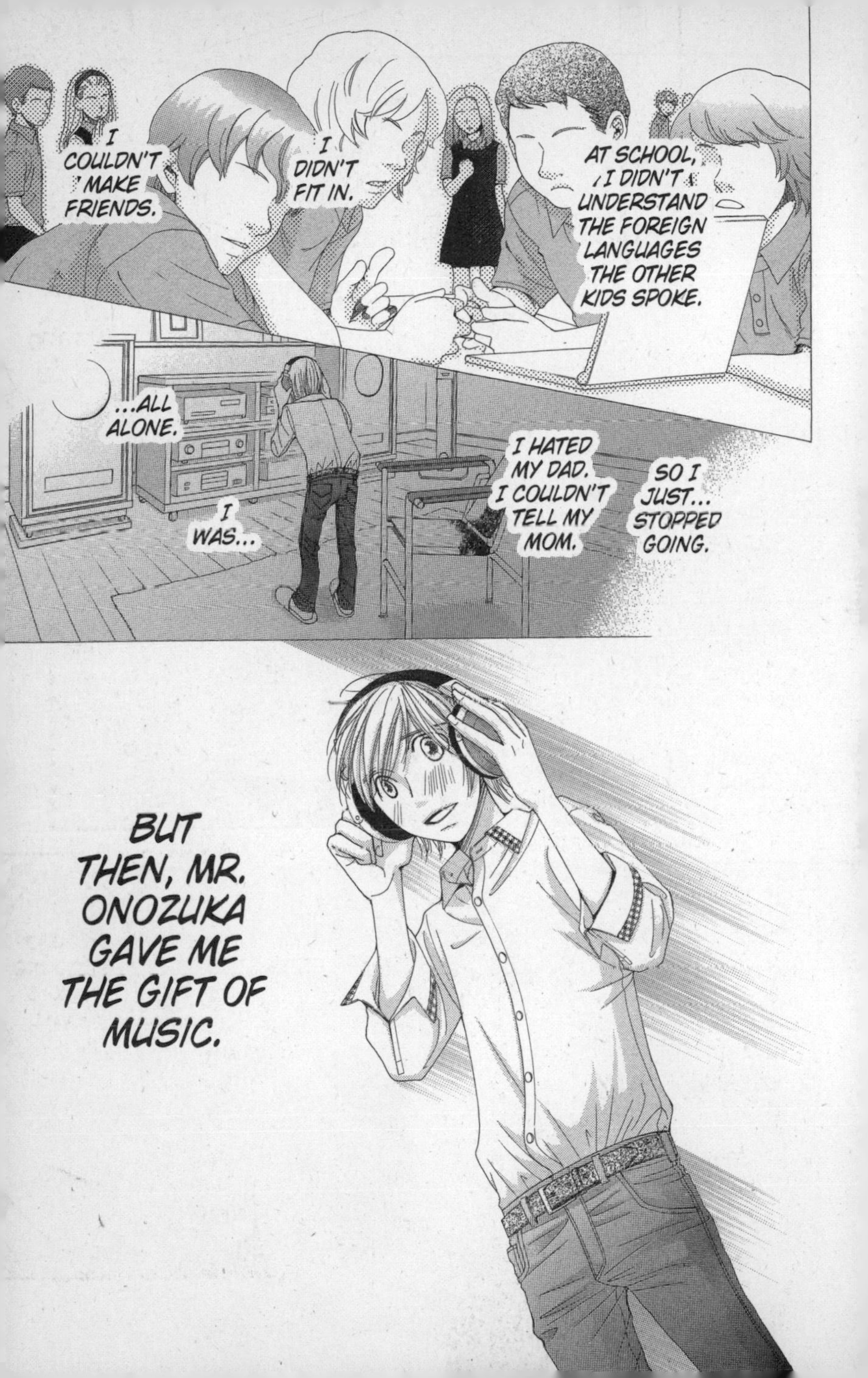
AT SCHOOL, I DIDN'T UNDERSTAND THE FOREIGN LANGUAGES THE OTHER KIDS SPOKE.
I DIDN'T FIT IN.
I COULDN'T MAKE FRIENDS.
SO I JUST... STOPPED GOING.
I HATED MY DAD. I COULDN'T TELL MY MOM.
I WAS...
...ALL ALONE.
BUT THEN, MR. ONOZUKA GAVE ME THE GIFT OF MUSIC.

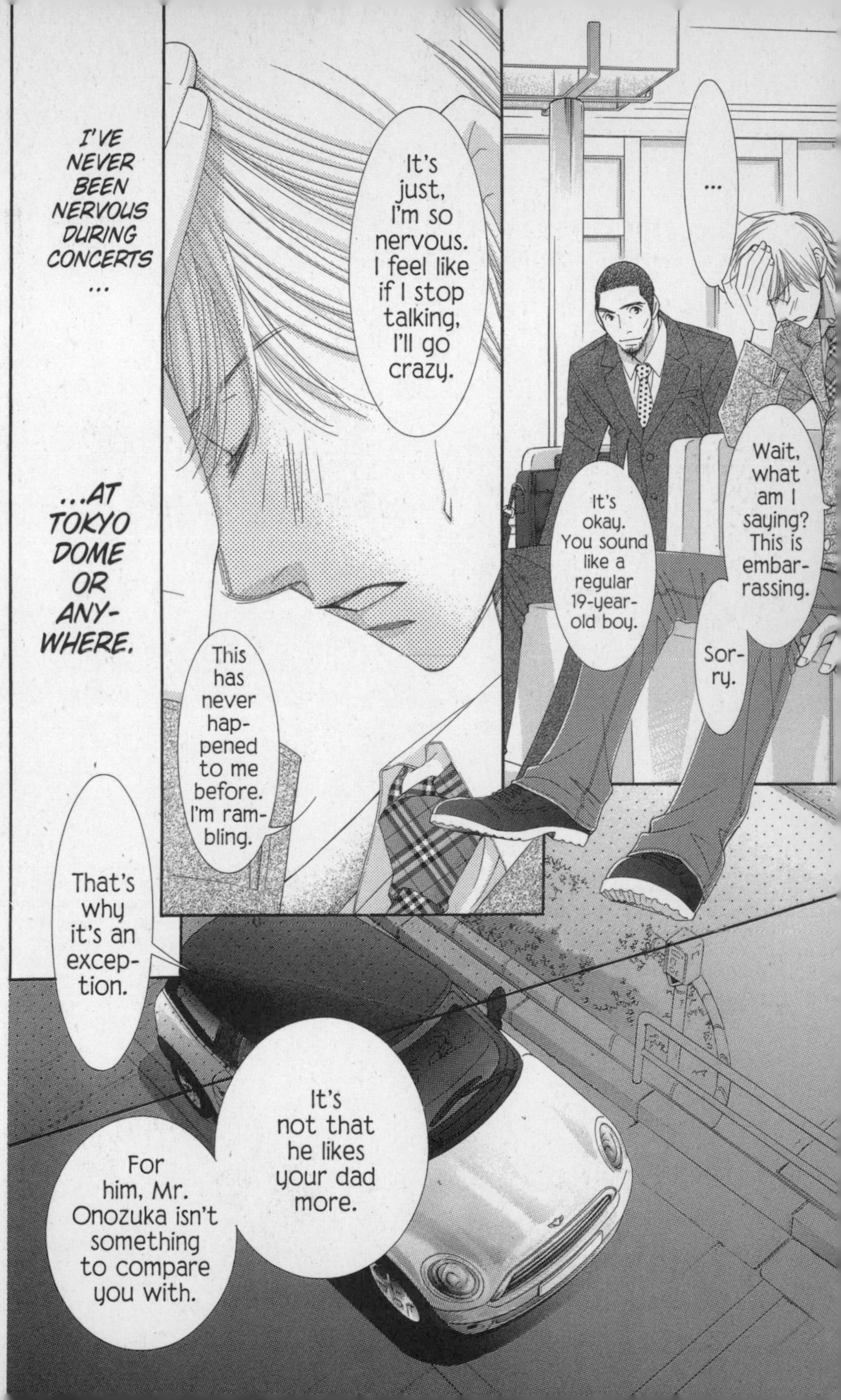
...
Wait, what am I saying? This is embarrassing.
Sorry.
It's okay. You sound like a regular 19-year-old boy.
It's just, I'm so nervous. I feel like if I stop talking, I'll go crazy.
This has never happened to me before. I'm rambling.
I'VE NEVER BEEN NERVOUS DURING CONCERTS...
...AT TOKYO DOME OR ANYWHERE.
It's not that he likes your dad more.
For him, Mr. Onozuka isn't something to compare you with.
That's why it's an exception.

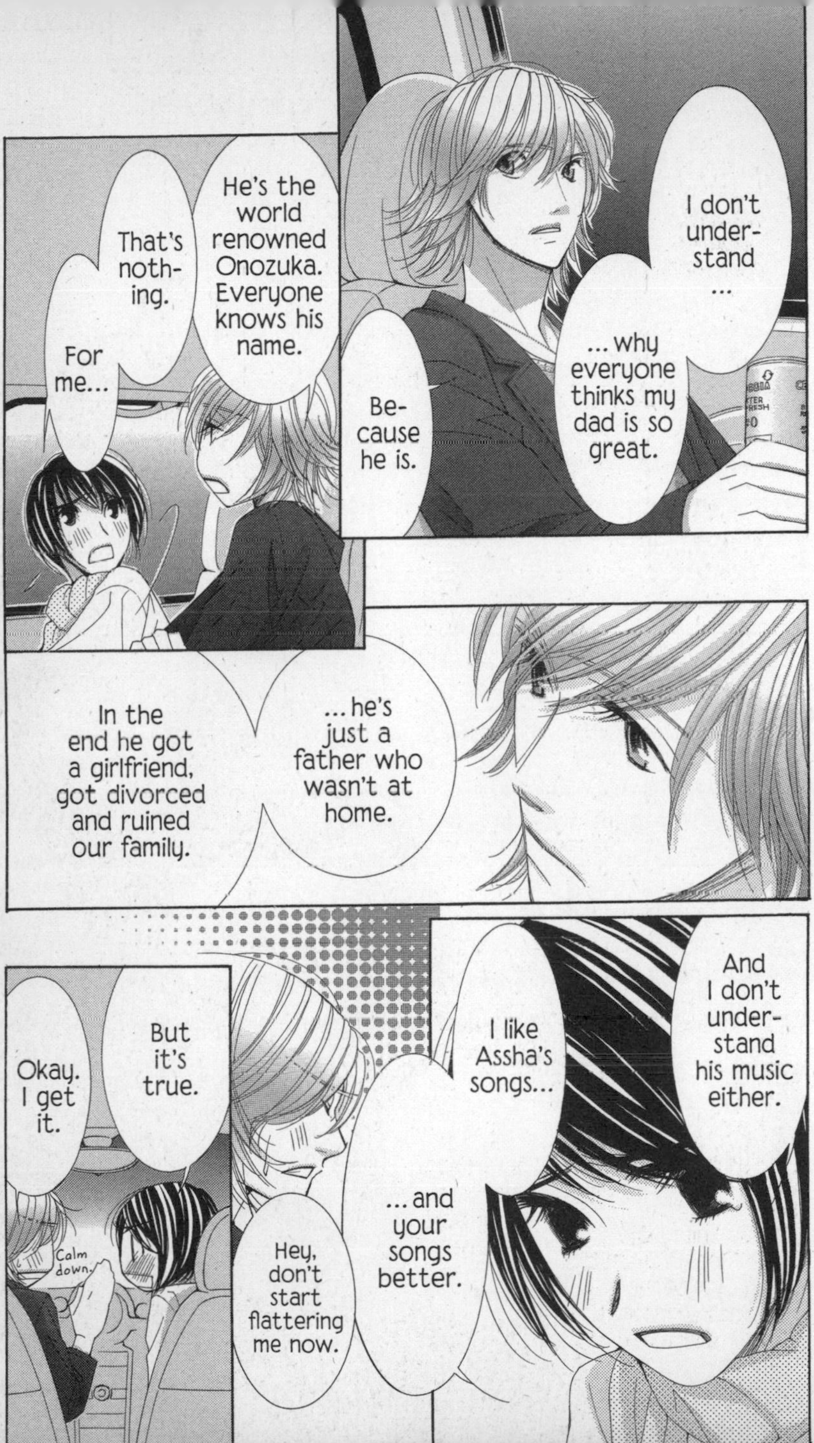
I don't under-stand ...
... why everyone thinks my dad is so great.
Be-cause he is.
He's the world renowned Onozuka. Everyone knows his name.
That's noth-ing.
For me...
... he's just a father who wasn't at home.
In the end he got a girlfriend, got divorced and ruined our family.
And I don't under-stand his music either.
I like Assha's songs...
... and your songs better.
Hey, don't start flattering me now.
But it's true.
Okay. I get it.
Calm down.

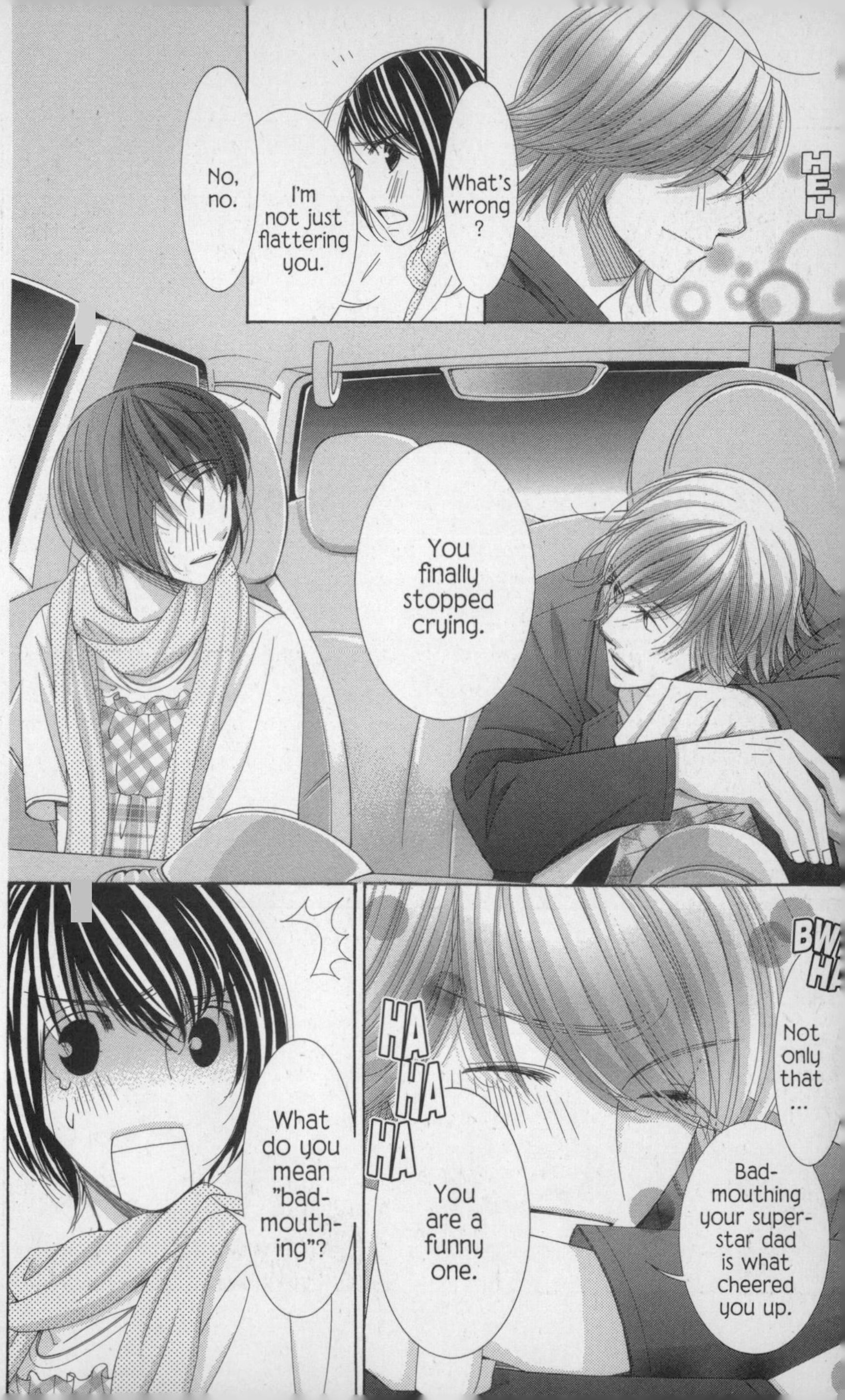
HEH
What's wrong?
I'm not just flattering you.
No, no.
You finally stopped crying.
Not only that...
Bad-mouthing your superstar dad is what cheered you up.
HA HA HA
You are a funny one.
What do you mean "bad-mouthing"?

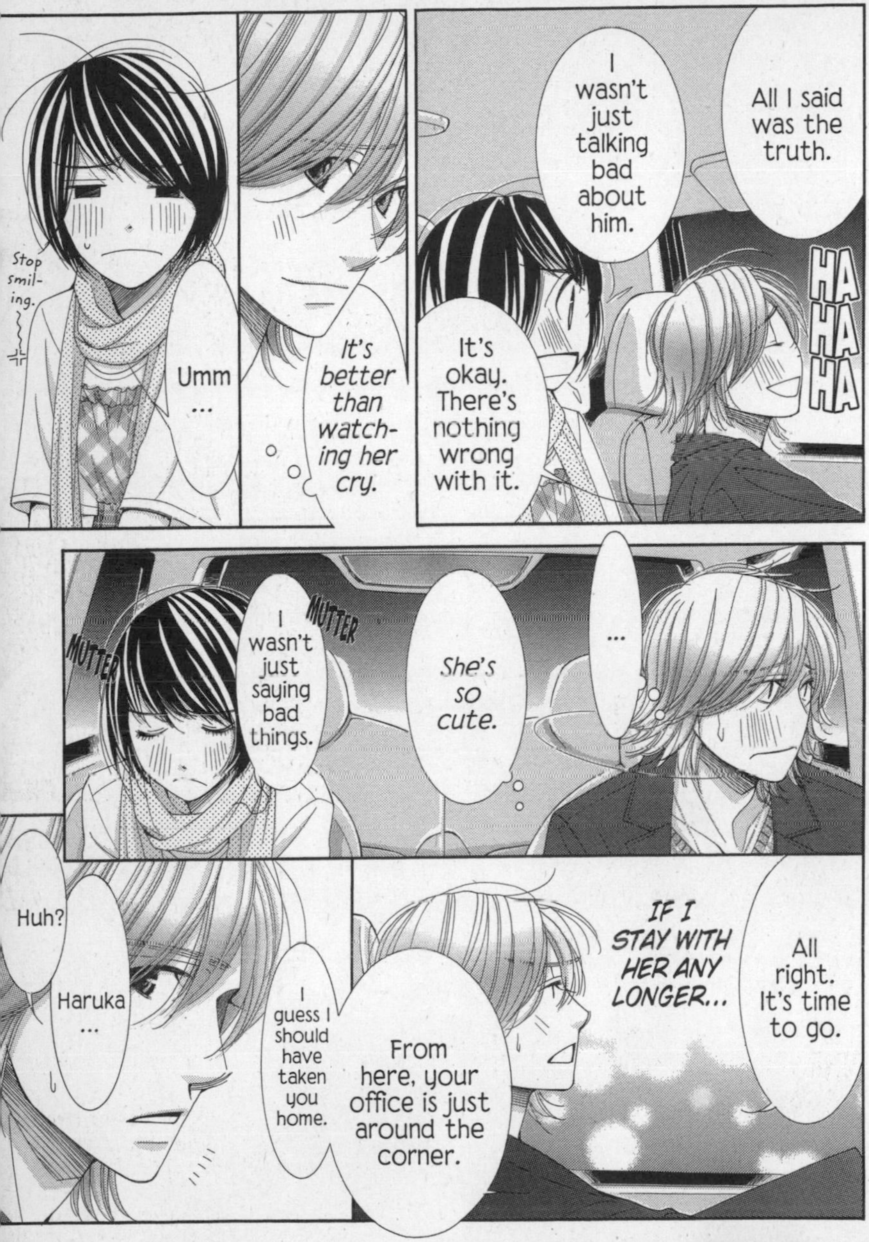
All I said was the truth.
HA HA HA
I wasn't just talking bad about him.
It's okay. There's nothing wrong with it.
It's better than watching her cry.
Stop smil-ing.
Umm ...
...
She's so cute.
MUTTER
MUTTER
I wasn't just saying bad things.
All right. It's time to go.
IF I STAY WITH HER ANY LONGER...
From here, your office is just around the corner.
I guess I should have taken you home.
Huh?
Haruka ...

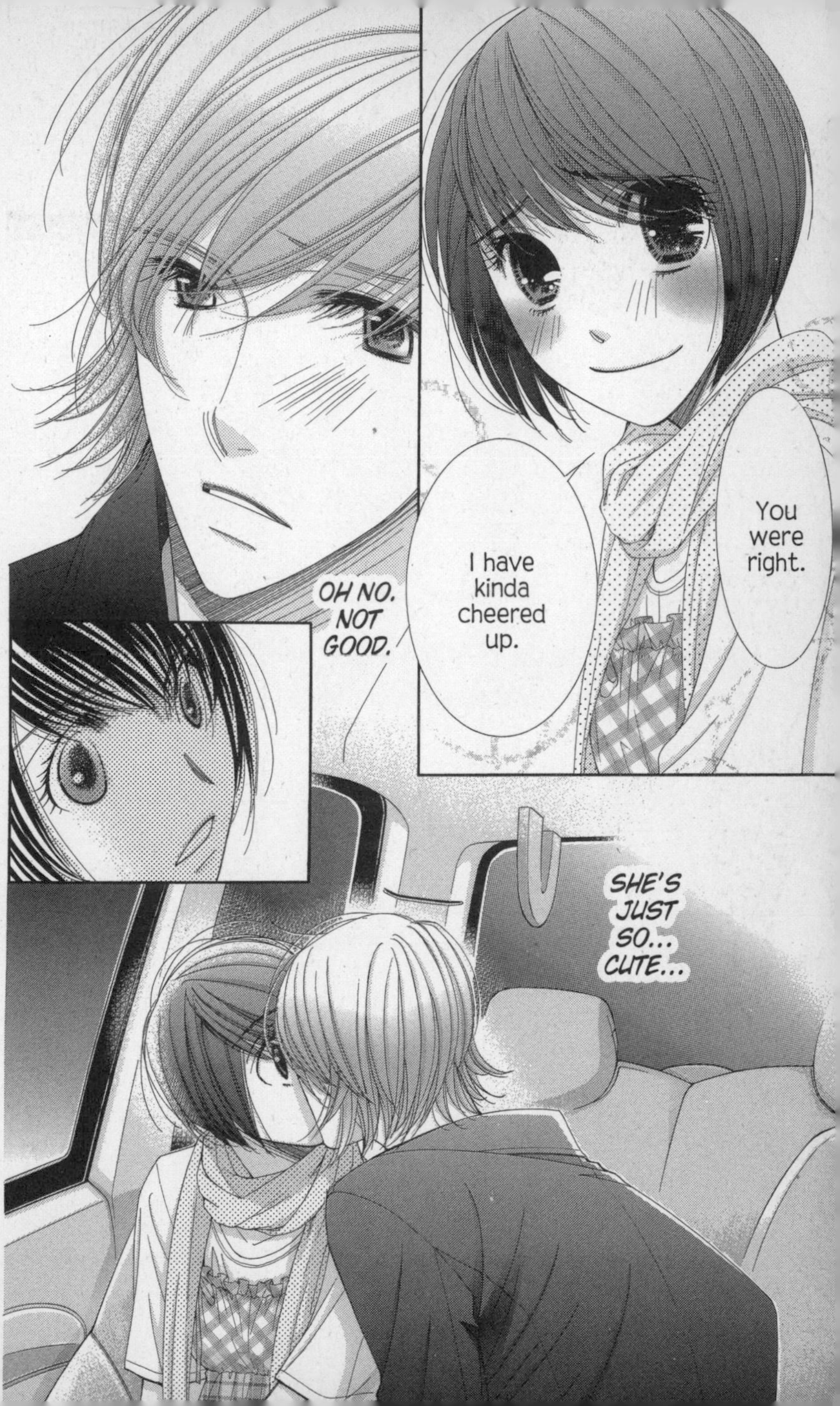
You were right.
I have kinda cheered up.
OH NO. NOT GOOD.
SHE'S JUST SO... CUTE...

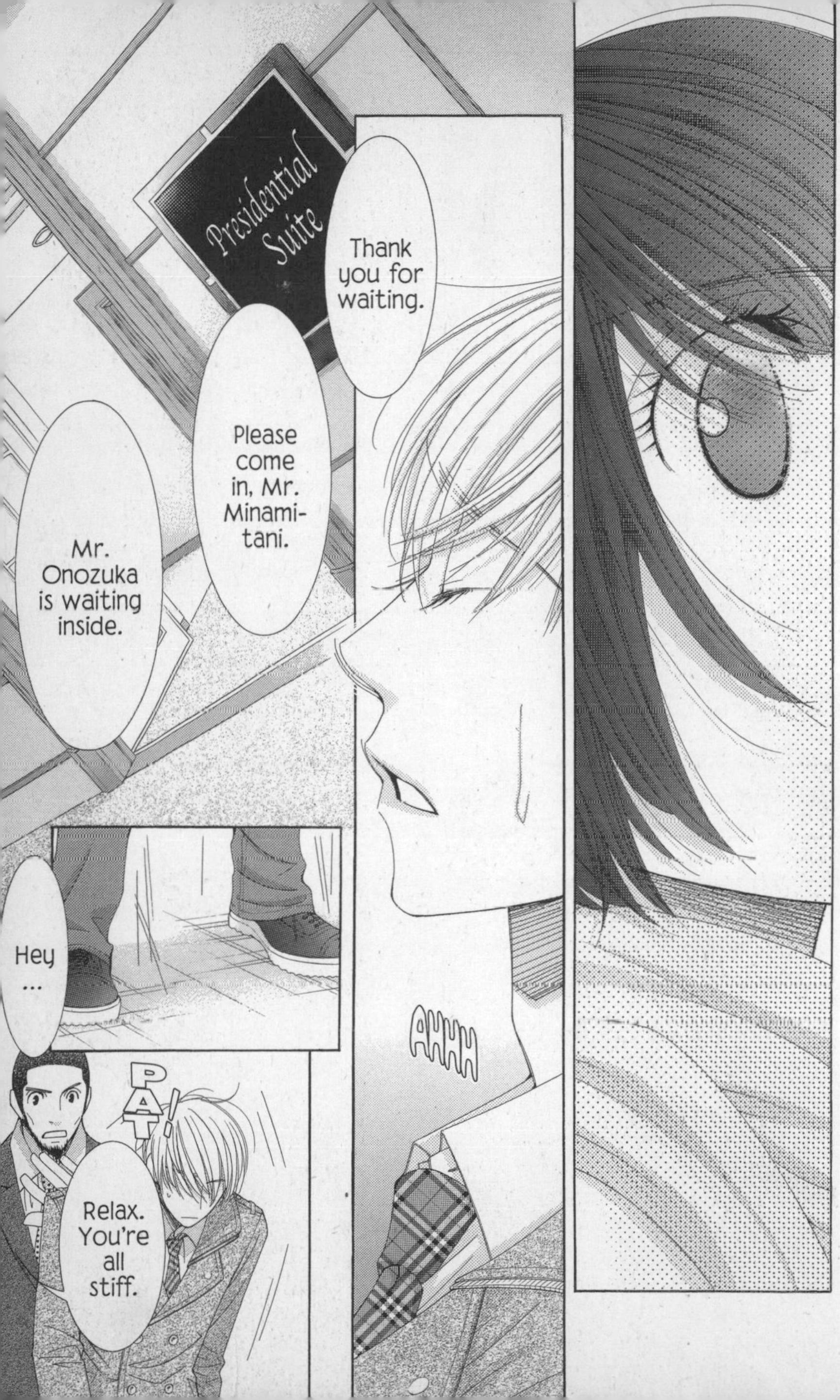
Presidential Suite
Thank you for waiting.
Please come in, Mr. Minami-tani.
Mr. Onozuka is waiting inside.
Hey ...
PAT!
Relax. You're all stiff.
AHHH

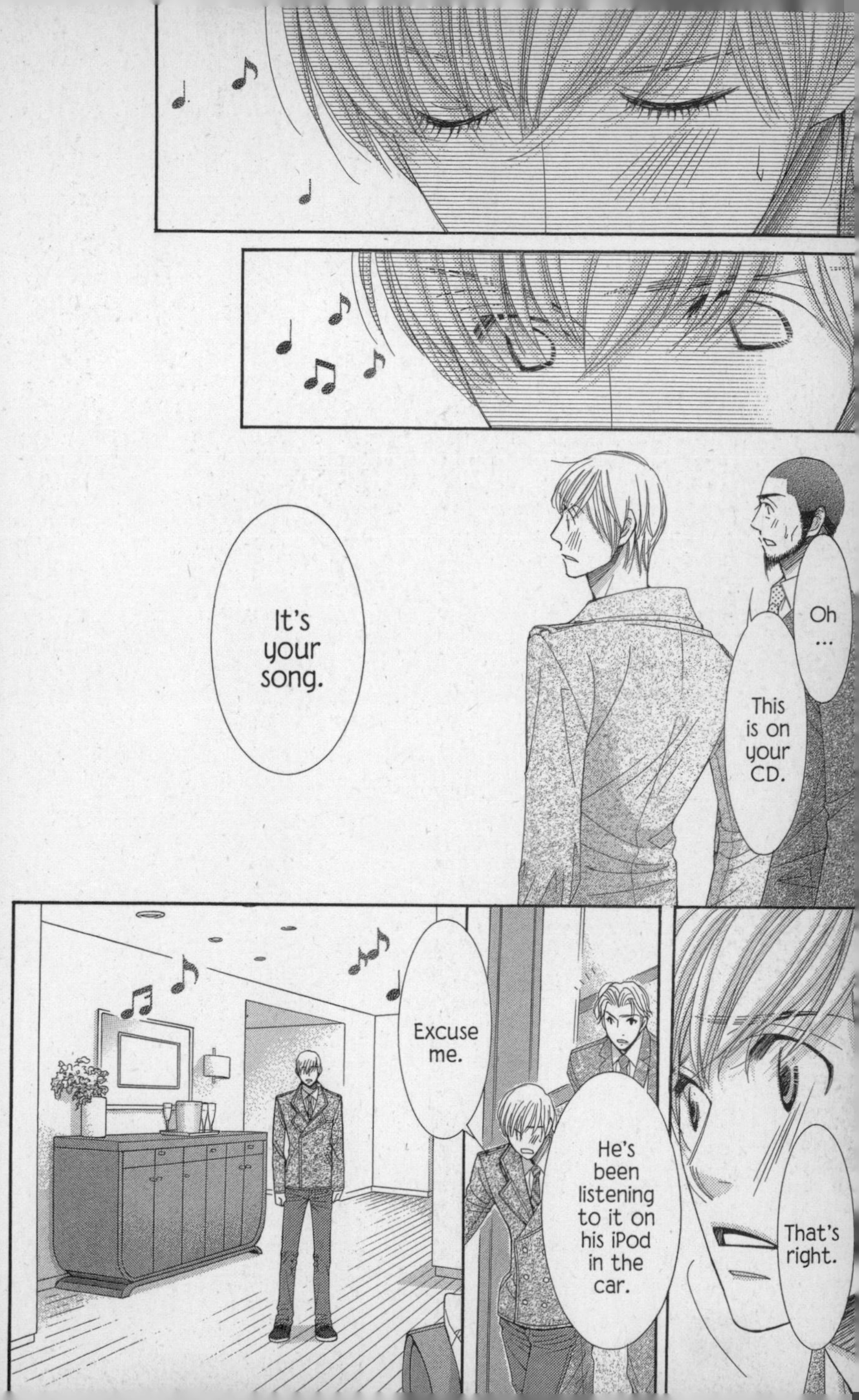
Oh...
This is on your CD.
It's your song.
That's right.
Excuse me.
He's been listening to it on his iPod in the car.

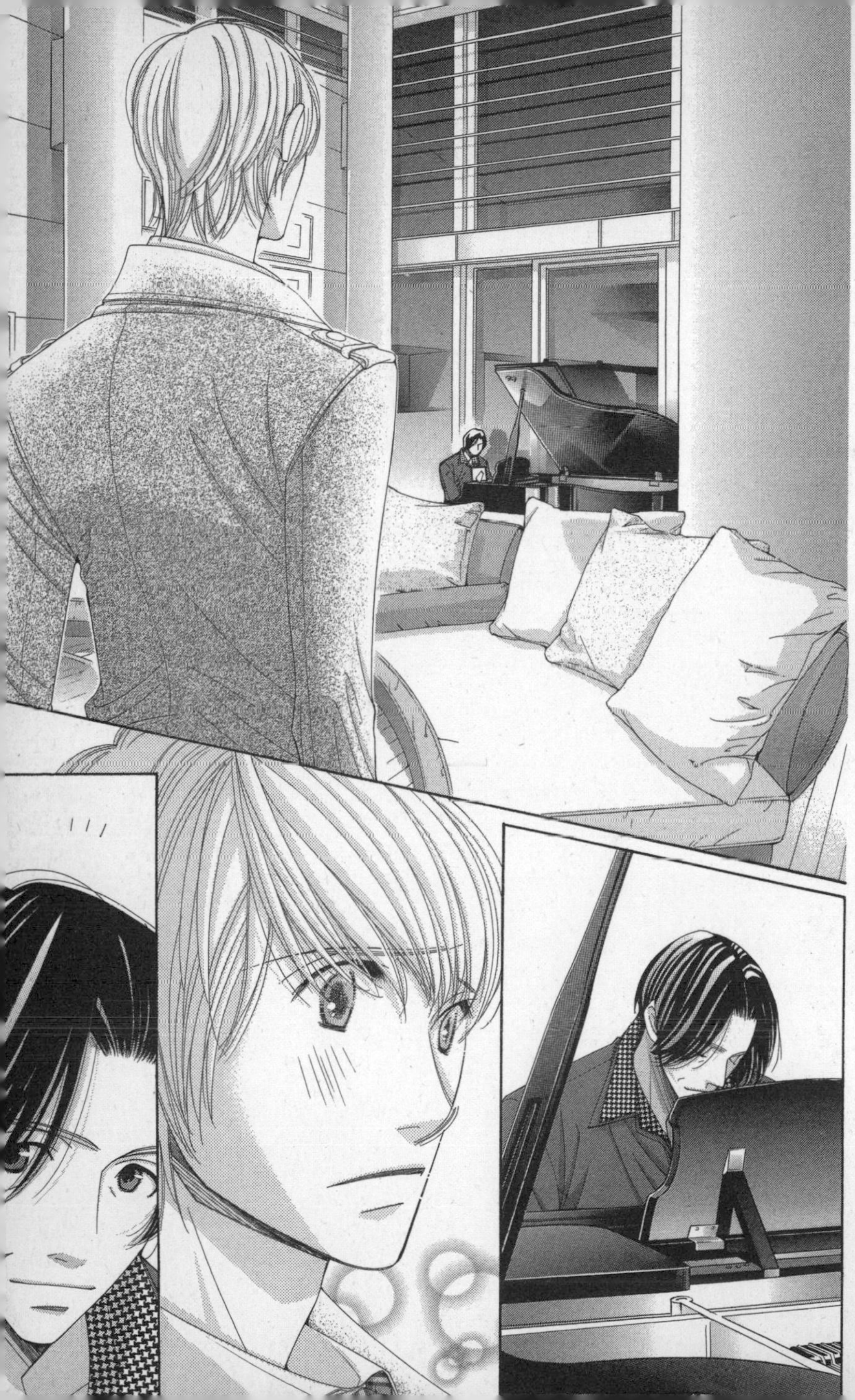

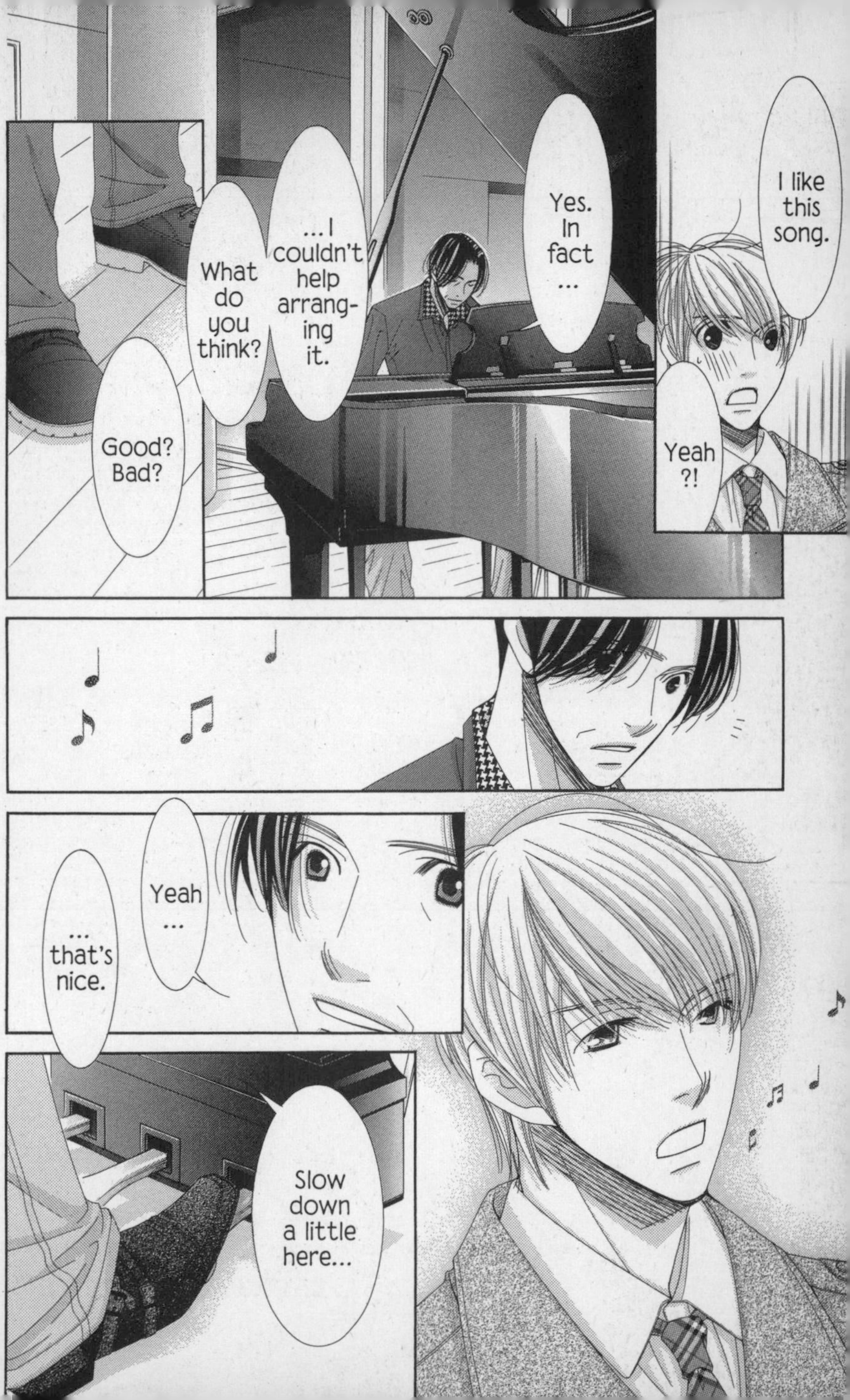
I like this song.
Yeah ?!
Yes. In fact ...
...I couldn't help arranging it.
What do you think?
Good? Bad?
Yeah ...
... that's nice.
Slow down a little here...

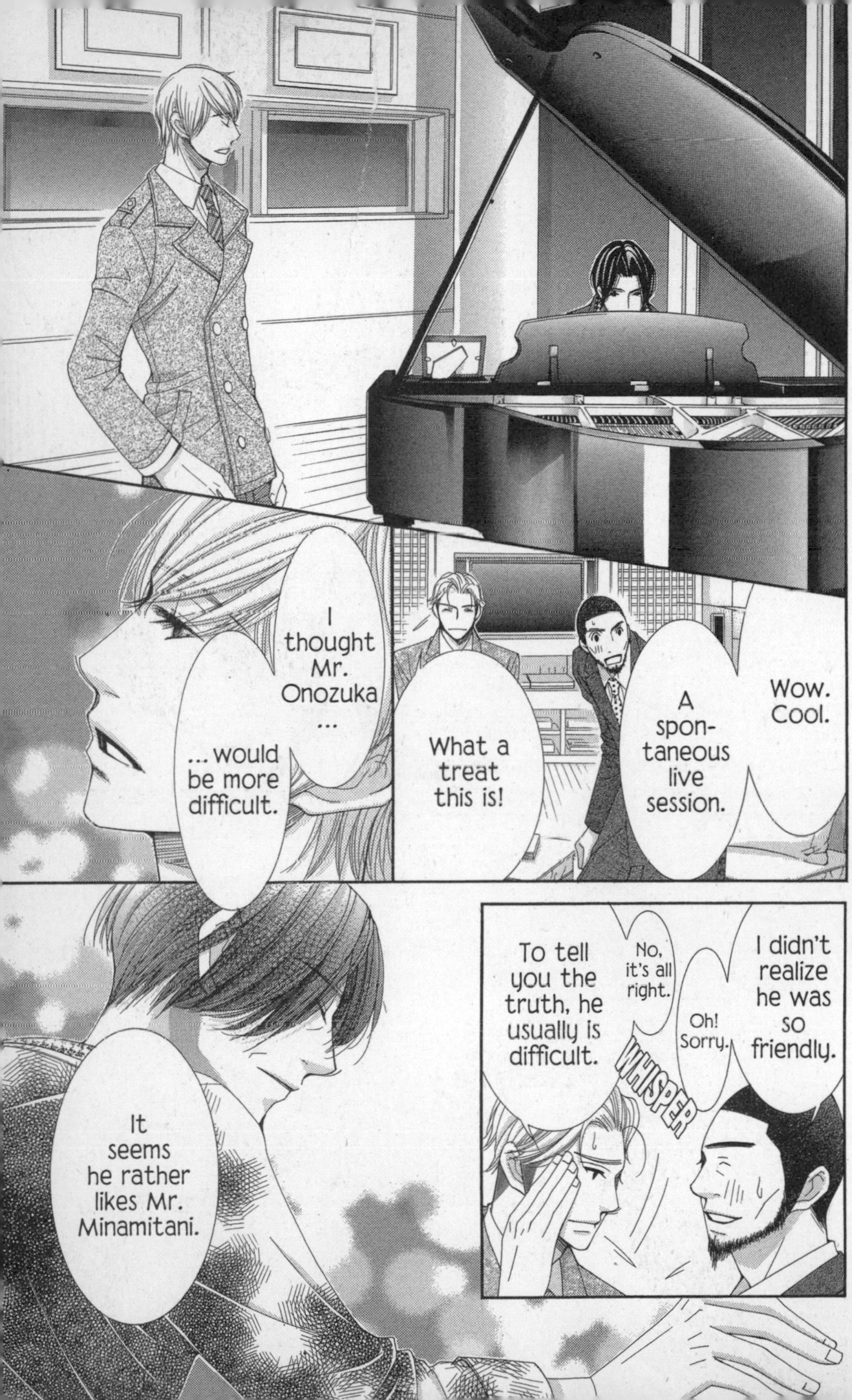
Wow. Cool.
A spon-taneous live session.
What a treat this is!
I thought Mr. Onozuka ...
... would be more difficult.
I didn't realize he was so friendly.
Oh! Sorry.
No, it's all right.
To tell you the truth, he usually is difficult.
WHISPER
It seems he rather likes Mr. Minamitani.

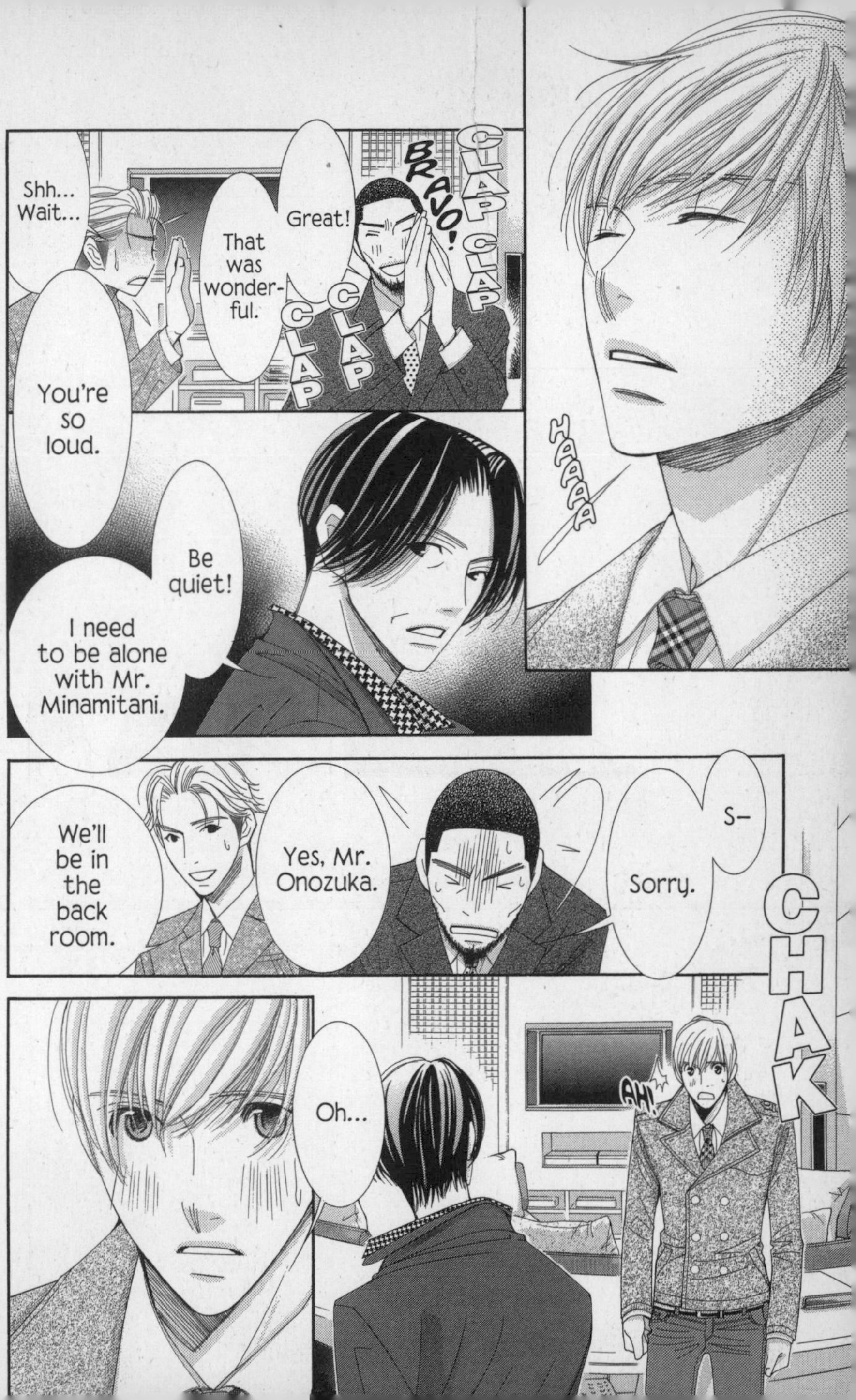
HAAAA
CLAP CLAP
BRAVO!
Great!
That was wonderful.
CLAP CLAP
Shh... Wait...
You're so loud.
Be quiet!
I need to be alone with Mr. Minamitani.
S–
Sorry.
Yes, Mr. Onozuka.
We'll be in the back room.
CHAK
AH!
Oh...

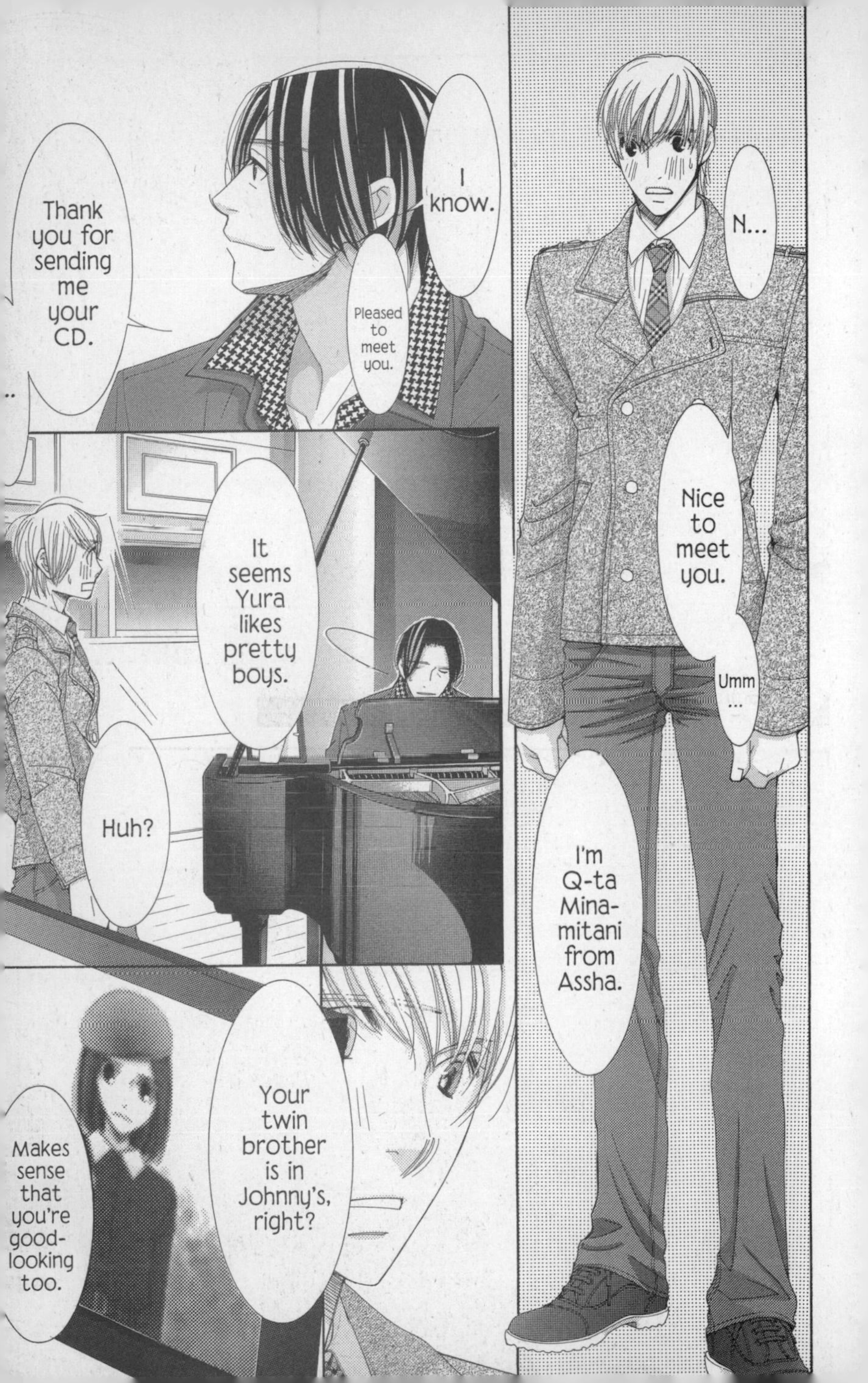
N...
Nice to meet you.
Umm...
I'm Q-ta Minamitani from Assha.
I know.
Pleased to meet you.
Thank you for sending me your CD.
It seems Yura likes pretty boys.
Huh?
Your twin brother is in Johnny's, right?
Makes sense that you're good-looking too.

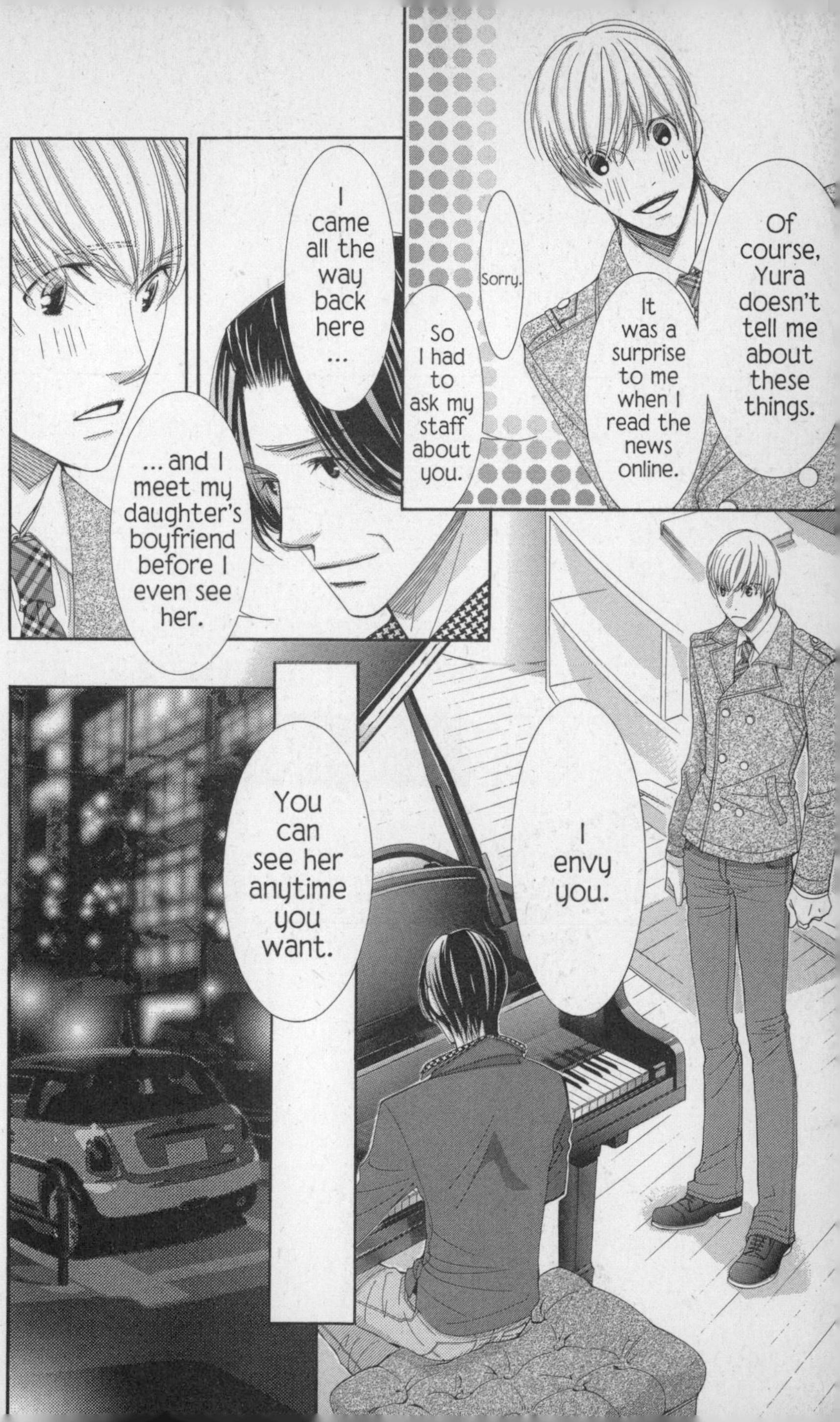
Of course, Yura doesn't tell me about these things.
It was a surprise to me when I read the news online.
Sorry.
So I had to ask my staff about you.
I came all the way back here ...
... and I meet my daughter's boyfriend before I even see her.
I envy you.
You can see her anytime you want.

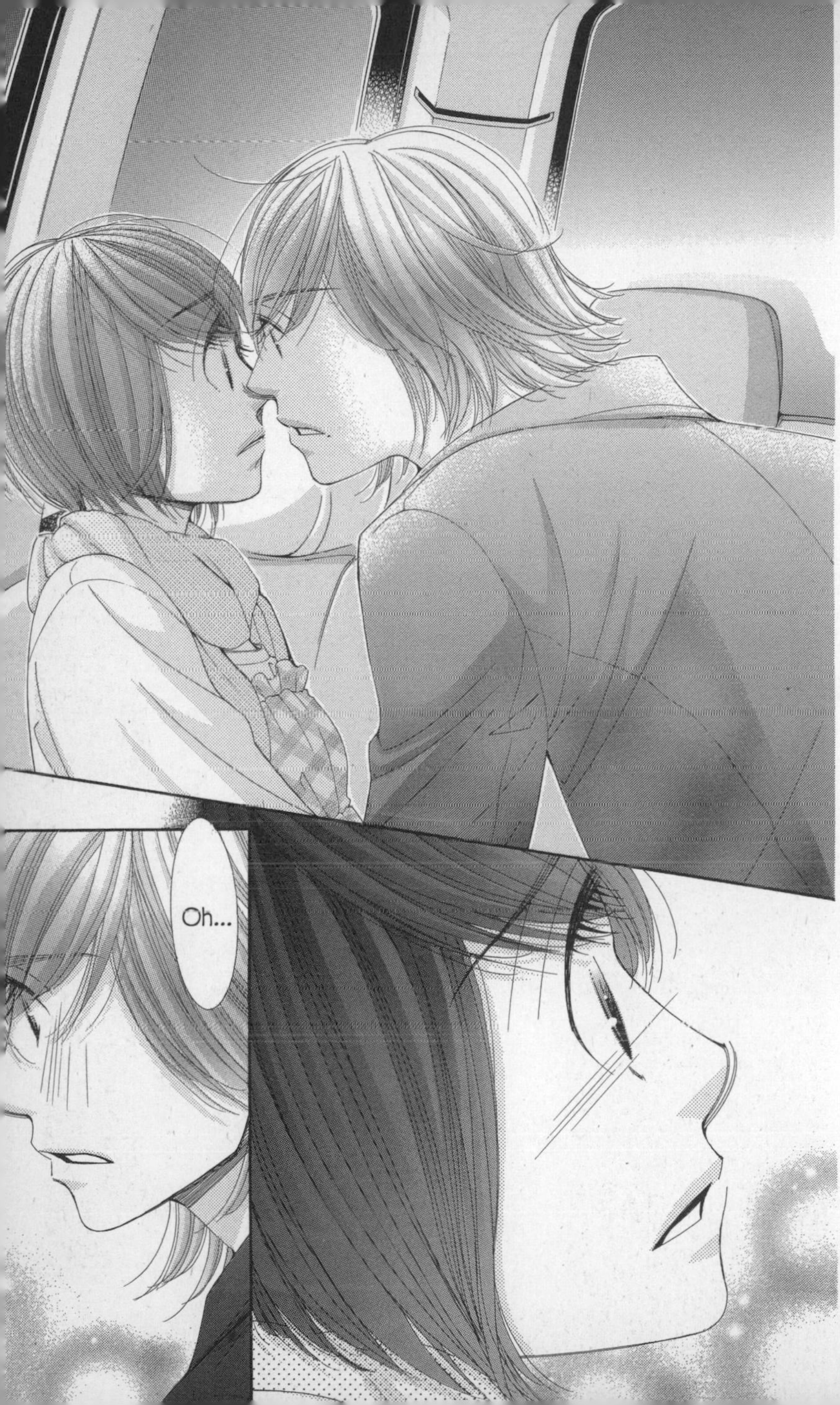
Oh...

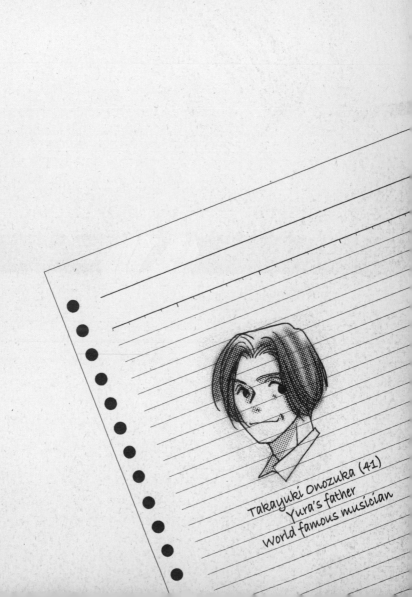

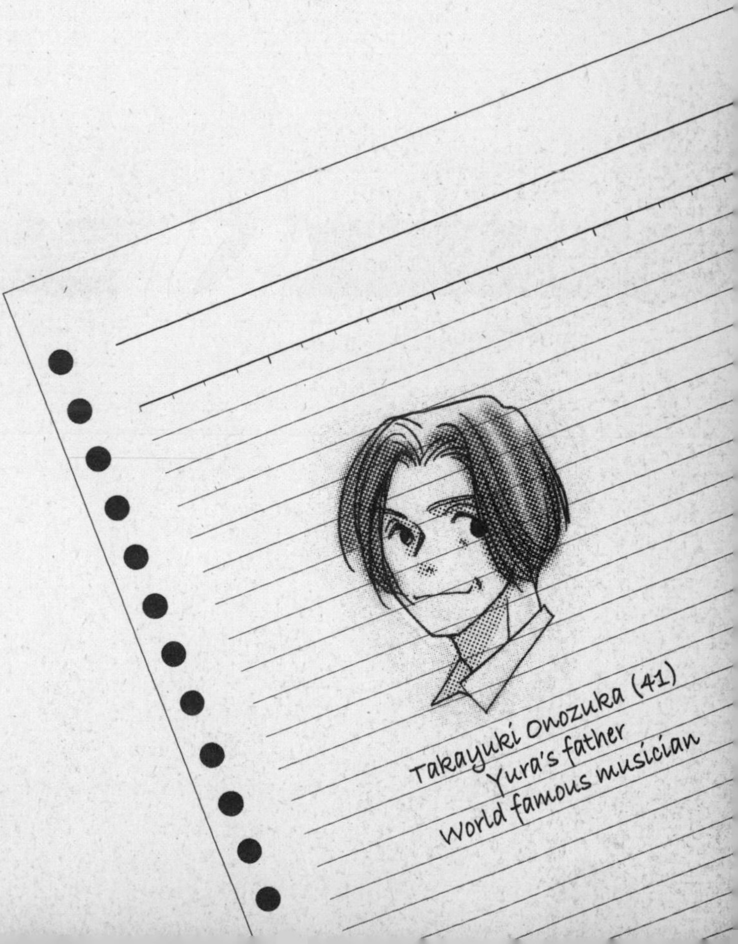
Takayuki Onozuka (41)
Yura's father
World famous musician

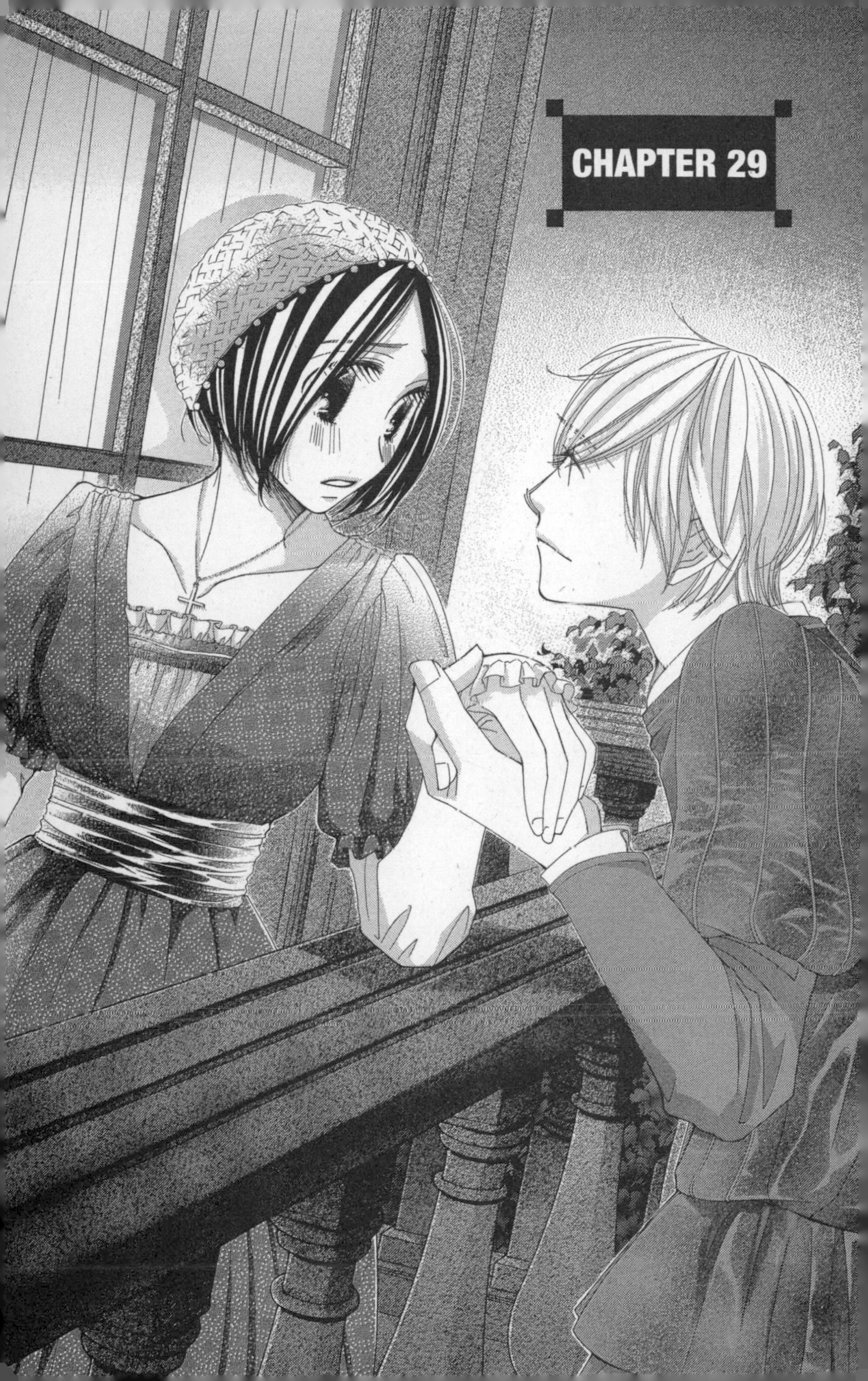
CHAPTER 29

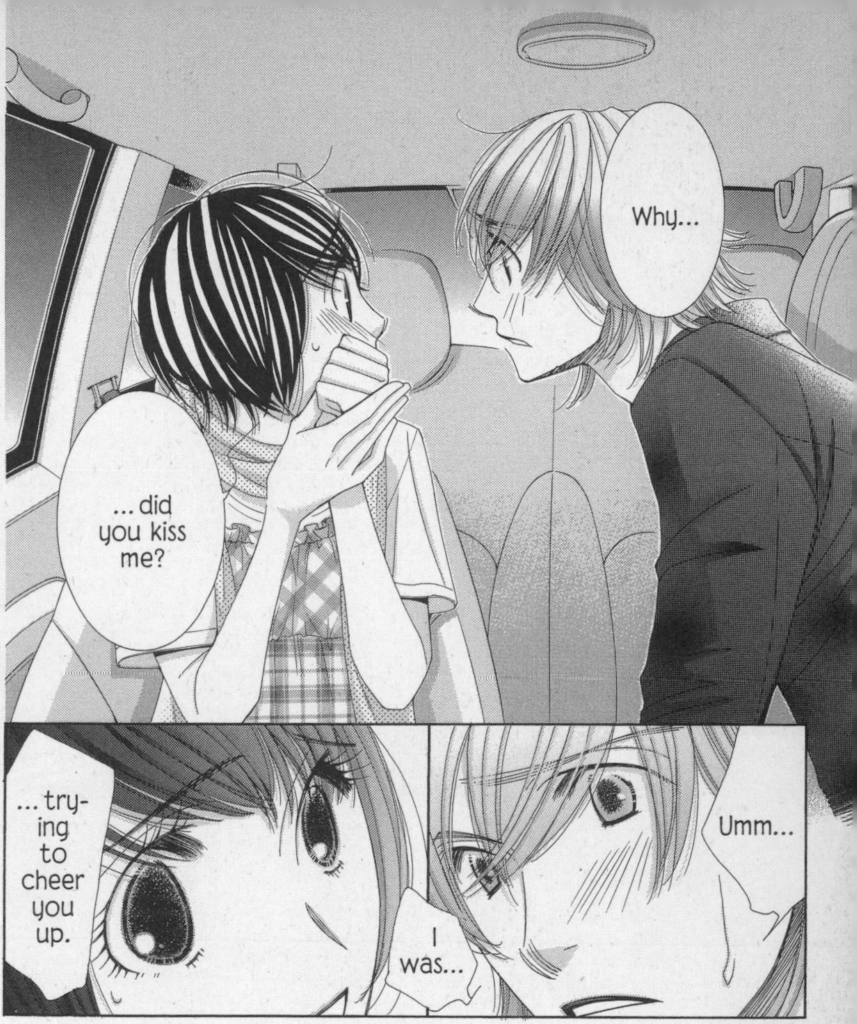
Why...
... did you kiss me?
Umm...
I was...
... try-ing to cheer you up.

Honey Hunt

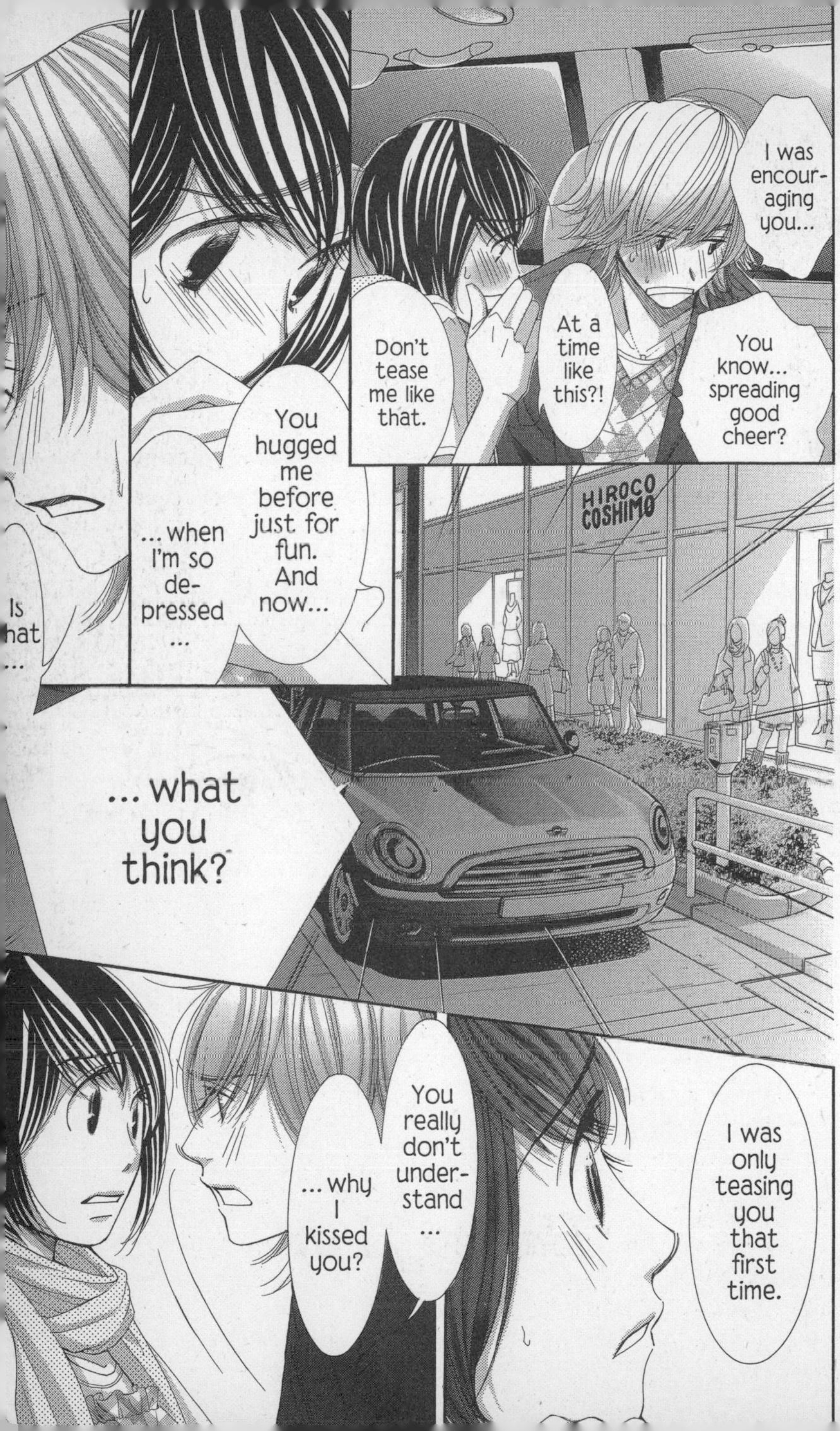
I was encouraging you...
You know... spreading good cheer?
At a time like this?!
Don't tease me like that.
You hugged me before just for fun. And now...
...when I'm so depressed...
Is hat ...
HIROCO COSHIMO
...what you think?
I was only teasing you that first time.
You really don't understand...
...why I kissed you?

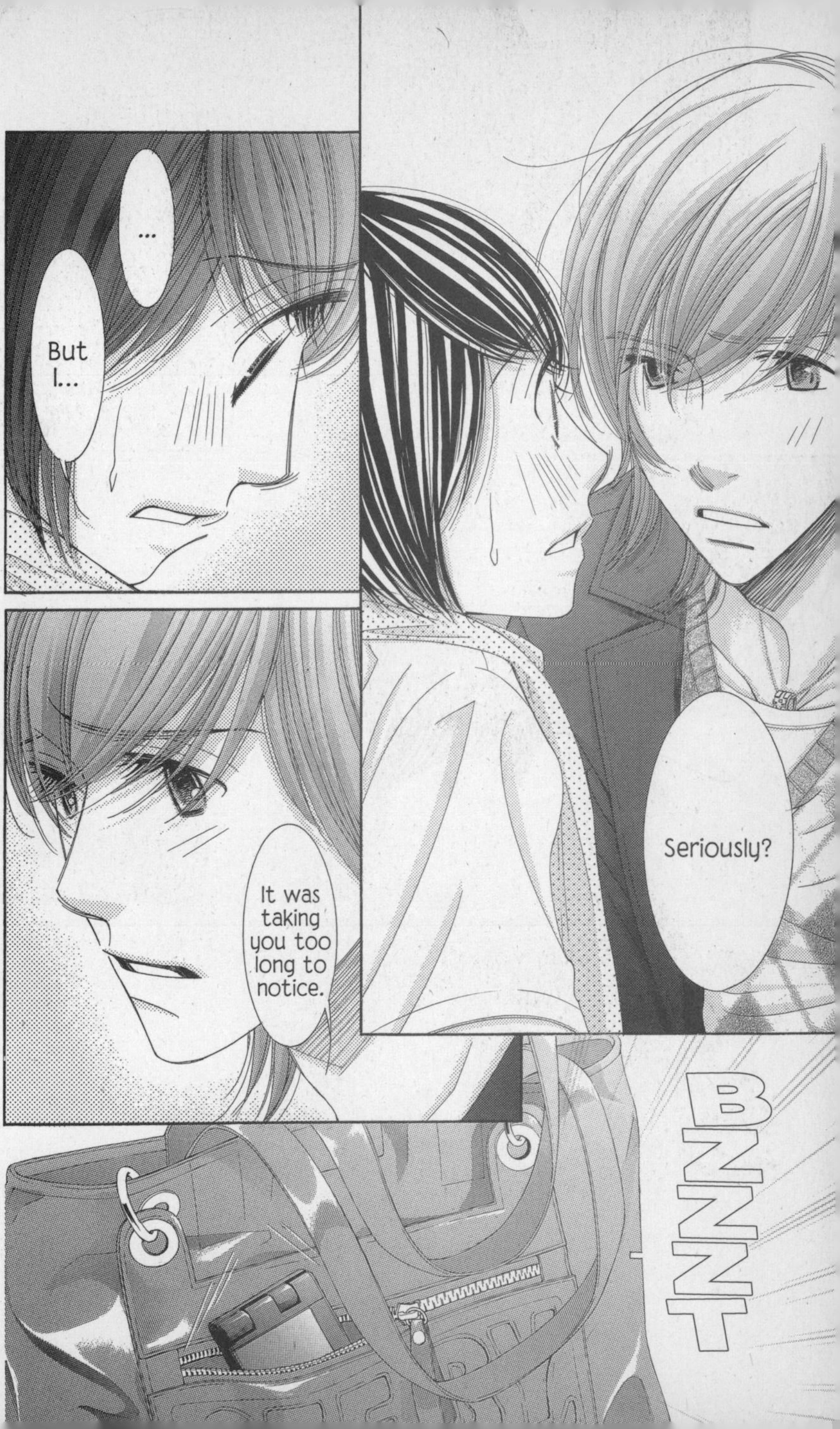
Seriously?
...
But I...
It was taking you too long to notice.
BZZZT

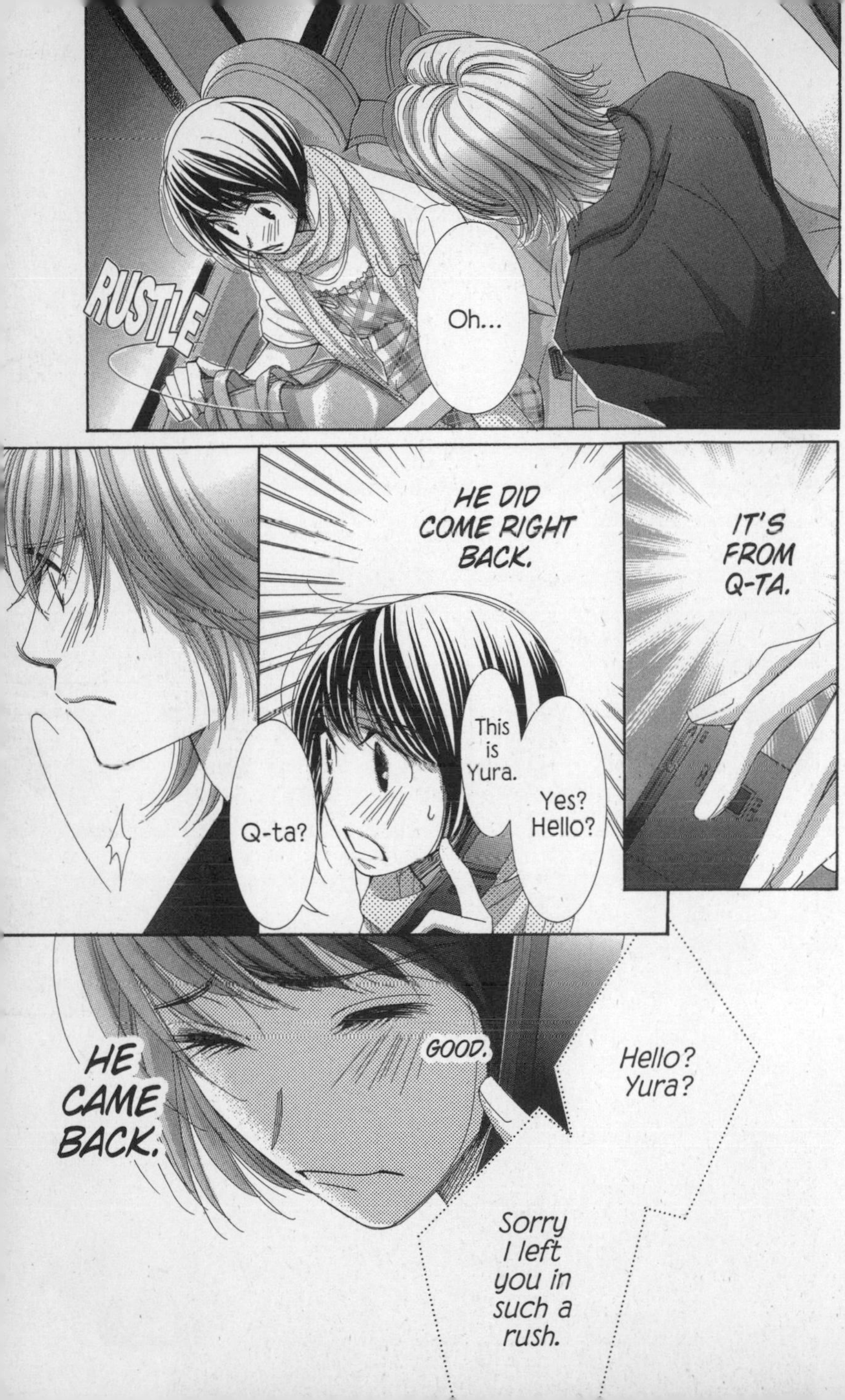
Oh...
RUSTLE
IT'S FROM Q-TA.
HE DID COME RIGHT BACK.
Yes? Hello?
This is Yura.
Q-ta?
Hello? Yura?
Sorry I left you in such a rush.
GOOD.
HE CAME BACK.

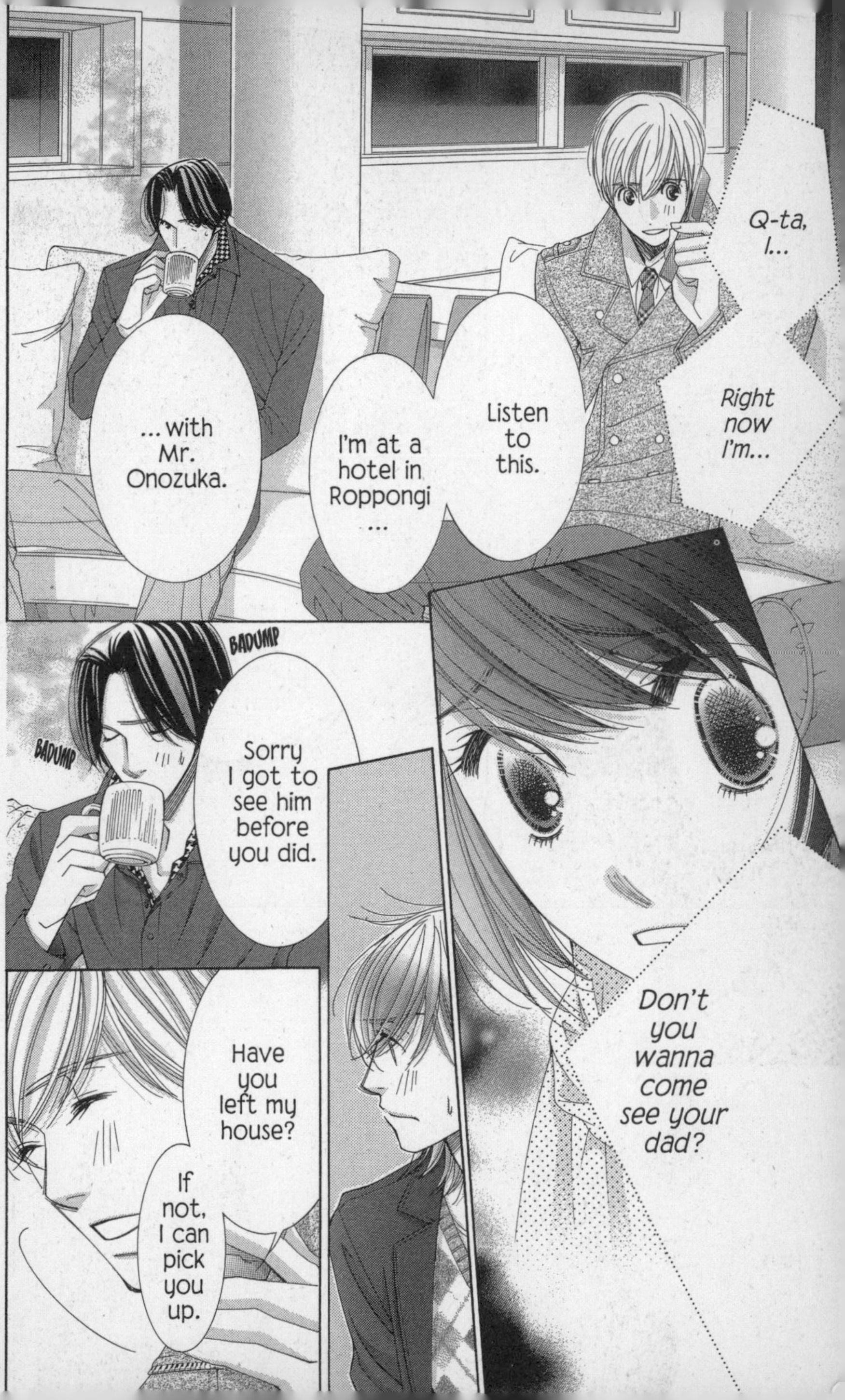
Q-ta, I...
Right now I'm...
Listen to this.
I'm at a hotel in Roppongi ...
...with Mr. Onozuka.
Don't you wanna come see your dad?
BADUMP
BADUMP
Sorry I got to see him before you did.
Have you left my house?
If not, I can pick you up.

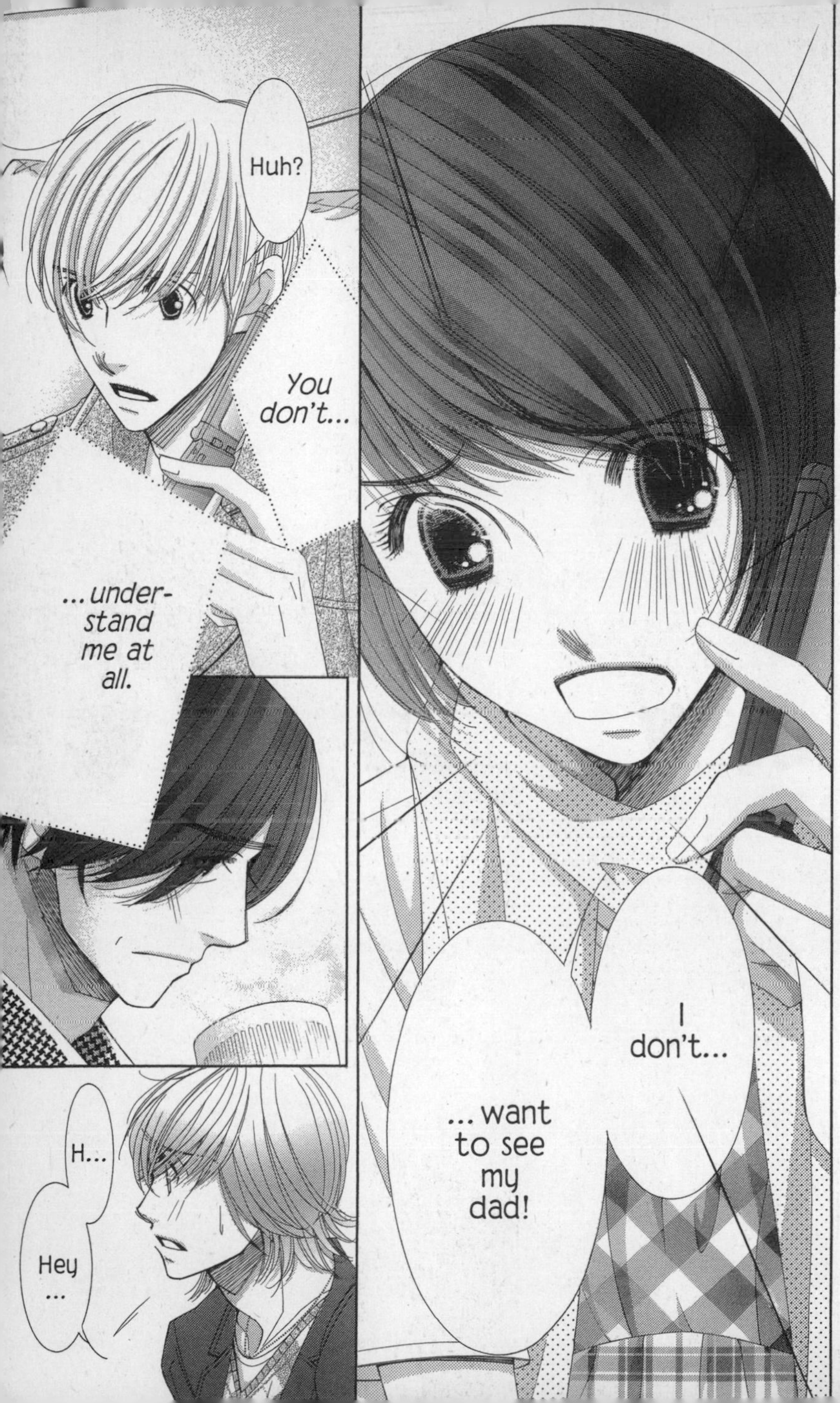
I don't...
...want to see my dad!
Huh?
You don't...
...under-stand me at all.
H...
Hey ...

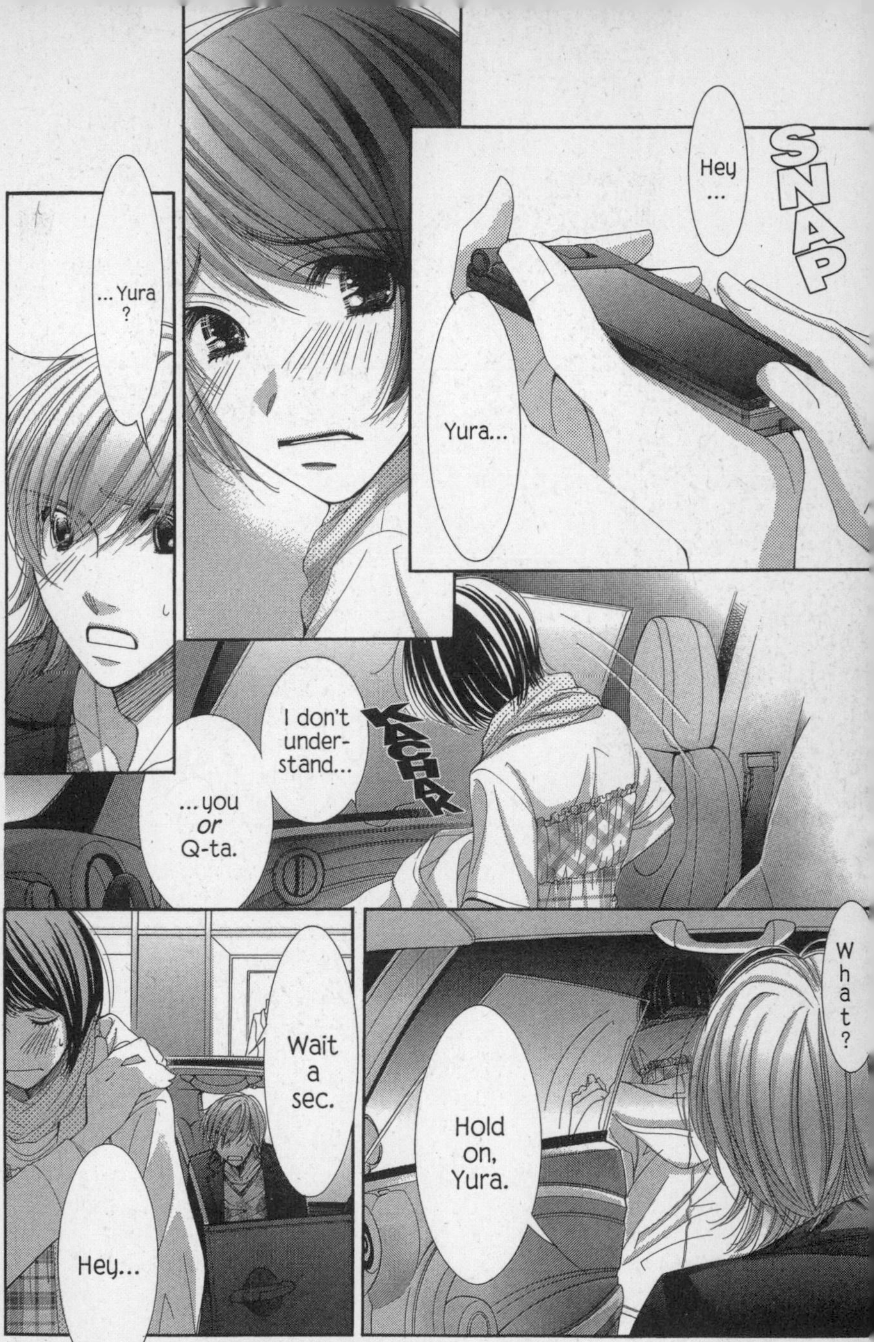
SNAP
Hey ...
Yura...
... Yura ?
KACHAK
I don't under-stand...
...you *or* Q-ta.
What?
Hold on, Yura.
Wait a sec.
Hey...

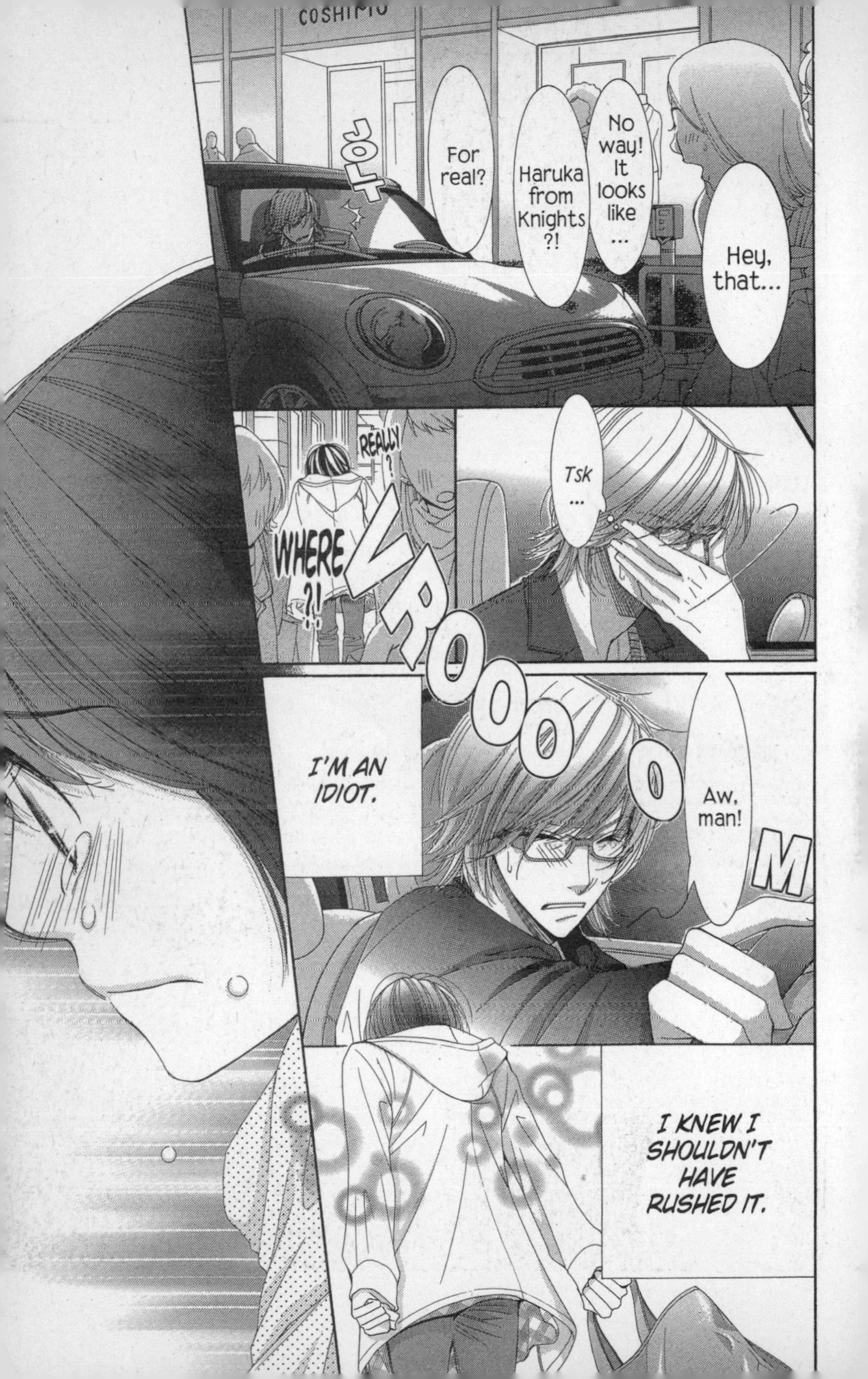
Hey, that...
No way! It looks like ...
Haruka from Knights ?!
For real?
JOLT
Tsk ...
REALLY ?
WHERE ?!
VROOOOOM
Aw, man!
I'M AN IDIOT.
I KNEW I SHOULDN'T HAVE RUSHED IT.

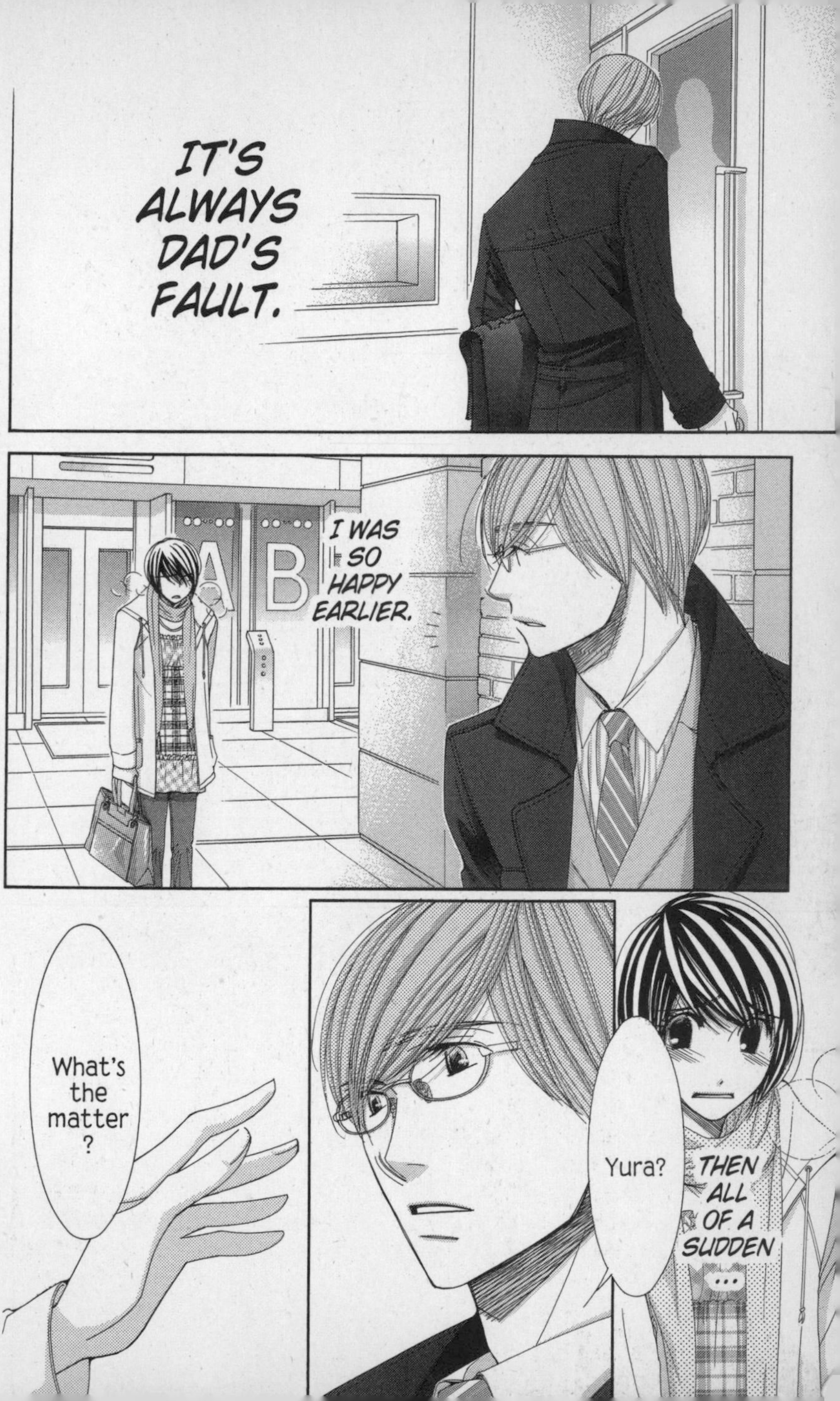
IT'S ALWAYS DAD'S FAULT.
I WAS SO HAPPY EARLIER.
THEN ALL OF A SUDDEN ...
Yura?
What's the matter?

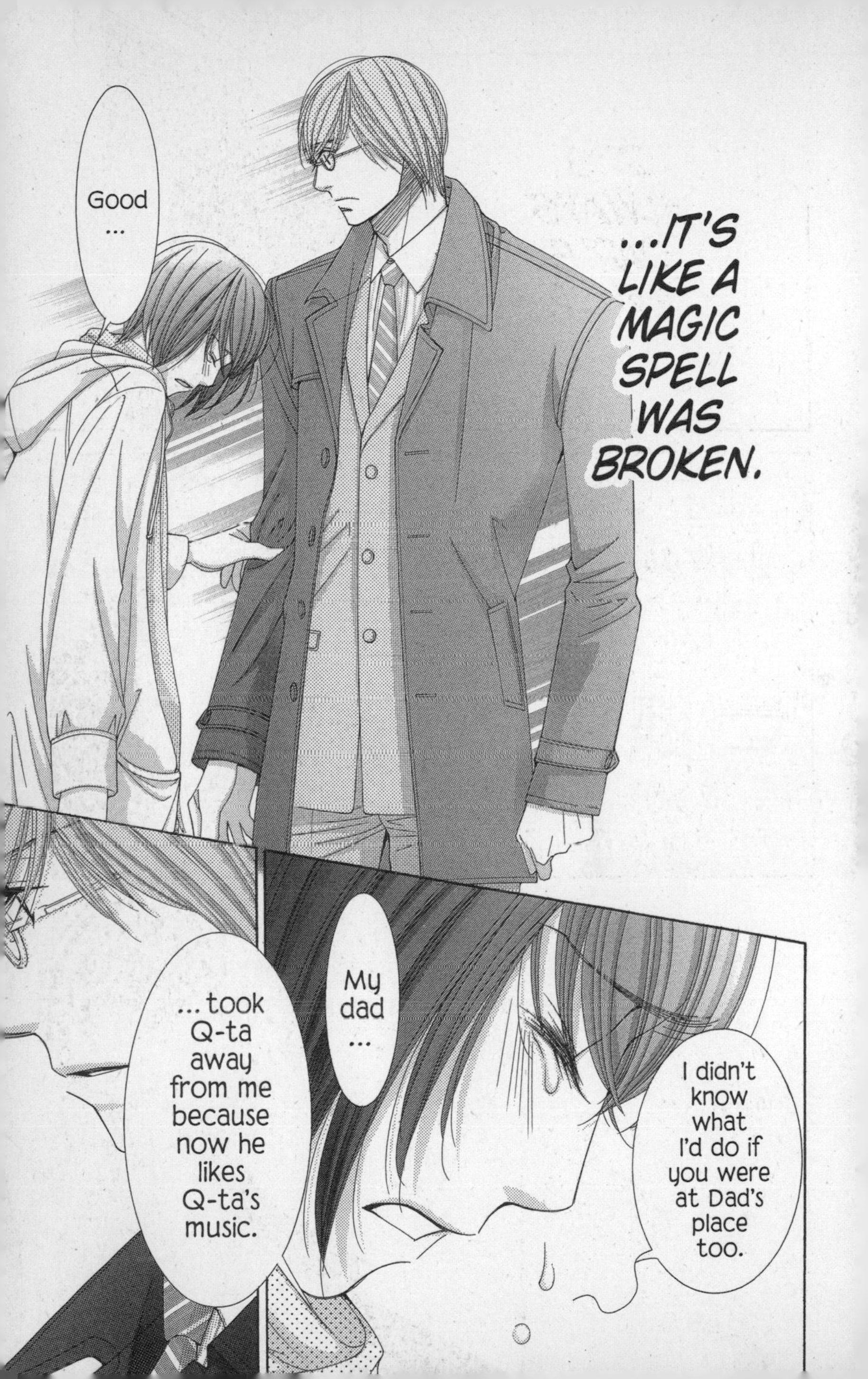
...IT'S LIKE A MAGIC SPELL WAS BROKEN.
Good ...
I didn't know what I'd do if you were at Dad's place too.
My dad ...
... took Q-ta away from me because now he likes Q-ta's music.

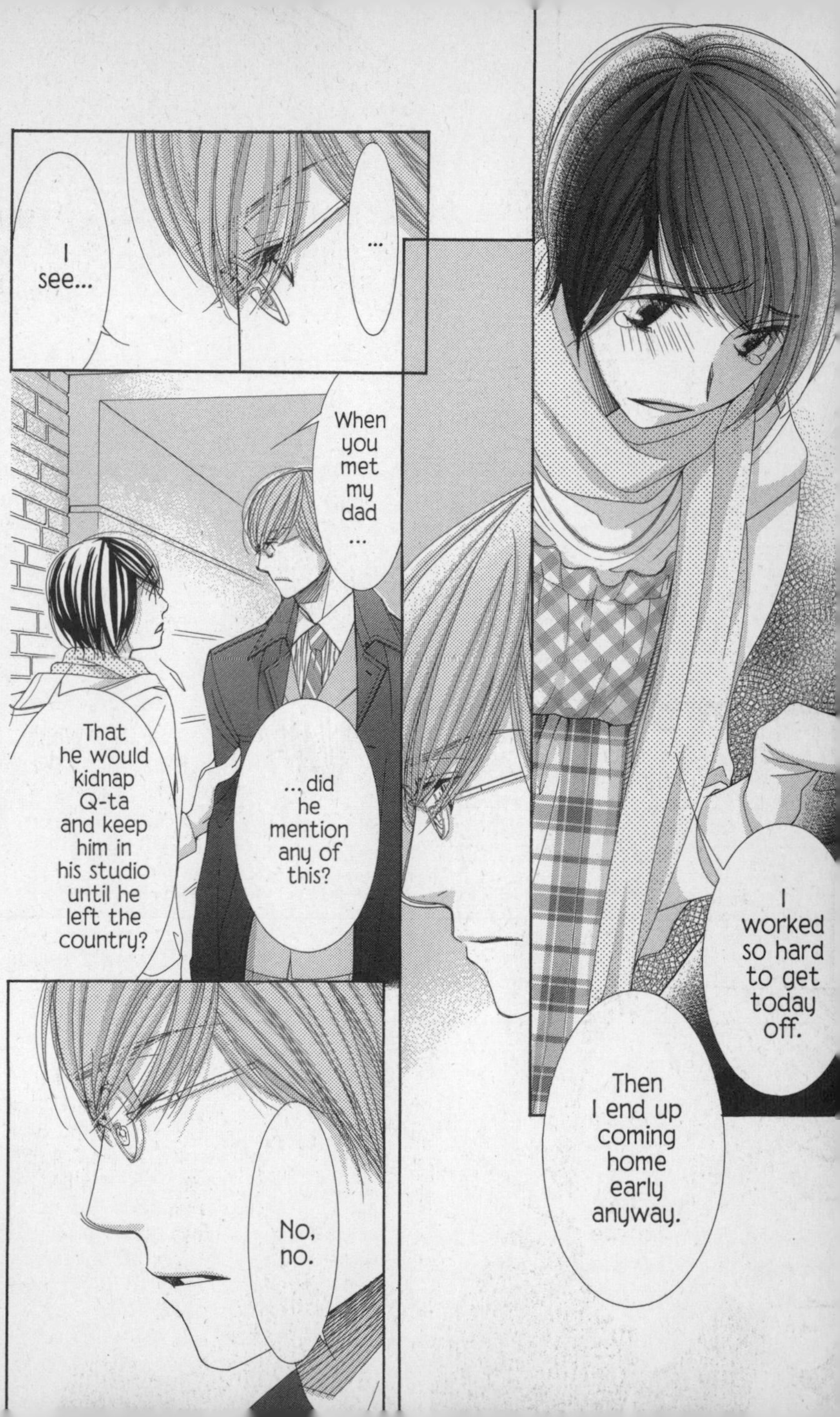
I worked so hard to get today off.
Then I end up coming home early anyway.
...
I see...
When you met my dad...
...did he mention any of this?
That he would kidnap Q-ta and keep him in his studio until he left the country?
No, no.

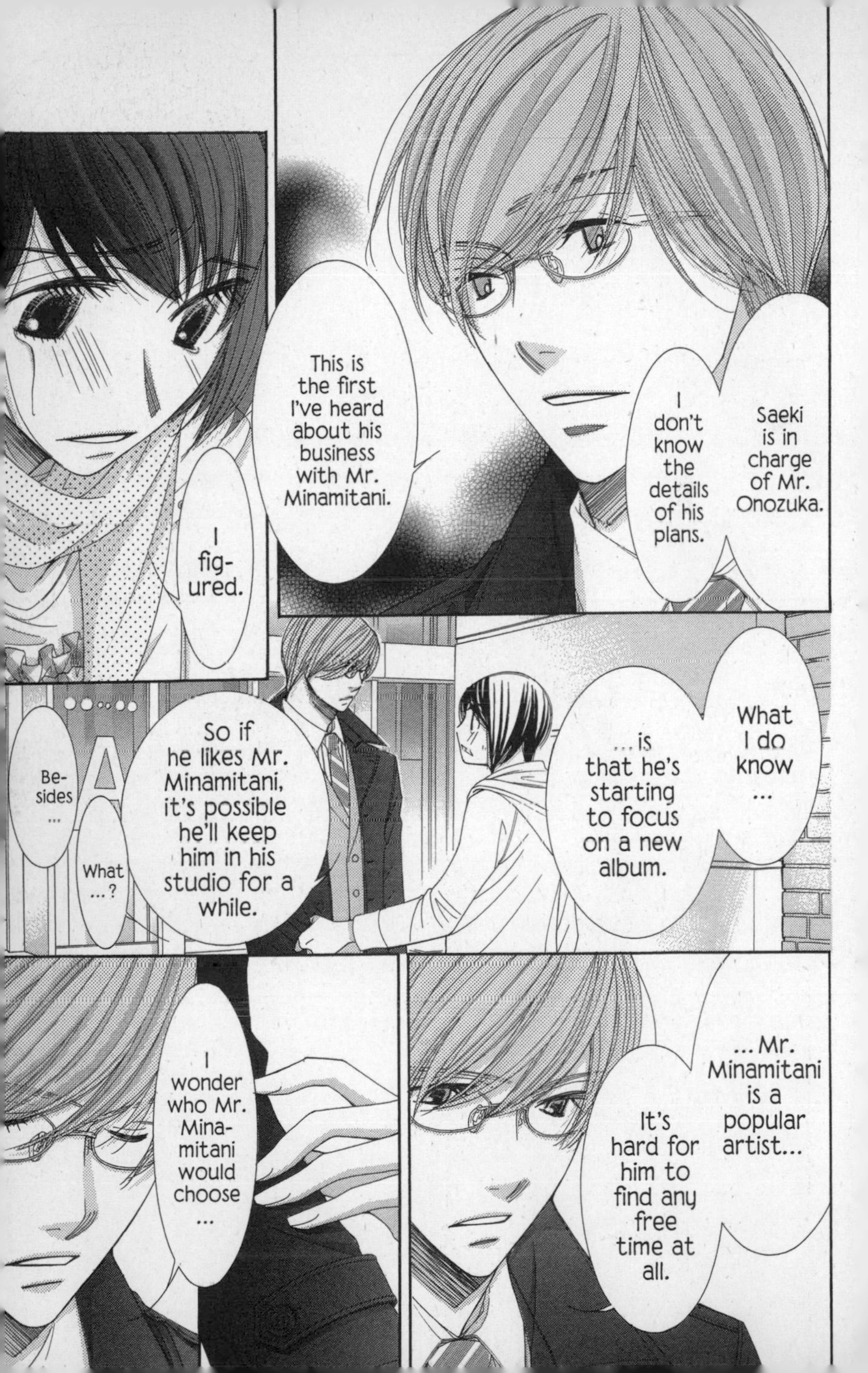
Saeki is in charge of Mr. Onozuka.
I don't know the details of his plans.
This is the first I've heard about his business with Mr. Minamitani.
I figured.
What I do know ...
... is that he's starting to focus on a new album.
So if he likes Mr. Minamitani, it's possible he'll keep him in his studio for a while.
Be-sides ...
What ...?
... Mr. Minamitani is a popular artist...
It's hard for him to find any free time at all.
I wonder who Mr. Mina-mitani would choose ...

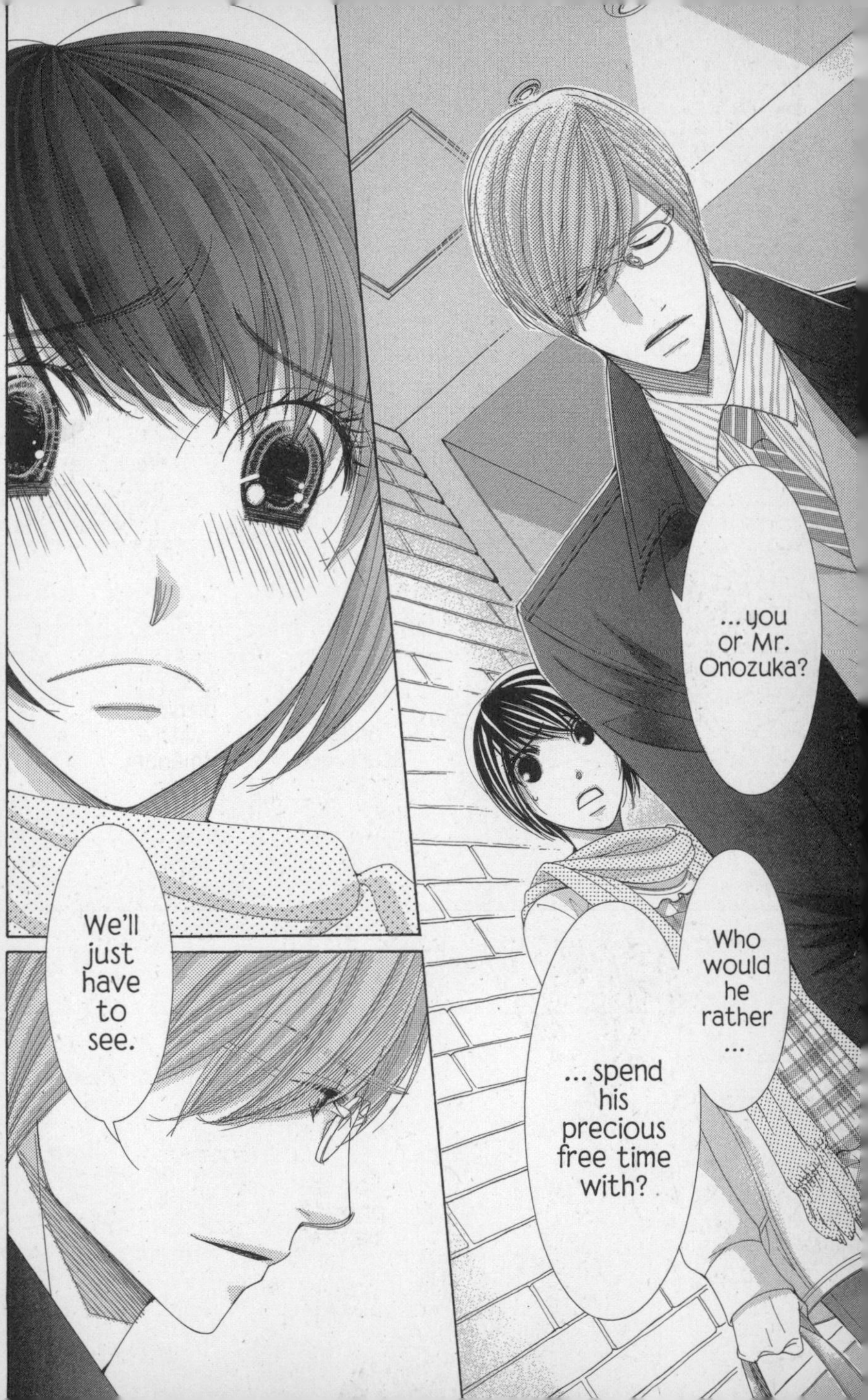
...you or Mr. Onozuka?
Who would he rather ...
...spend his precious free time with?
We'll just have to see.

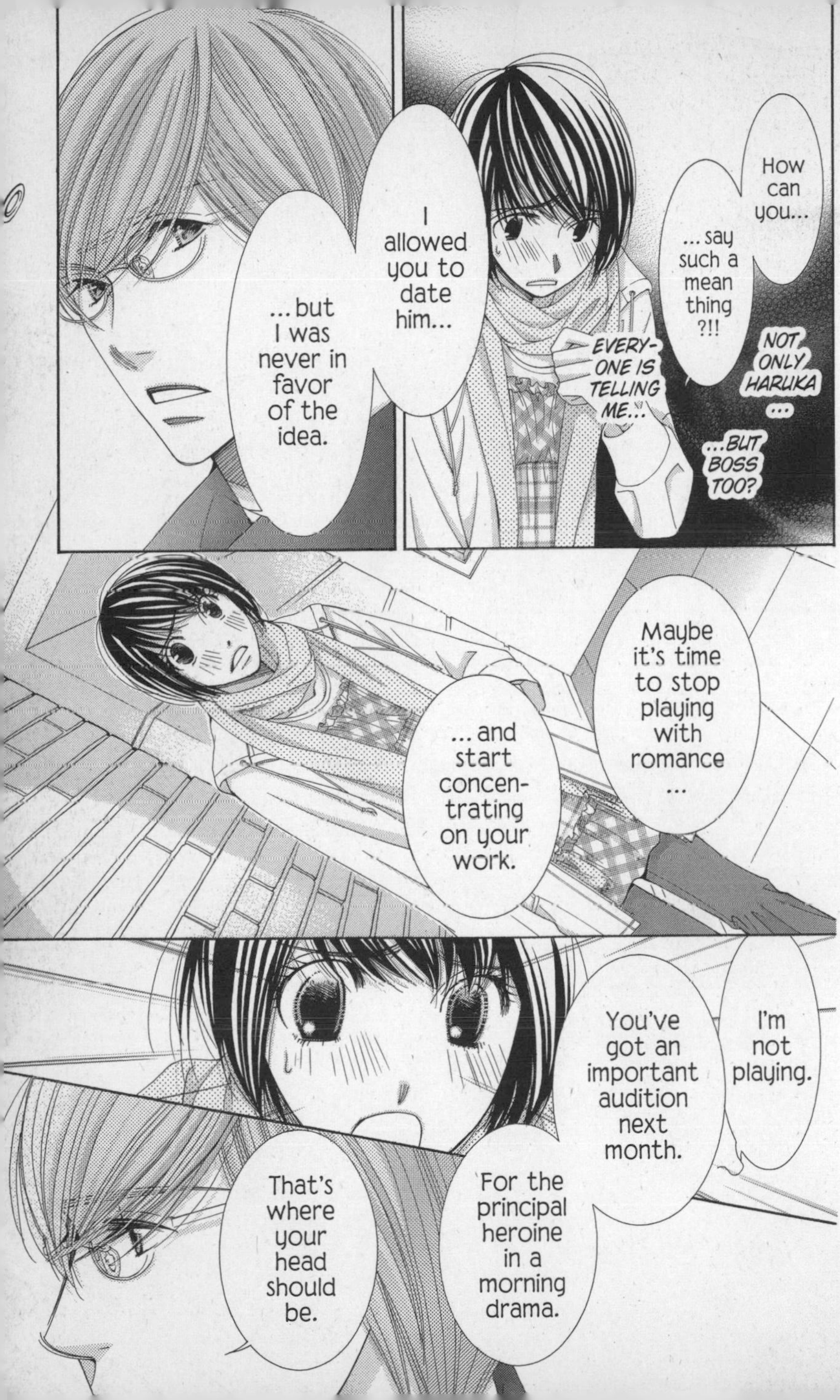
How can you...
... say such a mean thing ?!!
NOT ONLY HARUKA ...
...BUT BOSS TOO?
EVERY-ONE IS TELLING ME...
I allowed you to date him...
... but I was never in favor of the idea.
Maybe it's time to stop playing with romance ...
... and start concen-trating on your work.
I'm not playing.
You've got an important audition next month.
For the principal heroine in a morning drama.
That's where your head should be.

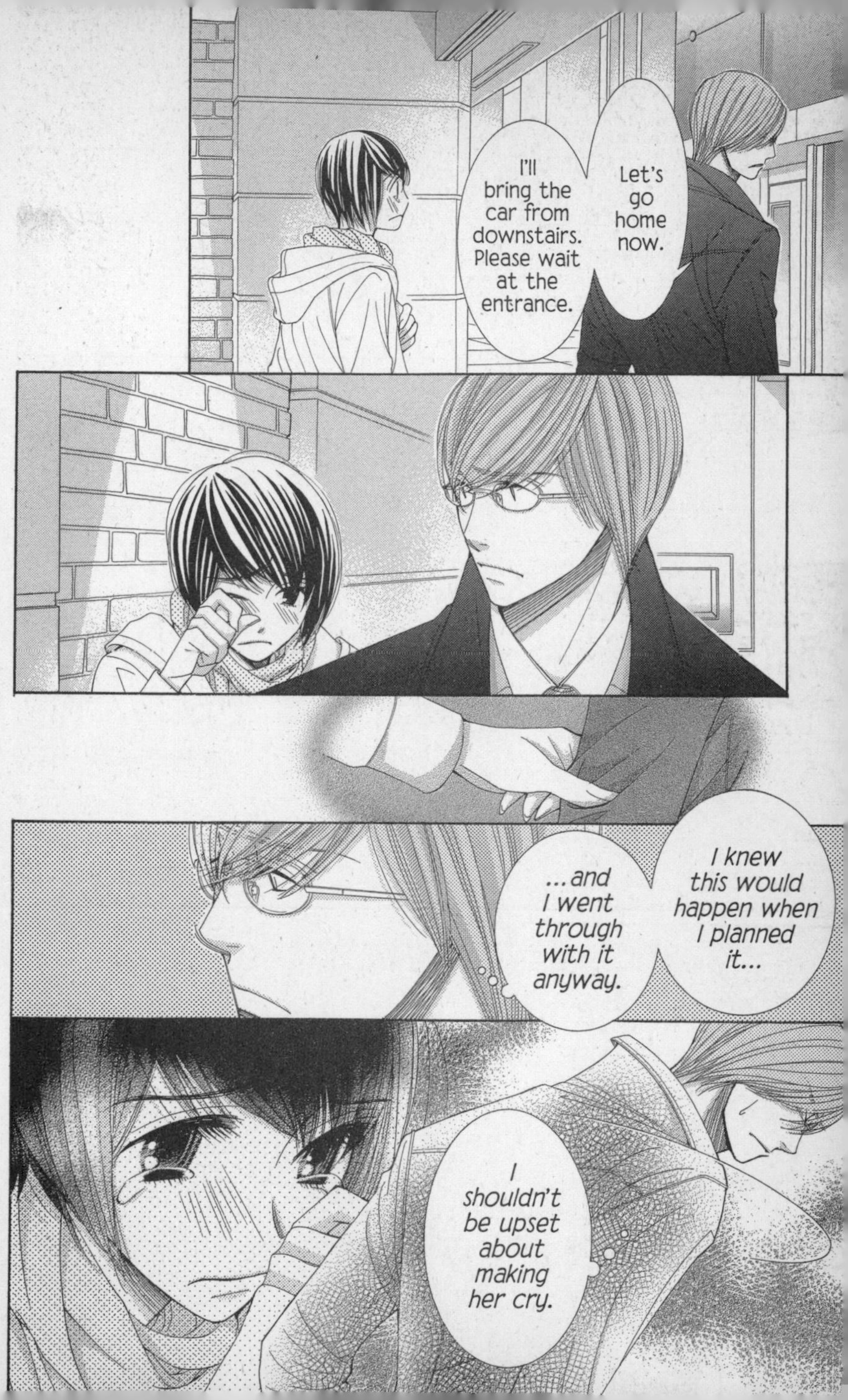
Let's go home now.
I'll bring the car from downstairs. Please wait at the entrance.
I knew this would happen when I planned it...
...and I went through with it anyway.
I shouldn't be upset about making her cry.

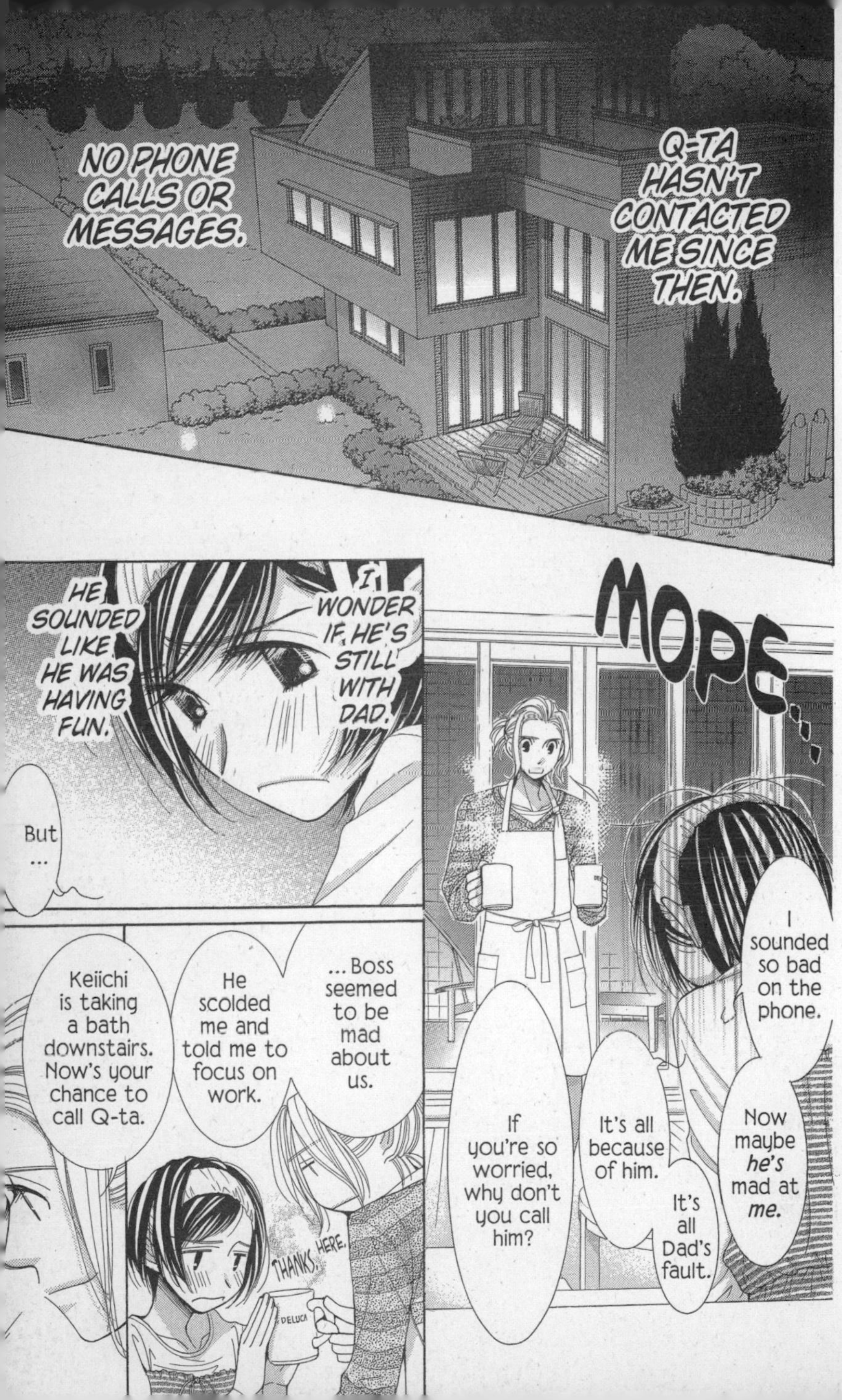
Q-TA HASN'T CONTACTED ME SINCE THEN.
NO PHONE CALLS OR MESSAGES.
MOPE...
I sounded so bad on the phone.
Now maybe *he's* mad at *me*.
It's all Dad's fault.
It's all because of him.
If you're so worried, why don't you call him?
I WONDER IF HE'S STILL WITH DAD.
HE SOUNDED LIKE HE WAS HAVING FUN.
But ...
... Boss seemed to be mad about us.
He scolded me and told me to focus on work.
Keiichi is taking a bath downstairs. Now's your chance to call Q-ta.
HERE.
THANKS.
DELUCA

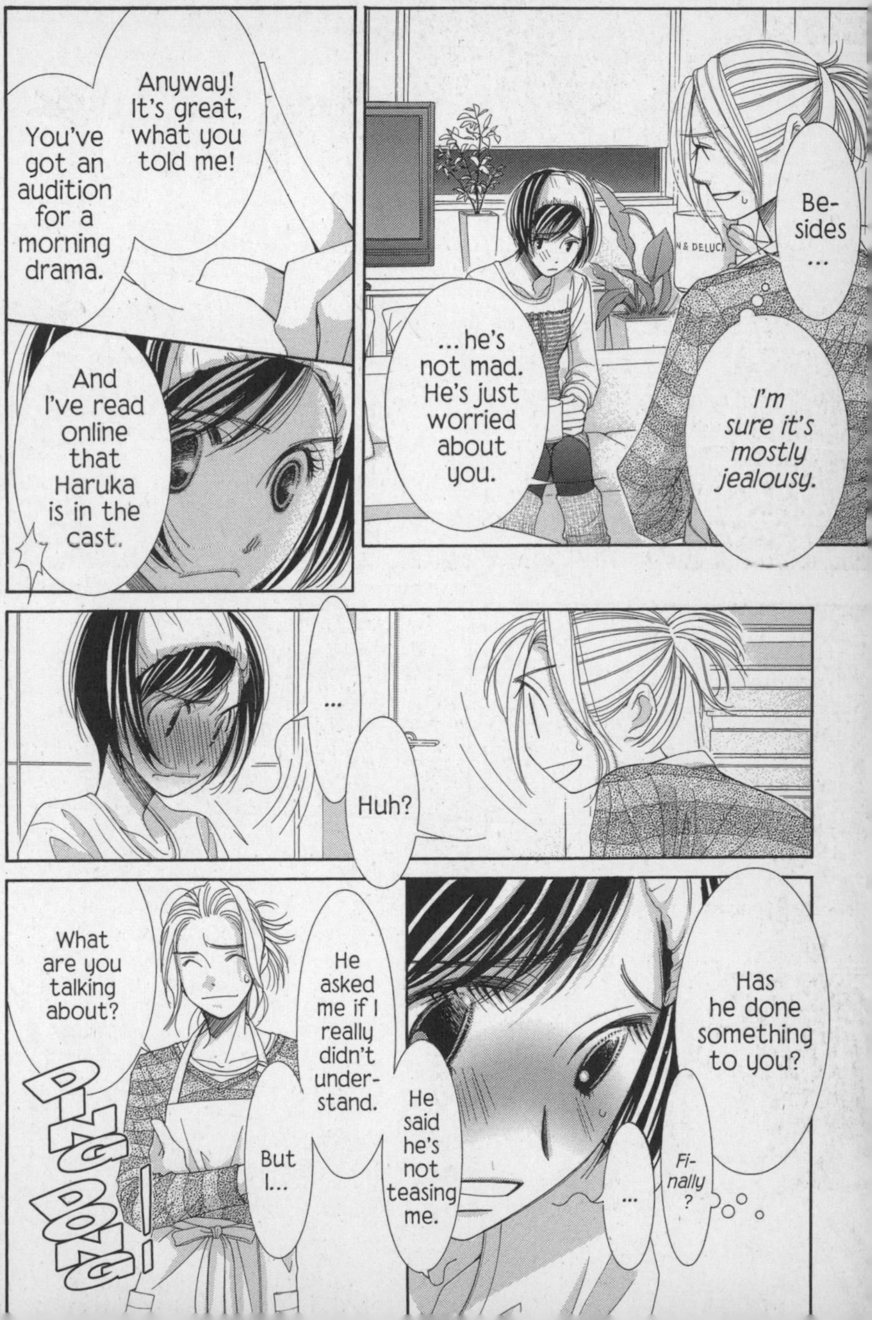
...he's not mad. He's just worried about you.
Be-sides...
I'm sure it's mostly jealousy.
Anyway! It's great, what you told me!
You've got an audition for a morning drama.
And I've read online that Haruka is in the cast.
...
Huh?
Has he done something to you?
Fi-nally?
...
He asked me if I really didn't understand.
He said he's not teasing me.
But I...
What are you talking about?
DING DONG

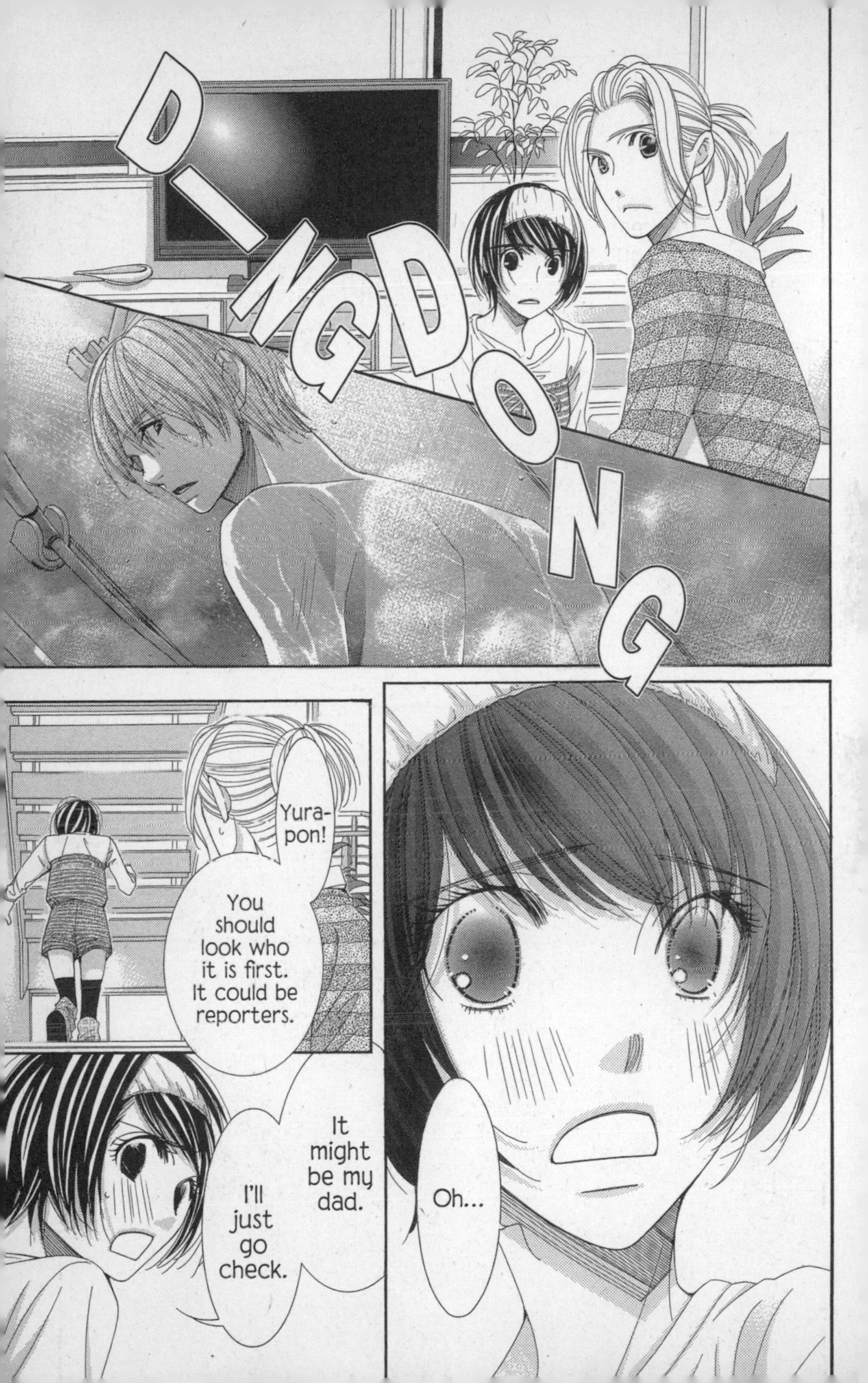
DINGDONG
Oh...
Yura-pon!
You should look who it is first. It could be reporters.
It might be my dad.
I'll just go check.

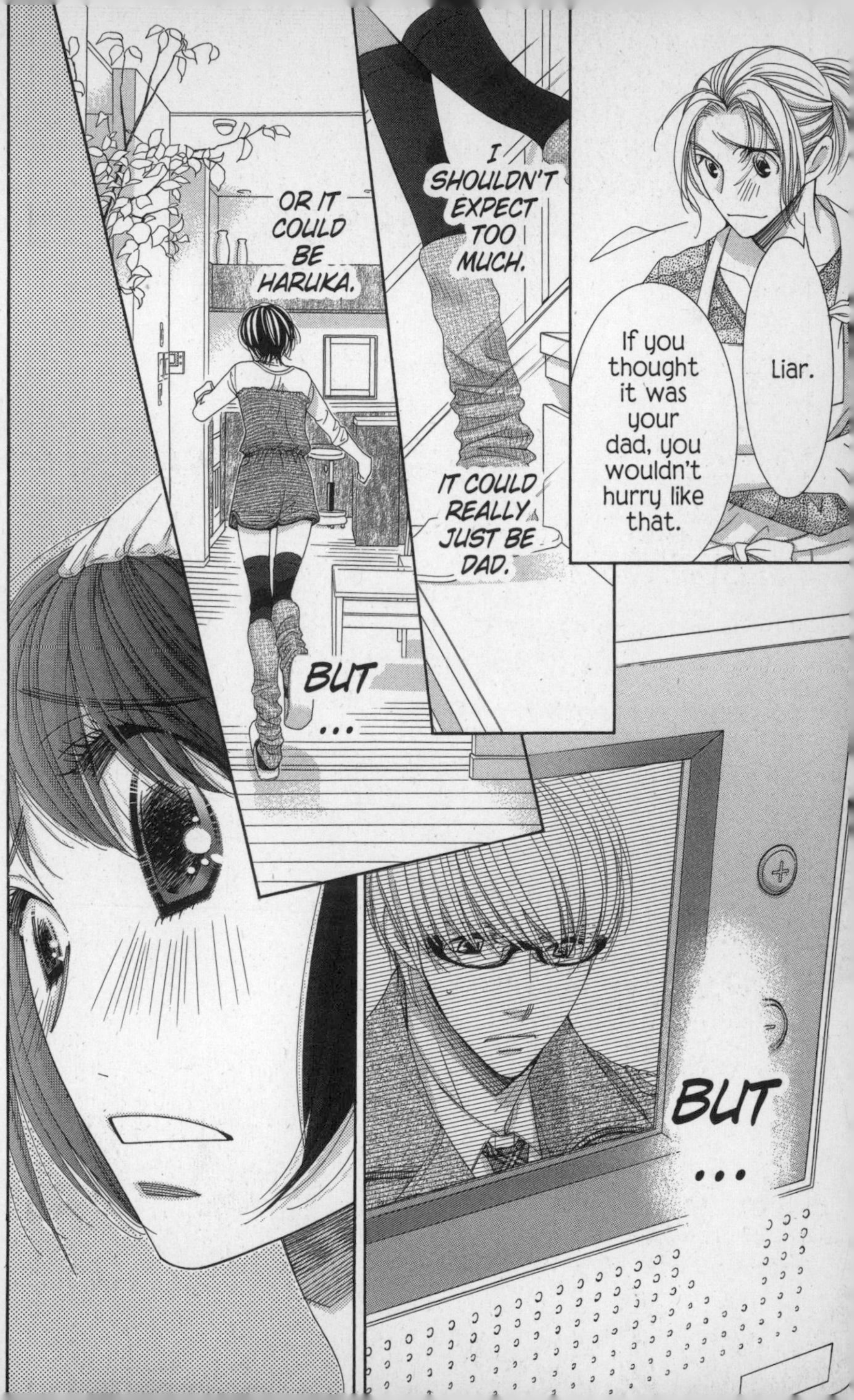

Liar.
If you thought it was your dad, you wouldn't hurry like that.
I SHOULDN'T EXPECT TOO MUCH.
IT COULD REALLY JUST BE DAD.
OR IT COULD BE HARUKA.
BUT ...
BUT ...

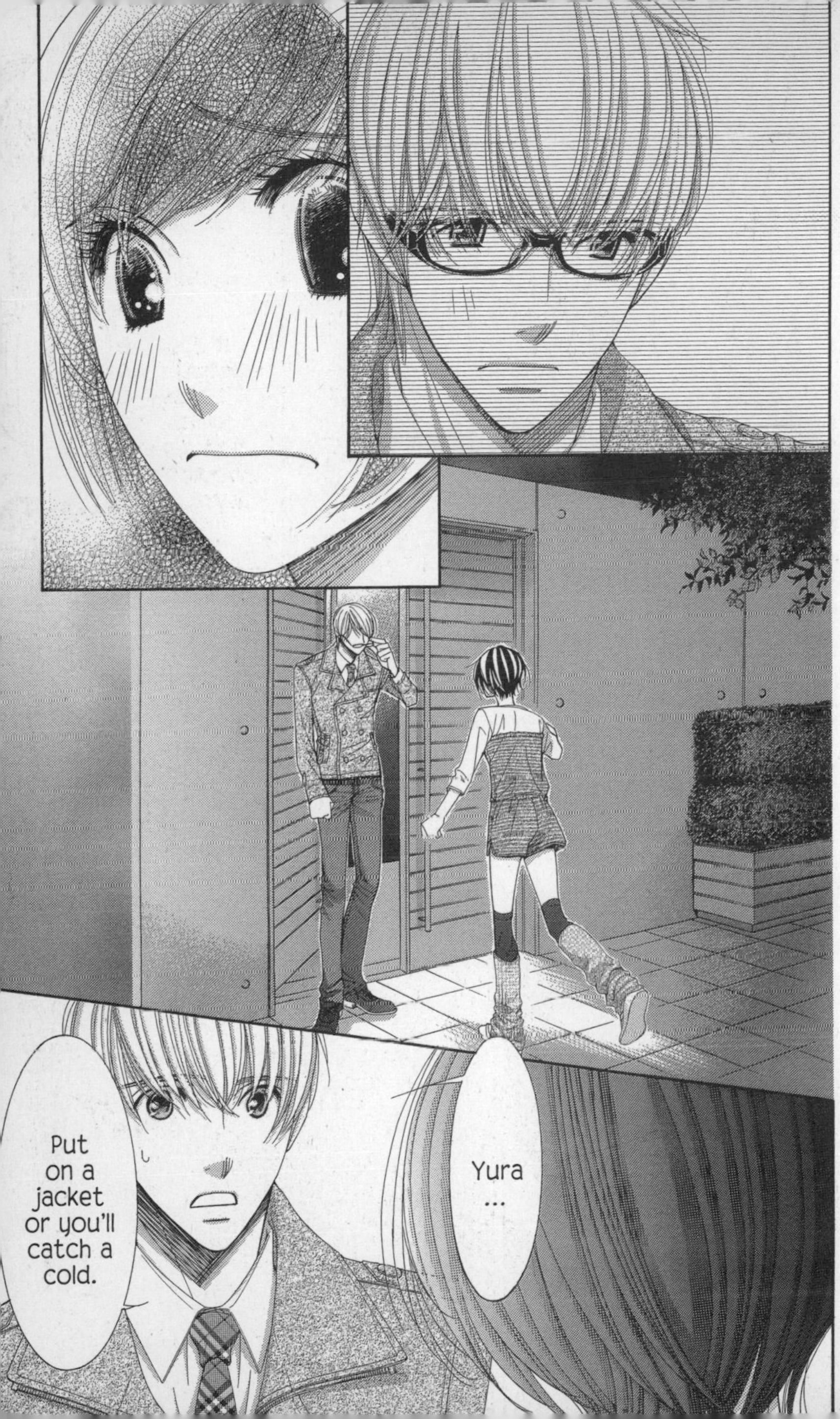
Yura ...
Put on a jacket or you'll catch a cold.

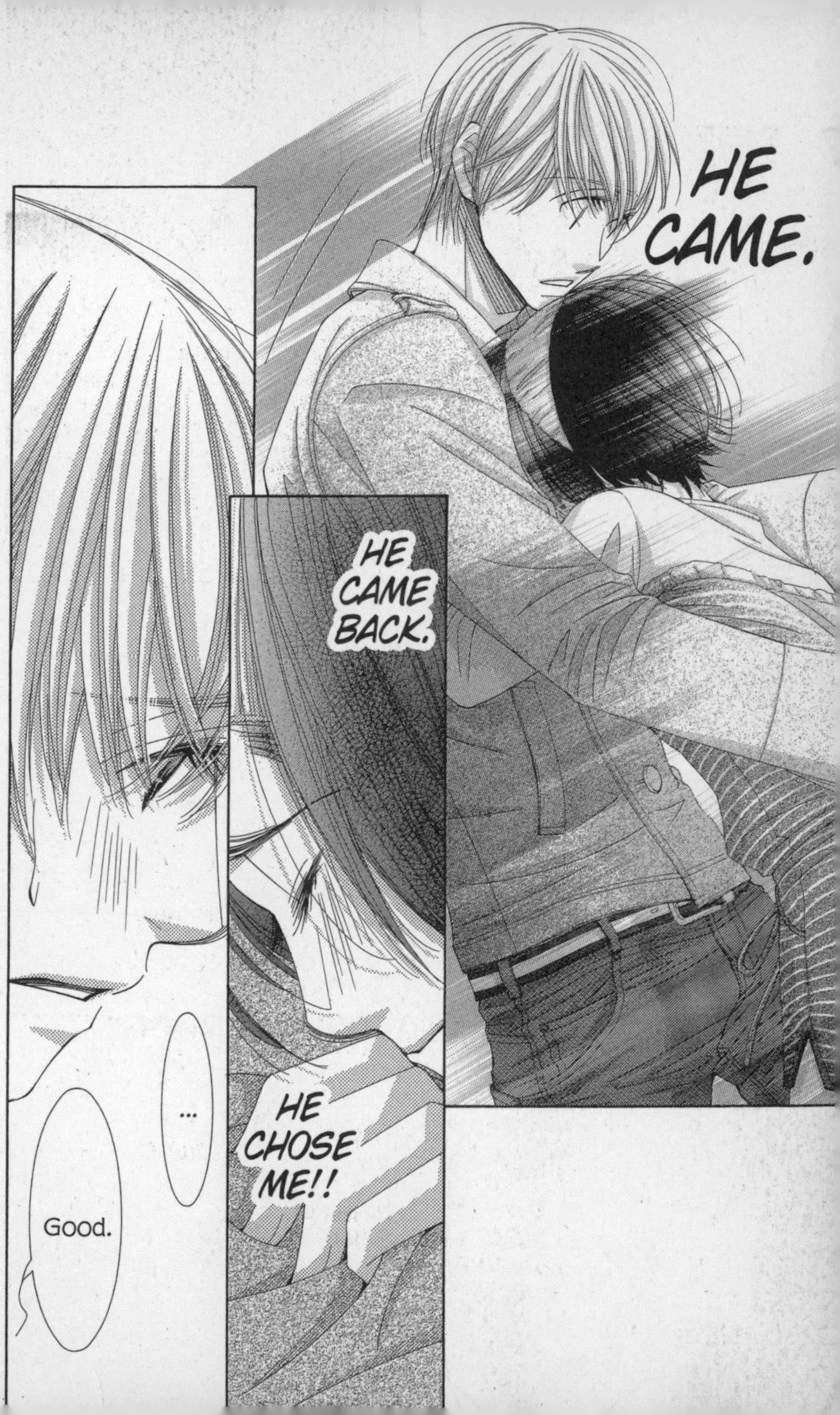
HE CAME.
HE CAME BACK.
HE CHOSE ME!!
...
Good.

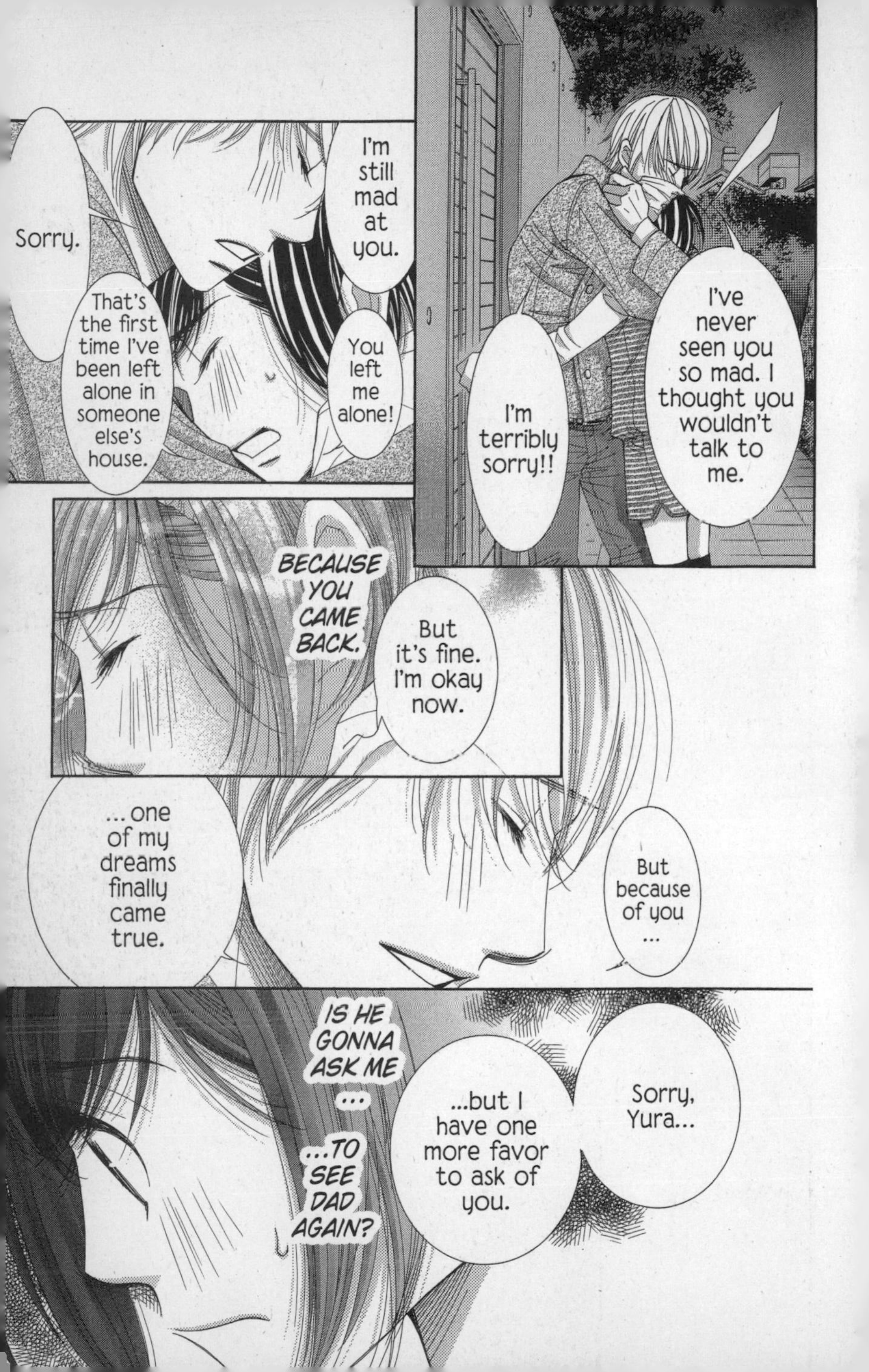
I've never seen you so mad. I thought you wouldn't talk to me.
I'm terribly sorry!!
I'm still mad at you.
You left me alone!
Sorry.
That's the first time I've been left alone in someone else's house.
But it's fine. I'm okay now.
BECAUSE YOU CAME BACK.
But because of you ...
...one of my dreams finally came true.
Sorry, Yura...
...but I have one more favor to ask of you.
IS HE GONNA ASK ME ...
...TO SEE DAD AGAIN?

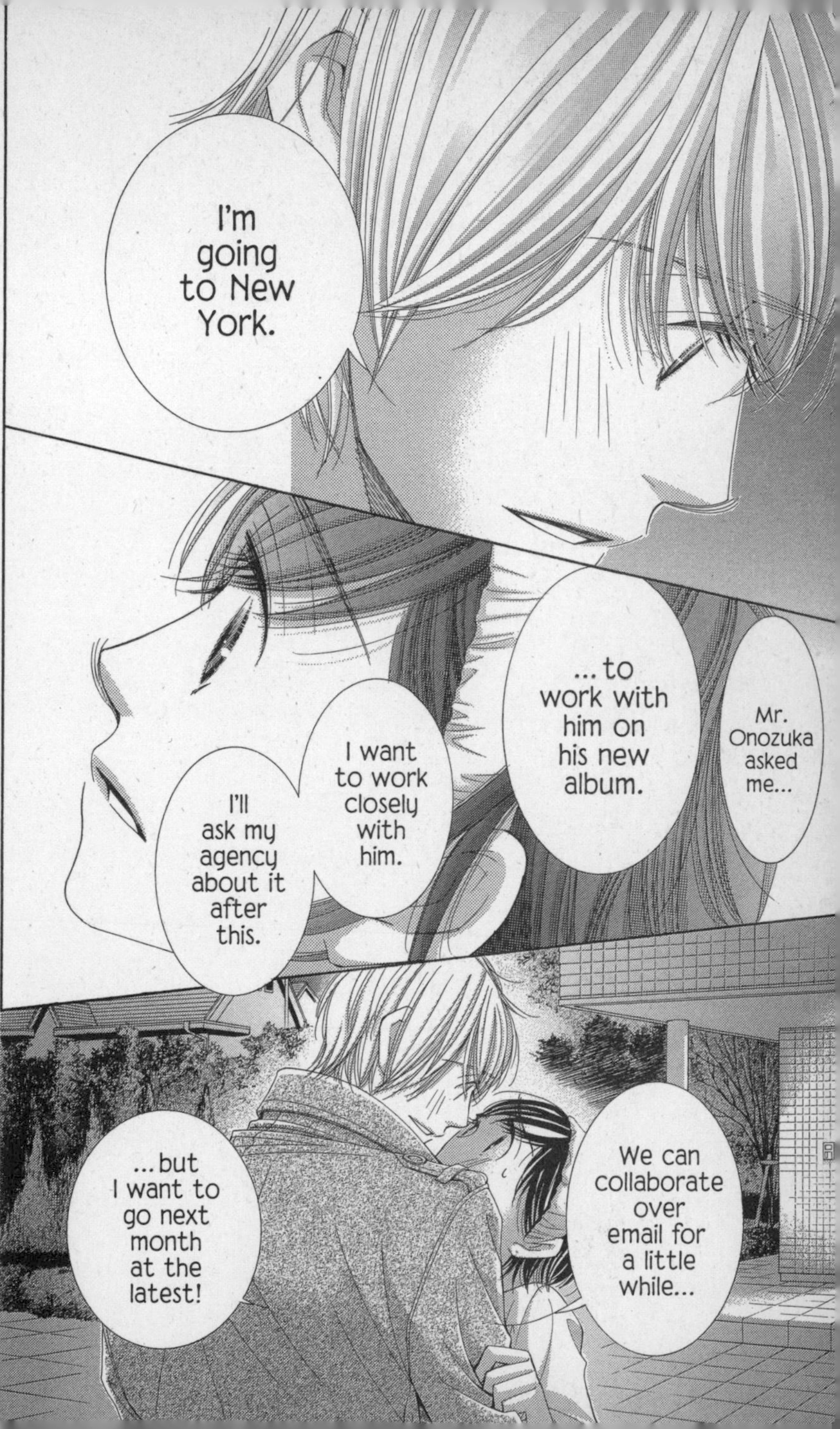
I'm going to New York.
Mr. Onozuka asked me...
...to work with him on his new album.
I want to work closely with him.
I'll ask my agency about it after this.
We can collaborate over email for a little while...
...but I want to go next month at the latest!

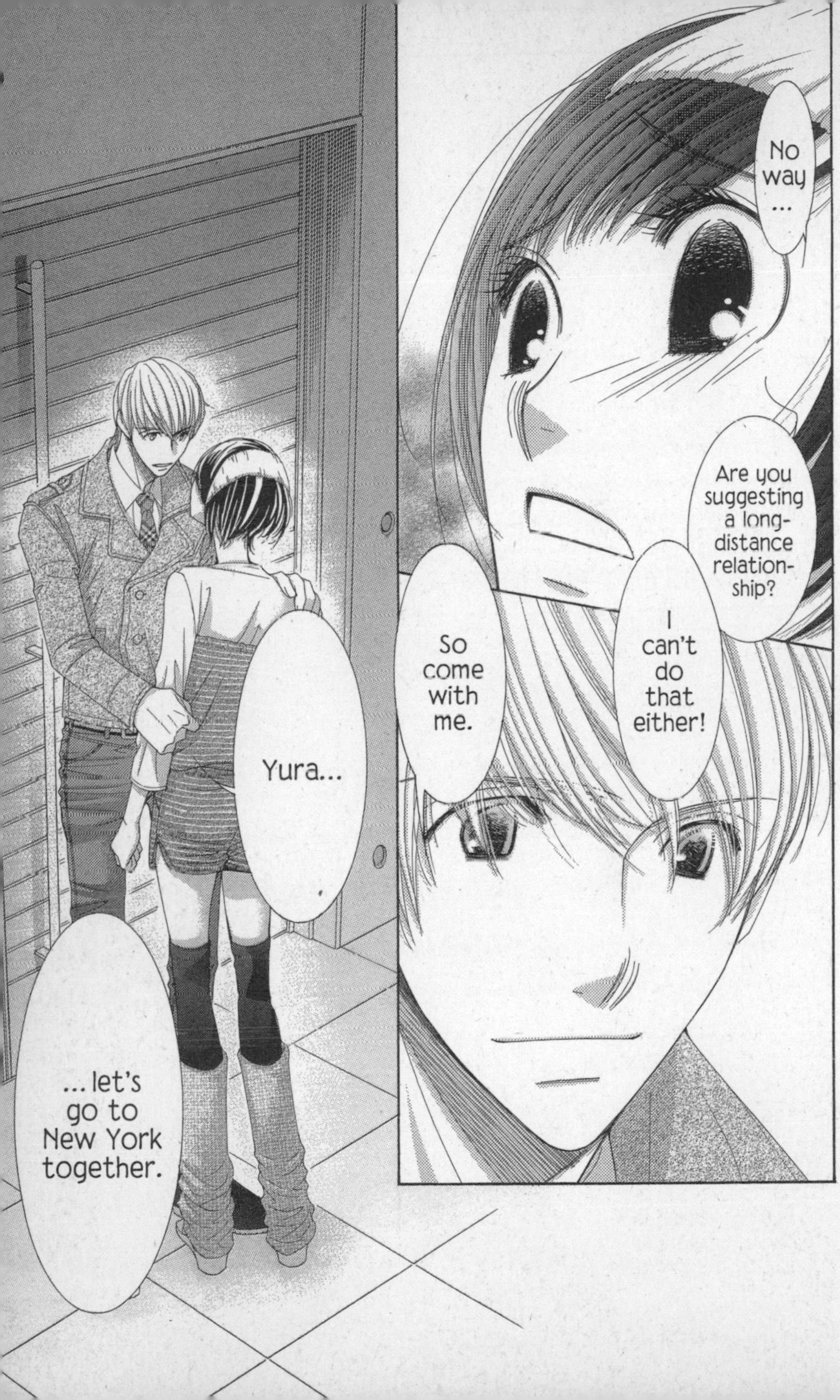
No way ...
Are you suggesting a long-distance relationship?
I can't do that either!
So come with me.
Yura...
... let's go to New York together.

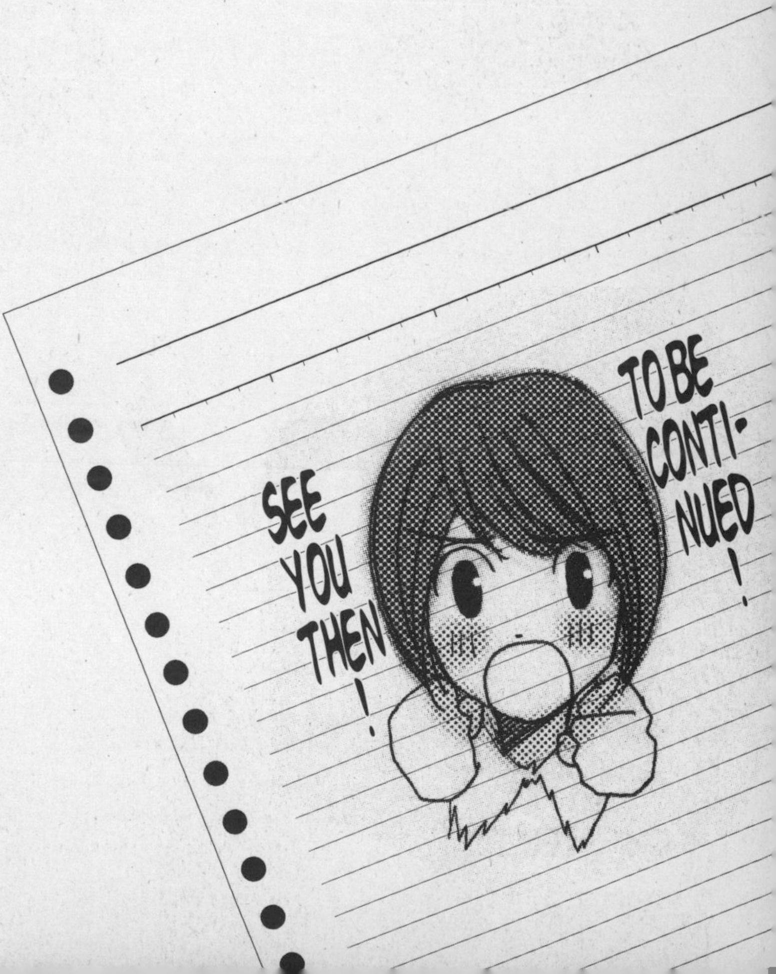
TO BE CONTI-NUED!
SEE YOU THEN!

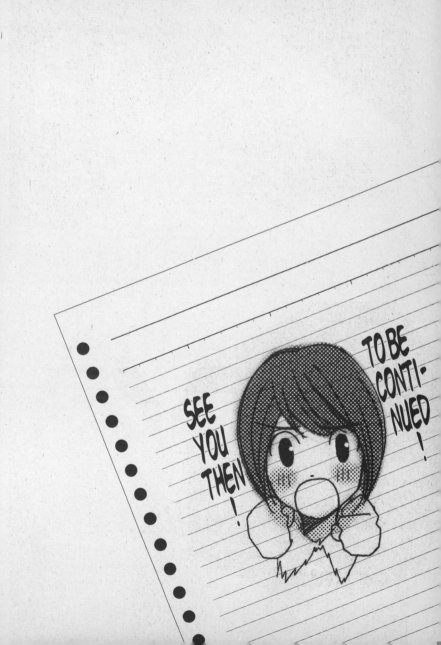

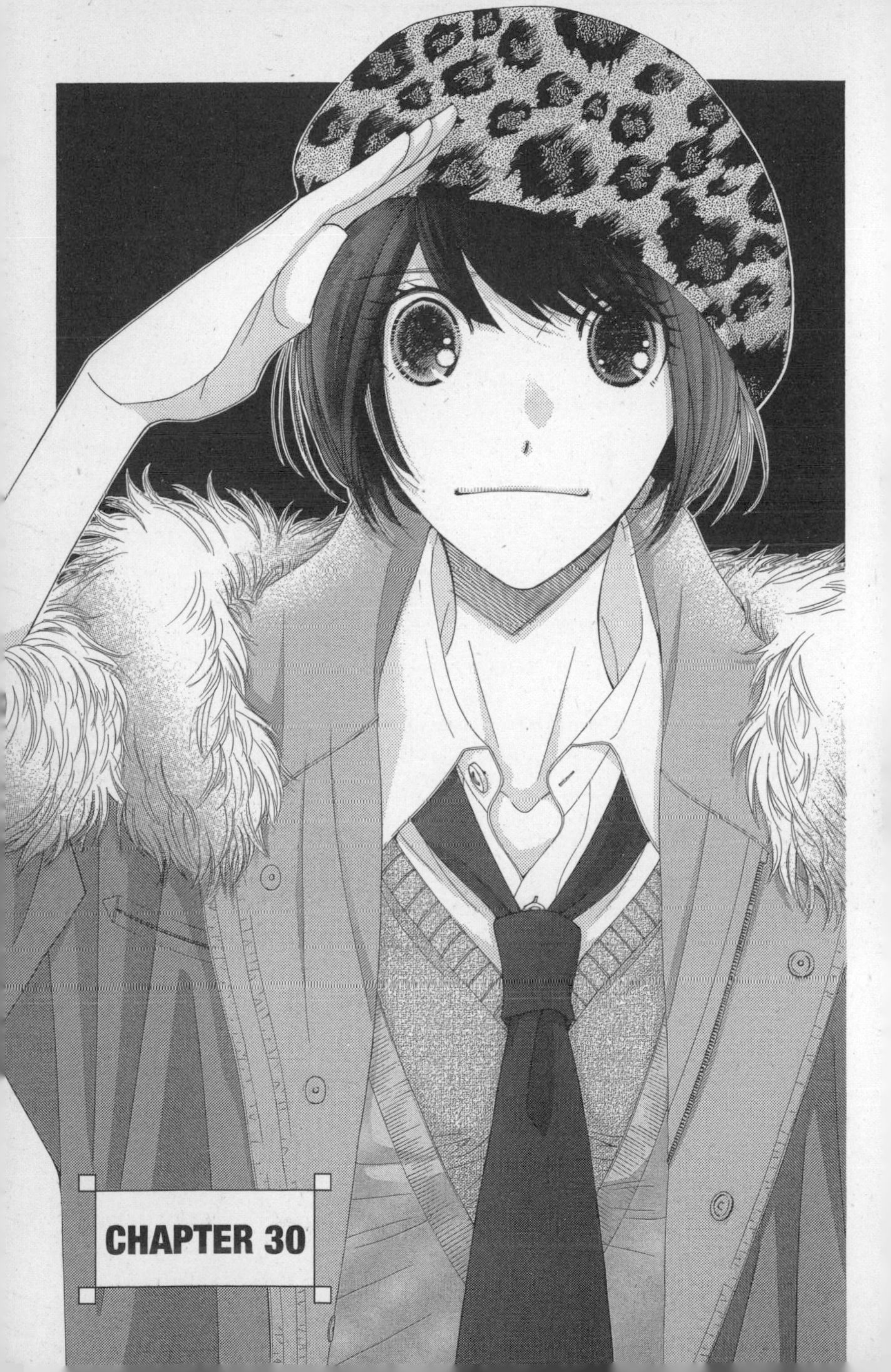
CHAPTER 30

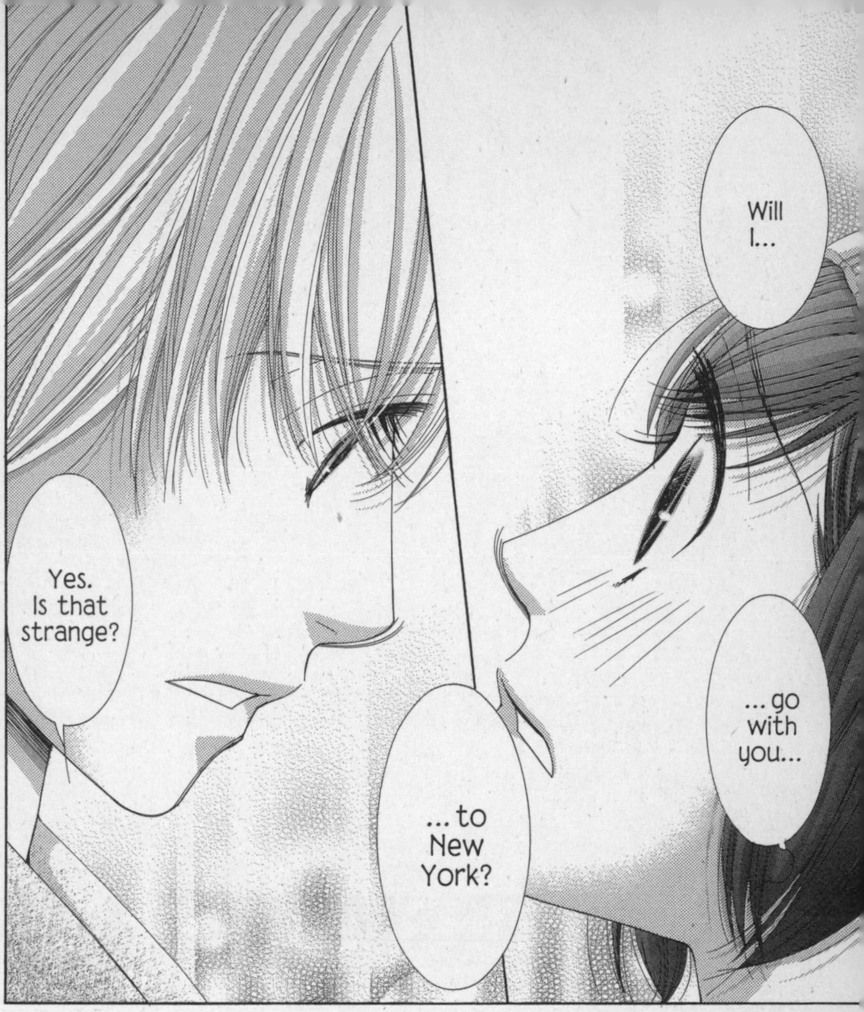
Will I...
...go with you...
...to New York?
Yes. Is that strange?

Honey Hunt

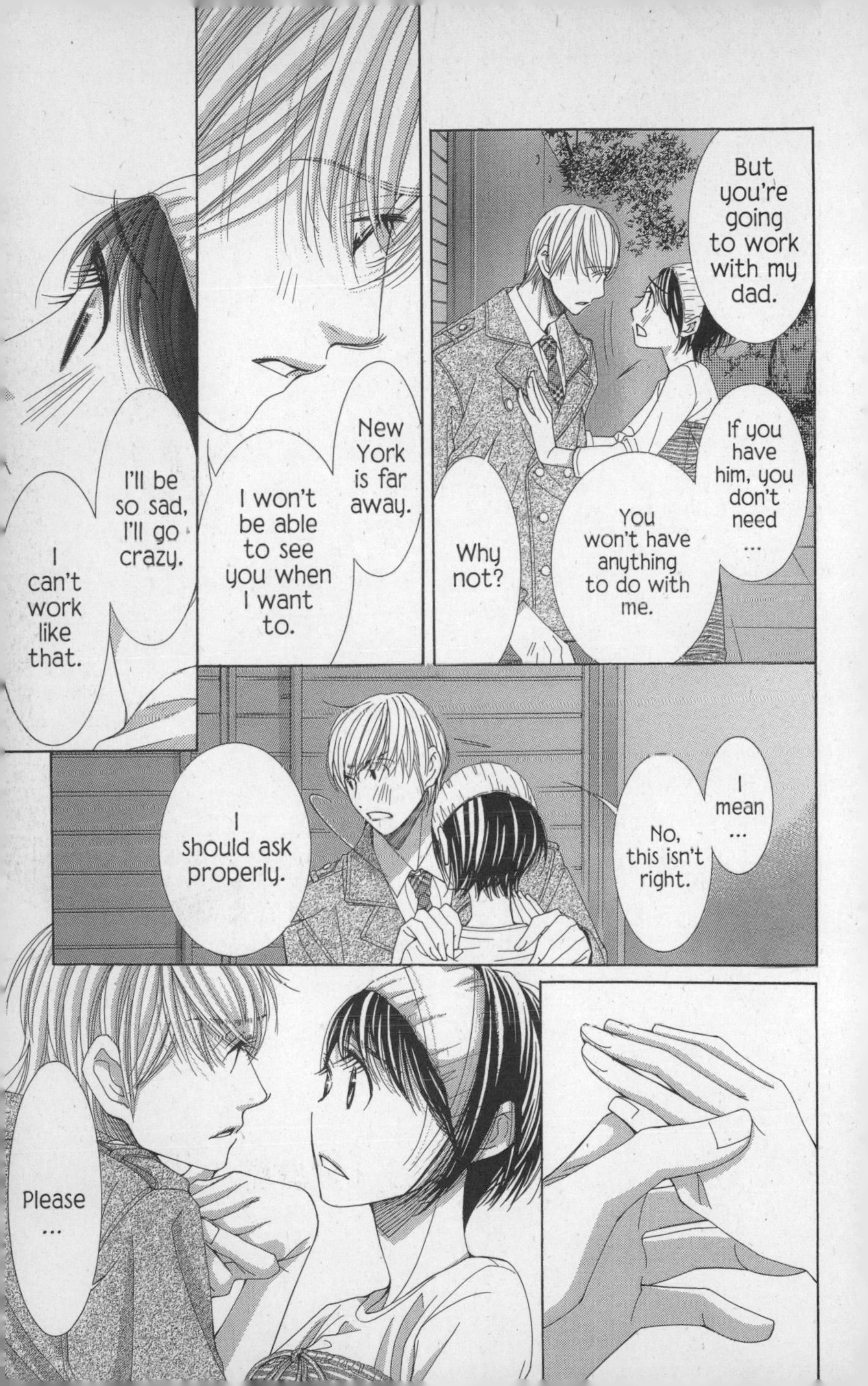
But you're going to work with my dad.
If you have him, you don't need ...
You won't have anything to do with me.
Why not?
New York is far away.
I won't be able to see you when I want to.
I'll be so sad, I'll go crazy.
I can't work like that.
I mean ...
No, this isn't right.
I should ask properly.
Please ...

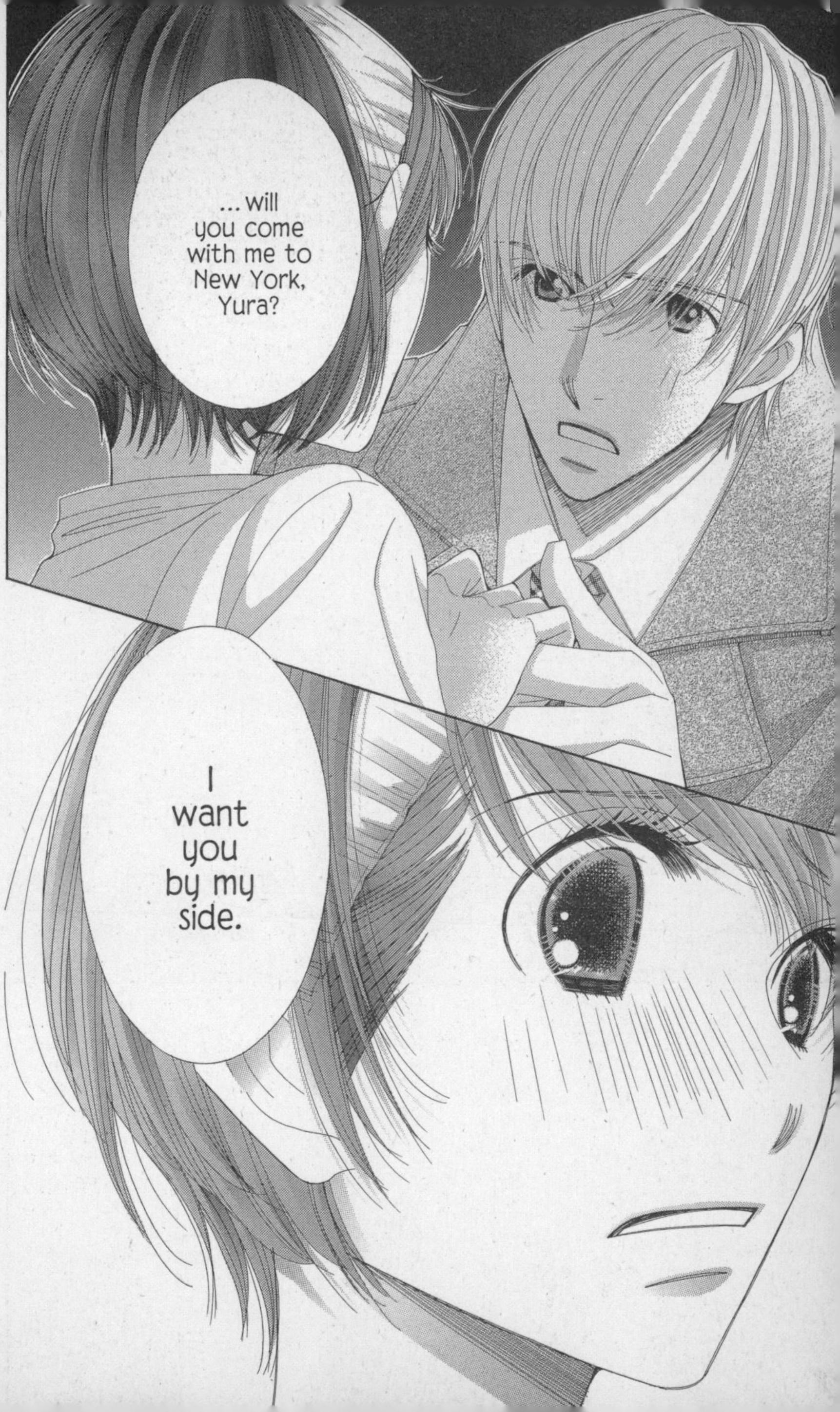
...will you come with me to New York, Yura?
I want you by my side.

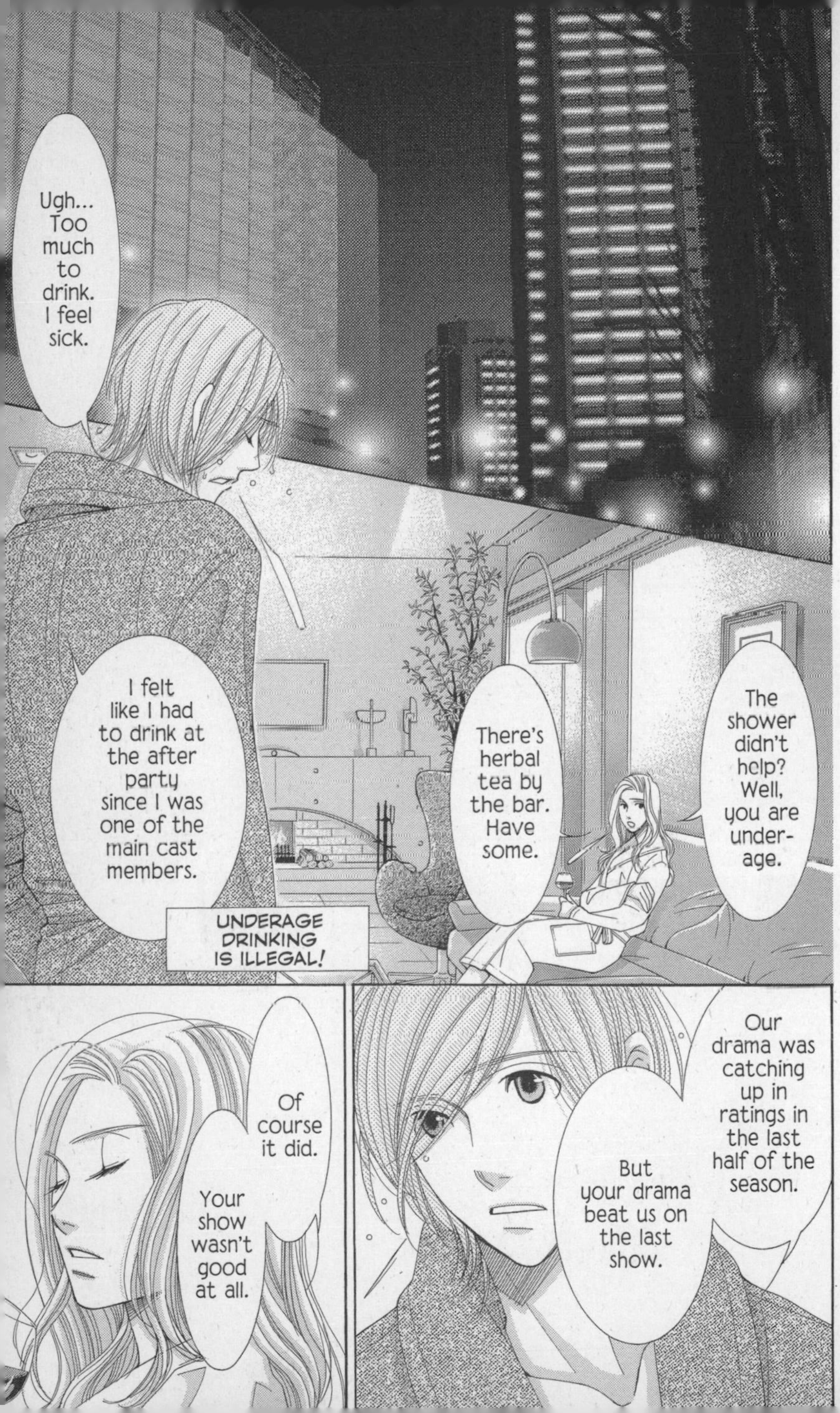
Ugh... Too much to drink. I feel sick.
The shower didn't help? Well, you are under-age.
There's herbal tea by the bar. Have some.
I felt like I had to drink at the after party since I was one of the main cast members.
UNDERAGE DRINKING IS ILLEGAL!
Our drama was catching up in ratings in the last half of the season.
But your drama beat us on the last show.
Of course it did.
Your show wasn't good at all.

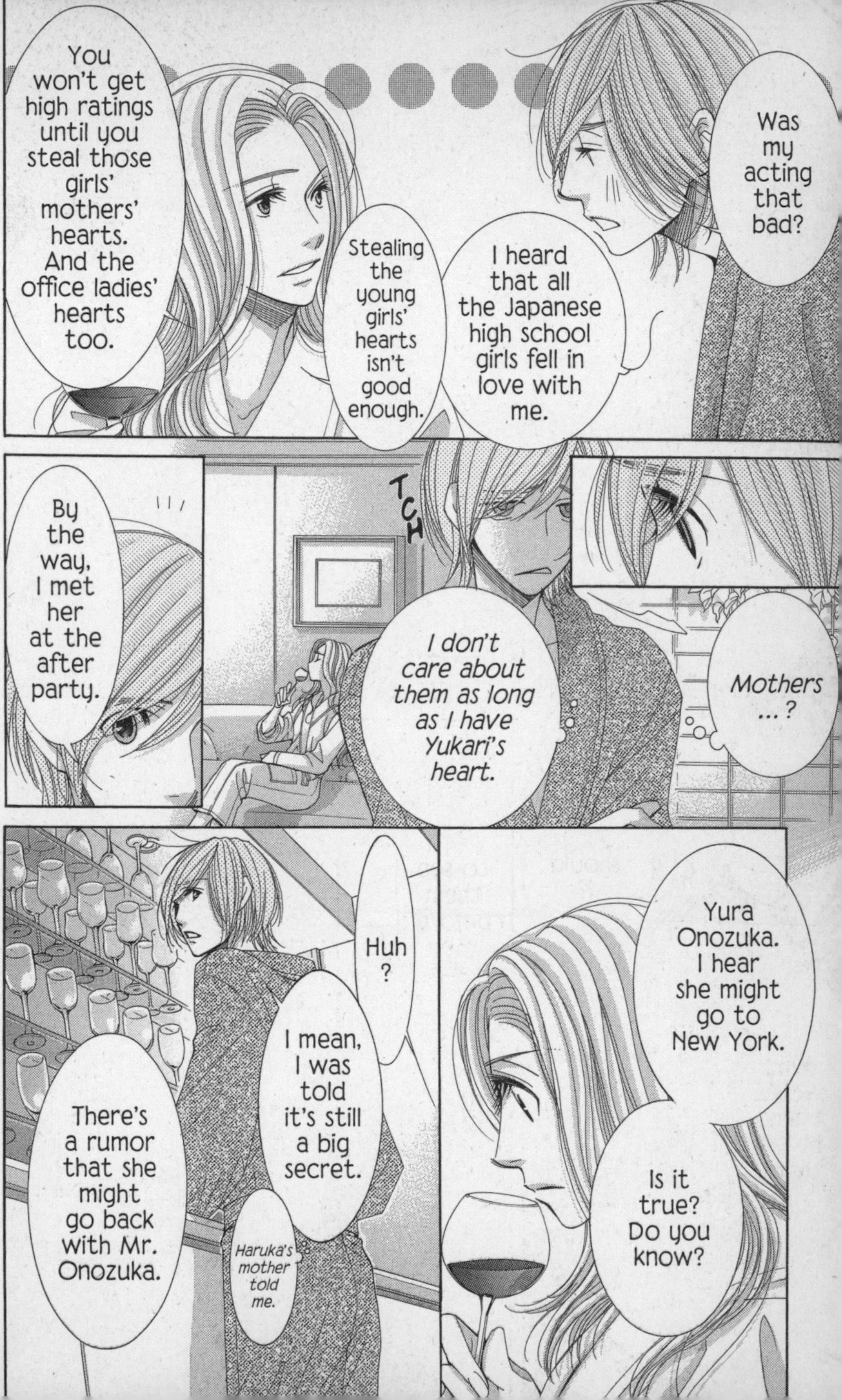
Was my acting that bad?
I heard that all the Japanese high school girls fell in love with me.
Stealing the young girls' hearts isn't good enough.
You won't get high ratings until you steal those girls' mothers' hearts. And the office ladies' hearts too.
Mothers ...?
TCH
I don't care about them as long as I have Yukari's heart.
By the way, I met her at the after party.
Yura Onozuka. I hear she might go to New York.
Is it true? Do you know?
Huh?
I mean, I was told it's still a big secret.
Haruka's mother told me.
There's a rumor that she might go back with Mr. Onozuka.

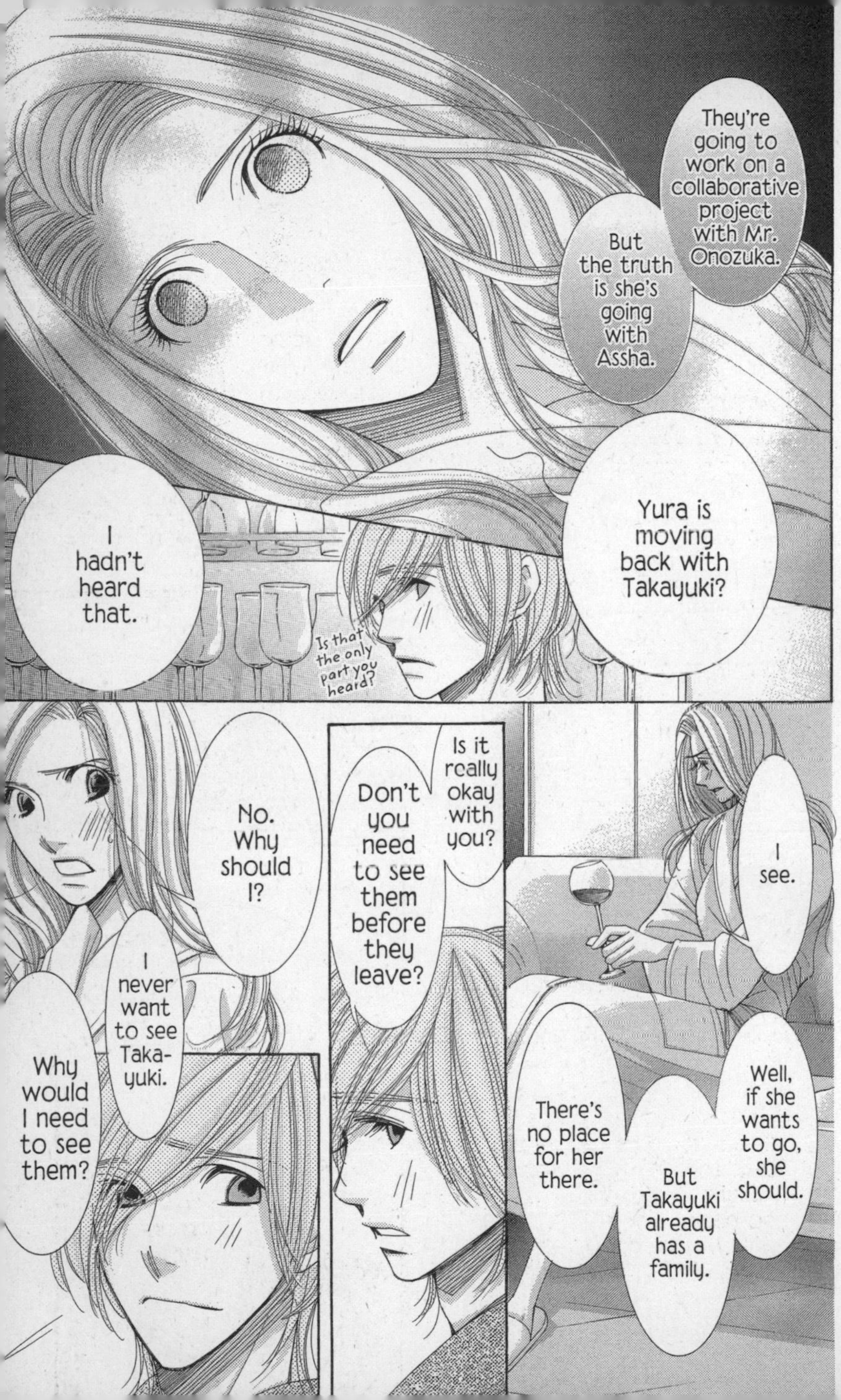
They're going to work on a collaborative project with Mr. Onozuka.
But the truth is she's going with Assha.
Yura is moving back with Takayuki?
I hadn't heard that.
Is that the only part you heard?
I see.
Well, if she wants to go, she should.
But Takayuki already has a family.
There's no place for her there.
Is it really okay with you?
Don't you need to see them before they leave?
No. Why should I?
I never want to see Taka-yuki.
Why would I need to see them?

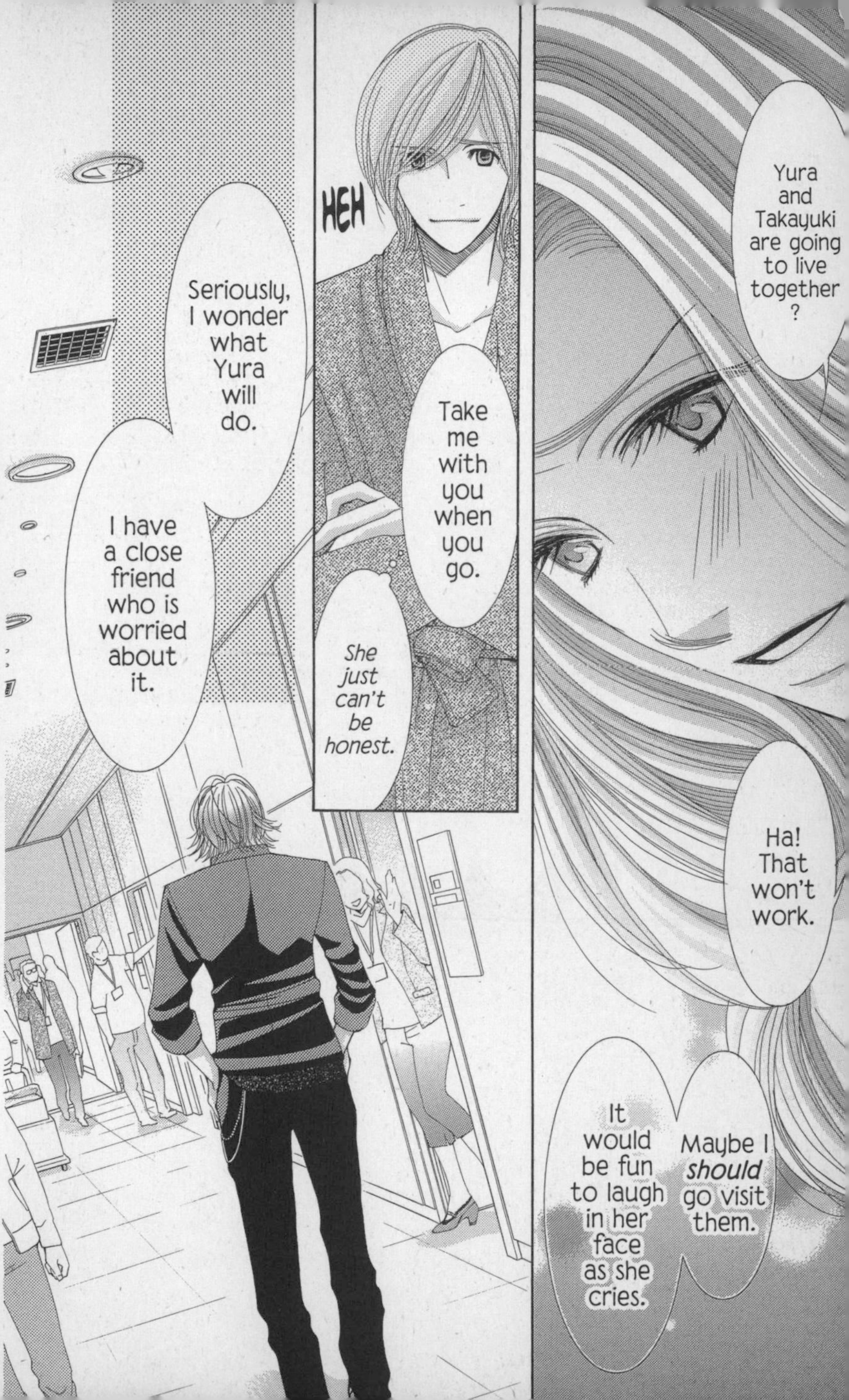
Yura and Takayuki are going to live together?
Ha! That won't work.
Maybe I *should* go visit them.
It would be fun to laugh in her face as she cries.
HEH
Take me with you when you go.
*She just can't be honest.*
Seriously, I wonder what Yura will do.
I have a close friend who is worried about it.

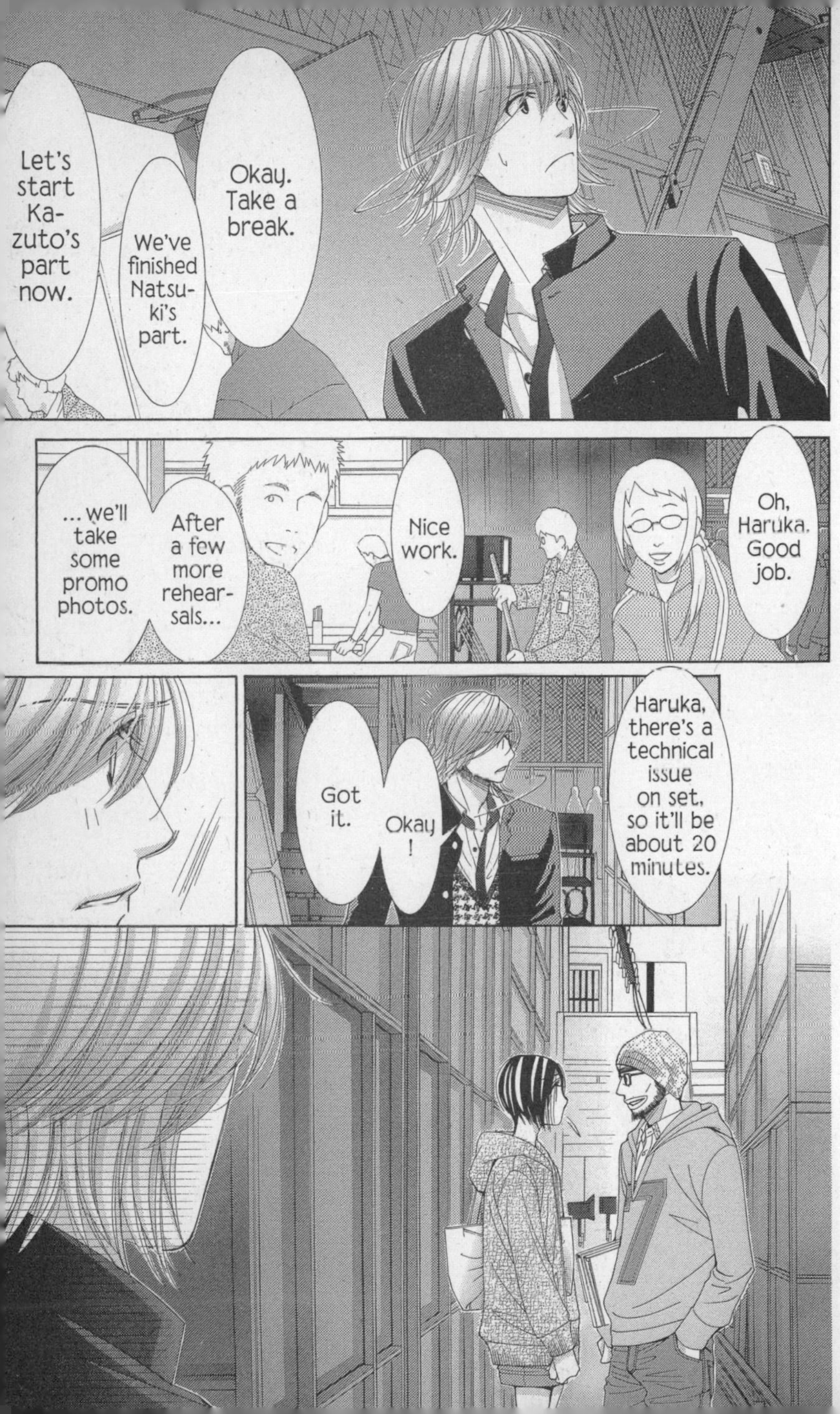
Okay. Take a break.
We've finished Natsuki's part.
Let's start Kazuto's part now.
Oh, Haruka. Good job.
Nice work.
After a few more rehearsals...
... we'll take some promo photos.
Haruka, there's a technical issue on set, so it'll be about 20 minutes.
Okay!
Got it.

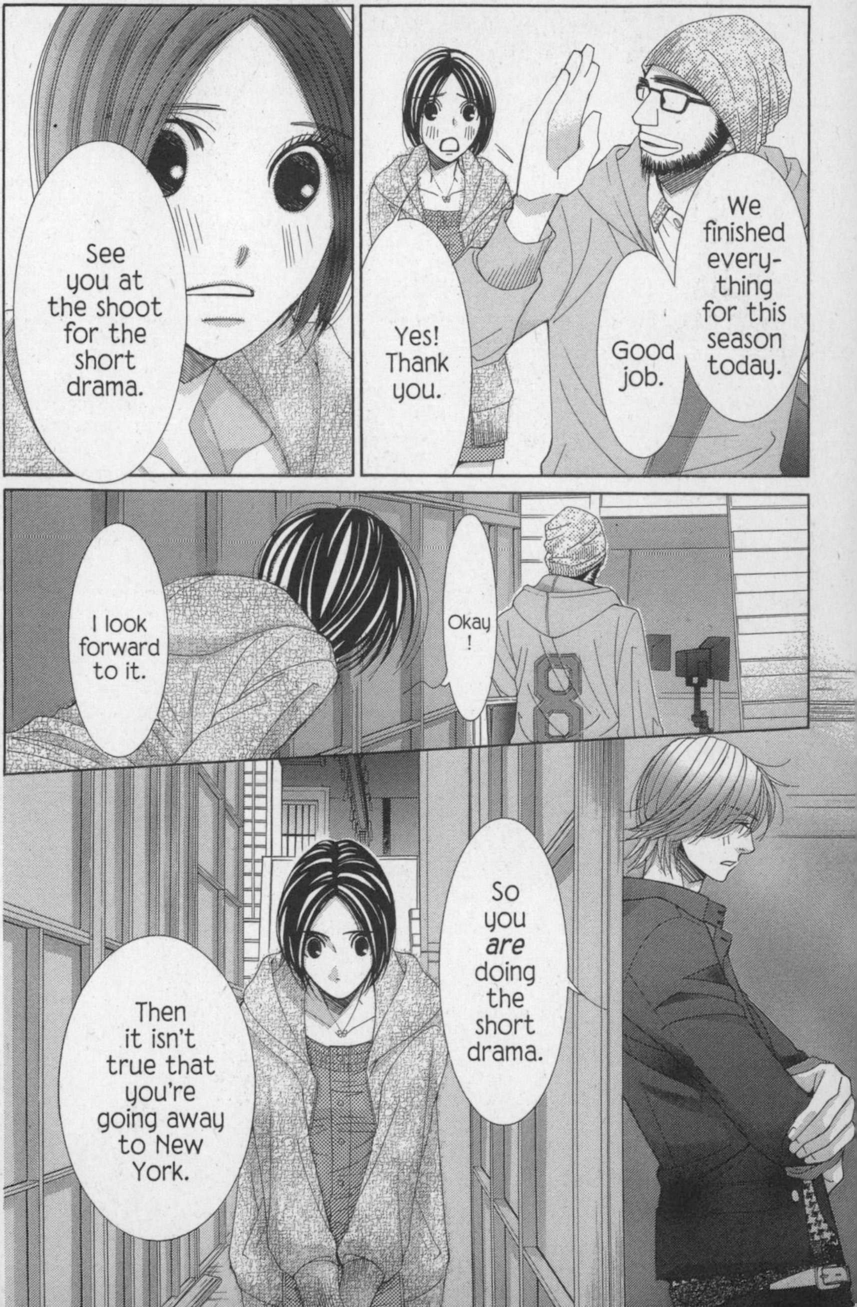
We finished every-thing for this season today.
Good job.
Yes! Thank you.
See you at the shoot for the short drama.
Okay!
I look forward to it.
So you *are* doing the short drama.
Then it isn't true that you're going away to New York.

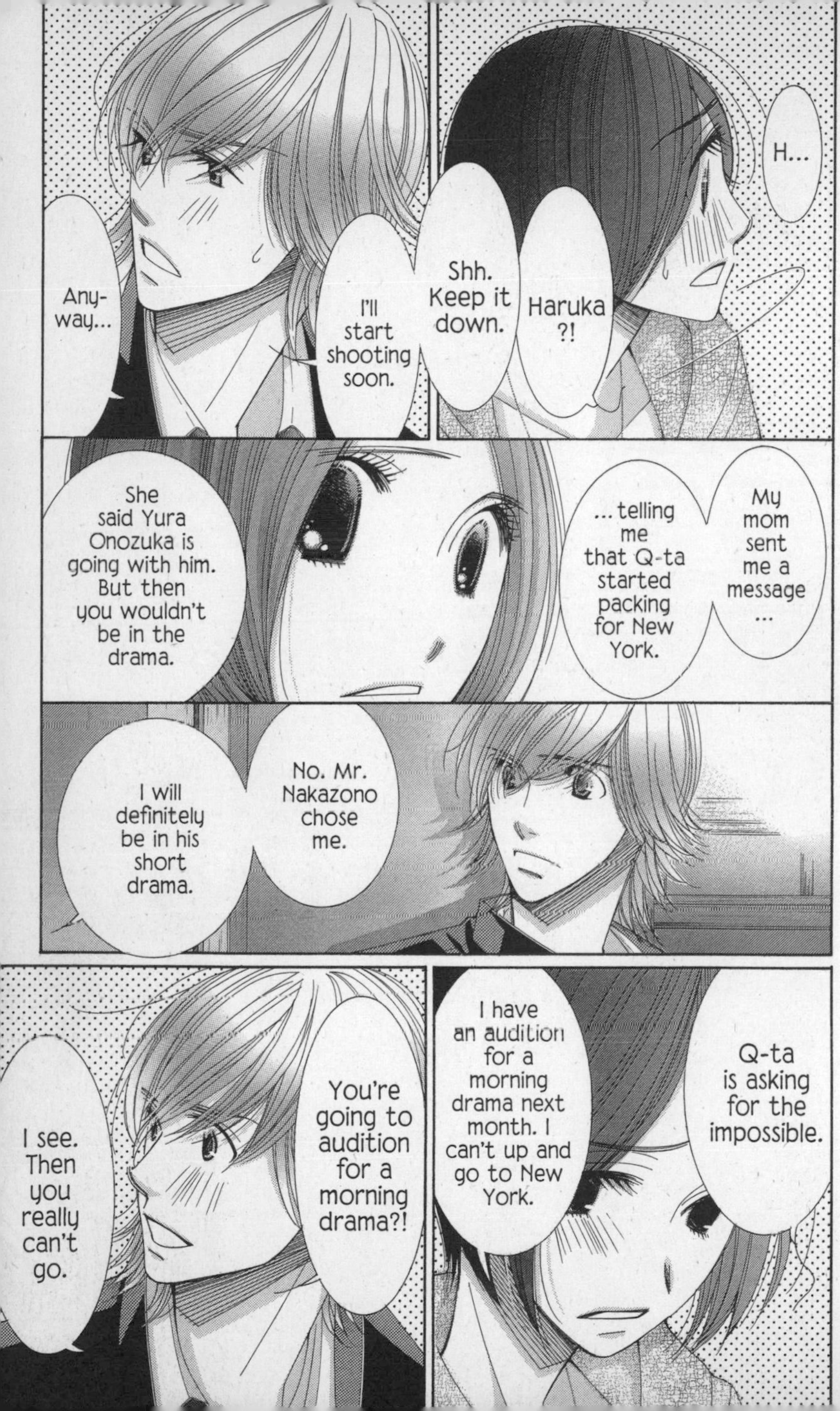
H...
Haruka ?!
Shh. Keep it down.
I'll start shooting soon.
Any-way...
My mom sent me a message ...
... telling me that Q-ta started packing for New York.
She said Yura Onozuka is going with him. But then you wouldn't be in the drama.
No. Mr. Nakazono chose me.
I will definitely be in his short drama.
Q-ta is asking for the impossible.
I have an audition for a morning drama next month. I can't up and go to New York.
You're going to audition for a morning drama?!
I see. Then you really can't go.

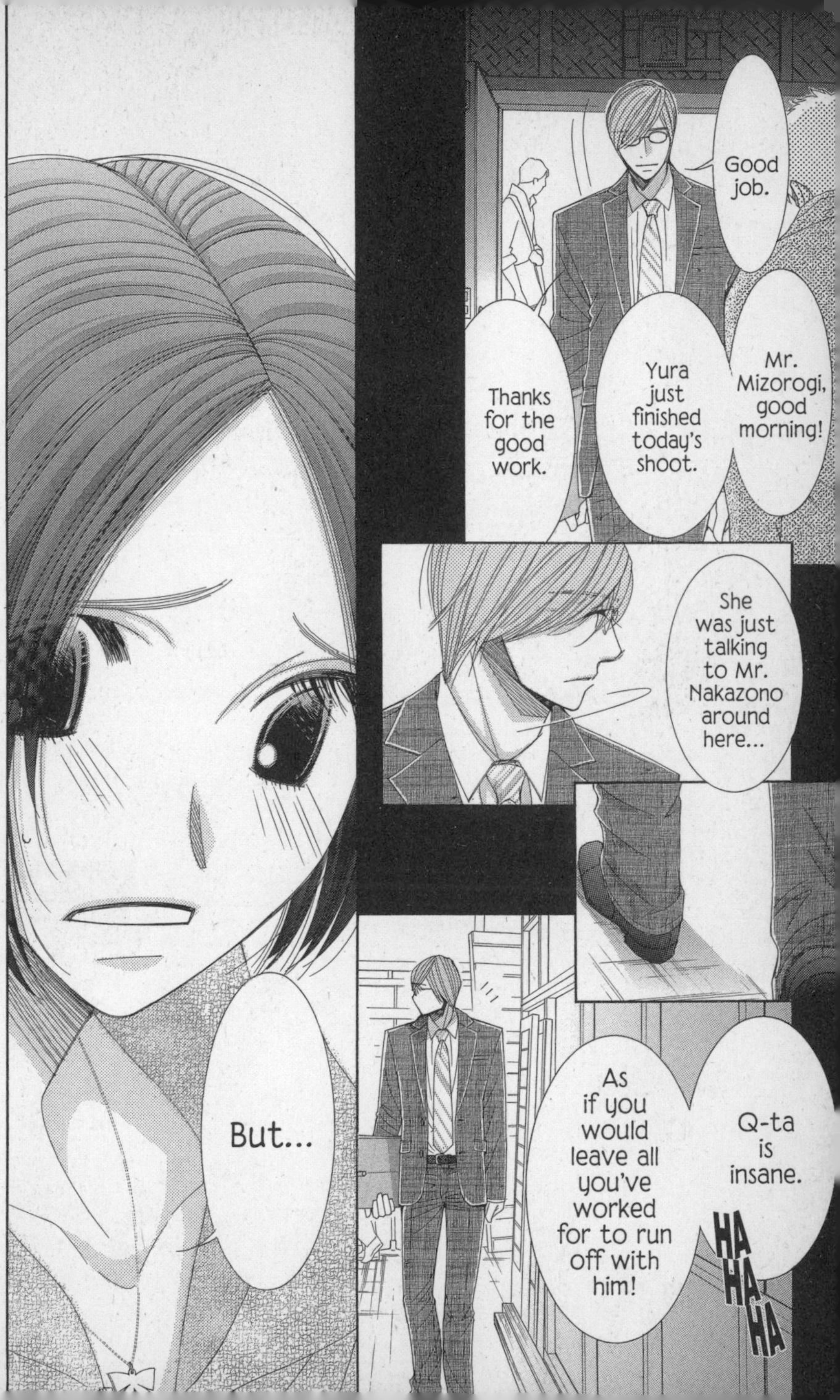
Good job.
Mr. Mizorogi, good morning!
Yura just finished today's shoot.
Thanks for the good work.
She was just talking to Mr. Nakazono around here...
Q-ta is insane.
As if you would leave all you've worked for to run off with him!
HAHAHAHA
But...

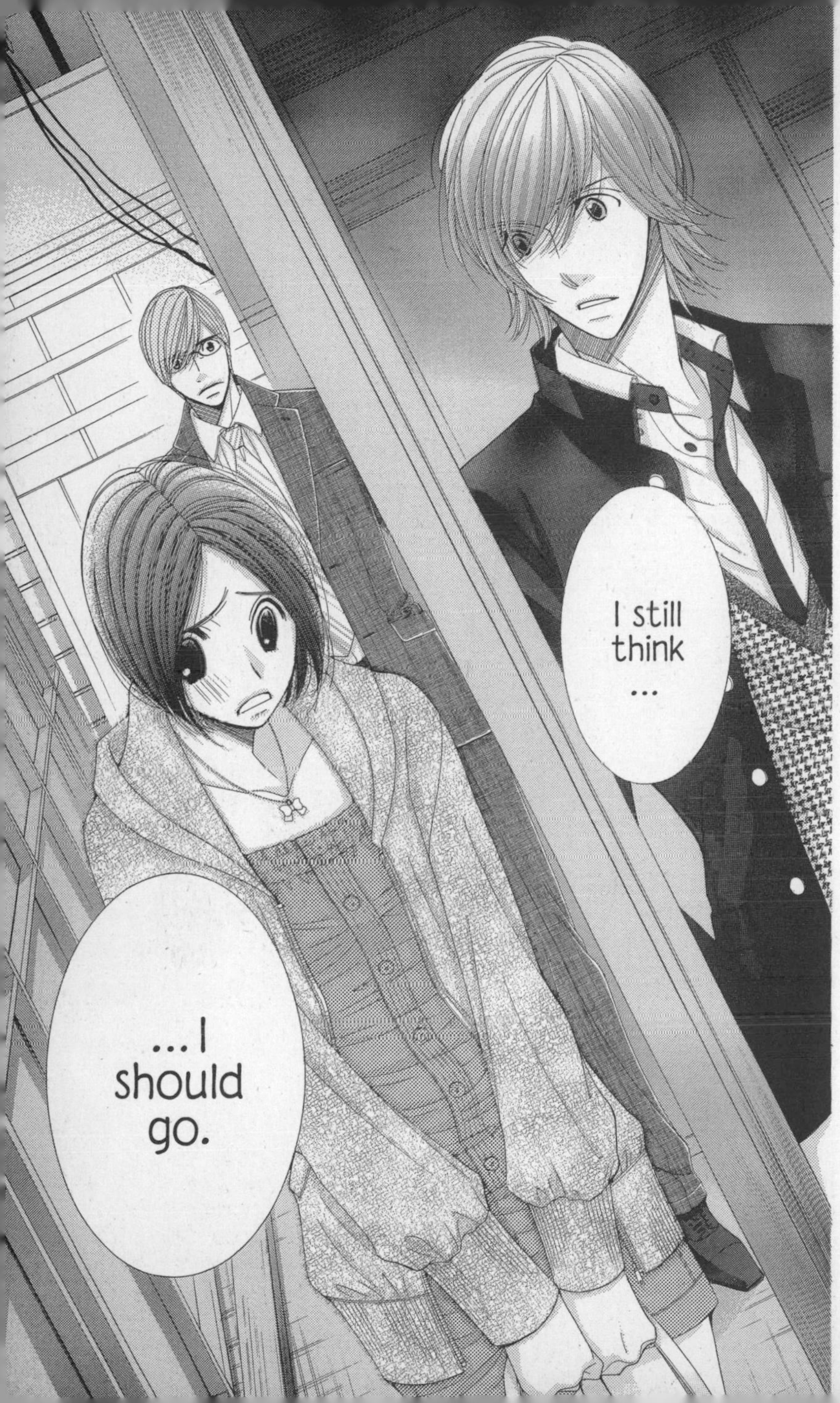
I still think ...
... I should go.

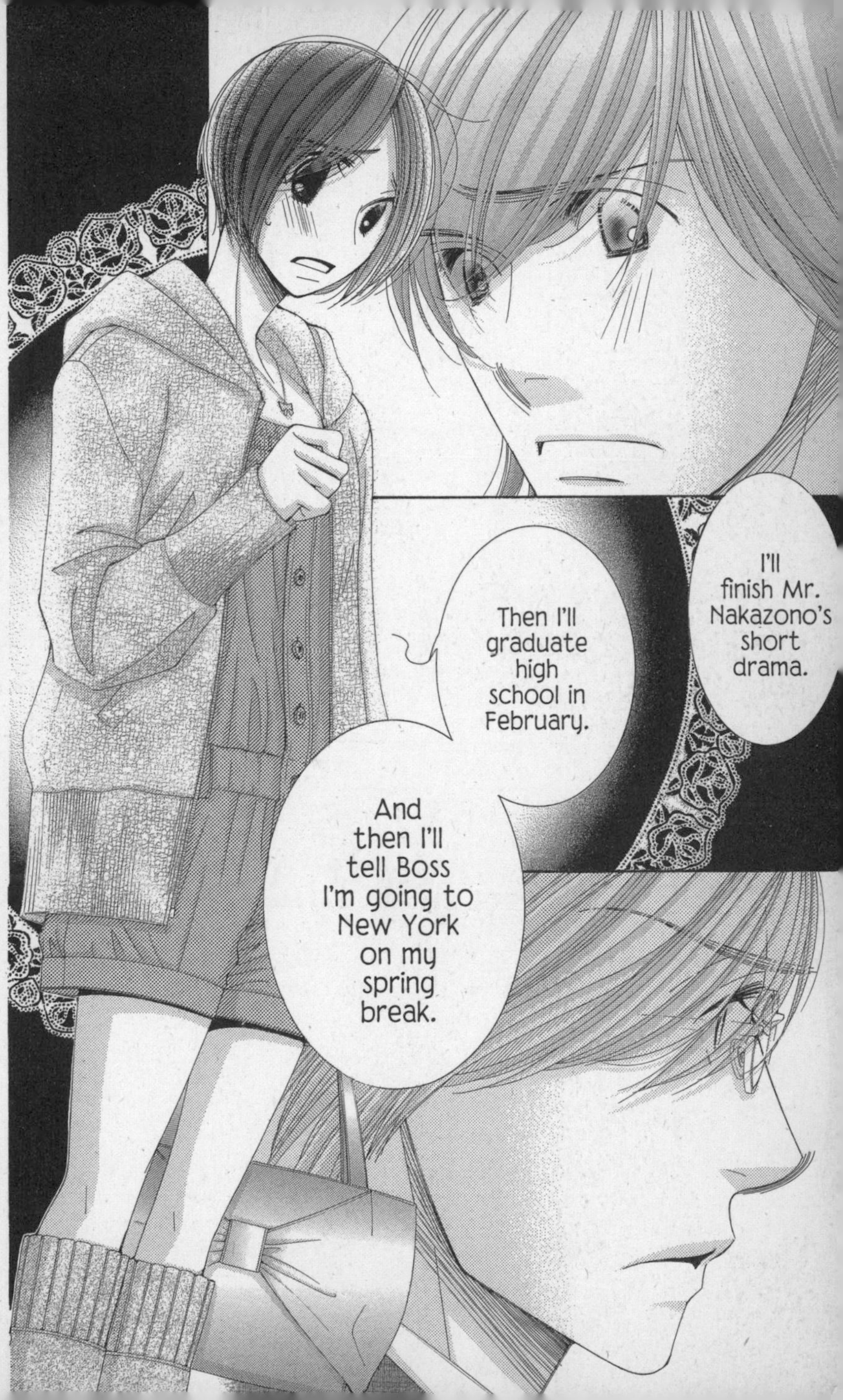
I'll finish Mr. Nakazono's short drama.
Then I'll graduate high school in February.
And then I'll tell Boss I'm going to New York on my spring break.

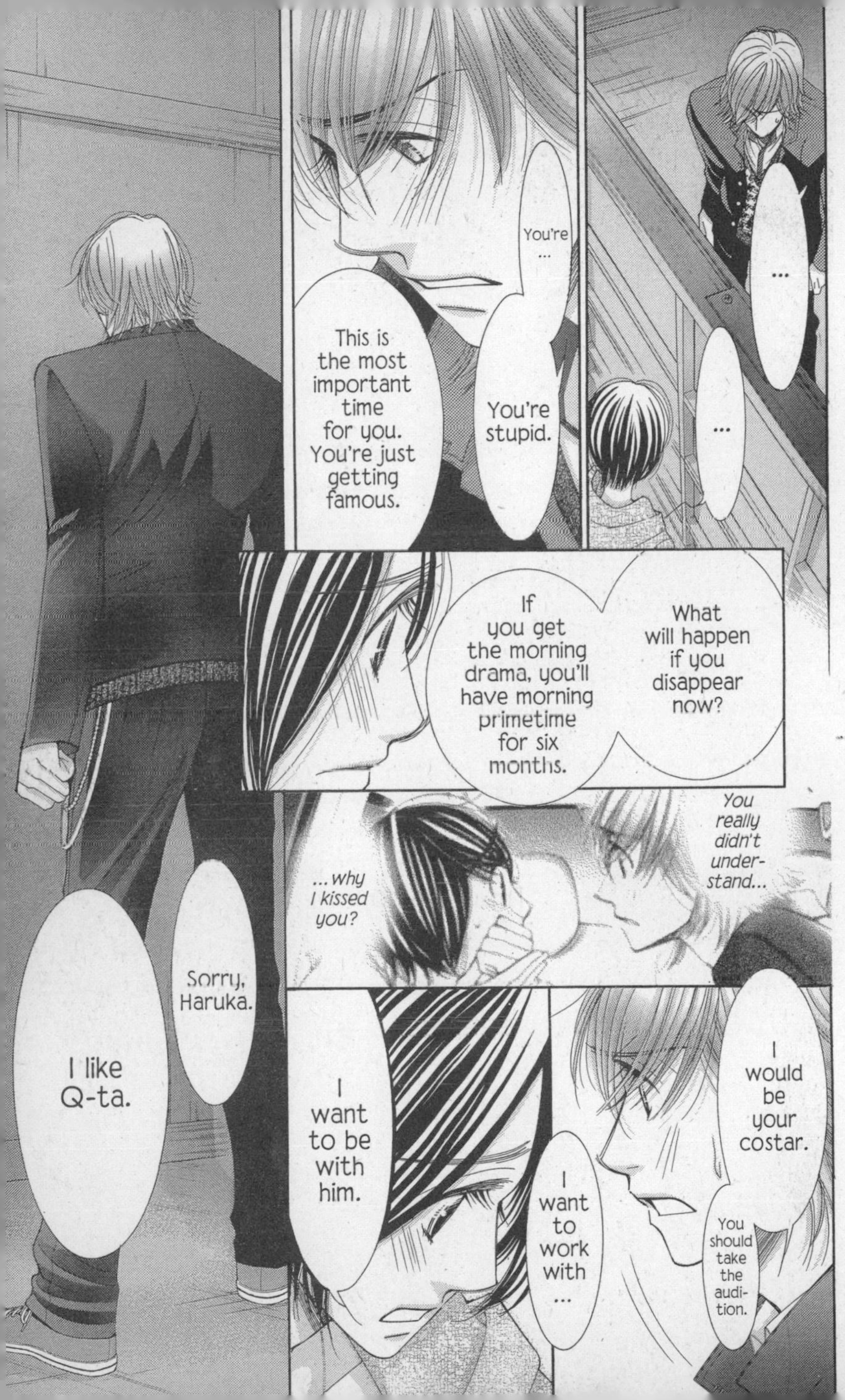
...
...
You're ...
You're stupid.
This is the most important time for you. You're just getting famous.
What will happen if you disappear now?
If you get the morning drama, you'll have morning primetime for six months.
You really didn't under-stand...
...why I kissed you?
I would be your costar.
You should take the audi-tion.
I want to work with ...
I want to be with him.
Sorry, Haruka.
I like Q-ta.

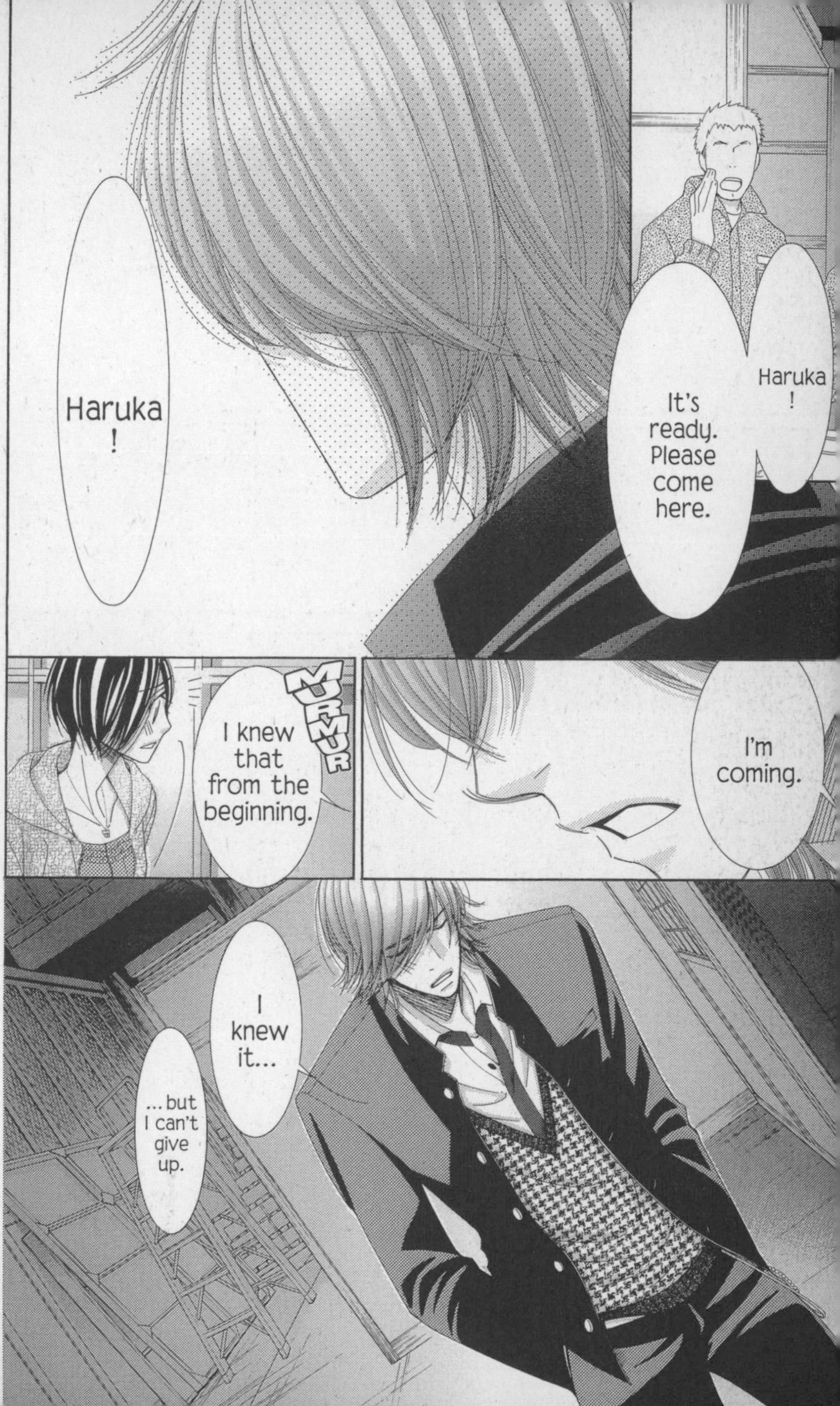
Haruka!
It's ready. Please come here.
Haruka!
I'm coming.
MURMUR
I knew that from the beginning.
I knew it...
...but I can't give up.

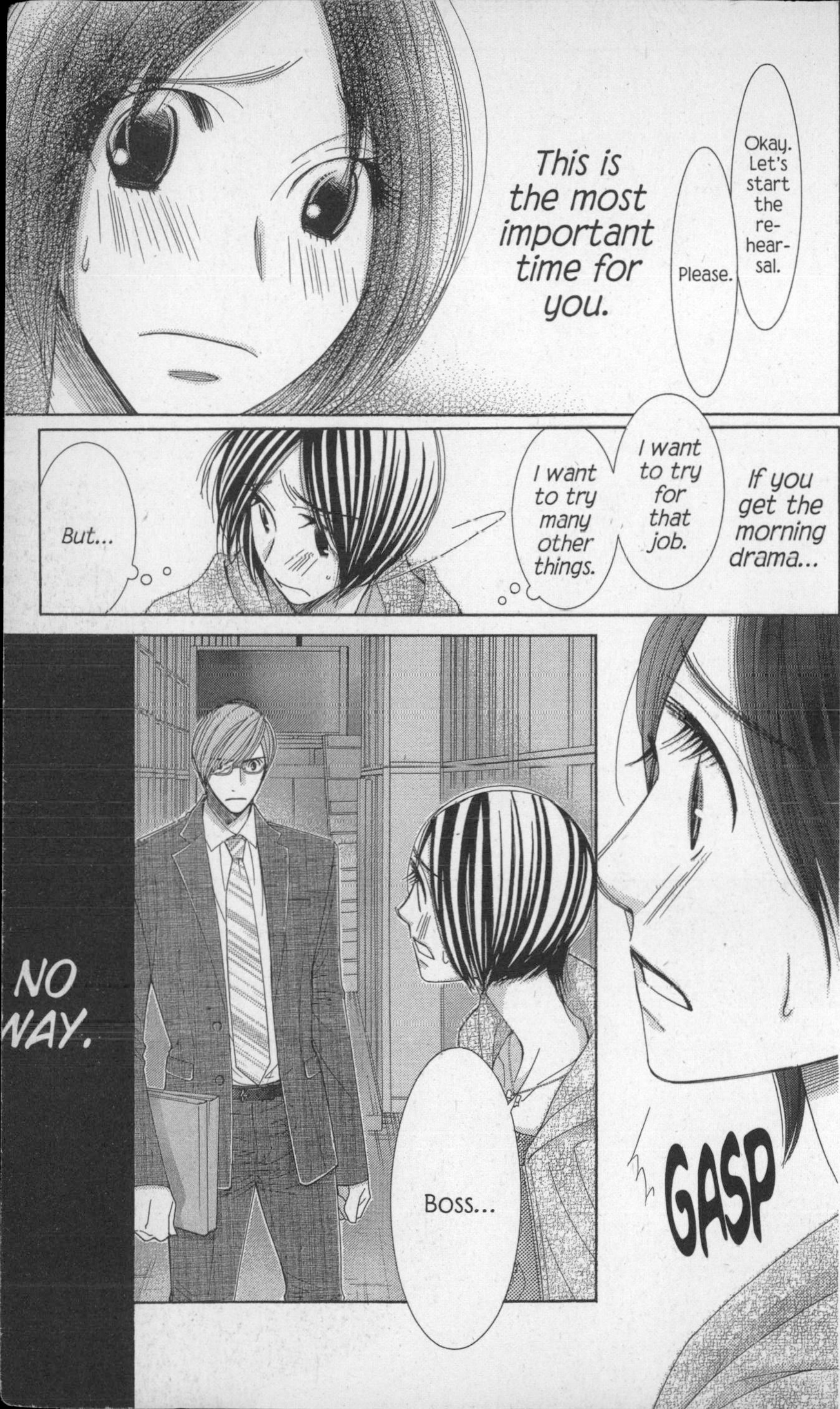
Okay. Let's start the re-hear-sal.
Please.
This is the most important time for you.
If you get the morning drama...
I want to try for that job.
I want to try many other things.
But...
GASP
Boss...
NO WAY.

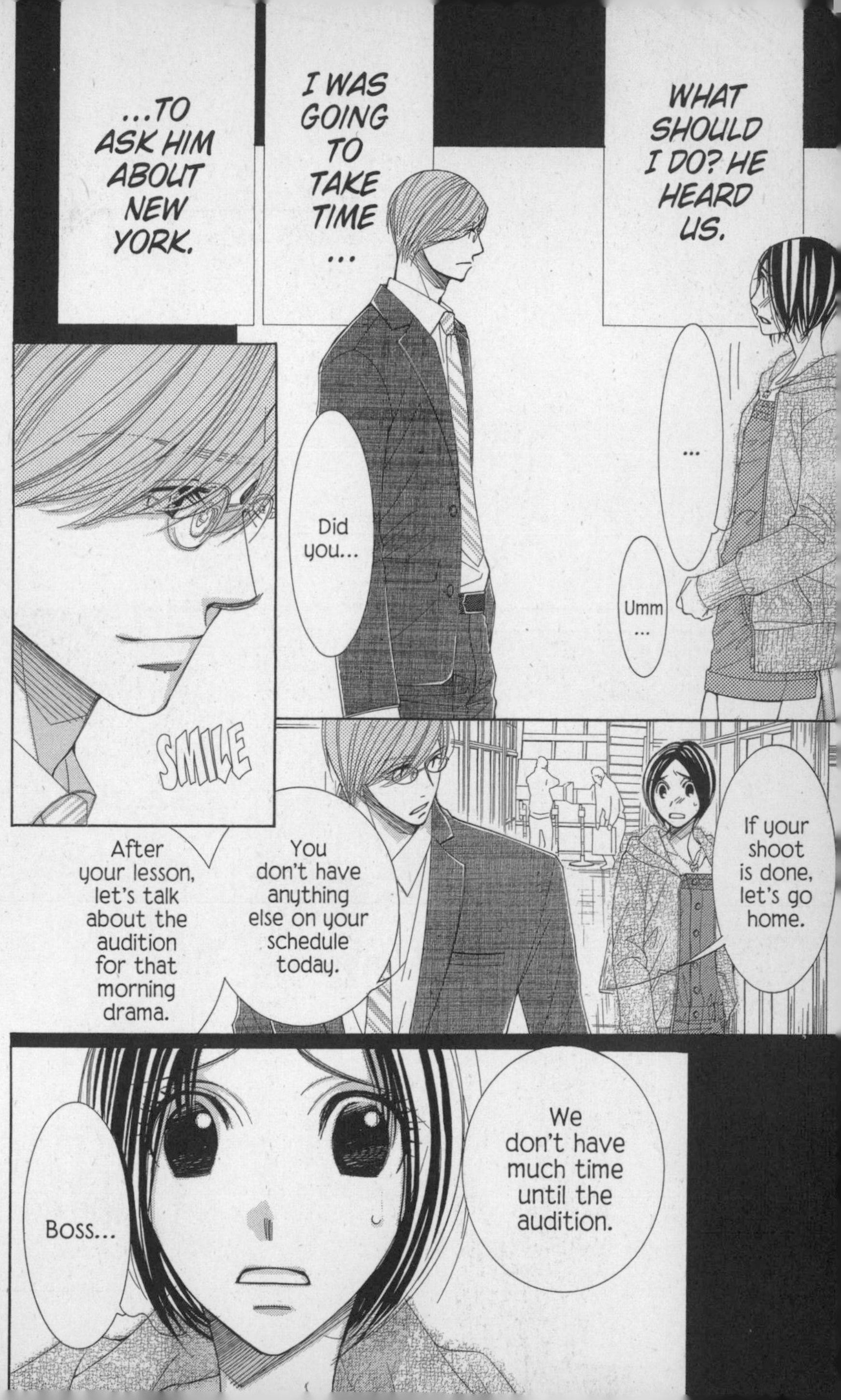
WHAT SHOULD I DO? HE HEARD US.
I WAS GOING TO TAKE TIME...
...TO ASK HIM ABOUT NEW YORK.
...
Umm...
Did you...
SMILE
If your shoot is done, let's go home.
You don't have anything else on your schedule today.
After your lesson, let's talk about the audition for that morning drama.
We don't have much time until the audition.
Boss...

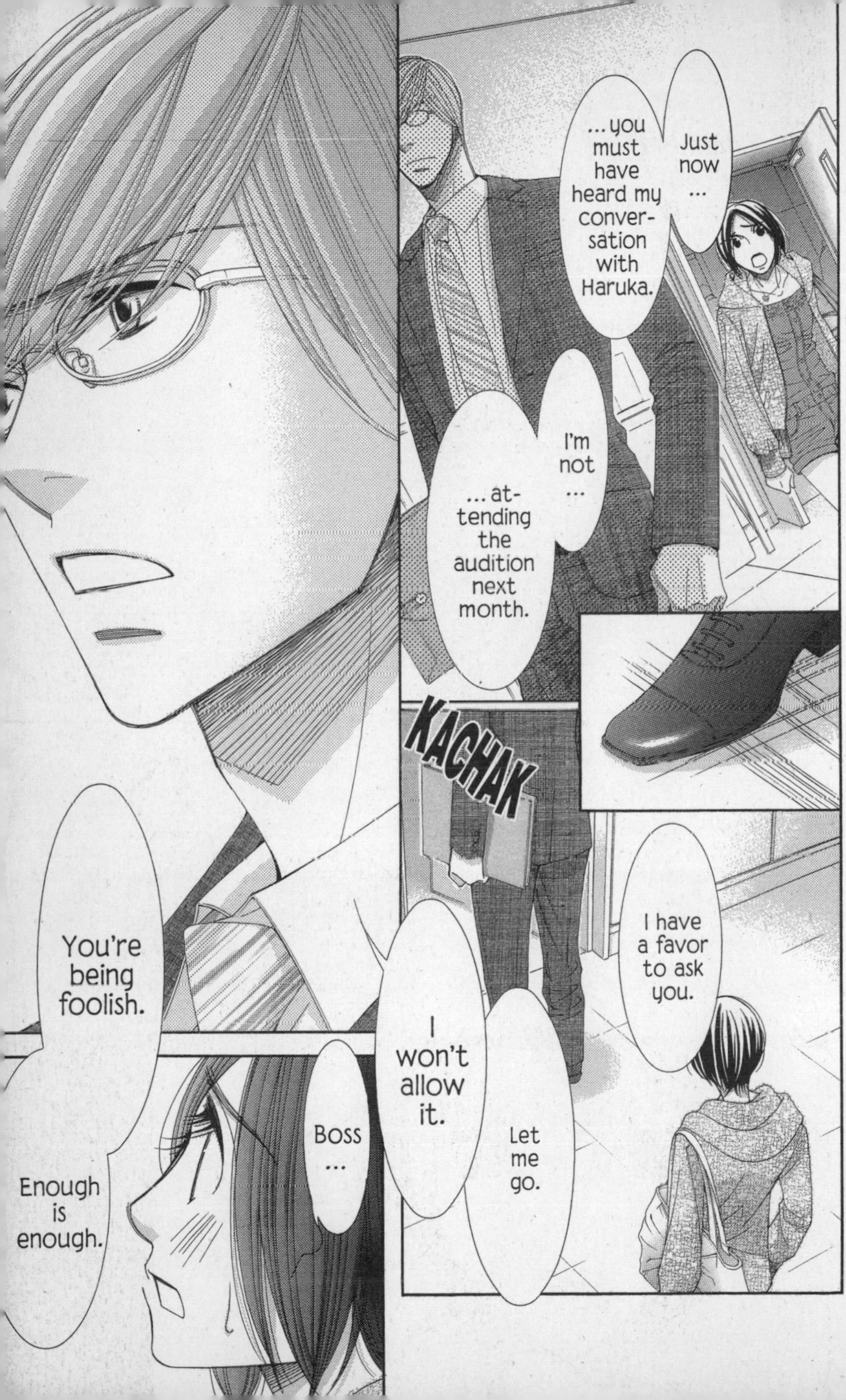
Just now ...
... you must have heard my conversation with Haruka.
I'm not ...
... attending the audition next month.
KACHAK
I have a favor to ask you.
Let me go.
I won't allow it.
You're being foolish.
Boss ...
Enough is enough.

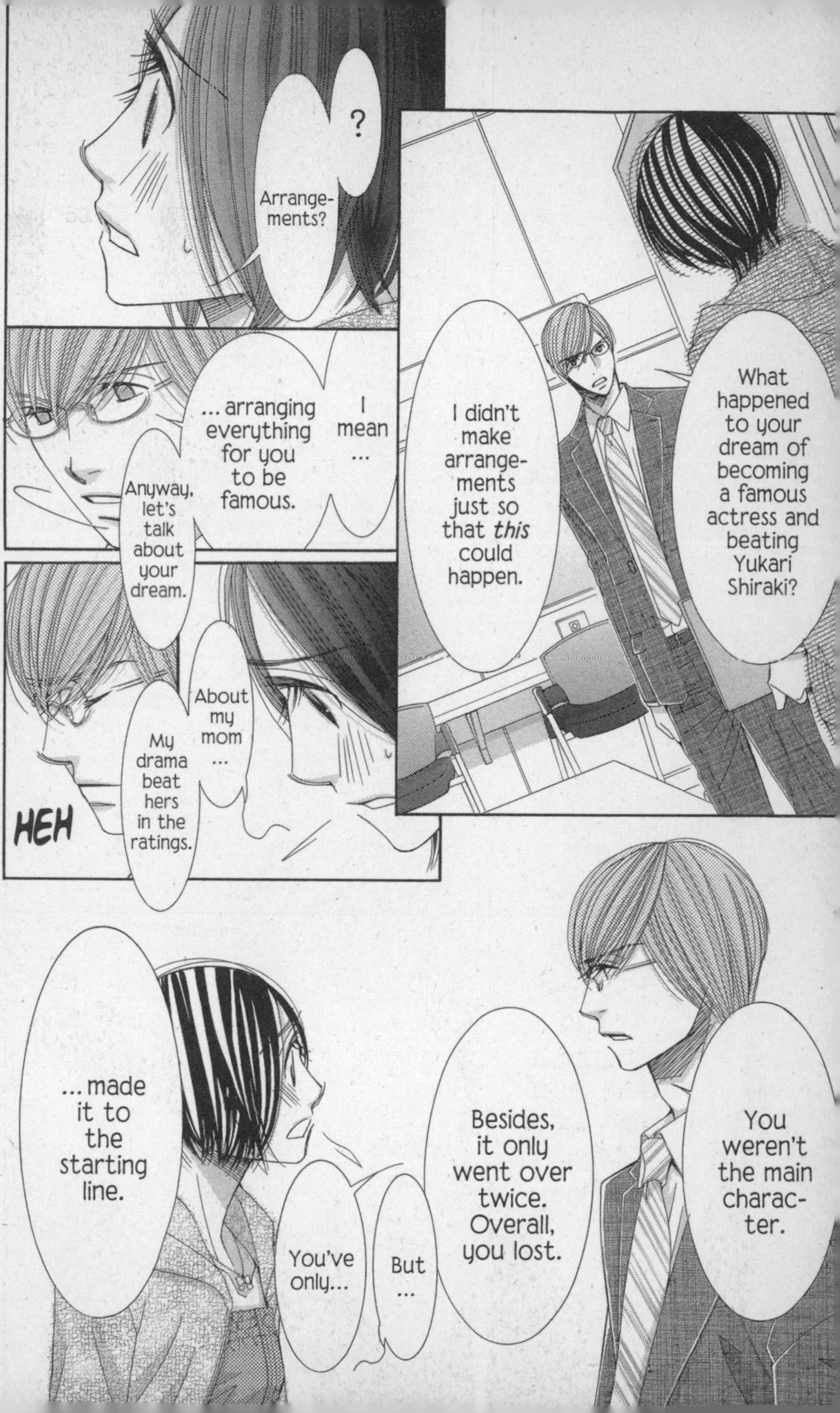
?
Arrange-ments?
I mean ...
... arranging everything for you to be famous.
Anyway, let's talk about your dream.
About my mom ...
My drama beat hers in the ratings.
HEH
What happened to your dream of becoming a famous actress and beating Yukari Shiraki?
I didn't make arrange-ments just so that *this* could happen.
You weren't the main charac-ter.
Besides, it only went over twice. Overall, you lost.
But ...
You've only...
... made it to the starting line.

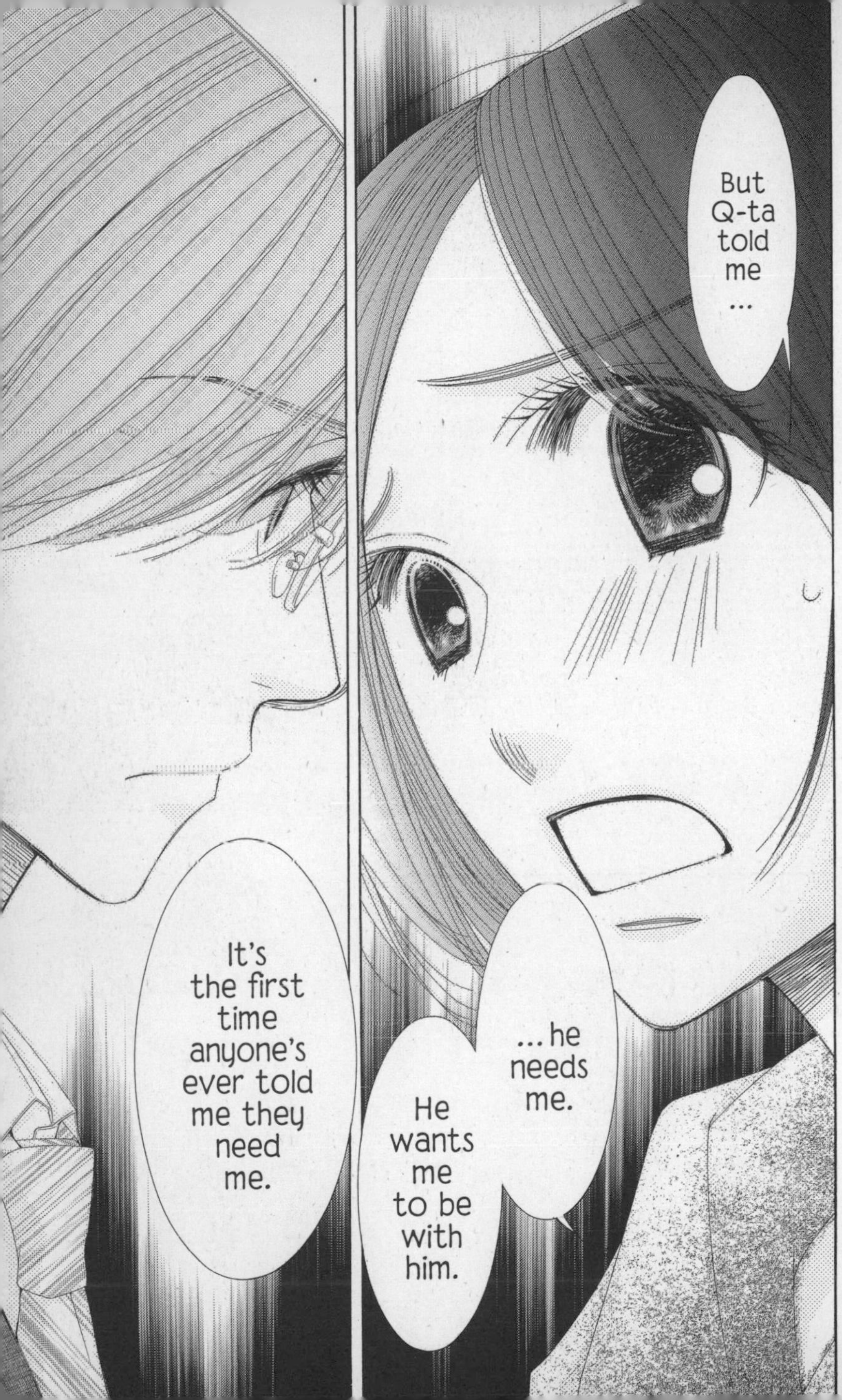
But Q-ta told me ...
...he needs me.
He wants me to be with him.
It's the first time anyone's ever told me they need me.

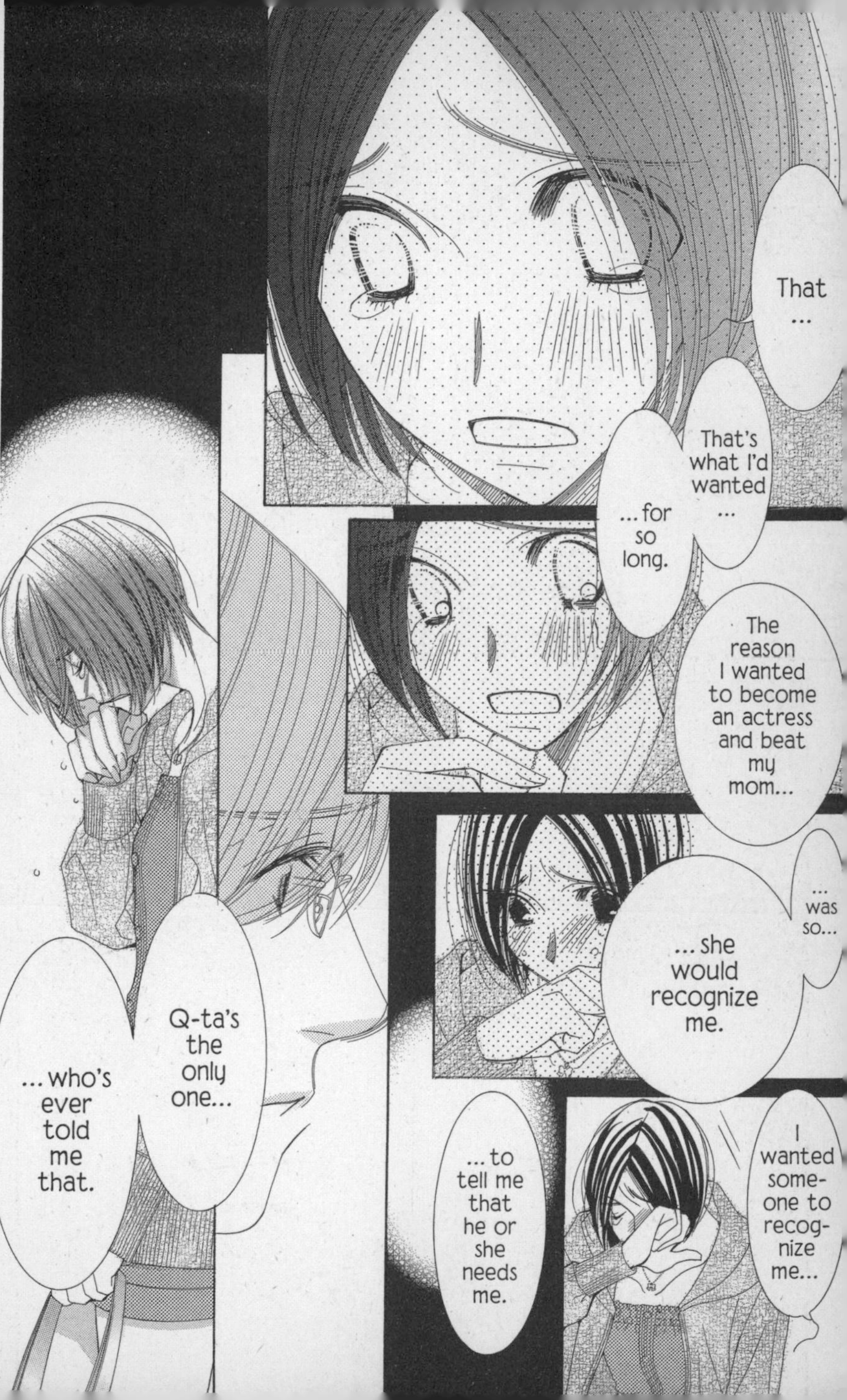
That ...
That's what I'd wanted ...
... for so long.
The reason I wanted to become an actress and beat my mom...
... was so...
... she would recognize me.
I wanted some-one to recog-nize me...
... to tell me that he or she needs me.
Q-ta's the only one...
... who's ever told me that.

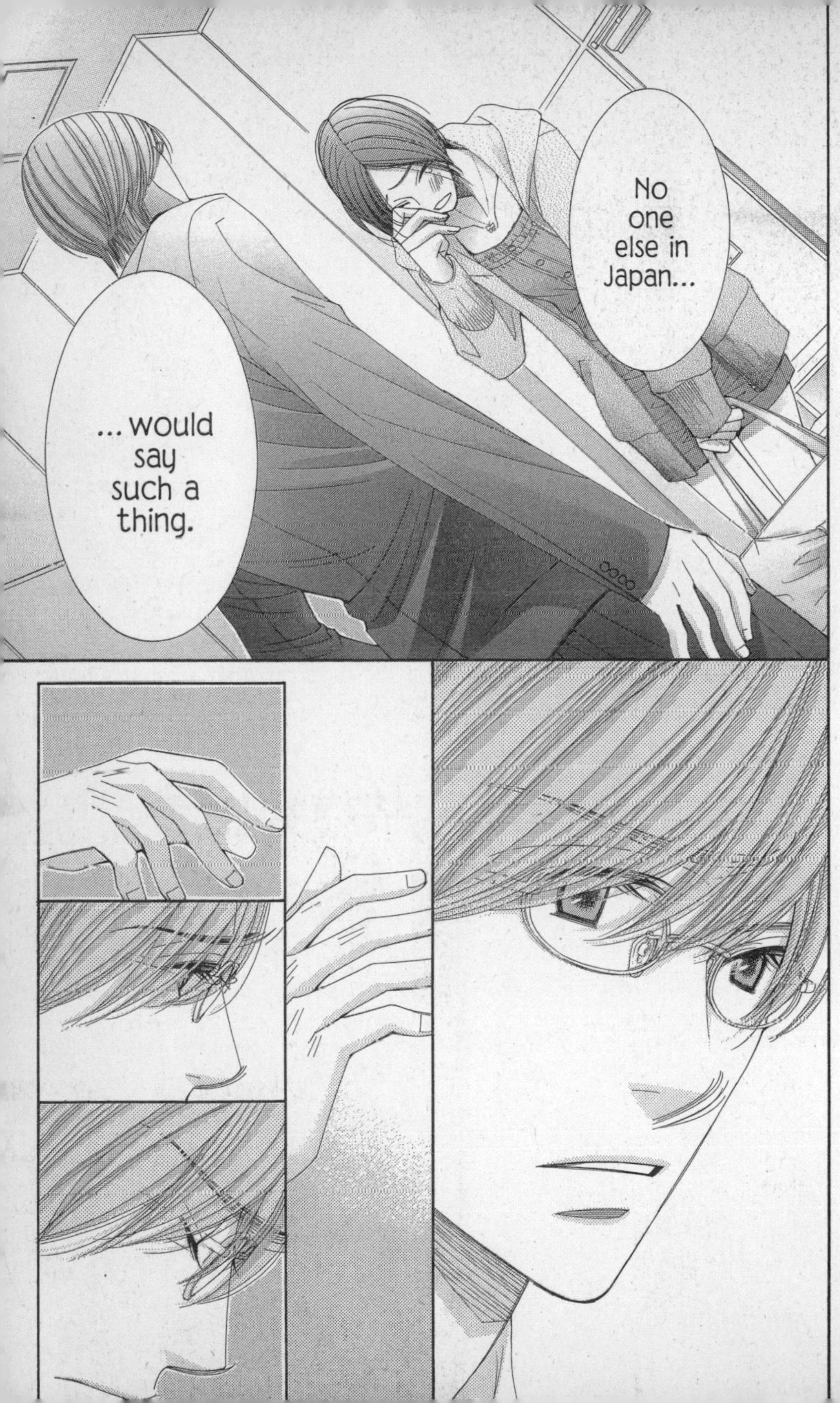
No one else in Japan...
...would say such a thing.

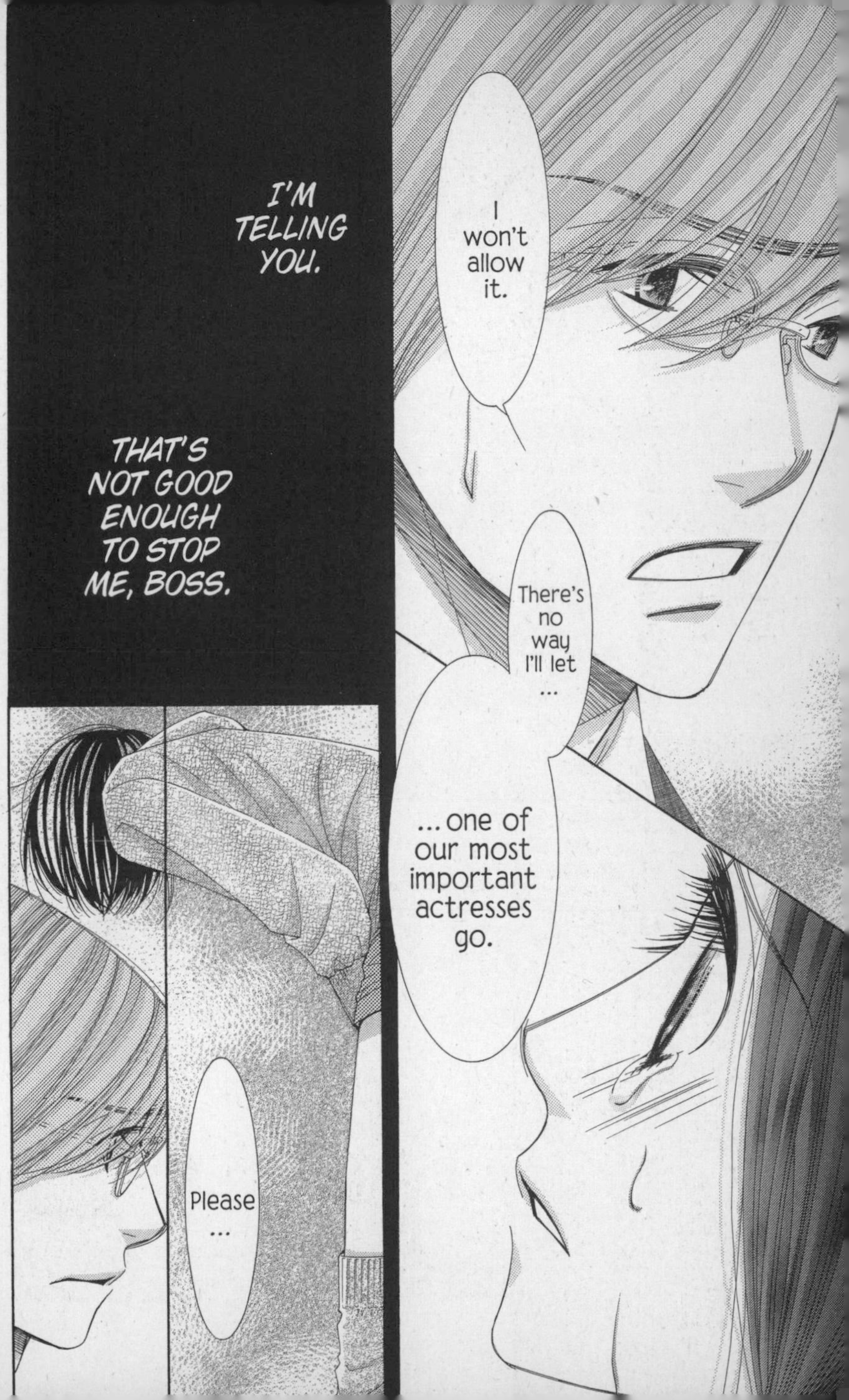
I won't allow it.
There's no way I'll let ...
... one of our most important actresses go.
I'M TELLING YOU.
THAT'S NOT GOOD ENOUGH TO STOP ME, BOSS.
Please ...

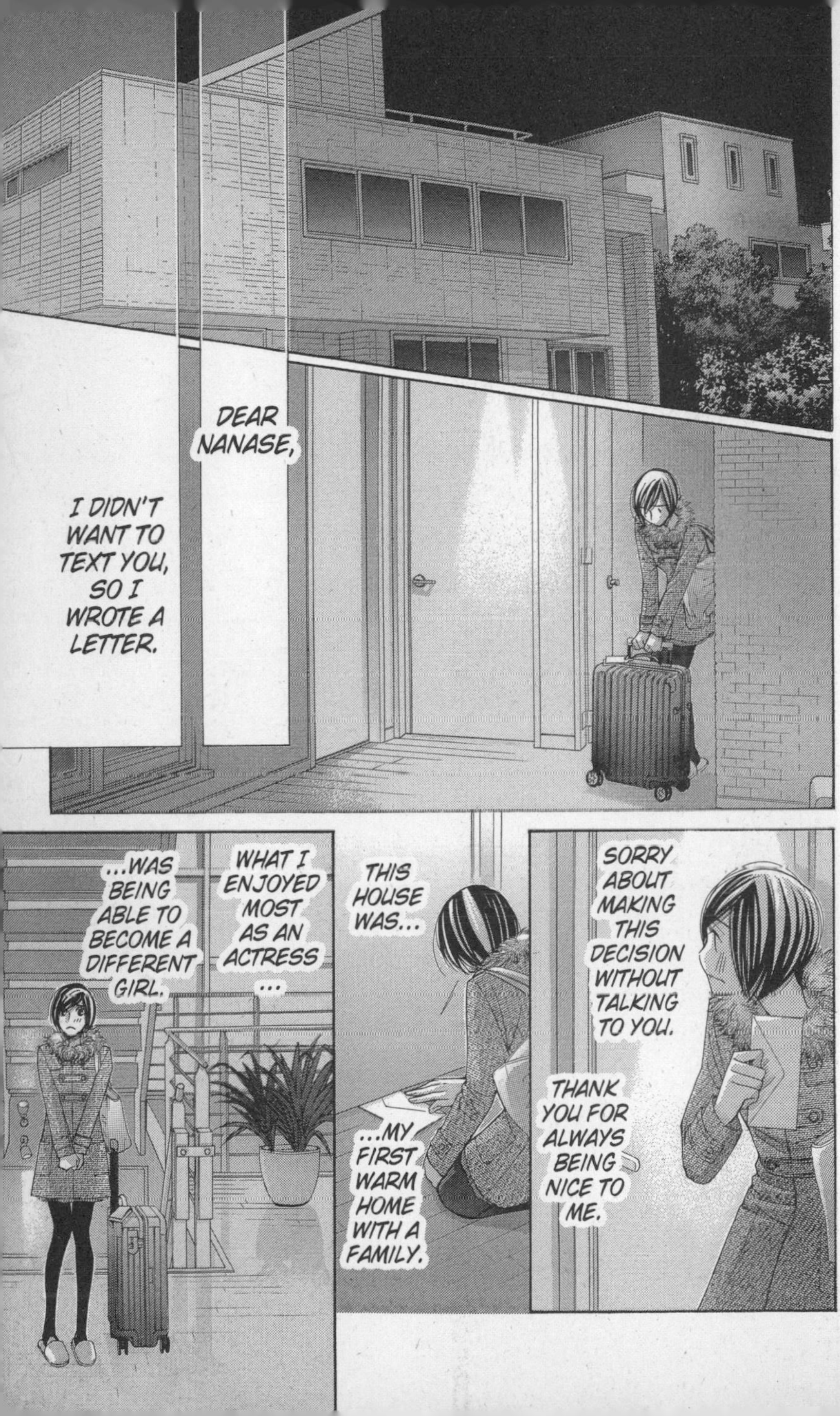
DEAR NANASE,
I DIDN'T WANT TO TEXT YOU, SO I WROTE A LETTER.
SORRY ABOUT MAKING THIS DECISION WITHOUT TALKING TO YOU.
THANK YOU FOR ALWAYS BEING NICE TO ME.
THIS HOUSE WAS...
...MY FIRST WARM HOME WITH A FAMILY.
WHAT I ENJOYED MOST AS AN ACTRESS...
...WAS BEING ABLE TO BECOME A DIFFERENT GIRL.

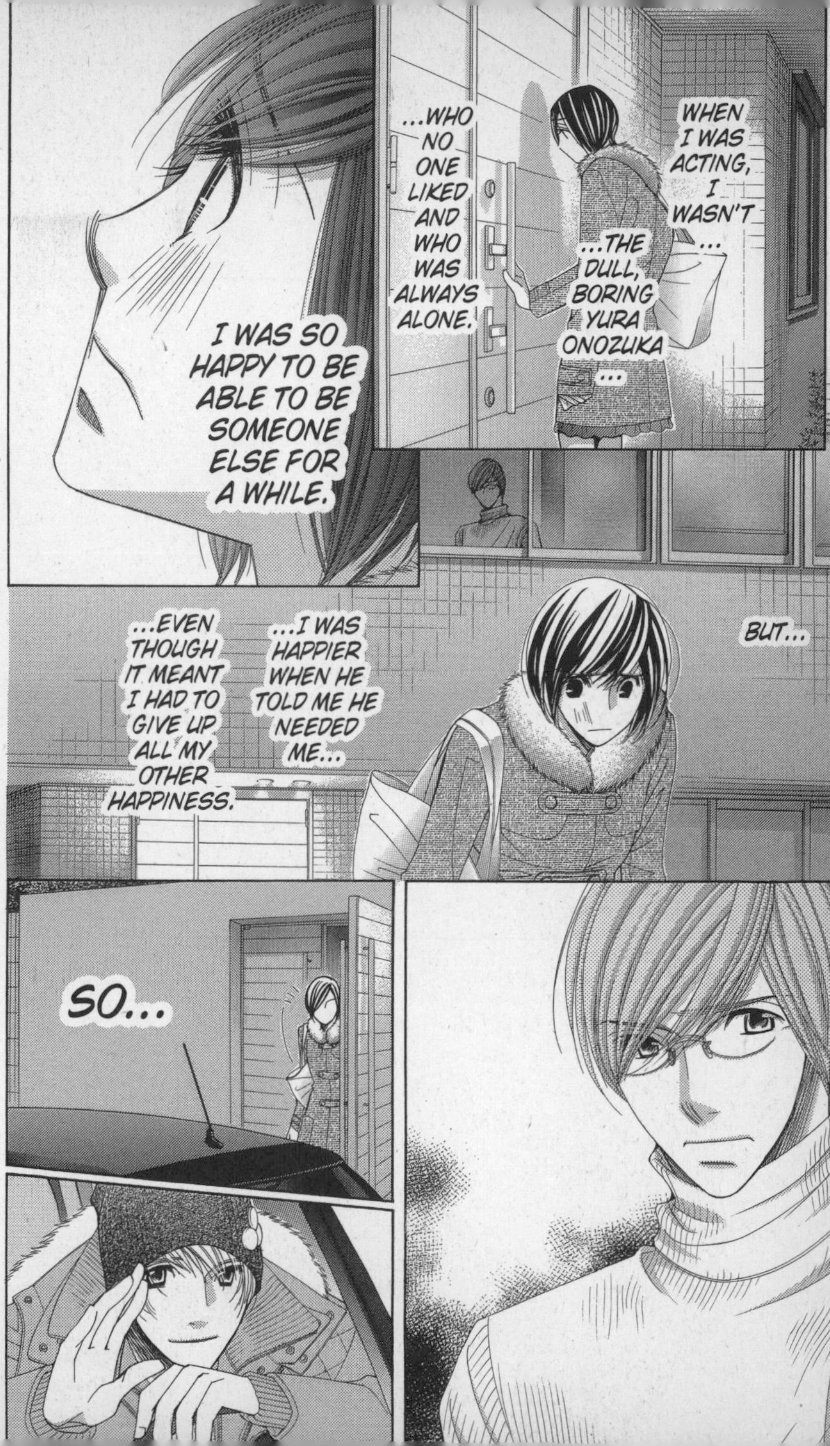
WHEN I WAS ACTING, I WASN'T...
...THE DULL, BORING YURA ONOZUKA...
...WHO NO ONE LIKED AND WHO WAS ALWAYS ALONE.
I WAS SO HAPPY TO BE ABLE TO BE SOMEONE ELSE FOR A WHILE.
BUT...
...I WAS HAPPIER WHEN HE TOLD ME HE NEEDED ME...
...EVEN THOUGH IT MEANT I HAD TO GIVE UP ALL MY OTHER HAPPINESS.
SO...

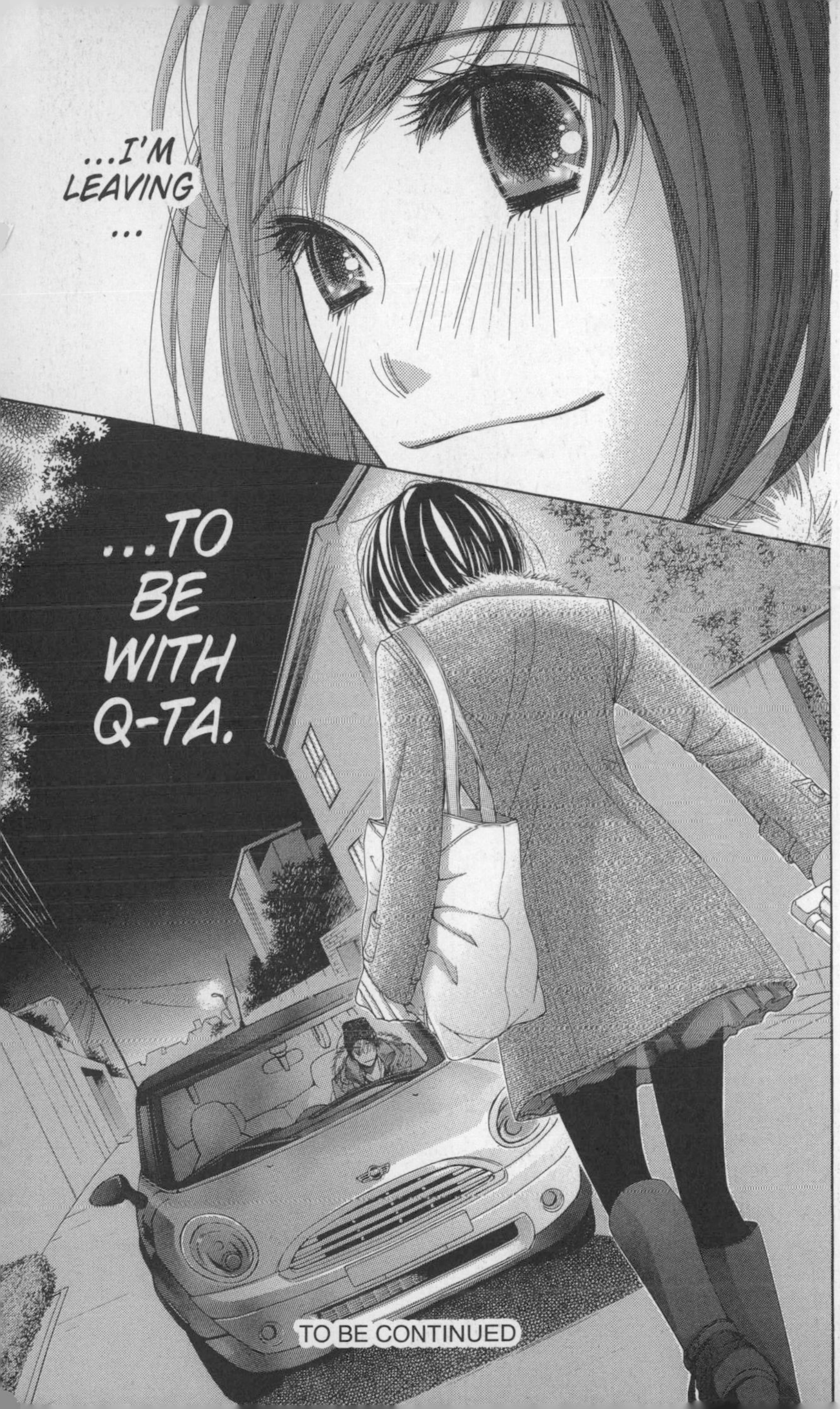
...I'M LEAVING ...
...TO BE WITH Q-TA.
TO BE CONTINUED

thank you
for reading,
and

to be continued
next
"Honey Hunt"

●blog
http://mikiniki.net (Japanese Only)

# MIKI AIHARA

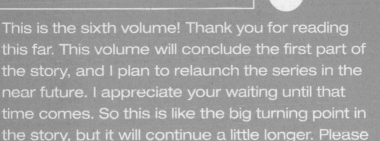

This is the sixth volume! Thank you for reading this far. This volume will conclude the first part of the story, and I plan to relaunch the series in the near future. I appreciate your waiting until that time comes. So this is like the big turning point in the story, but it will continue a little longer. Please follow my blog Miki Nikki for updates on when the series will start up again. Thank you very much!

Miki Aihara, from Shizuoka Prefecture, is the creator of the manga series *Hot Gimmick*. She began her career with *Lip Conscious!*, which ran in *Bessatsu Shojo Comic*. Her other work includes *Seiten Taisei* (The Clear, Wide Blue Sky), *So Bad!*, and *Tokyo Boys & Girls*. She's a Gemini whose hobbies include movies and shopping.

# HONEY HUNT
## VOL.6

Shojo Beat Edition

STORY AND ART BY MIKI AIHARA

© 2007 Miki AIHARA/Shogakukan
All rights reserved.
Original Japanese edition "HONEY HUNT" published by SHOGAKUKAN Inc.

English Adaptation/Liz Forbes
Translation/Ari Yasuda, HC Language Solutions, Inc.
Touch-up Art & Lettering/Rina Mapa
Design/Ronnie Casson
Editor/Alexis Kirsch

Printed in Canada

Published by VIZ Media, LLC
P.O. Box 77010
San Francisco, CA 94107

10 9 8 7 6 5 4 3 2 1
First printing, December 2010

www.viz.com          www.shojobeat.com